# Pro Agile .NET
# Development with Scrum

**Jerrel Blankenship**
**Matthew Bussa**
**Scott Millett**

Apress®

**Pro Agile .NET Development with Scrum**

Copyright © 2011 by Jerrel Blankenship, Matthew Bussa, and Scott Millett

ISBN-13 (pbk): 978-1-4302-3533-0

ISBN-13 (electronic): 978-1-4302-3534-7

President and Publisher: Paul Manning
Lead Editor: Jonathan Hassell
Technical Reviewer: Russ Lewis and Damien Foggon
Editorial Board: Clay Andres, Steve Anglin, Mark Beckner, Ewan Buckingham, Gary Cornell,
    Jonathan Gennick, Jonathan Hassell, Michelle Lowman, Matthew Moodie, Duncan Parkes,
    Jeffrey Pepper, Frank Pohlmann, Douglas Pundick, Ben Renow-Clarke, Dominic Shakeshaft,
    Matt Wade, Tom Welsh
Coordinating Editor: Jessica Belanger
Copy Editor: Kim Burton-Weisman
Compositor: Bytheway Publishing Services
Indexer: SPI Global
Artist: SPI Global
Cover Designer: Anna Ishchenko

Distributed to the book trade worldwide by Springer Science+Business Media, LLC., 233 Spring Street, 6th Floor, New York, NY 10013. Phone 1-800-SPRINGER, fax (201) 348-4505, e-mail orders-ny@springer-sbm.com, or visit www.springeronline.com.

For information on translations, please e-mail rights@apress.com, or visit www.apress.com.

Apress and friends of ED books may be purchased in bulk for academic, corporate, or promotional use. eBook versions and licenses are also available for most titles. For more information, reference our Special Bulk Sales–eBook Licensing web page at www.apress.com/bulk-sales.

The source code for this book is available to readers at www.apress.com. You will need to answer questions pertaining to this book in order to successfully download the code.

*To my wife, Stacy, my son, Tyler, and my family*
*–Jerrel*


*To my wife, Rebakah, and my family*
*–Matthew*

# Contents at a Glance

# Contents

# About the Authors

 **Jerrel Blankenship**, software craftsman, specializes in Microsoft technologies. He has been an application developer on the .NET platform for more than six years. He is a Certified ScrumMaster and a Microsoft Certified Professional.

During his career, Jerrel has developed a number of .NET-based software projects that run on desktop, web, and mobile environments. He enjoys working with impassioned developers and sharing the knowledge of agile and Scrum to teams that want to build software more effectively.

Jerrel is passionate about many things, including his family, fishing, chess, Cleveland-based sports teams, and gaming. He currently resides in Columbus, Ohio, with his wonderful wife, Stacy, and son Tyler. You can read Jerrel's ramblings at www.jerrelblankenship.com and he can be reached via e-mail at jerrel@jerrelBlankenship.com.

 **Matthew Bussa** is software craftsman specializing in Microsoft technologies. A Certified ScrumMaster and a Microsoft Certified Technology Specialist, Matthew has developed .NET-based solutions for both the web and the desktop. He enjoys helping transform agile teams through working together more effectively—so that they can build awesome software!

Matthew currently resides in Columbus, Ohio, with his wife, Rebakah. He maintains a blog at www.matthewbussa.com and can be reached via e-mail at matthew@matthewbussa.com.

# About the Technical Reviewers

■ **Russ Lewis** has been helping organizations build better software since the late 80s. An engineer by training, and entrepreneurial by background, he places the highest value in identifying and satisfying customer requirements. Agile principles and solid architecture have long driven his projects, even before the terms "Agile" and "Architecture" became fashionable.

He was one of the first to recognize the business benefits of service-orientation, developing training courses for Microsoft and Learning Tree International on Web Services and COM+.

Lately, he has been consulting with some of the world's leading organizations including Randstad, Toyota, Transport for London, and the Government of Angola, as software architect and agile lead.

■ **Damien Foggon** is a developer, writer, and technical reviewer in cutting-edge technologies and has contributed to more than 50 books on .NET, C#, Visual Basic and ASP.NET. He is the co-founder of the Newcastle based user-group NEBytes (online at http://www.nebytes.net), is a multiple MCPD in .NET 2.0 and .NET 3.5 and can be found online at http://blog.fasm.co.uk.

# Acknowledgments

The thought of trying to put to paper all who have helped me get to where I am is nearly impossible. I have been fortunate in my life to have met wonderful people who have each helped me both personally and professionally. I may forget some of you and for that I am sorry. Please remember that without all of you I would not have gotten where I am.

First and foremost, I want to thank my wife, Stacy, for her love, encouragement, and understanding through everything I have been through. She is my rock, my companion, and my friend. I want to thank my son, Tyler, for always bringing a smile to my face whenever he enters a room. I want to thank my parents and family for their love, encouragement, and support.

I want to thank Tom Maier for giving me my first shot at showing the world what I can do and guiding me through the early stages of my career. I want thank Jared Conway for giving me insight and showing me what a great developer and friend can do.

I want to give a tremendous thanks to Jared Richardson, Tim Wingfield, and Michael Kramer for showing me the wonderful world that is agile. They were all mentors to me and helped shaped my career. Without these guys, my involvement with this book would have been non-existent. Thank you guys!

I thank my co-authors, Matthew Bussa and Scott Millet, who helped make this book awesome. I wish to thank everyone at Apress who gave me a way to share my voice and love of development with the world, especially Jessica Belanger, Jonathan Hassell, and Tom Welsh.

—Jerrel Blankenship

I'm not going to lie to you. The Acknowledgments section of the book is a scary proposition for me. The notion that I (or anyone) could quantify, or prioritize, the contributions (direct and indirect) by which this book was made possible is fantasy. I'll do my best, but it's entirely possible I'll forget somebody, and for that, I apologize in advance.

I foremost thank my wife, Rebakah, for her love, eternal patience, indulgence, support, and encouragingly witty comments. She is my love, my companion, and my best friend. I want to thank Michael Hoffer for his friendship and for Fridays. I thank my parents, sister, and my in-laws for their influences, grace, support, and love.

I want to thank Jared Richardson, Tim Wingfield, and Michael Kramer for first introducing me to the practices of Scrum and the Agile Manifesto, and teaching me the importance of building a great team and that software can remain soft with good engineering practices. Their mentorship made a difference and also made this book possible.

I thank my co-authors, Jerrel Blankenship and Scott Millet, who helped make this the most exciting book I've ever worked on! I also want to say thanks to the people at Apress who helped ensure the highest standards in quality every step of the way.

—Matthew Bussa

# Introduction

The Agile Manifesto set forth a set of principles on how we as developers create software for our customers. Over the past 10 or so years, we have seen those ideas and principles expanded upon by developers all over the world.

Transitioning into an agile team takes hard work and may be a bit overwhelming. What we hope to show in this book is what this transition might look like for a .NET development team.

## Who This Book Is For

This book is for software developers who want to learn how to work in an agile environment and develop software using a test-first/behavior-first approach. This book is for developers who want to start with the business, not a column in a table.

This book assumes that you have some familiarity with the .NET framework. When it comes to the testing and mocking frameworks, this book assumes you have little familiarity.

## How This Book Is Structured

This book contains ten chapters and seven appendices.

Chapter 1: "The Art of Agile Development" gives a general overview of agile. This overview includes the difference between plan-driven and value-driven development.

Chapter 2: "Managing Agile Projects with Scrum" provides an introduction to Scrum.

Chapter 3: "eXtreme Programming" discusses the fundamentals of eXtreme Programming (XP) and its relationship with Scrum and behavior-driven development.

Starting in Chapter 4, the book provides a fictional case study about a team utilizing the concepts and ideas from the previous chapters to develop a web-based blackjack game.

Chapter 4: "Sprint 0: Generating the Product Backlog," covers establishing a baseline sprint to develop three different user stories: Initial Bet, Start Game, and Deck of Cards. We'll establish the logistical fundamentals of a sprint and set the tone for the next four chapters.

Chapter 5: "Sprint 1: Starting a Game" introduces the team experiencing their first sprint in the project. It shows how the daily stand-up, retrospective, planning, and product demo meetings work in the real world.

Chapter 6: "Sprint 2: Playing a Basic Game" shows the team dealing with their second sprint and the user stories they have completed.

Chapter 7: "Sprint 3: Changing the Game" finds the team dealing with a change in their group dynamics.

Chapter 8: "Sprint 4: The Release" presents the culmination of four sprints' worth of work for the first release of the blackjack game to the customer.

Chapter 9: "Code Review" gives a brief overview of the behind-the-scenes framework used on the blackjack web application.

Chapter 10: "What's Ahead for You and Scrum," is our retrospective of the product release; it takes a look at what we've covered and gives some pointers on where to go from here.

Appendix A: "TDD Primer with NUnit" is a tutorial on installing and using NUnit to begin to build an automated test suite.

Appendix B: "BDD Primer with SpecFlow" gets you started with the basics of SpecFlow and shows how to transform specifications into workable code.

Appendix C: "Mocking with Moq" is a tutorial explaining why mocking is important and showing you how to mock using the Moq framework.

Appendix D: "Manage a Product Backlog with Pivotal Tracker" is an introduction to a free, online agile management tool to track user stories throughout their lifecycle.

Appendix E: "Web Testing with WaitiN" discusses how to use WaitiN, an automated GUI framework for the browser.

Appendix F: "Source Control with SVN" discusses how to set up and use a version control system for your source code.

Appendix G: "Continuous Integration with CruiseControl .NET" explains how to install and configure a continuous integration server using CruiseControl .NET.

## Conventions

You will notice a tremendous amount of dialog among the team members in the case study chapters. These conversations are italicized.

In instances where a code line is too long to fit the page's width, we break it with a code continuation character. Please note that when you try to type the code, you have to concatenate the line without any spaces.

## Prerequisites

A knowledge of C# and ASP.NET MVC is tremendously useful. No other previous knowledge is required.

To make the most of this book, install Visual Studio 2010 Express with Service Pack 1 or higher and SQL Server 2008 Express R2 or higher. Both are available for free download from www.microsoft.com/visualstudio/en-us/products/2010-editions/express.

# Downloading the Code

The source code for this book is available from the Apress web site (www.apress.com) in the Source Code / Download section.

# Contacting the Authors

We always welcome your questions and feedback regarding the contents of this book. You can reach Jerrel Blankenship by e-mail at jerrel@jerrelblankenship.com or via his web site at www.jerrelblankenship.com. You can contact Matthew Bussa via e-mail at matthew@matthewbussa.com or through his web site at www.matthewbussa.com.

# CHAPTER 1

# The Art of Agile Development

In this chapter you will be introduced to the principles and practices that constitute agile development. You will learn that agile development is as much a philosophical and cultural shift as it is a set of practices and processes. You will understand why the need for an agile approach to software development has developed, the issues it helps to solve, and the reasons for its rapid rise in popularity.

In this chapter you will also dive into the Agile Manifesto, the document that started the agile movement. You will then examine the key features of agile by digging deeper into the principles and values as laid out by the manifesto and understand what they mean at a more granular level.

Finally you will be introduced to a number of practices that all fall under the agile umbrella. These practices share a common goal of striving to make your development effort more flexible, adaptable, and ultimately of more value to the business.

The aim of this chapter is to provide you with the knowledge that will form the foundations on your road to becoming a master agile practitioner over the course of this book.

## Why the Need for Agile?

So where did the need for an agile software development methodology come from and what was so bad about agile's predecessors?

### It's What I Asked for But Not What I Need

Previously, when a team would develop software they would use plan-driven development. This type of development was characterized by *gated stages*, where one would gather all the requirements the customer would need on the project, and then do an analysis of the problem. Next, the whole application was designed before the first line of code was ever written.

One of the most widely adopted methodologies associated with plan-driven development was the *waterfall* approach to software development. The waterfall approach uses gated stages of requirements gathering, planning, designing, development, testing, and then, eventually, deploying, as seen in Figure 1-1.

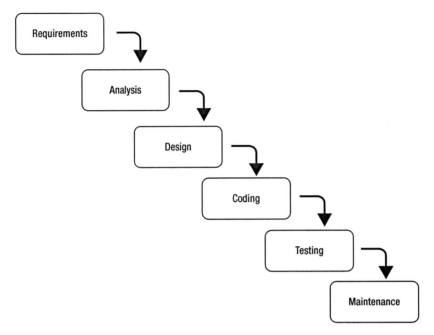

*Figure 1-1. The waterfall process*

The plan-driven method, while great for industries like construction—where requirements remain fixed throughout the project, has its drawbacks when applied to an industry where requirements can change during the lifecycle of the project, as is often the case with software development. Real-world software projects change, not every requirement can be gathered up front, things get missed, and the business is always learning and figuring out better ways to do things. We want the software to outlive the business requirements; not the business requirements outliving the software.

Plan-driven development relies on unchanging requirements. That is to say, once they have been gathered and agreed they may not be changed. If they have to be changed, it is at a great cost to the development team as well as the customer. The notion that a business would remain static for nine to thirty-six months, which is what an average project lasts, is almost absurd. Businesses and project stakeholders are constantly looking to improve process and innovate, and cannot jeopardize this evolution because they are waiting on a software tool to be completed. During the lifecycle of a plan-driven project, the business would find it difficult to give feedback on requirements and design documentation. Because requirements are a gated stage in the process, many plan-driven projects would proceed without the stakeholders really understanding what was to be delivered. Many times stakeholders are uncertain about what they want. A 400-page requirements document is not the ideal way to communicate what the new system will do. However, this was necessary to satisfy a gated stage of the plan-driven method, and development would not start until the project was through that gate.

With this gated process there is not a convenient mechanism for the development team to show their work and for the stakeholders to offer feedback on that work. Therefore, oftentimes the first opportunity that stakeholders would have to offer feedback on the project was during the QA (quality assurance) stage of the process, which would happen after the coding gate was completed. What this means is that a stakeholder would ask for a solution to a problem and would not see a response from the team for a year or more. This is a black-box type of development environment. The customer sends issues in and doesn't see a possible resolution for a year or more.

In this situation, the stakeholder and business would have to accept that they met the requirements as they were defined at the beginning of the project, even if the needs of the business and the environment that the business works in had changed since the requirements' gated stage. A plan-driven approach can only expect to deliver up to the requirements that were agreed upon at the beginning. What the business knew then has been eclipsed by what they know now, perhaps making the software redundant, or worse, obsolete.

One of the biggest issues with the plan-driven process is the lack of any real return on investment to the business until the end of project, during the deployment stage. There is no tangible benefit or value to the business during the months of design and detailed requirement documents. The business cannot just take that 400-page requirements document and use it in their day-to-day operations. It is only when the project is finally finished that the business can expect to see any inkling of business value.

The plan-driven method makes no provision for the unknown. You could say that the plan-driven method of software development's goal is to eliminate the unknown from a project precisely because it has no mechanism for dealing with it. Hence the need for gated stages: you cannot move to the next stage until all the unknowns are known. Because of this need to remove the unknown from a project, no provision is made for altering the initial design when technical issues surface that require these changes.

A by-product of this need to remove the unknown from a project is the way estimation is handled. By removing the unknown and agreeing on the time estimates of the project, all delays that occur in the project are stacked up to the end of the project. In plan-driven development, there is no correction mechanism for estimation errors and the only buffer on this is the amount of over-estimation (slack) that was originally added on to the project.

It is also true that the process does not take into consideration the technical expertise of the developers who will carry out the implementation. These developers carry the responsibility for the eventual implementation of the project. The smallest coding error can have major consequences that may go unnoticed for years, so it is appropriate to think of developers as engineers who make a myriad of decisions, implement technical designs, and solve problems many times during their working day.

The plan-driven method has some shortcomings that do not adequately support the needs of certain organizations. Experiencing projects that overrun or under-deliver also highlights the weaknesses of this method.

Plan-driven development only works in a situation where product managers and business stakeholders know exactly what they want, will not change their minds, are clear on priorities, and are sure that the business process does not change. We have not been able to find any examples of this mythical project, but if you happen to find yourself working on one, then please give us a call and we will be more than happy to join you!

Putting too much emphasis and time into upfront design and requirements gathering can be a risk to the business in terms of both opportunity and cost. The need for a more reliable and iterative approach, where risk is minimized, and that can give businesses maximum return on their investment, is where agile comes in.

## Iterative Change

Software development is simply a means to an end. It enables organizations to automate, streamline, and improve their business processes to solve business problems in order to ultimately reach their goals. By adopting an agile development methodology, and its idea of value-driven development, you will be able to understand and meet the challenges of today's businesses, and in turn you will be able to offer much more value to your stakeholders.

Frequent feedback and interaction between the development team and the stakeholders, domain experts and sponsors, means that agile projects deliver value very rapidly. Task prioritization ensures urgent needs are satisfied first. Iterative development cycles minimize risk, and regular delivery of working software leads to smooth roll-outs, user satisfaction, and reduced training and maintenance costs.

As the software development discipline has matured, agile methods were developed as an evolution from earlier methodologies.

The agile methodology is as much a philosophical shift as it is a process shift. Agile has a firm emphasis on customer satisfaction and a quick return on investment via an iterative approach to software development. Figure 1-2 shows the process of an agile workflow.

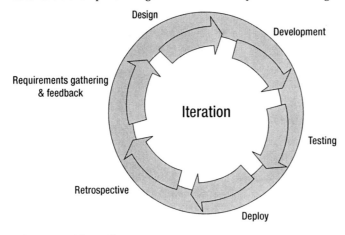

*Figure 1-2. The agile process*

Instead of upfront design and planning stages that strive to remove the unknown from a project before development, agile focuses on small, feature-driven iterations that strive to solve specific business problems. These iterations usually occupy a time box of a fixed two to four weeks' duration. These iterations include all steps of the plan-driven process and enable the business to give frequent feedback on working software in a very short time. The difference between an iteration and doing a project using the plan-driven method of software development is that each iteration is working on small chunks of the project. These chunks are what the stakeholders have designated as the highest priority requirements in the system.

The ability to give working software back to the business within a short time enables the business to start working with that software and gaining value from it—even if that value is to learn that this is not what they really wanted after all. Because agile is so closely aligned with the business, domain experts are considered first-class team members and often meet with the development teams.

Unlike the relaxed start and frantic finish of the more traditional waterfall-based approach, agile promotes a more sustainable working pace.

By breaking down the deliverables of the project into smaller pieces that can be completed in an iteration, agile is providing a mechanism for improving the accuracy of the team's estimates. This mechanism is missing in a plan-driven project. Typically, by the third or fourth iteration the team will be producing fairly accurate estimates. With more accurate estimates, the project manager or sponsor can get a good prediction of the time required to complete the whole system.

Agile is very much like a business, where it is always focusing on improvement of the process by learning and refining its processes. Constant feedback loops from business and development stakeholders help to hone these skills and processes, enabling more efficient delivery of valuable software.

In the end, by applying the agile methodology and using value-driven software development, you as a developer are delivering software that meets the needs of the business in an iterative timeframe.

Now that you have a handle on some of the problems agile has been designed to tackle, let's take a closer look at how to be an agile developer—starting by looking at the Agile Manifesto and some key features that it contains.

# Defining Agile

This section will provide you with a clear definition of the agile development process and some of the key features it encompasses.

## The Agile Manifesto

In the 1990s there were several people in our profession who were talking about changing the way we wrote software. These discussions came to a head in 2001, when a number of software development luminaries, including the likes of Martin Fowler, Kent Beck, Bob Martin, Ken Schwaber, Jess Sutherland, and Dave Thomas met in a lodge at the Snowbird ski resort in the Wasatch Mountains of Utah. What came of this meeting became known as the Agile Manifesto (see Figure 1-3).

---

**Manifesto for Agile Software Development**

We are uncovering better ways of developing
software by doing it and helping others do it.
Through this work we have come to value:

**Individuals and interactions** over processes and tools
**Working software** over comprehensive documentation
**Customer collaboration** over contract negotiation
**Responding to change** over following a plan

That is, while there is value in the items on
the right, we value the items on the left more.

---

*Figure 1-3. The Agile Manifesto*

In addition to the manifesto, twelve principles of agile, shown in Figure 1-4, were created to expand on the manifesto's declaration.

```
+--------------------------------------------------------------------+
|             Principles behind the Agile Manifesto                  |
|                                                                    |
|                  We follow these principles:                       |
|                                                                    |
|          Our highest priority is to satisfy the customer           |
|               through early and continuous delivery                |
|                      of valuable software.                         |
|                                                                    |
|           Welcome changing requirements, even late in              |
|            development. Agile processes harness change for         |
|                 the customer's competitive advantage.              |
|                                                                    |
|            Deliver working software frequently, from a             |
|            couple of weeks to a couple of months, with a           |
|               preference to the shorter timescale.                 |
|                                                                    |
|             Business people and developers must work               |
|               together daily throughout the project.               |
|                                                                    |
|             Build projects around motivated individuals.           |
|          Give them the environment and support they need,          |
|                 and trust them to get the job done.                |
|                                                                    |
|             The most efficient and effective method of             |
|           conveying information to and within a development        |
|                  team is face-to-face conversation.                |
|                                                                    |
|        Working software is the primary measure of progress.        |
|                                                                    |
|           Agile processes promote sustainable development.         |
|           The sponsors, developers, and users should be able       |
|                to maintain a constant pace indefinitely.           |
|                                                                    |
|           Continuous attention to technical excellence             |
|                 and good design enhances agility.                  |
|                                                                    |
|           Simplicity--the art of maximizing the amount             |
|                  of work not done--is essential.                   |
|                                                                    |
|         The best architectures, requirements, and designs          |
|                 emerge from self-organizing teams.                 |
|                                                                    |
|             At regular intervals, the team reflects on how         |
|            to become more effective, then tunes and adjusts        |
|                   its behavior accordingly.                        |
+--------------------------------------------------------------------+
```

*Figure 1-4. The Twelve Principles behind the Agile Manifesto*

Let's expand on the manifesto and its principles to define a set of key features that an agile process should have.

# Key Features of Agile

Looking through the Agile Manifesto and, in particular, the twelve principles, we can identify some key features that define the process and mindset. Let's explore these at a deeper level.

- *Embracing change by understanding the needs of the business:* Being agile is a realization that change is inevitable, nobody gets it right the first time, business priorities change, and people get things wrong. Agility comes about by embracing change, and learning from and with the business. With this in mind agile defines the ability to adapt and be flexible, to embrace change rather than resist it or sit around and moan that the goalposts have moved. Agile teams embrace change and actively identify changes in applications that will increase business value.

- *Focusing on the business value and return on investment (ROI):* Agile development is a development mind shift and a refocusing of efforts and priorities. There are a number of techniques that you will be introduced to in this book that will help you become a more agile developer. However, becoming truly agile is so much more than the sum of its parts. The tools, project methodologies, and programming methods can certainly go some way to help one become agile, but it is the ability to apply these techniques to an ever-changing business that will truly reap the rewards. Fundamentally you must understand the business domain you are working within and align your efforts, practices, and process to realize its value.

- *Continuous delivery via incremental and iterative development:* Being agile is all about delivering working software of value as often as possible. Success of software development is not measured in the amount of design work. Businesses measure success in working software; this should be your measure of progress as well.

- *Continuous improvement by learning from and with the business:* As part of the software development team, it's our job to turn the language and processes of the business into software systems. In order to do this it is vital that we work closely with the domain experts themselves, that is, the people that will use the software. The users aren't always domain experts. They have experience using the existing process, but do not necessarily understand why it is that way. That is where the domain experts come in. The more you as a developer understand about the business you are writing software for, the better the software will be.

  - Eric Evans in his book Domain-Driven Design: Tackling Complexity in the Heart of Software (Addison-Wesley Professional, 2003) picks up on this point when he mentions the "ubiquitous language." This is a language that is shared between the developers and the business to describe the business domain being modeled.

- *Keeping the process lean by continuous reflection on process and the removal of waste:* Keeping process and practices lean is all about eliminating waste. Don't bother with lots of documentation before developing systems. Create the documentation when it is needed. You should be able to cope with a few architectural diagrams that any member of the team can reproduce on a white board. Instead of masses of requirements documentation, use story or tasks cards and write features that can act as reminders for conversations when it is time to build the feature. Lots of upfront documentation is no good to the business—there is simply no value in it. The amount of documentation that is produced in an agile project is defined as a requirement. It is not true that agile equals no documentation. Agile equals the removal of useless information. The code and the user stories with their corresponding acceptance criteria become the documentation of the project. Not a 400-page, stagnant requirements document.

    - Keeping lean is also achieved with regular retrospectives on work carried out and meetings on what's working and not working with the current processes. Continuously refining how we work and concentrating on the work at hand will contribute towards a leaner and more effective working practice.

- *Strong focus on team effort that spans more than developers in order to reduce risk and find better ways of working:* Agile is about working together with a strong focus on the team in an effort to improve your working practices and ultimately deliver more value for your business. Domain experts, product managers, business analysts, security and IT infrastructure stakeholders, and testers should be first-class citizens along with developers during the project. Including non-developers in the team helps to increase knowledge and shared ownership and decreases the "them and us" gap between developers and everyone else in more traditional methods.

    - Agile development can be the proverbial silver bullet. The problem that occurs has to do with changing the people around you. That being said, an agile project methodology can be very valuable to any organization with a need to be flexible when prioritizing application development.

## The Flavors of Agile

There are various forms of agile methodologies, but they all share similar characteristics. You can think of these various methodologies as branches of the same religion. The cornerstone of each branch is the idea of customer satisfaction. They also feature many of the key ideas listed previously, as well as the practices and principles laid out in the Agile Manifesto. The key thing to remember about all the agile flavors is that every one of them is iterative.

## Scrum

The Scrum methodology consists of a series of "sprints," typically lasting two to four weeks, each delivering some working, potentially shippable software. The workload of each of these sprints is driven from the "product backlog." The product backlog consists of new features, bug fixes, technical debt, and anything else that will contribute to the end deliverable. A product owner, with help from the customer, prioritizes the product backlog and works closely with the team via regular stand-up meetings and sprint retrospectives. The iterative aspect of Scrum is that this cycle is repeated over and over until the project is complete.

You will look at Scrum in more detail in Chapter 2.

# eXtreme Programming (XP)

eXtreme Programming (XP) is strongly focused on customer interaction and involvement. It has the following five values:

- Simplicity
- Communication
- Feedback
- Courage
- Respect

It also follows these twelve practices:

1. Planning Game
2. Small Releases
3. Customer Acceptance Tests
4. Simple Design
5. Pair Programming
6. Test-Driven Development
7. Refactoring
8. Continuous Integration
9. Collective Code Ownership
10. Coding Standards
11. Metaphor
12. Sustainable Pace

In XP, user stories are created to capture requirements from customers. These stories are then estimated by the developers, prioritized by the customer, and then developed into working software on an iteration-by-iteration basis. Continuous planning and delivery underpin the disciplined XP process. It is also worth noting that many of the practices in XP are shared by other branches of agile, like Scrum.

You will take a closer look at XP in Chapter 3.

# Crystal

The Crystal group of agile methodologies focuses more on people rather than process. It has a simple set of principles that enhances teamwork by concentrating on communication and the removal of project management noise. It also concentrates teams on the priorities and critical paths of the software development. Like Scrum and XP, it also encourages frequent delivery of working software.

## Dynamic Systems Development Method (DSDM)

The Dynamic Systems Development Method (DSDM) is based on the 80/20 rule, in that 80 percent of the benefit a system will be derived from only 20 percent of the systems requirements. With this in mind, only work that is deemed critical for the system to operate is prioritized; that is, the first 20 percent of requirements. DSDM is prioritized using the so-called MoSCoW method, which is as follows:

> **M**: Must have
>
> **S**: Should have, if at all possible
>
> **C**: Could have, but not critical
>
> **W**: Won't have this time, but potentially later

All "must have" work is committed to being completed in the course of the project; all other work is deemed a "nice to have" and is picked up only when the core requirements have been implemented.

## Feature-Driven Development (FDD)

Feature-driven development (FDD) begins by creating a model of the domain under development. Once this is completed, an iterative process of feature design and implementation begins. Features represent a useful grouping of functionality to the customer. FDD is made up of the following five simple activities:

1. Develop the Domain Object Model
2. Create a feature list
3. Plan by feature
4. Design by feature
5. Build by feature

## Lean Software Development

Lean software development comes from the Lean manufacturing principles that were derived mostly from the production system created by Toyota. Lean focuses on customer value and the elimination of waste. It achieves this by following these next seven principles:

1. Eliminate waste: Selects only the most valuable features for a customer.
2. Amplify learning: Learn by doing and testing things rather than documenting.
3. Decide as late as possible: Delay decisions in order to enable more facts to be gathered and changes to take place.
4. Deliver as fast as possible: The sooner software is delivered, the sooner feedback is received and incorporated into the next release, giving fast return on investment to the business.

5.   Empower the team: Make the team responsible and increase motivation by including all members in the decision-making process.

6.   Build integrity in: Re-factor regularly to keep code flexible and adaptable to change.

7.   See the whole: Ensure that domain knowledge is spread throughout the team in order for problems to be identified at any level of the system.

Throughout this book we will be using the more popular agile methodologies, Scrum and XP, to show you what it means to be agile.

## Summary

This chapter has introduced you to the need for agile with its idea of value-driven development. You first read about the failings of the traditional plan-driven approach to software development. Many of its shortcomings were based on the following presumptions:

•   Requirements won't change.

•   There will be no obstacles or surprises.

•   The business can wait for several months before taking delivery of the first version of the software.

A new process that could react and embrace changes while working alongside the business and treating its people as first-class team members was badly needed to deliver real business value on investment.

With a firm knowledge of why we needed value-driven development you then examined the characteristics of agile by looking at the Agile Manifesto. Some key features you have learned about the agile methodology include:

•   Focusing on the business value and ROI

•   Embracing change by understanding the needs of the business

•   Continuous improvement by learning from and with the business

•   Keeping lean by continuous reflection on practices and the removal of waste

Lastly, you were introduced to a number of popular flavors of agile, each having its own terminology but all sharing a common focus on customer satisfaction through working closely with the business and giving a fast return on investment. The agile methodologies you will follow in the remainder of this book are Scrum and XP, although many of the concepts in this book can be applied to the other methodologies.

In the next chapter you will look at the Scrum process in more detail, as this will be the project methodology that you will follow for the case study that forms the second part of this book.

# Managing Agile Projects with Scrum

In this chapter you will learn all about the Scrum project methodology. You will be introduced to the iterative nature of Scrum, which defines a process skeleton containing a set of roles, activities, and artifacts, all focused on supporting a team committed to delivering a product.

The case study that features in Part Two of this book follows the Scrum methodology, so you will get to see a practical implementation of all of the key characteristics of Scrum as discussed in this chapter, which will help to cement the process and benefits of the methodology.

## What Is Scrum?

Scrum is an iterative approach to software development tightly aligned with agile principles and the Agile Manifesto. Scrum is made up of a series of time blocks called *sprints*, which focus on delivering working software. A sprint is typically two to four weeks in length and is defined by a goal or theme that helps to clarify the objective of the sprint. Sprints are isolated from change, allowing the team to focus on delivering working software without distraction. Scrum focuses on helping the people committed to develop the project deliver that project.

Work is prioritized from a product backlog that is managed by a product owner. Before each sprint occurs, a feature from the product backlog is chosen and the team commits to deliver it by the end of the sprint.

To keep things running smoothly, a *ScrumMaster* is appointed to ensure there are no obstacles impeding the team from delivering the features that the team committed to. Daily stand-up meetings help the team communicate about any issues preventing them from delivering. Retrospectives at the end of each sprint help to improve process.

Figure 2-1 shows a graphical representation of the Scrum methodology, including all of the roles, activities, and artifacts that you will read in more detail in the following sections of this chapter.

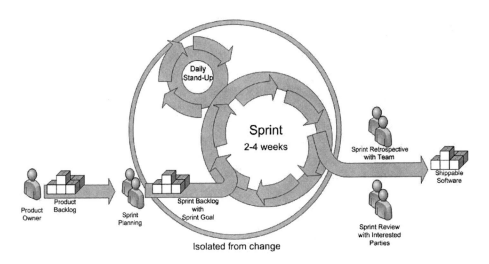

*Figure 2-1. The Scrum process*

The consistent sprint duration combined with the team being time boxed to work on features that cannot be changed in that time frame, as well as short meetings and regular retrospectives, improve development practice by generating a development rhythm. This rhythm enables the team to concentrate on designing and developing high-quality software.

Now that you have an overview of what Scrum is, let's dive deeper into the wonderful world of Scrum.

# Plan-Driven vs. Value-Driven Methods

When looking at the differences between the Waterfall method and the Agile method you need to look at the core behind each method. One method is driven by the plan that was created at the beginning of the project and the other method is driven by the value that you give the customer.

## Waterfall Method (Plan Driven)

The waterfall method can be thought of as a plan-driven method of software development. In the past, this method of development was used by many—not because it was the best way to develop software, but because it was the only method known.

A project that used the waterfall method involved a large amount of risk, mainly because everything was done at the beginning of the project. All the requirements gathering, and discovery and scope definition was completed before the first line of code was ever written. Customers had to know up front everything that they needed or wanted the system to do. At times customers did not know exactly what they wanted, but yet, they had to define every last detail of their needs; and once they defined the details, they could not change them—even if they later realized that their needs had changed.

This approach destined the project for failure before it even began. The entire process led to problems that were hidden until toward the end of a project, simply because the customer had not considered every little detail, and there was no way make changes as the need arose. Sometimes it was too expensive to make a change. Scope creep was rampant in these kinds of projects; developers didn't understand the problem that the customer was trying to solve—and the customer didn't either.

Plan-driven development could be like a hoop jumping process: you started at discovery and once you jumped through that hoop, it was on to the requirements-gathering hoop, and from there you went on to the design hoop. You could not jump through one hoop until you had jumped through the previous hoop, and once you were through a hoop it was near impossible to go back to a previous hoop if the need arose. There was no allowance to do a little bit of everything and then pause to make sure you were still on the right path. The waterfall process did not foster an environment where developers could go to a customer and say, "I would like to show you what I am working on to make sure it is what you want."

Usually the big issues would surface toward the end of a project, which was rather late in the process. This led to many development teams being behind on their projects. When teams got behind on a project, they would just throw more bodies at the project, with the hope that the more people on the project, the faster it would get done. That rarely happened. Most of the time the project would remain behind schedule, so the team had to cut the scope, cut testing, or both.

## Scrum Method (Value Driven)

Scrum is considered a value-driven method for software development. Scrum is a dramatic change over the waterfall method for a number of reasons. Instead of first gathering all the requirements needed for every feature of the project, completing all the designs based on these requirements, and then coding the application based upon these up-front designs, Scrum looks at doing iterative, incremental development.

Scrum is all about taking small passes at a problem and reassessing that problem after each pass. Scrum is all about small:

- Small time blocks called *sprints*

- Small features

- Small teams

Small time blocks are how the team works on a solution for the customer. Each sprint can be looked at as a mini waterfall project. This is because in every sprint you are doing everything you would normally do in a waterfall project, except you are doing it on a smaller scale. In each sprint, you take a feature and you gather requirements on that feature, you design that feature based on those requirements, and you code and test that feature based on those designs. In Scrum, unlike waterfall, you are not trying to do everything up front; you are doing everything you need to do when you need to do it. The goal of each sprint is to deliver an increment of the final product—but an increment *that is potentially releasable.*

So how can we do numerous waterfall projects in each sprint, when we could barely do one waterfall project before? By doing these sprints against small features. Small features are pieces of a project that try to solve a particular problem for the customer; they don't attempt to create the whole application. The massive features of the project are broken down into smaller chunks that can still provide value to the customer and are able to be completed more quickly. As more and more of these features are completed, the customer will start seeing the entire application coming into view.

All of this is done with a small team of developers, testers, and designers that are dedicated to getting the project done. This team is cross functional in that every member knows how to do everything. Each member may not be the best at everything, but everyone knows how to do everything necessary to complete the project. Think of them as a SEAL[1] team, where every member knows how to do everything needed, but there are also experts on every aspect of the operation.

By doing things on a small scale, problems are less likely to arise near the end of the project. In fact, Scrum works to expose problems as soon as possible. Issues can't hide because the process is broken down to a manageable scale. When a problem does surface, it causes major discomfort for the team until they address and fix it. They can't ignore the problem because it is visible to everyone.

There is one important thing to realize about Scrum, however: it works to expose problems to the team as soon as possible, but it is not designed to fix the problems. It exposes the mud, but it is still the team's job to clean it up.

With Scrum, you are not just creating features for the sales and marketing teams to show the customers, you are creating solutions for the customer. This is done by prioritizing the features that need to be completed based on the customer's needs and wants. If a customer deems feature A to be more important than feature B, then the developer would be wasting his time working on feature B before feature A. Give the customers what they want when you say you can deliver it.

## Fixed vs. Variable Factors

There are three key factors or constraints to every software project: time, resources, and scope. Unfortunately you can't have all three at the same time. In a triangle-like fashion, you can work within the influence of two of them at any one time and those two will dictate what happens with the third.

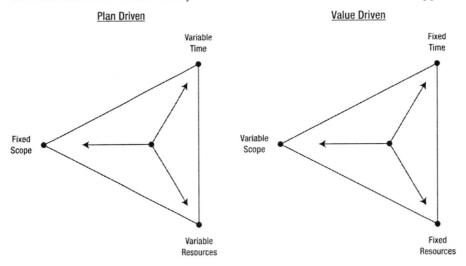

*Figure 2-2. The triangles*

In the plan-driven development model, the project's scope is usually one of the two fixed items, with the project's resources and time being variable. In this case, scope dictates resources and time. This all sounds well and good until you are in the middle of the project and *scope creep* rears its ugly head. In such a case the scope will increase, but neither the resources nor the time can be changed to

---

[1] An elite US Navy special operations force.

reflect that increase. This is when you experience the desperation of throwing more bodies and technology at the project, hoping for the best, ultimately achieving varying degrees of success.

In the value-driven development model, resources and time are fixed on the triangle. You know the size of your team and you roughly know their velocity from their work on previous sprints. The scope of the project becomes the variable in the triangle. In other words, the project's resources and time dictate the project's scope.

You may be asking: how is this even possible with customers always changing their minds? Well, since the team is able to release workable and valuable software to a customer at the end of each sprint, scope creep becomes nearly impossible. As new features are requested by the customer, they are prioritized against other items already in the product backlog that the team has yet to start. After this prioritization, the customer's "must haves" move to the top of the list and their "would like to haves" are pushed to the bottom of the list. Over-commitment is prevented because the team is only working on features that the customer wants right away.

Now let's talk about the pieces and parts of the Scrum framework.

# Scrum Artifacts

Scrum contains three main artifacts: product backlog, sprint backlog, and the burn-down chart. These artifacts are the by-products of the Scrum activities and help give direction and transparency to the team. In addition to these main artifacts, there is also an important secondary artifact: acceptance criteria.

## Product Backlog

The product backlog is a list of all work remaining on a project that the team needs to complete. This list represents the customer's product needs and wants. At the heart of this list is the *user story*, a key component of Scrum. It defines the increment of value to the customer that the developer is trying to deliver.

The product backlog is managed by the product owner, who is responsible for adding and removing user stories to and from the list. The product backlog is constantly prioritized by both the product owner and the customer. This constant prioritization is the key to Scrum. It ensures that the user stories that provide the greatest value to the customer are listed at the top of the product backlog. As user stories are added, they are compared to the user stories already on the list to see where they fit in value to the customer. During a sprint, user stories can be added to the product backlog, however, they will not be presented to the team until after the current sprint is completed.

## User Stories

As mentioned earlier, the product backlog is nothing more that a prioritized list of user stories. A user story is a card that describes an increment of value to the customer. The user story is written for the developer in order to express the increment of value. The key to a good user story is that it is a vertical slice through the product. A horizontal slice is a feature that just touches one level, such as the database level or the UI (user interface) level. A vertical slice, on the other hand touches all the levels of the product, as illustrated in Figure 2-3. This is the smallest amount of work that touches all levels of the product and still provides value to the customer. By writing the user stories in a way that allows for vertical slicing, you can create basic functionality in the first user story and then easily add functionality to this feature as the customer needs it.

Vertical Slice

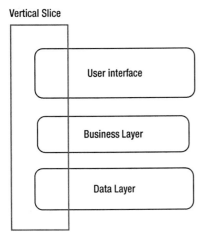

***Figure 2-3.*** *Vertical slicing of the product*

A way to make sure that a user story accomplishes the goal of being a vertical slice through the system is to make sure that it fits the INVEST acronym. INVEST[2] stands for:

- Independent: The user story should be self contained, so that there is no inherent dependency on another story.

- Negotiable: User stories, up until they are a part of a sprint, can always be changed and rewritten.

- Valuable: A user story must deliver value to the end user.

- Estimable: You must always be able to estimate the size of a user story.

- Sized appropriately: User stories should not be so big as to become impossible to plan/task/prioritize with a degree of certainty.

- Testable: The user story or its related description must provide the necessary information to make test development possible.

## Backlog Sizing

Sizing the product backlog is a measure of the pace at which the Scrum team can deliver items. People are not good at estimating work. We all know how terrible we are at accurately estimating how long something will take us to complete. How many times have we heard or said ourselves, "I am 80 percent complete on this. The remaining 20 percent will be done in an hour." Yet two days later, it's still not done. People are just naturally bad at estimating.

---

[2] This mnemonic is hard to attribute, as it has become pervasive. See
`www.scrumalliance.org/articles/80-keep-your-team-seeing-red` for more information.

We may not be good on our estimates, but we are great at comparing things. For example, we are able to look at two cooking recipes and tell which one is more complex without being a professional chef. We can look at two items and see that one is larger than the other. Sizing the backlog is all about making decisions based on the complexity and amount of work, not on how long it will take to do the work. Sizing is not equal to estimating.

You may ask: how do I know how long something will take? Consider, as an example, a manager who wants to know how long it will take your team to produce a widget. You can derive the time estimate of completing the widget from the complexity of the widget. After your team has gone through a sprint, you can then look at that sprint and calculate how long it took the team to complete it. The team is only concerned with how complex a task is.

To perhaps better explain the idea of estimating the amount of work over the time to complete it, let's compare it to painting your house. Let's say you went to your local hardware store and bought several gallons of paint to paint your house. Then you call three contractors to give you an estimate on painting the house. The first contractor comes out and walks around the house, looks at all the buckets of paint you bought, and explains that he has old rusty ladders and handheld brushes and a scrawny kid to help him, so it will take him two days to do the job.

The second contractor comes out and walks around the house, looks at the buckets of paint, and explains that he just recently purchased new ladders and brushes, and the local high school varsity football team is working for him that weekend. With all those hands and the new equipment it will only take him a day to paint your house.

The third contractor comes out, walks around the house, looks at the paint, and explains that he owns some brand new mechanical paint sprayers and top-of-the-line machinery and he can have the house painted by lunch time.

What you see in this story are three contractors with three different time estimates on how long it will take to paint the house, but there is one thing that did not change throughout all of this and that is the size of the house and the amount of paint. No matter who was doing the job, the house size never changed, even though the time estimates did. The moral of the story is to do your best not to estimate the duration of the work, but instead estimate the amount of effort it will take to complete the work. Once you have the estimation of the amount of work, you can derive the duration to complete the work.

## Sprint Backlog

The sprint backlog is a list of all work remaining in a sprint that needs to be done by the team. Think of the sprint backlog as a subset of the product backlog. Whereas the product backlog lists all the user stories remaining for the product, the sprint backlog contains all the user stories and tasks remaining for the sprint. Typically when a user story is chosen for a sprint, the team will split that user story into tasks.

A task is a small chunk of the user story that can be done by any member on the team. Examples would be a task to implement the database changes needed for the user story, or a task to implement the UI for the user story. These tasks are displayed on a task board—also known as a Kanban[3] board—that is visible to the entire organization. Other items can appear on this board as well, including information on set-up meetings to gather requirements, review checks, research, testing, design, and stages of coding. Figure 2-4 shows an example.

Team members take a card from the board and during the sprint commit to doing the task the card describes. As team members work through tasks, other tasks may emerge and original estimates are adjusted. All members of the team are responsible for updating the Kanban board based on new information gained on the feature being worked on.

---

[3] Japanese for "signboard" or "billboard."

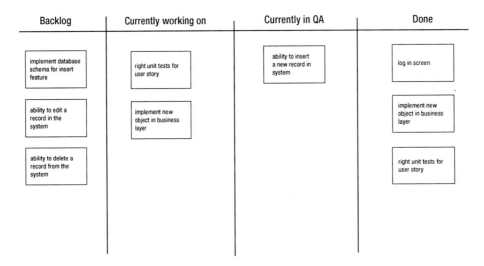

| Backlog | Currently working on | Currently in QA | Done |
|---|---|---|---|
| implement database schema for insert feature | right unit tests for user story | ability to insert a new record in system | log in screen |
| ability to edit a record in the system | implement new object in business layer | | implement new object in business layer |
| ability to delete a record from the system | | | right unit tests for user story |

*Figure 2-4. An example Kanban board with a sprint backlog*

The sprint backlog supplies the information needed by the burn-down chart. At the end of each sprint, the sprint backlog is emptied. Any remaining items on the backlog are pushed back to the product backlog, where they are reprioritized against user stories currently in the product backlog, in addition to any new user stories that were added during the sprint.

## Burn-down chart

A burn-down chart is a visual way to track how the sprint is progressing. The chart graphically shows the amount of remaining work on any given day of the sprint, as seen in Figure 2-5. It is usually displayed in a public area where anyone can see it. This aids the communication among team members and anyone else in the organization. This chart can also act as an early indicator that there is a problem in the sprint and the team may not be able to fulfill the commitment.

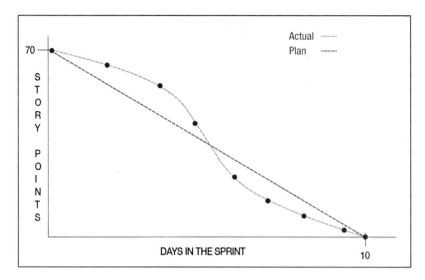

*Figure 2-5. Example burn-down chart for a sprint*

## Acceptance Criteria

Although product backlog, sprint backlog, and the burn-down chart are the primary parts of Scrum, acceptance criteria is a very important secondary artifact in the Scrum process. Without good acceptance criteria a project is doomed to fail.

Acceptance criteria is essentially a clarification of the story. It gives the developer a set of steps that must be completed before the story can be considered done. The acceptance criteria are created by the product owner with the help of the customer. It sets the expectation of the user story. With this in place, a developer has a great starting point in which to write automated tests or even use test-driven development (TDD). In this way, the developer is creating something that the customer needs and wants with the understanding of how the customer will use it.

Another benefit of acceptance criteria appears when a feature cannot be completed in a sprint and needs to be spread out across sprints. Then the team can use the acceptance criteria as a tool to see where the user story could be broken into smaller pieces that still provide value to the customer, but *can* be completed in a sprint.

## Scrum Roles

Scrum makes a strong distinction between the people *committed* to the project and those that are just *interested* in it. The most famous way of explaining this concept is via the fable of the pig and the chicken.

A pig and a chicken are walking down a road. The chicken looks at the pig and says, "Hey, why don't we open a restaurant?" The pig looks back at the chicken and says, "Good idea, what do you want to call it?" The chicken thinks about it and says, "Why don't we call it 'Ham and Eggs'?"

"I don't think so," says the pig, "I'd be committed, but you'd only be involved."

The "Pigs" are the people who are committed to the project. They are the ones that handle the creating, testing, and deploying of the project. The "Chickens," on the other hand, are less committed. They are the stakeholders and/or interested parties who benefit from the project, but are not responsible for delivering it. Input from people classified as Chickens on the project should be taken into consideration; however it should not prevent the team from delivering the project.

Scrum promotes the support of the Pigs, but values and takes into account the views of the Chickens.

## Pig Roles

The following are the three Pig roles that make up a Scrum team:

- ScrumMaster

- Product owner

- Delivery team

## ScrumMaster

If the team is the engine of a Scrum project, then you can think of the ScrumMaster as the oil that keeps the engine running. The ScrumMaster is responsible for ensuring that the Scrum process is understood and followed. A ScrumMaster facilitates the team meetings and removes any blockages that the team may have in the course of the doing their work. He ensures that there are no obstacles keeping the team from achieving their goals and also isolates the team from outside distractions, all of which ensures focus is kept on the job at hand.

The ScrumMaster also liaises with different parts of the team, from product owners to testers and business stakeholders, ensuring that all members of the team are productive and share the common goal of delivering the sprint. Don't liken the ScrumMaster position to that of a traditional project manager because the role is much more than that.

The key characteristic of a ScrumMaster is to be a "servant leader." A ScrumMaster is not the boss of the team, but is there to help the team achieve what it needs to accomplish in the sprint. The ScrumMaster is there to help the team align the work in order to deliver value to the customer. A ScrumMaster is the team coach. He facilitates the decision-making aspects within a team. He is the point person for the team to those outside the group, and thus needs to be a top-notch communicator. When issues arise among a team, it is up to the ScrumMaster to manage that conflict and get the team back on track.

There are times, however, when the ScrumMaster stops being the servant leader and starts becoming a dictator. Since a key responsibility of the ScrumMaster is to ensure that the practices of Scrum are being followed as a team, any issue or attack against the framework should be handled by the ScrumMaster. Hopefully this is something that rarely happens.

## Product Owner

A product (or project) owner represents the customer and is responsible for maximizing the value of the work that the team produces. The product owner meets with the customers to determine their wants and needs, and prioritizes those items so that the team is always working on the items of highest customer value. A product owner manages the product backlog and is the only person who can prioritize the user stories for a sprint; all features are developed for her and she is responsible for the sign-off of sprint deliverables. The product owner's responsibilities change from being classified as a "Pig" before and after a sprint to being a "Chicken" during a sprint.

The product owner role is also vital in that this person is the customer's representative to the team. A product owner is similar to a ScrumMaster, but the main difference is the nature of the roles: the ScrumMaster is looking after the *team's* best interest during a sprint while the product owner is looking after the *customer's* best interest during the sprint.

In a Scrum team, the product owner is the one role that cannot be miscast. A product owner who is unable to accurately portray the customer's wants and needs will result in failure. The product owner is key to delivering a product that brings value to the customer and success to the team.

## Delivery Team

The delivery team is the group of people responsible for actually delivering the product. The team usually consists of two to ten people and includes a combination of programmers, testers, front-end designers, and members from any other required disciplines. The team works on each sprint to move the user story and related tasks through the different stages on the Kanban board until completion.

The key characteristic of a Scrum delivery team is that it is a self-organizing unit. There is no one leader; everyone decides as a group what they can commit to each sprint. Team members also decide what tools they need to be successful for the project. This level of autonomy was unheard of in a waterfall method.

Delivery teams are designed to optimize flexibility and productivity. They are cross functional in that each member of the team should know all aspects of the product to varying degrees. Each individual on the team is not an expert at everything in the application, but each is a generalist in everything and an expert on a few aspects of the product.

The delivery team, along with the ScrumMaster and product owner, work together to complete the user stories and successfully accomplish each sprint. The ScrumMaster is geared to look after the team's interests and the product owner is geared to look after the customer's interests. With those two roles in place, the team does can concentrate on creating the application that the customer wants.

## Chicken Roles

The people classified in the Chicken roles vary, ranging from business managers and directors to stakeholders such as customers, vendors, and sponsors. The Chickens are not actively involved in the development of the project; rather they are an interested party. Ultimately, the project is developed *for* these people, so their views are important and must be taken into account, but not at the expense of the development. This is why the ScrumMaster liaises between other people and the team and makes sure that these interested other people provide the resources that the team needs to get the job done, but don't act as a distraction. Chicken roles are only involved in the process during sprint reviews, when feedback from stakeholders and other interested parties is of high value.

Because Chicken roles typically enjoy higher salaries in an organization they are not usually called chickens! Instead, they are told the pig and chicken story and then invited (and actively encouraged) to attend the Scrum meetings from time to time. Generally they do so and are very happy to observe and hear firsthand about what is going on.

# Scrum Activities

The activities involved in Scrum center around project planning, review, and meeting.

# Sprint Planning

Before the start of each sprint, a planning meeting is held to determine which features will be included in the sprint. Features come from the product backlog, which is prioritized by the product owner. The first time that this meeting occurs on a project the product backlog is created. You can think of this as sprint 0. The user stories chosen by the product owner to be included in the sprint are given to the team and through a tool called *Planning Poker*, they are resized to show the complexity of a story related to the other stories in group (this will be further discussed in the following section). Once the user stories are sized, they are turned into a number of tasks by the team and a time estimate on how long each task will take is determined. Once all this is done, the team will look at the entire list of submitted work for the sprint and decide if they can commit to completing the work by the end of the sprint. To decide this, the team does a five-finger vote to gauge individual members' opinions.

A team member simply raises his hand and through the number of fingers he is holding up, he displays what bests reflects his confidence level. A hand value of a "1" means that the team member is very doubtful of the proposal. A hand value of a "5" means the team member is extremely confident in the proposal. If no one holds up a value of a "1" or "2" then the team commits to that work for the sprint. If a value of "1" or "2" is shown, then the team discusses why that team member voted this way and adjusts the proposal accordingly.

Once the team commits to delivering the list of user stories and tasks within the sprint, the ScrumMaster enacts a change freeze to allow the team time to develop the user story as written before any changes can be made (to prevent scope creep). A sprint backlog is made up of all the user stories and tasks required to complete the sprint. All members of the team, including the ScrumMaster and the product owner, are involved in sprint planning meetings. Once the planning meeting is over, the team will get together without the product owner to discuss the high-level design of the system.

## Planning Poker

Planning Poker is a game that encourages the team members to give their honest assessment of the complexity of a user story in relation to other stories. The tools required for the game are simple: you can use your hand or purchase a set Planning Poker cards to handle it.

To play this game, the product owner will read the user story and explain it to the team. The team is free to ask questions about the story. Once all the questions have been answered, the ScrumMaster will ask the team to privately determine a number that best represents the complexity of the story. Team members should not share their numbers with anyone in order to prevent inadvertently influencing other team members. Once the team members have each come up with a number, the ScrumMaster asks everyone to reveal their numbers. If all the team members decided the same number, that number is assigned to the user story and everyone moves on to the next one. If the numbers do not match, then the team members with the lowest number and the highest number are asked to explain why they selected the number that they did.

After the discussion, another round of poker is played with each member deciding on a number for the user story. This goes on until the team has unanimously settled on a number. On average, there will be no more than three rounds to agree on numbers. If at the end of three rounds there is still no consensus, however, we suggest that the ScrumMaster take the number in the middle and move on to the next user story.

Planning Poker accomplishes a conversation about a user story among the entire team. When this discussion occurs, "rabbit holes" and "gotchas" are usually avoided for the developer.

## Daily Stand-Ups (Scrums)

During a sprint, the team, the ScrumMaster, and the product owner commit to meeting once daily in the same place and at the same time to discuss any issues that are preventing work from being done. Meetings are held with everyone standing and time boxed to no longer than 15 minutes. Anyone interested is invited to attend these meetings; however, only the people classified as Pigs are allowed to speak at these meetings.

At the meeting, each team member answers the following three questions:

- What have you done since yesterday?

- What are you planning to do today?

- Do you have any problems preventing you from accomplishing your goal? What progress has been made on existing impediments? Can the blockage be removed or must it be escalated? (The ScrumMaster looks after this area.)

To keep the meeting from becoming a long, drawn-out ordeal and to stay within the 15-minute time box, team members agree to meet after the meeting to further discuss any problems raised during the stand-up. The daily stand-up meetings are about team members committing to work and giving a platform to talk about issues early in the process.

## Sprint Review

The sprint review is held at the end of the sprint. Its purpose is for the team to present the user stories it has completed during the sprint. The team, product owner, and ScrumMaster are present at the review, along with any interested parties—especially managers and customers. The review consists of an informal demo of the developed software as it stands at the end of the sprint. This product demo meeting is a chance for the customer to give feedback on the product to the team. This opportunity for the customer to see the product and provide feedback on it gives the customer the chance to see a return on investment that was not possible in the waterfall development process. The aim of the review is to show the actual working software; there should be no formal slide show presentation or masses of preparation for this review. This meeting aligns with the agile principle of satisfying the customer through early and continuous delivery of valuable software.

## Sprint Retrospectives

Along with the sprint review, a sprint retrospective occurs at the end of a sprint. The sprint retrospective is an opportunity for the team to reflect on the sprint that was. This is the team's chance to congratulate itself for the things that went well and discuss the things that went wrong. This is an open area where the team should feel free to discuss any issue that affects the team and their ability to deliver the product to the customer. During this meeting, the entire team is present, including the ScrumMaster and the product owner.

At the beginning of this meeting the ScrumMaster gives each person three stacks of Post-it notes in three colors. One color is designated to mean "things that went well during the sprint;" another color is designated to mean "things that were confusing during the sprint;" and the third color is designated to mean "things that were bad during the sprint." The group is then given a time box (three to five minutes) to write down as many thoughts as they can about the sprint onto the Post-it notes. This is quiet time with everyone writing. Once the time is up, all the notes are gathered and put on a wall in the office room. The cards are then organized into similar categories. As time progresses on the product, you start to see some common categories that come up with every sprint.

The ScrumMaster reads the notes for each category and the team discusses them. If during the discussion an action item is presented, the ScrumMaster will write it down. Once the team has finished discussing the category, the ScrumMaster will move on to the next category. This is done until all the categories are discussed.

---

▨ **Note**  To keep the meeting moving and to avoid having a four-hour retrospective, the ScrumMaster may time box the discussion of each category.

---

Toward the end of the meeting, the ScrumMaster reads all the action items that were presented and the team assigns members to be responsible for making sure the action items get addressed.

This is a good time for the team to try new ideas on how to fix problems. Do not be afraid to try something new with a sprint. If it does not work for the team, then throw it out and try something else. This meeting aligns with the agile principles of continuous improvement of practices and process, and owes much to Lean principles.

# Summary

This chapter has examined the details of the Scrum methodology and its differences compared to the waterfall method of development. The Scrum process is designed to support all who are committed to the delivery of a product and it promotes continuous improvement via regular, short, team meetings in the form of sprints, sprint retrospectives, and daily stand-ups.

Scrum is aligned with many of the key features of the Agile Manifesto and agile principles that Scrum values, as follows:

- Customer satisfaction through regular delivery of software demonstrated in the sprint review.

- Embracing change by allowing customers to add to the product backlog and permitting changes to be incorporated in the next sprint.

- Business and developers communicating regularly and during sprint reviews.

- Team members communicating daily at the stand-ups.

- Building projects around motivated individuals, allowing teams to self-organize, shielding teams from outside distractions, and rapidly removing obstacles.

- Effective face-to-face communication via sprint planning, daily stand-ups, sprint reviews, and sprint retrospectives.

- Providing working software by committing to deliver software of value for each sprint.

- Reflecting on how to become more effective via sprint retrospectives.

- Sustainable development by a consistent sprint duration and team estimation of workloads.

This chapter also examined the artifacts of Scrum, which include the following:

- Kanban board
- Sprint burn-down charts
- Product backlog
- Sprint backlog

Scrum roles were covered, as follows:

- ScrumMaster
- Product owner
- Delivery team

And Scrum activities were also covered, including the following:

- Sprint planning
- Daily stand-ups
- Sprint retrospectives

Scrum is a process that embraces the principles and themes of agile development. It has a great lightweight framework for supporting teams in delivering quality software at regular intervals. Because Scrum doesn't dictate how to develop, it can easily be complemented by other flavors of agile development.

In the next chapter you will take a closer look at the features of eXtreme Programming (XP). You will use XP in conjunction with Scrum during the case study that starts in the second part of this book.

# eXtreme Programming

A number of different implementation frameworks have been conceived within the spirit of the Agile Manifesto. eXtreme Programming (XP) is such a framework and focuses on delivering business value through a lean process, customer satisfaction, and short development cycles. Whereas Scrum is primarily focused on the project management side of things, XP is more focused on development details. Thus Scrum and XP are complementary, and are often used together to become more efficient in delivering customer valued software.

In this chapter, you will learn about the concepts behind the XP methodology and see how closely it's aligned with the Agile Manifesto's principles and practices. Following the values of XP, we will discuss the following XP practices: Planning, Environment, Self-Organization, Shared Understanding, Commitment to Development Excellence, and Quality Assurance.

## XP Values

eXtreme Programming is based on the following five core values:

- *Respect*: Respect is a two-way street: it needs to be given to fellow teammates so that everyone feels respected as a valued team member; and it is also required from management so that the team owns and is responsible for what they have committed to.

  Respect is not attacking a fellow developer for the code that he has written. Respect implies criticizing the code, not the developer, and working with that developer to increase his level of code quality. Respect is being humble and leading by example to bring others on your team up, not disrespectfully tear them down.

- *Communication*: In order to develop quality software efficiently, clear and frequent communication is required between the customer and team members. If possible, sit down with the customer and flush out ideas, point to things, make communication highly visible and interactive, and avoid "pie in the sky" types of conversations. Stick figures and a whiteboard or pointing at the computer screen to bring across a point go a long way. Such methods often work better than trying to write a multi-page document attempting to get the same point across.

  Clear and frequent communication is required by code as well as people. XP practices such as simple design, refactoring, pair programming, and test-driven development (TDD) help define a simple system architecture that is understood by the team and represents the domain that the model is based on.

- *Simplicity.* Albert Einstein had it right he said, "Make everything as simple as possible, but not simpler." Simplicity is an art form. Keeping the code simple means doing what is required and nothing more, rather than over-complicating things that may never be needed. The value of having a simple code base is that it enables developers to quickly understand and work with the code, which in turn enables features to be added and modified easily and quickly.

- 
  *Feedback.* Feedback is an essential part of XP programming and it can come in various flavors. Feedback is important when working with the code base to ensure that it is not broken when making a modification. This is achieved through TDD and a continuous integration process. Feedback is also valuable when demoing working code to a customer. The customer's feedback can be integrated into the code right away, or added to the next iteration. Having customers sit with the team allows constant feedback to happen. Finally, feedback from the rest of the development team is crucial in XP. Team feedback can help validate system design decisions and ensure the design remains simple. Feedback from the team via pair programming enables knowledge sharing and increased technical excellence; for when a member of the team learns a new technique, she can share it. Team feedback is enabled by the team sitting together, which is an XP practice that you will read more about later.

- *Courage.* Last, but certainly not least, courage is a must. The XP methodology empowers developers to self-organize and estimate their work; and to be honest and transparent with estimates and roadblocks. To have courage opens the possibility of failure; but the key is to fail early, change course, and continue along the path to success. Courage is needed for developers to leave preconceptions behind when they start a project. Thus they are able to embrace new ideas and come up with the simplest design for the project they are working on, rather than (for instance) trying to reuse a design that is familiar from a previous project.

The project management methodology of XP, as you'll see, is very similar to Scrum; we will discuss similarities. Now let's take a look at the practices of XP, which can help you achieve an agile software development process.

## XP Practices and Principles

XP is made up of a set of twelve practices that can be used independently, but are far more powerful when used in concert. Figure 3-1 shows all twelve XP practices and where they fit in relation to the development process.

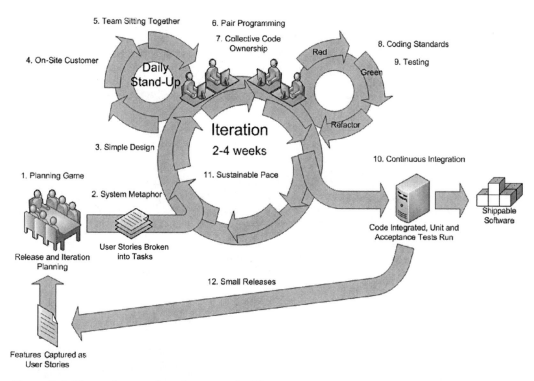

**Figure 3-1.** *The twelve practices that comprise XP*

Let's take a look at how these practices relate to the iterative development process.

1.   Planning Game: The planning game captures the features of the system as user stories, and defines the releases of the project. During iteration planning, user stories selected for the iteration are broken down into development tasks.

2.   System Metaphor: When communicating with the business, it helps to have a ubiquitous language so that complex systems can be explained easily.

3.   Simple Design: High-level system design occurs at the start and during an iteration.

4.   On-Site Customer: During an iteration, it is ideal for the customer to be on-site to aid in quickly answering details of a user story. While physical meetings are ideal, virtual meetings are better than no meeting at all. The important point is to have an available customer who can quickly provide answers as the developers explore the details of a user story.

5.   Team Sitting Together: It's important for all of the team committed to the project to be within shouting distance of each other. This improves communication and imparts a feeling of camaraderie.

31

6.  Pair Programming: Pair programming is a development practice that pairs developers so that they can work on a problem together. A pair will share a development machine, and while one codes, the other will assist with design decisions and look ahead to the next feature. With pair programming, code reviews become "real time," producing a level of quality that "inspection-only" cannot. With two people developing, it's highly unlikely that they will both overlook the same mistake.

7.  Collective Code Ownership: Through sitting together and pair programming, the entire team shares a collective ownership of the code base. All developers are allowed to fix and work on any part of the code base.

8.  Coding Standards: To help with collective ownership, best practices are used to keep a simple design and ensure all code is created in a consistent manner. This ensures that source code can be understood quickly when working on any part of the system and with any other developer.

9.  Testing: To ensure quality is delivered to the customer, emphasis is placed on testing through the XP process. Testing starts by identifying acceptance criteria from user stories. These acceptance criteria are used to write unit tests and start development in TDD style. User acceptance testing also derives from the acceptance criteria and will be automated as much as possible.

10. Continuous Integration: To ensure that all of the code that the team is collectively developing actually works, the team integrates often and early. A continuous integration (CI) server will pull the code base from a source control repository, build it, and run all the automated tests to ensure the build is not broken. The publicly published output of the CI server can be notified instantly to developers, customers, and project managers. This report includes the number of tests that are pass/fail at this point. Daily tracking provides an indicator of progress in creating customer value. This quick feedback loop also enables developers to fix the build. The sooner an issue is identified, the cheaper it is to fix.

11. Sustainable Pace: Because of the short release cycles and the iterative nature of XP, requirements gathering, design, development, testing, and deploying all happen often. This means that issues found after review and testing can be incorporated into the next iteration. This quick feedback model ensures that developers can work at a sustainable pace. Thus, they save long weeks compared to more traditional development methodologies that have clearly defined stages for the development life-cycle, leaving feedback and testing until the end. Sustainable pace also helps management to plan more efficiently for staff holidays, unplanned absences, and the occasional production "fire" that needs to be extinguished immediately.

12. Small Releases: XP is all about customer satisfaction and delivering business value through quality software. As far as the business is concerned, the more often this can happen, the better. XP promotes frequent releases, which may be relatively small, but highlights the features prioritized by the business. XP does not allow the development team to go into hiding for months on end, hoping that the project completes on time. This transparency of frequent

releases encourages customers by showing them the team is adding value to the project all along the way.

Each of these twelve practices forms the practical application of XP, which realizes the five values discussed in the previous section.

The remainder of this chapter will take a more detailed look at the twelve XP practices, starting with project planning.

# Planning

Planning is an important part of any project and an XP project is no different. In XP, the planning phase occurs before each iteration.

## User Stories

Developers estimate features by capturing requirements as user stories and assigning points to them based on relative complexity. With a list of sized stories and a development time budget, customers are able to select features for inclusion in the next iteration. The development budget is made up of the amount of work the development team can commit to in an iteration. The budget for Iteration 1 is simply an educated guess. Be comfortable in the knowledge that the budget estimate will be wrong initially, but it will be correct by the start of the next iteration. At the end of the iteration, add up the points from each completed story. The total of completed points becomes your *velocity*. This velocity will be a good indicator of how to budget for the next iteration. Once enough data points have been gathered, another good budgeting indicator is a "rolling velocity," which is the average of the last three iterations.

Now that you have a high-level overview of the planning phase, let's take a more detailed look at all of the methods that make up the planning game.

The planning game is divided into two phases: the exploration phase and the planning phase. The exploration phase brings the developers and customers together to discuss the requirements of the system being designed. Remember, this is just-in-time planning and development, so discuss only enough features to begin working. Know that this list of captured features is not complete. Customers oftentimes don't know or can't articulate what they want, so this list will typically be fluid. As features are refined, more will be added; or you can remove some features that are no longer as relevant. During exploration, features are broken down and documented as user stories.

A user story is a short description of a feature that represents a single unit of business value to the customer. User stories are told from the user perspective and are written using the following template:

As a <type of user>, I want <some action> so that < business benefit>

Or,

In order for <some reason>, as a <user role> I want <some action>

Typically user stories are recorded on index cards during meetings with the customer, using terms and a language that the customer understands. You may think that the documenting of requirements goes against the agile theme given that agile values working software over comprehensive documentation. In fact, user stories simply act as reminders or a commitment for a more detailed conversation to happen at a later date and are deliberately kept short and focused. This requires more communication between developers and customers to understand lower-level details, in line with the agile principle that states, "The most efficient and effective method of conveying information to and within a development team is face-to-face conversation."

When capturing features as user stories, use the mnemonic INVEST to ensure good user stories, as follows:

- *Independent*: The user story should be independent of others. This is important because a customer can reprioritize or even toss out user stories that aren't in an iteration. Having a user story that has a number of dependencies is apt to reduce this flexibility.

- *Negotiable*: Until a story card is in an iteration, user stories need to be negotiable and considered fluid. This allows the customer to continue refining the user story as more information is gathered.

- *Valuable*: A user story must deliver value to the end user.

- *Estimable*: Estimation is a mix between art and science. Humans are better at estimating relatively smaller things than larger things. We are also good at comparing things ("this user story is larger than that user story").

- *Sized Appropriately or Small*: This is iterative development and we want relatively quick turnaround so define tasks that are relatively small. Small tasks are much easier to manage and estimate.

- *Testable*: How can we test this user story? The user story must be able to be tested. Determining that a user story is testable and identifying what those tests are will aid in determining in the definition of done. Based on these tests passing, we know that this user story is complete. Not defining done allows for ambiguity. A definition of done is important and needs to be agreed to by both the Customer and the team.

Figure 3-2 shows an example of a user story that describes the feature of a customer adding a voucher to a basket. "Receive a discount" is the business benefit to the primary actor (the Customer). "Add a voucher to (my) basket" is the name of the process or use case.

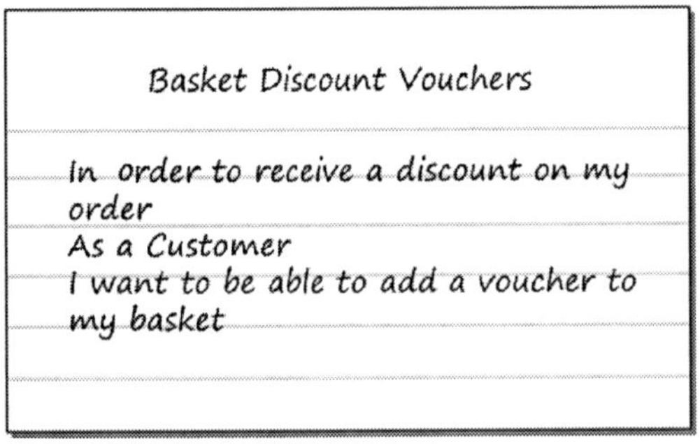

Basket Discount Vouchers

In order to receive a discount on my order
As a Customer
I want to be able to add a voucher to my basket

*Figure 3-2. Add discount voucher to basket*

User acceptance criteria can also be captured during the story generation. Story cards can be turned over and the acceptance criteria should be captured on the reverse side, as shown in Figure 3-3. Using the opposite side of the card allows team members and customers to gather information in one location.

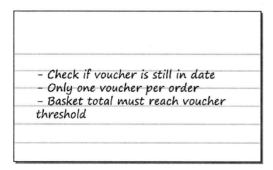

*Figure 3-3.* *User acceptance criteria on the back of a story card*

The acceptant criteria also aids in flushing out more details or identifying dependencies. In the case of Figure 3-3, what is the definition of "in date" and what determines the "voucher threshold"? Typically there should be a minimum of three acceptance criteria.

You will learn more about user stories when you create them for the case study that begins in the next chapter. A great resource for more information is *User Stories Applied: For Agile Software Development* by Mike Cohn (Addison-Wesley Professional, 2004).

When the customers and the team feel as if they have 75 percent of the most important features, the developers estimate the size of the stories to get them ready for the customer to prioritize.

## Estimating

Estimation is hard, no doubt about it. It's both a science and an art. When a project first begins, estimation is really difficult, as there are many unknowns. XP meets the challenge by relative estimation and adjusting estimates as the project progresses, for example, when the developers gain a greater understanding of the system that they are creating. Estimates are captured as story points. Story points can be a combination of complexity and time or the concept of a perfect day.

One tool in group estimation is a technique called Planning Poker. Planning Poker incorporates all the technical members of the team. In the case of Planning Poker, the team is composed of software developers, analysts, and security and infrastructure experts who each bring a different technical perspective. The customer is involved in Planning Poker only to answer questions that the team might ask in order to develop a better estimate.

A member of the team picks up a user story and explains it to the team. The team discusses the feature with the customer to discover more details. After the team has a good understanding, the voting begins. Each team member can vote with a pack of cards with the numbers 0, 1, 2, 3, 5, 8, 13, 20, 40, and 100.

The team should start with a story that is relatively small and easy to size. It becomes the baseline. Each user story's effort estimate should be relative to this baseline story. The baseline story is important. It is key that this estimate is accurate, as it forms the basis for future estimates. If the baseline story is wildly incorrect, the rest of the estimates will also be incorrect.

If all team members vote with the same number, then that's the estimate for that story. If, however, they don't vote with the same number, the moderator—anyone who is not voting—will ask the persons who voted the highest and the lowest to each explain the reasoning behind their vote. The team further discusses the feature and another round of voting commences. From experience, it's good to have a reasonable time block for each discussion. This keeps the group focused on the task at hand.

If a story is too difficult to estimate due to the lack of technical knowledge, it can be useful to leave the story and instead create another story to spike the unfamiliar technology. After the spike has been completed, the development team should be in a better position to estimate the story. The difference between a spike and a dependency is that a spike involves gaining enough technical knowledge to be able to provide an estimate, whereas a dependency occurs when the technical knowledge exists but another task or feature needs to be completed first. A spike could be to learn Silverlight in order to develop a Windows Phone 7 application versus a dependency where a subscreen needs to be developed, but the home screen needs to be developed first.

Stories that total more than one week's worth of work are known as *epic* stories and are usually too big to estimate. Realistically, these stories will be broken into smaller stories that are easier to comprehend and estimate. One way to break down a task is using vertical slices. This means taking a large feature and creating a user story that will provide less functionality, but will work through all layers of architecture instead of slicing it horizontally by architecture layer. The advantage of this is twofold. One, since a vertical slice runs through all layers of architecture, it provides immediate customer value. Two, it provides a proof of concept to verify that implementing this feature works as intended through all layers of architecture.

For the first iteration, if the team hasn't worked together before, the estimates will either be too low or too high. But as each iteration goes by and more experience and knowledge is gained by the team, story estimation should improve.

There are many benefits of using Planning Poker. You get more accurate estimates because there are many different technical perspectives involved. It also helps the team to "speak with one voice" because everyone hears what is said and everyone is on the same page. Planning Poker is a great tool to facilitate conversation and come up with a well-rounded estimate.

After the stories have been estimated, the customer and product owner will work with the team to produce a release plan.

## Release Planning

Although potentially shippable code can be released at the end of each iteration, an XP project is delivered in a series of releases. A release is made up of just enough stories to offer business value, which helps to keep it small. It's good to have a theme or a goal during a release, as this helps to keep the release focused on some element of business value that drives the release. Typically a release is made up of four iterations, as depicted in Figure 3-4.

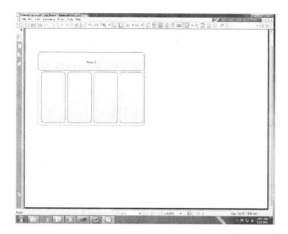

**Figure 3-4.** *Release versus Iteration*

During release planning, an iteration length is also determined, which is usually between two and four weeks. From experience, if your environment is one of constant interruption, you may want to initially limit the iteration to one week.

One project we worked on was a legacy application that was very difficult to maintain and extremely unstable. The team received frequent calls from the customer, who reported critical bugs and "production down" issues. Initially we had an iteration length of one week due to the number of frequent, yet unknown interruptions. This kept the feedback loop small and we were able to focus on stabilizing the product one iteration at a time. Once the product became a bit more stable, the customer calls became more infrequent, and we could plan for an iteration more accurately because there were few interruptions.

A one-week iteration length is good if you need a tighter feedback loop as well as the ability to deploy that shippable code at the end of the iteration. But it does incur an additional amount of overhead from breaking user stories down into smaller segments so that they can be completed within one iteration. As we'll discuss later, each iteration includes a planning meeting and a retrospective. While these meetings tend to be shorter due to a smaller iteration length, they still represent additional overhead.

As the team becomes more familiar with the process and comes to have fewer high-priority issues, it can move to two-week iterations. The iteration length is largely set by the team environment and the customer. If the environment is a high-context switching environment or the team is just starting out, one-week iterations are often better. If, however, you're developing larger features that cannot be broken down into one-week iterations and the team is still learning, then a longer iteration is acceptable.

With the iteration length and an initial story budget set (made up of the team's estimated points), the customer selects which stories included for the first release will be completed during the first iteration.

Customers need to prioritize stories to determine which delivers the most business value at the earliest time. Since the customer owns and is responsible for the user stories, the team needs to explain that there are often some stories that need to be created for purely technical reasons. Let's say that the team is working on a large legacy system that needs to be refactored. Then, they should add a user story to refactor a component of the system and write automated tests around the newly refactored code. This type of user story needs to be sold to the customer as an investment. The team knows there are a lot of changes happening in this one component and if they take the time to refactor now, this will pay off later, as the code will be easier to maintain in a refactored state with automated tests. This is known as "paying back technical debt."

Typically user stories that entail high risk or a larger set of unknowns should be added in the first one or two iterations. Because they are higher risk, it may be acceptable to continue working on them over two iterations. Perhaps the user story was grossly underestimated or it was not broken down properly. While it is not ideal or even recommended, a single user story may occasionally span multiple iterations. If this happens, commit to these user stories early so that even if they do span multiple iterations, no "half-done" user story ever goes into a release.

Once the customer has used up the budget, then no additional stories can be piled on. Customers and/or managers are notorious for adding additional items. When this happens, it needs to happen earlier rather than later, but once an additional user story tries to get into the release, the team needs to be courageous and push back and communicate that this new user story can be done, but an existing user story that has not yet been started will need to be eliminated from this release; or if the team thinks they are budgeted light, they can choose to take the new user story and communicate that they did not commit to it but will put the story in their "stretch" backlog. A stretch backlog consists of stories that were not committed to, but if time remains, the team can work to complete it.

Once the first release plan has been defined, the team can plan their first iteration.

## Iteration Planning

Once the customer has selected the stories they want included in the iteration, a set of acceptance criteria is defined for each of the stories. As you'll notice, at each phase we are spending more and more time gathering more and more details for each user story and digging deeper into each one. This is beneficial because if a user story is created at the beginning of a project, it may be determined not to be a high priority or deemed unimportant and get tossed out before time is spent on it.

If we spend a lot of time detailing all stories at the beginning, a lot of time would be wasted if a story is discarded later. So the further along a story gets in the process, the more detailed it gets. At the iteration planning level, we define a set of acceptance criteria for each user story. The acceptance criteria help the developer to know when a user story is done. They are typically written in terms of a scenario in the Given/When/Then template.

The following example describes the scenarios and steps for a customer adding items to their basket:

Feature Title: Add Products to a Basket
  As a Customer
  I want to be able to add products to my basket
  So that I can continue shopping

Scenario: An Empty Basket
  Given I have an empty basket
  Then the total number of products available to order in my basket should be "0"

Scenario: Add a Product to a Basket
    Given I have an empty basket
    When I add product id "1" to my basket
    Then the total number of products available to order in my basket should be "1"

Scenario: Add Products to a Basket
    Given I have an empty basket
    When I add product id "1" to my basket and product id "2" to my basket
    Then the total number of products available to order in my basket should be "2"

Scenario: Add the Same Product to a Basket Twice
    Given I have an empty basket
    When I add product id "1" to my basket
    And I add product id "1" to my basket again
    Then the quantity of product "1" in my basket should be "2"

Scenario: Add a Product that is Out-of-Stock to a Basket
    Given I have an empty basket and that product id "2" is not currently in stock
    When I add product id "2" to my basket
    Then the total number of products available to order in my basket should be "0" and alert the user
    that the product is out-of-stock

As acceptance tests are written in ordinary language, business rules tend to emerge. In the basket example, let's say that questions arise about how to remove an item from a basket. And, if an item is not currently in stock and the user is alerted, what should happen next? Scenarios help the team to uncover the implications, explicitly declare them, and write additional scenarios to test for them.

These scenarios are used by developers as the starting point of their unit tests during test-driven and behavior-driven development, which you will read about later in this chapter. The scenario also helps with acceptance testing, allowing the developers and testers to agree upon when a story is complete.

After the stories' acceptance criteria has been defined, the development team sets about splitting each story into the development tasks that are required to complete the story. Tasks that relate to the story are then added to a task wall and the development team assigns estimates in some unit of measure (man hours, gummy bears, etc.) to them. Figure 3-5 shows a task board.

An example of tasks may include creating a database schema for a story, or integrating with an existing part of the system. Tasks can also include technical items such as adding a logging subsystem or an exception handler framework. Often these types of tasks are overlooked when it comes to tracking a user story. A user story will have many tasks associated to it; for example:

User Story: As a User, I want the ability to manage a user.

The following tasks could come out of that:

Create a database schema to store the user in
Create a User class to manage the user programmatically

Any team member can sign up for and work on any task on the board; this enables collective code ownership and shared knowledge. When a team member picks a task, he simply needs to add his initials to the task card in order to show the rest of the team that the task is being worked on. Typically, but not always, one developer will take ownership for all tasks related to a story. Taking ownership of a story means that that developer, with the support of the team, will see that story to completion. The developer may need to acquire additional information on a user story, but the developer is the responsible party for getting a user story done. The responsible party for the user story also serves as a point of contact if anyone else on the team has questions regarding the user story.

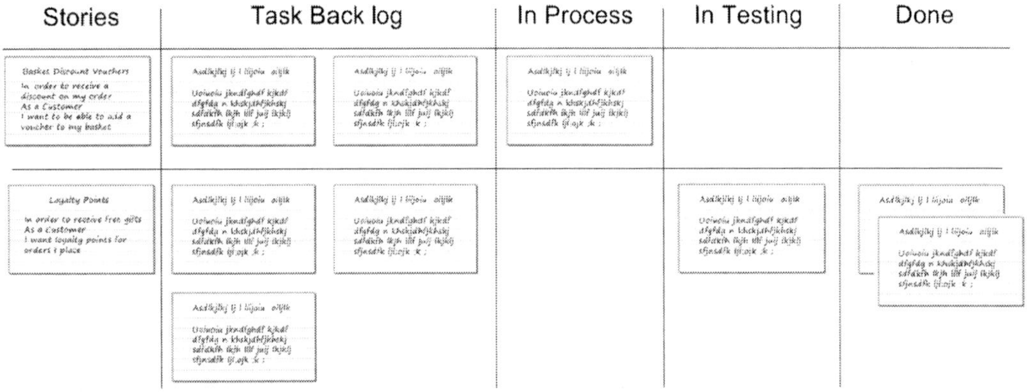

*Figure 3-5. A task board showing project progress*

Typically, at the start of the iteration, the architecture and lead developer develops and documents a high-level architecture design to support the system design for the iteration. This document outlines how the components or any third-party application interacts.

As with Scrum, once an iteration has begun, the stories being worked on cannot be changed. It is important not to change the iteration plan during the iteration because this leads to context switching. Context switching, for developers, is very costly, both in time and money. Once developers get "in the zone" and are highly focused on what they are doing, they become very productive; but initially, it takes a while to get into that zone. Unfortunately, it takes very little to get them out of the zone. Switching stories (and thus requiring developers to switch context) leads to them not getting anything done because they are being shifted around.

Instead of trying to change an iteration in midstream, determine if the additional work or additional user story can wait until the next iteration. Customers or managers typically can accept something going into the next iteration because they realize they are not going to have to wait months to get it. If the additional work really cannot wait, then to the team should courageously explain the risk of pulling the existing code out and switching to other functionality. The team should also warn that, if extra work is added to the iteration, some previously planned work may get pushed into the next iteration. The rule of thumb is that if something new comes in and cannot wait, then something of equal or greater value must come out. Again, this being the case, typically customers and managers are willing to wait for the next iteration.

Velocity shows us what the team completed during an iteration and it is used for planning future iterations. In order to track velocity, a burn-down chart is used. A burn-down chart (see Figure 3-6) shows the number of story points left in a project and the number completed in each iteration. Velocity is calculated at the end of each iteration; it is defined by the number of story points completed in the last iteration. Based on the current velocity and the number of story points remaining, an estimate can be given as to when all story points will be completed, as shown by the dashed lines in Figure 3-6.

The burn-down chart gives managers a good tracking tool to see if the team will be finished by the target date or not; and if not, how management should react to it. Should they add more bodies (which doesn't always help)? Should they decrease the number of features or extend the end date?

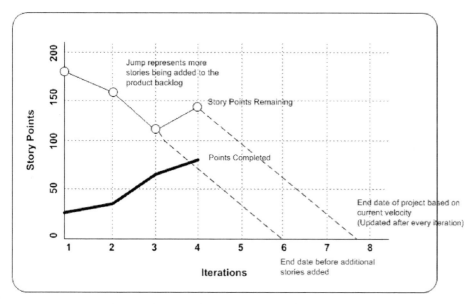

**Figure 3-6.** *Burn-down Chart*

During an iteration, a stand-up meeting with all committed team members starts each day and, as with Scrum, any issues that may prevent the team from delivering the business value that day are discussed. The team also updates the task list and the board to make visible the progress they are making or any roadblocks that are in their way.

# Environment

Having a working environment that is conducive to open communication and team work is a big factor in the success of a project. XP promotes a dedicated, open work space where open communication from all members of the team is actively encouraged. The ability to have impromptu conversations within earshot of everyone means that the entire team is aware of what is going on and can get involved if the conversation is relevant to what they are working on.

Other factors that contribute to a better XP working environment include, ideally, having the customer on site, but at the very least reachable. The option of impromptu meetings is highly important to quickly delivering business value. If a customer is not available, this immediately slows down development and becomes a roadblock because waiting on the customer is preventing the developer from completing the user story; therefore, velocity goes down and decisions from management have to be considered since the target date cannot be hit.

Having the team—including the business analysts, the testers, and the project manager—sit together encourages open dialogue and impromptu meetings. As with customers, having timely conversations with the rest of the team is critical to getting user stories completed in a timely fashion. There are times when a stand-up conversation will solve an issue, but holding it in a room with whiteboard is preferable. Whiteboard drawings and explanations help to get at the heart of solving a problem. Sometimes the entire team needs to be involved, but more often than not it's only one or two individuals working to solve a particular problem.

## On-Site Customer

The commitment and availability of the customer is vital to a successful XP project. Because the process trades documentation for working software, more often communication needs to occur between the developer and the customer. The customer needs to be available in order to do this. With the waterfall methodology, requirements analysis ends when developers begin coding and then picks back up during the release. In reality, the business process or requirements may have changed during the development process. XP works with the customer to become reactive to the business and deliver real value, not potentially outdated value, to the customer. In order to keep up-to-date with the business, a clear and constant communication must occur with the customer.

By sitting with the rest of the team, customers will solidify their commitment and responsibility to the project. The developers can also learn much from constant feedback and knowledge sessions with the customer. Bottom line: the more involved the customer is, the greater the likelihood that the development team can deliver real value.

## Sit Together

Sitting together is essential for effective pair programming, a practice that you will learn about later in this chapter. Perhaps at a more fundamental level, seating the team together with customers is essential for easy and effective communication, which is the underpinning of the XP process and one of the five core values. Sitting together increases the shared understanding of the team and helps to build team spirit, which is crucial when committing as a team to a project. Building team spirit is important because, over time, relationships begin to form with team members; you become invested with your team members. Good relationships and team spirit really boosts productivity. All tasks are handled by the team rather than "tossed over the wall" to someone that you don't know. People have a more vested interest in those they know than some "voice" at the other end of the phone line. And, a large part of personal vocabulary is in body language—and this can only be noted from sitting together.

# Self-Organization

The operation of XP teams is based on trust and self-organization. Trust is a big part of the XP methodology. Developers are trusted to estimate fairly, to work together in a dedicated environment, to self-organize, to be responsible for selecting their own tasks, and for the quality and state of the code base.

Team members need to trust each other. This is vital to the success of the project and is earned by team members consistently completing their tasks on time and with a high standard, as well as by helping fellow teammates. In the XP environment, it is every team member's duty to help teammates. Team members should practice offering "servant leadership" to other team members. This is demonstrated by leading by example and getting tasks completed on time, and, again, by helping and encouraging other team members.

There must also be trust between the team and management. Trust is typically earned at the first review meeting, when managers hear exactly what the team has achieved in the iteration. Developers learn to trust their customers as they communicate more fully. The first review meeting should also make known any roadblocks and clearly communicate if and why something did not get done. The principles of Agile have unique ways of exposing failures, roadblocks, and weaknesses, but don't always address ways to resolve them. A successful project means identifying these issues and solving them. Problems can no longer be shoved under the rug as often done with older development technologies. Agile encourages teams to clearly communicate the state of the project with each other, with the customer, and with management.

Two other factors under the umbrella of self-organization are working at a sustainable pace and having a collective code ownership.

## Sustainable Pace

Working at a sustainable pace is essential to avoiding burnout. A sustainable pace means working a standard workweek and not putting in overtime. XP promotes a sustainable development pace, which is feasible due to the iterative process, the short release cycle, and continuous integration. These ensure that there are no surprises during the lead up to product releases, which in turn makes for a more stress-free working environment.

Working at a sustainable pace is achieved by planning the work. Most often overtime is the direct result of a lack of planning or surprises. With iteration planning and the team committing to a certain amount of work, these surprises should not occur; the team can work at a sustainable pace. Since the team is involved during story and task estimation, they commit to a certain amount of work; this prevents over-committing, which can occur in non-agile methods and can lead to working many late nights. Consistently working at a non-sustainable pace leads to burnout, which leads to sloppy code being written, which increases the amount of technical debt that will need to be paid back later. Companies don't want to lose good developers to burnout nor do they want an unreasonable amount of technical debt. Creating burn-down charts and communicating with managers about the progress of work produces a big and visible metric that prevents surprises at the end date. We have the necessary information to get the job done earlier rather than later. It is management's responsibility to react appropriately.

Agile also ensures that customers work with the development team to define release plans, rather than enforcing an unrealistic delivery date that can never be met by the team.

## Collective Code Ownership

The programmers within the team are responsible for the state of the source code on a project and any member can work on any part of the system and perform changes. Collective code ownership ensures that every part of the system is accessible to all programmers, which in turn empowers any member of the team to fix a bug when it is found, regardless if they have been working on that part of the code base.

We can provide a real-life story demonstrating the importance of collective code ownership. During a project, we introduced continuous integration to the team. The builds broke quite frequently as team members checked-in code. One day a team member checked-in code and then left for a meeting before the build could complete. Consequently, the build broke due to his check-in. As a result, another team member became angry, interrupted the meeting that the "build breaker" was in, pointed his finger accusingly, and yelled, "YOU! You broke the build!"

Though we still laugh about this story, it was not an example of teamwork. The team member responsible for breaking the code should not have walked away before the build completed; nor should the other team member have lost his temper. By the time he returned to his desk, a third team member had already fixed the error and checked-in the code.

We tell this story to urge you to be patient with your teammates. Everyone has different personalities and different skill sets. If there's an issue, remain calm, approach the teammate who may have caused the issue, and ask how you can help resolve it. Supporting fellow teammates goes a long way in building trust, building effective communication, and delivering quality and value.

To encourage team building and collective code ownership, make it clearly visible when the code breaks on the CI server. Our team hung a big, traffic light from the ceiling and wired it to the CI server to make it clearly visible when the code was broken (red), a build was running (yellow), or a build was successful (green). Make team members accountable for breaking the build. Peer pressure goes a long way in making sure that your code doesn't break the build. Create a "doughnut-able offense" rule that says if a person breaks the build and leaves for the day before it is fixed, then that person must bring in doughnuts the following morning for everyone. Or, have some fun with it. If a build breaks, turn on a lava lamp. If the lava lamp bubbles up before a successful build, that's a "doughnut-able offense."

On the flip side, praise and reward the team when they do well. Promote an attainable, automated testing goal in which after a certain number of tests are built, pizza is brought in to celebrate. Also celebrate the end of an iteration whenever the team goes above and beyond to make it happen. Peer pressure can have a positive influence and is an effective tool for collective code ownership.

Encourage brown-bag lunches where team members who are learning new, more efficient ways of doing things present these ideas to the team. Let the team decide if they want to adopt the new ideas.

Collective code ownership is also achieved through sitting together and pair programming, getting involved in each other's code, and doing code reviews often. Rather than making code reviews a big, formal process, have them frequently through the valuable impromptu conversations that you have while sitting together.

## Shared Understanding

An understanding of the domain that you are working within is fundamental to the success of a project. Understanding complex business logic, workflow, and rules and modeling them in a programming language becomes more difficult without a shared understanding of the business domain between the team and the domain experts.

A lot of this domain knowledge should come at Iteration 0. By the end of Iteration 0, a good understanding of both the project and the business domain should be shared by the team. This gives the team the foundational knowledge for building software. The earlier the domain knowledge is shared, the clearer and more concise the communication becomes.

## Simple Design

A simple design is fairly free of code smells. A *code smell* is any symptom in code that indicates a potential deeper problem and makes the system more difficult to maintain. Duplicated code, over-engineering, large classes, dead code, and uncommunicated names are all examples of code smells.

Simple design allows for a maintainable, understandable, and, therefore, changeable system. Simple design allows the code to outlive the business process, not for the business process to outlive the code.

As an example, a project that we were on required significant modifications to a legacy application that had been written by a programmer who had long ago left the company. After many developers read this code, no one could get a sense of what it was doing or even how we could begin making changes to it. We told the company that we would spend more time trying to figure out this needlessly overly-complex system than if we rewrote the application from scratch. We rewrote the application, added the new functionality, and wrote the code in a maintainable way. This is an example of the business outliving the code. The goal of simple design is for the software to outlive the business, not the other way around.

Coding to well-known patterns and best practices (when appropriate), and refactoring regularly can help to reinforce the idea of a shared language and promote a simple design.

Other XP practices, such as TDD, behavior-driven development (BDD), and refactoring also keep the design of a system simple and concise. TDD and BDD are especially useful, as they adhere to the YAGNI ("You ain't gonna need it") Principle, which states that you should only implement features that you actually need rather than ones you *might* need later.

## System Metaphor

In *Extreme Programming Explained: Embrace Change* (Addison-Wesley Professional, 2004), authors Kent Beck and Cynthia Andres explain the System Metaphor as a practice that allows all team members, customers, and stakeholders to explain the system under development in simple terms. He also mentions how code should adopt the System Metaphor in order for source code to be self-describing.

Agile encourages developers to go light on documentation and heavy on delivered value. The System Metaphor equates a system to objects and develops thoughts, ideas, and naming conventions around them. Let the code document what the system actually does, rather than producing heavy paper documentation that will become outdated as soon as changes are made to the system. Using the System Metaphor should allow anyone, even a non-programmer, to look at the code and have a general understanding of what the system does based on how things are named and how they relate to each other. This becomes possible because the domain language is consistent with the way in which a customer would describe processes.

In projects that we work on that use XP, we adopt the domain-driven design (DDD) methodology as laid out by Eric Evans in his book *Domain-Driven Design: Tackling Complexity in the Heart of Software* (Addison-Wesley Professional, 2003).

---

■ **Note** One challenge of methodologies is that they are ideas. There is no "silver bullet" methodology that will solve every problem. Instead, look at methodologies as tools. For example, in order to make a wooden chair, a combination of tools needs to be used: a saw, wood glue, measuring tape, pencil, and so forth. Think of this when building software. Use hybrid models when it makes sense. A methodology can be read from a book, but what really matters is how it is implemented in the "real world," and the discernment of knowing what will or what will not work in a particular situation.

---

DDD has the notion of a "ubiquitous language," which is a language shared by the business and the developers. This shared language should be found within the code base so that when developers are working on complex problems, they are able to communicate with business users in a language that the latter clearly understands.

DDD also has a number of building blocks that—along with architectural patterns such as the domain model, design patterns, and best practices and principles—help keep developers focused on business problems rather than infrastructure concerns. As a by-product, they also help to form a shared vocabulary for developers when communicating complex design scenarios.

These practices that focus on modeling a problem domain make it easier for developers to understand the business processes and rules that the code base is trying to replicate. This focus on the business model creates a shared vision among the team, both for technical and non-technical people.

## Refactoring and Design Improvement

Refactoring code is the process of improving and simplifying the design of existing code; keeping the same functionality, but producing a better (because it's simpler) design. Refactoring allows automated tests to be written and makes the application more maintainable. Legacy applications often need to be refactored in order to strip away dependencies so that automated tests can be performed.

As an example, consider a 200-line function. A general guideline for the length of a function is the height of your screen. If it's larger than the height of your screen, seriously consider refactoring the function into smaller, more manageable sections of code.

Refactoring is as much an art as a science. Experienced developers gain a sense for good design and can quickly see how to refactor with minimal impact. A number of standard refactoring patterns can be found in the classic book *Refactoring: Improving the Design of Existing Code*, by Martin Fowler, Kent Beck, John Brant, William Opdyke, and Don Roberts (Addison-Wesley Professional, 1999).

XP practices such as simple design and TDD/BDD promote the idea of doing just what is needed to meet the feature request. As systems get bigger, however, there is a need to ensure that the structure and design of code is not ignored in favor of adding features. Refactoring can help to make code more maintainable and adaptable to change. Popular frameworks such as JetBrains' ReSharper make refactoring code very easy, and with a suite of unit tests, the design of code can be changed with confidence as behavior can be tested and confirmed very easily.

Refactoring towards well-known patterns and best practices is another way of simplifying the design of a system and introducing a common design vocabulary. In his book *Refactoring to Patterns* (Addison-Wesley Professional, 2004), Joshua Kerievsky shows how code can be refactored to well-known design patterns in order to further improve design.

## Commitment to Development Excellence

The XP process is nothing without technically proficient developers. In order for developers to hone their skills and become better craftsmen, it's important to have an automated environment that helps, rather than hinders, development.

A continuous integration environment ensures code that is worked on by many developers is tested when code commits are made, and that notifications are sent to all team members in case of a break to the source code. Coding standards and pair programming also increase technical ability within the team by the sharing of ideas and experience. XP encourages technical knowledge sharing. Pair programming creates the opportunity for a senior developer to elevate a junior developer by teaching best development practices. This mentorship is a win-win situation because both the domain and code knowledge is shared. This would also be true of any new hire, whether it be a programmer or a business analyst. By extending the idea of pair programming to business analysts, the more senior analyst can mentor the junior in a shared, collaborative environment. This is in stark contrast to the notorious knowledge silos that have to be torn down at high cost when someone leaves a project.

## Continuous Integration

Continuous integration (CI) checks quality continuously throughout the process, rather than leaving all the quality checking to be performed at the end of a project.

The components of a CI system include a source control repository, a build script, automated tests, and a notification system to alert developers of a broken build. This notification system could be as simple as a web page or a little tray icon on your computer that indicates the build status.

Figure 3-7 shows the workflow of a basic CI environment.

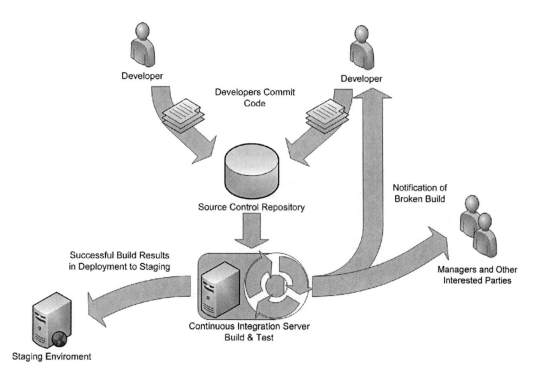

***Figure 3-7.*** *Continuous integration process*

Developers should commit to the source control system early and often. They should also ensure before committing changes that they update their code to the latest version of the code base and run their automated test suite in order to ensure a successful build. A CI process will then pull the latest code from the repository, either at a specified interval or once code is committed by a developer, and then will run through the build script.

A build tool is used by the CI environment to build the solution and run all of the automated tests that confirm the behavior of the system in order to ensure that the latest commit has not broken the build. Tests can be developer unit tests, as well as complete end-to-end user acceptance tests defined by the customer and testers.

Once the build process finishes and is successful, the CI environment can optionally deploy the compiled assemblies to a staging environment for more user testing. If the build does not succeed or tests fail, the developers and any other interested parties should be notified so that they can resolve the error and fix the build.

The benefits of CI are a reduction in large integration issues towards the end of a project and the ability to deploy a consistent build of the software quickly and easily.

## Coding Standards

Traditionally the XP practice of coding standards focused on a set of rules that the development team agreed upon for the formatting and naming conventions of code. In our experience, coding standards go far beyond formatting and naming conventions. We are far more concerned with overly long methods and poorly named variables than the need to underscore local variables.

Coding standards dictate such things as keeping each method's source code no longer than the height of your monitor, and having self-documenting code. That, in turn, entails properly naming variables—avoiding such mysterious names as i or j—and instead giving each variable a meaningful name so that the next programmer can quickly understand the role it plays. A good software craftsman will not program only for himself, but "program ahead" and write easily maintainable code for the next person coming in to add a new feature.

A standard code style throughout a project will certainly contribute to collective ownership and help people working on different parts of the system to recognize the style and formatting. Popular tools such as JetBrains' ReSharper can highlight coding that does not adhere to a defined set of coding standards, so when a coding style is agreed upon it is easy to implement.

We feel it is important to ensure that code is well written and clearly conveys its intention. A great resource that can help with creating clean code is *Clean Code: A Handbook of Agile Software Craftsmanship* by Robert Martin (Prentice Hall, 2008). Another way to ensure coding standards are adhered to is to have all developers understand the SOLID set of design principles as catalogued in *Agile Principles, Patterns, and Practices in C#* by Robert Martin (Prentice Hall, 2006).

Briefly, the SOLID design principles are as follows:

- *Single Responsibility Principle*: An object should have only a single responsibility—a focused task.

- *Open/Closed Principle*: Software entities should be open for extension, but closed for modification.

- *Liskov Substitution Principle*: Objects in a program should have the ability to be replaced by instances of their subtypes without altering the correctness of that program. Typically, this is accomplished through design by contract.

- *Interface Segregation Principle*: Many client-specific interfaces are better than one general-purpose interface.

- *Dependency Inversion Principle*: Develop against abstractions and do not depend upon concretions.

## Pair Programming

Pair programming comes from the understanding that two heads are better than one. In pair programming, two developers share the duties of completing a user story task; the idea is that both developers have time at the keyboard. There's a driver and a navigator. The driver is the one sitting at the keyboard typing in code, while the navigator is the one reviewing the code being written, thinking about how to code the next step, and guiding the driver down a focused path.

At first, management is often skeptical of this idea. They think that productivity will be cut in half because you have two developers doing what one developer could do. In reality, productivity increases in the following areas:

1. *Programmers stay focused:* While we may not like to admit it, developers tend to be easily distracted. If they are stumped with a problem they typically go to the web to find some inspiration. This inspiration time typically slides into checking Twitter or Facebook or reading the latest blogs. With pair programming, each programmer is held accountable to the other to stay focused on the task at hand. Besides, it's easier to bounce ideas off one another and come up with a solution quicker.

2. *Increase the "bus factor:"* When one developer works on a feature, he works in a silo. His knowledge is therefore "siloed," leading to a "bus factor" of 1. This colorful term focuses attention on the question: If you get hit by a bus or leave the company, what happens? Typically someone else needs to get ramped up on the code, but that takes time. With pair programming, the "bus factor" is increased to 2, which makes maintaining the system easier because two people have the knowledge. Moreover, they can usually add new features more quickly than if they were siloed.

Pair programming is typically a developer practice, but it can be extended (for instance) to having a business analyst and a developer sitting down together. They can discuss the tests to be written, so questions and ideas can be answered quickly.

## Quality Assurance

Quality assurance is essential when creating software. It's no good having great practices for gathering requirements, working closely with the customer, and understanding what you are doing if you don't get the final product right. Knowing when you have completed a story, feature, or task is essential if you are to truly satisfy your customer's expectations. XP promotes the practices of TDD and User Acceptance Testing (UAT) to ensure quality working software is delivered at the end of each iteration.

## Testing

TDD is the process of driving the design of your system using test-first coding. The fundamental concept behind TDD is to write a test that proves the behavior of a feature before writing any production code; and then write just enough code to get the test to pass. Figure 3-8 shows the famous red, green, and refactoring steps.

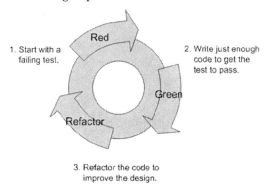

*Figure 3-8. The test-driven development process*

While the chance of finding a bug with TDD decreases dramatically with good unit tests, a bug may still be found. If a bug is found, it needs to be fixed and a unit test created to verify that the bug is permanently gone and to make sure it isn't introduced again. With legacy systems, a defect-driven methodology can be used. Defect-driven testing involves refactoring not the entire system, but only the parts where bugs are prone to occur. Fixing those bugs is critical, but refactoring the area of code each bug occurred in and wrapping automated tests around those areas, ensures that the bug is not introduced again.

A primer on TDD featuring a TDD code kata[1] and deeper details on the process can be found in Appendix A.

Another important testing discipline in XP is UAT. This is used to confirm that the behavior of a story has been completed. UAT is typically carried out by the testing team. The testers will not wait until a story is complete to start UAT; rather testers will work with the development team on test plans. In this phase, new requirements and edge cases will be discovered—including those overlooked during story capturing. This information will allow the developers to resolve issues before customers use the software, ensuring a higher-quality, production-ready product is delivered.

BDD is a relatively new way of driving design using a test-first approach. BDD is an evolution of TDD; it also takes concepts from DDD and UAT.

The BDD process focuses first on the behavior of a system from a user's point of view. Testing the outside behaviors of the system first enables lower-level objects to be discovered through all of the various architectural layers. The steps for each of the story scenarios gathered during the planning phase form the initial tests. Figure 3-9 shows the process of the BDD methodology.

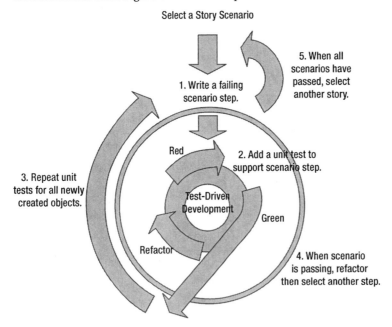

*Figure 3-9. Behavior-driven design process*

You will find a premier on BDD in Appendix B, with a code kata exercise that delves deeper into the methodology and practice of BDD.

The result of using methods such as TDD, BDD, and UAT is that you can confidently deliver quality software that satisfies the requirements of the customer. These three methodologies combine to cover all of the architectural layers of an application. They also act as a confidence layer for refactoring and

---

http://en.wikipedia.org/wiki/Kata_(programming)

modifying code, due to the automated "safety barrier" that offers immediate feedback if changes have altered the behavior of the system.

## Summary

This chapter detailed the values and practices of XP. Although XP and Scrum are similar in that they both adhere to the agile principles of using short development cycles and working closely with the customer, the XP practices give a more practical way of implementing the principles and themes of agile.

This chapter covered the five values of XP, as follows:

- Respect
- Communication
- Simplicity
- Feedback
- Courage

The bulk of the chapter then discussed the practices of XP. These twelve practices enable the theme of XP to be realized in various practical applications and bring about certain specific benefits. These practices are as follows:

- The Planning Game
- System Metaphor
- Simple Design
- On-Site Customer
- Team Sitting Together
- Pair Programming
- Collective Code Ownership
- Coding Standards
- Testing
- Continuous Integration
- Sustainable Pace
- Small Releases

In Part Two of this book you will work on a case study that will employ the Scrum methodology and feature the practices of XP covered in this chapter. During the case study you will be introduced to many of the open-source tools that can assist you with the practices of XP. You will also see how these practices are applied to a real working application.

# Sprint 0: Generating the Product Backlog

Welcome to Kojack Games! Over the next five chapters you will be watching a development team from the Kojack Games Company. You will watch as this team delivers a new and exciting product that will be implemented using agile development methods: Scrum for project management and eXtreme Programming for the day-to-day work.

This chapter introduces you to the project that the team will be working on and ends with a product backlog of work, a release plan, and the user stories that the team will be committed to completing during the first sprint. Essential to delivering a successful project is understanding exactly what the customer wants. In order to do this effectively, the team will be working closely with the product owner to capture what business value this software brings.

Without further ado, let's jump right in!

## The Project: Online Blackjack Gambling

The online gaming market is huge—and Kojack Games believes that there is room for a simple, no-nonsense blackjack gaming site of its own. You will work on developing the company's online game, and based on the success of this project, Kojack Games will look to expand its online game portfolio.

Let's meet the team. Table 4-1 lists each team member along with a description of his or her individual role and responsibilities.

*Table 4-1. Meet the Team*

| Name | Role | Responsibilities |
| --- | --- | --- |
| Bill | Customer/Senior Sponsor | Our main point of contact with the customer. |
| Simon | Product Owner/Business Analyst | Responsible for prioritizing the features that go into the product. |
| | | Responsible for communication with the customer to gather all of the business requirements. Serves as the domain expert. |

| Name | Role | Responsibilities |
|------|------|------------------|
| Tim | ScrumMaster | Responsible for guiding the team and ensuring that the agile process is followed, as well as maintaining big, visible charts, such as the burn-down chart. |
| Sarah | Technical Lead/Senior Developer | Responsible for the programming. |
| Tyler | Junior Developer | Work-pairs with Sarah and is responsible for coding. |

## Mission Statement

Bill: *Let's start with a mission statement. "Kojack Games is dedicated to stylish, simple, and easy-to-play games, packed with fun for our players."*

## Team Name

Tim: *Now let's have some fun. Since we are a team and every team has a name, I open up the floor to suggestions on our team name. Now, some may wonder, what is the need for having a team name? Well, having the team create its own name is a great way to liven the mood and build relationships within the team. It's a way for every member of the team to build ownership of the team.*

Tyler: *How about "The Agile Enforcers"?*

Sarah: *That is a nice name, but how about "Agile League of America"? It would be a nice play on comics.*

Tyler: *That sounds great! It has my vote.*

Tim: *If no one else has any suggestions and if everyone is okay with Sarah's submission, then I say "welcome to the first meeting of the 'Agile League of America'."*

## Team Ground Rules

Tim: *The next thing we want to do is to set a level of expectation among ourselves. We are all adults, but getting the ground rules established will prevent some unwanted drama later on. This is a chance for us as a team to state what we expect from our fellow team members, as well as ourselves.*

Tyler: *Is this really necessary?*

Simon: *I think it is necessary. With the ground rules established, we will all be on the same page from the beginning, and it gives us one less thing to worry about. How about we start with our core hours?*

Tim: *That's a good idea. I know we all work different hours, but how about we set aside a core time range where we all agree, developers and customer, to be available to one another.*

Bill: *I can get on board with that. That way if you all need something from me, you know where I will be at that time and if I need to ask one of you a question, I know where you will be. I propose a time frame of 10 AM to 2 PM.*

Tim: *I will put that down. For now, let's stop with that. This is a fluid list and I don't want to overburden everyone at the beginning trying to come up with rules for the team. If the need arises, we can revisit this list, but for now this is it.*

Simon: *I agree. Only create a rule when we have a need for one.*

## Technical User Stories

As a means to efficiently deliver quality code to our customer, proper software development infrastructure must be put in place, including source control, a continuous integration (CI) server, and a development environment. Doing this up front enables us to focus on the behaviors of the system and also proves that we can integrate our system with existing servers, databases, and so forth. Let's walk the development skeleton to ensure that we have our infrastructure in place.

---

▨ **Note** You can learn more about *BDD Primer with SpecFlow* in Appendix B, *Source Control with SVN* in Appendix F, and *Continuous Integration with Cruise Control.NET* in Appendix G.

---

## Walking the Development Skeleton

Walking the development skeleton enables the full implementation of a small part of the system from end to end. It helps you to discover potential stumbling blocks, such as deployment problems or trouble accessing external resources like databases or web services, early in the project.

Given what the team knows about the project at this point, the team needs to make some decisions. This includes the types of tools to use, such as any third-party tools like NUnit or WatiN; which programming language(s) to use; and how the project structure should be set up. Coming to these decisions depends on the team's experience with the tools or its willingness to learn new tools, as well as the way the customer plans to deploy the application.

The team decided to use ASP.NET MVC as its programming framework, NUnit as its unit testing framework, and WatiN for its acceptance tests. The customer decided on a web application, but didn't have a preference on anything beyond that.

The team also wants the flexibility to easily add tools to the project, if need be. A source control tree structure will be set up to allow this flexibility.

On to setting up a folder structure for source control!

## Setting Up for Source Control

To kick off the project, you will create a folder structure that is set up to be stored within a source control management system, as shown in Figure 4-1.

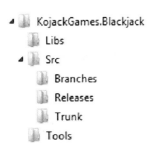

***Figure 4-1.*** *Solution folder structure*

The folders are used as follows:

- *Libs*: This folder contains all of the libraries required to run and test the application. This allows us to be scalable. If we need to add an additional third-party DLL (dynamic link libraries) later, just place it in the Libs folder and reference it. It's a centralized solution for referencing compiled DLLs. Having this consistency is important for ease of referencing DLLs and it makes creating the build script more streamlined.

- *Src*: This folder contains the source code for the application, and includes the following sub-folders:

    - *Branches*: This folder contains development branches, spiking sessions, and longer development efforts that span a release.

    - *Releases*: This folder contains all of your application release stages.

    - *Trunk*: This is your working directory. You create release and branches from the trunk. The trunk is a work in progress.

- *Tools*: This folder contains all of the tools that are used to develop, test, package, and deploy your application. It's important to keep these under source control so that your CI server can find dependent toolsets with ease, because it will not have the same tools installed as your development machine.

With the folder structure created, we now need somewhere for the code we create to be stored.

## Setting Up the Solution

Fire up Visual Studio and create a new solution named KojackGames.Blackjack within the Trunk folder, as shown in Figure 4-2, consisting of four, class-library projects and one ASP.NET MVC web application project.

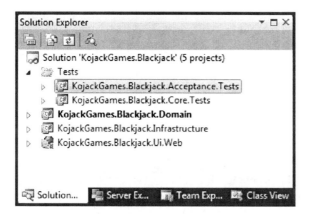

*Figure 4-2. Initial solution structure*

Let's take a look at the roles of each of the projects.

- *KojackGames.Blackjack.Domain*: The domain project represents the domain of blackjack game, all business rules and logic that govern and represent the world of blackjack, and repayments residing in the project. This project is free of any infrastructure and persistence concerns.

- K*ojackGames.Blackjack.Core.Tests*: The core tests project contains all tests aimed at the domain and the MVC project. The tests in this project are unit tests focused on small units of functionality. The tests are designed to be run often and fast; this is the reason they are kept separate of the slower acceptance tests.

- *KojackGames.Blackjack.Acceptance.Tests*: The acceptance tests project contains integration tests that test the system end to end with no fake or mock implementation of dependant classes or infrastructure. These tests typically run a lot slower than the core tests, hence the need to separate them.

- *KojackGames.Blackjack.Infrastructure*: The infrastructure project represents the plumbing of the application. This project contains all of the supporting framework for the domain model and CQRS implementation.

- *KojackGames.Blackjack.Ui.Web*: The MVC project contains the controllers, view models, and views that represent the user interface for the application. The MVC project will have a dependency on the domain project.

- When you are starting out, having both the acceptance and unit tests run after each build is acceptable because the test suite is small and can run quickly. Over time, as the test suite grows, (particularly in the Tests.Acceptance project), to continue quick feedback to the developers it is acceptable to run the Tests.Acceptance just a few times a day rather than after every check-in.

## Installing Open Source Libraries with NuGet

In this chapter you will utilize a number of open source tools to aid the development of each feature. In order to make finding and installing open source components easy, a package manager has been developed for the .NET community, its name is NuGet. A package manager makes it easy to find online projects or DLLs that you can easily install. Once installed, NuGet will also check for and prompt you to install updates for all of the packages that you have installed. This makes the life of a developer easy because she doesn't have to search for all of these components and then search later to check for updates; it's all managed through NuGet.

To install the NuGet package extension from within Visual Studio, click Tools and then Extension Manager. To find the NuGet Package Manager extension, select the Online Gallery tab, and enter "nuget" in the search box when the Extension Manager Dialog box appears. When found, download the NuGet Package Manager and run the installer. You will need to restart Visual Studio after the installation completes. When Visual Studio has restarted, select Library Package Manager from the Tools menu, and then click Package Manager Console.

In order for NuGet to download the packages to the Lib folder that we have already set up, you will need to include a config file named NuGet.config. Add this file to your solution, rather than a project, and then create it in the root of your solution, as follows:

```
<settings>
  <repositoryPath>../../../../libs</repositoryPath>
</settings>
```

With the destination for packages configured, switch to the NuGet Package Console, select the Core.Tests project from the drop-down, and type the following into the console:

```
PM> Install-Package MvcContrib.WatiN
```

Hit Enter and the package will be pulled down and install a new folder within your Libs folder, and also add a reference to them to the Core.Tests project, as shown in Figure 4-3. The MvcContrib.WatiN package allows you to perform automated GUI tests using WatiN (pronounced *What-in*).

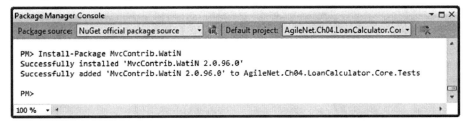

*Figure 4-3. Using NuGet to install dependencies*

## Setting Up the Acceptance Tests Project

We will be using SpecFlow to drive the design of our project directly from the acceptance criteria shown previously. The KojackGames.Blackjack.Acceptance.Tests project will be organized as shown in Figure 4-4.

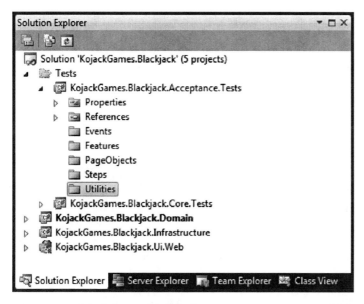

*Figure 4-4. KojackGames.Blackjack.Acceptance.Tests project folder layout*

With the structure of the Tests.Acceptance set up, you can now install SpecFlow and NUnit respectively. Make a point of adding the SpecFlow.MSI installer to the tools folder of the folder structure and ensure you add a folder each for the SpecFlow and NUnit libraries that you will reference in the Tests.Acceptance project. You can reference the SpecFlow library using NuGet or by locating the TechTalk.SpecFlow.dll from the installation folder. Similarily, with NUnit you can download the tool or add it from NuGet. Once it is all set up, your folder structure should look like Figure 4-5. The Libs folder contains the TechTalk.SpecFlow.dll that should be referenced by the Tests.Acceptance folder and the Tools folder contains the MSI that can be used by other developers who pull the code out of source control, alleviating the need to scour the web for the correct version of the SpecFlow tool.

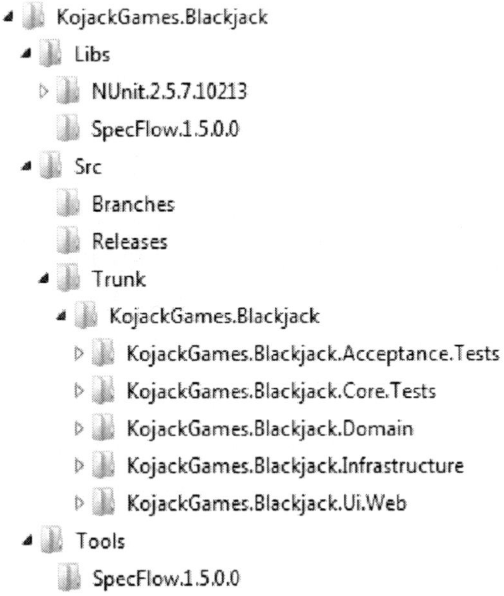

```
▲ 📁 KojackGames.Blackjack
  ▲ 📁 Libs
    ▷ 📁 NUnit.2.5.7.10213
      📁 SpecFlow.1.5.0.0
  ▲ 📁 Src
      📁 Branches
      📁 Releases
    ▲ 📁 Trunk
      ▲ 📁 KojackGames.Blackjack
        ▷ 📁 KojackGames.Blackjack.Acceptance.Tests
        ▷ 📁 KojackGames.Blackjack.Core.Tests
        ▷ 📁 KojackGames.Blackjack.Domain
        ▷ 📁 KojackGames.Blackjack.Infrastructure
        ▷ 📁 KojackGames.Blackjack.Ui.Web
  ▲ 📁 Tools
      📁 SpecFlow.1.5.0.0
```

*Figure 4-5. Bet folder structure with NUnit and SpecFlow libraries*

Now we have our project structure and our source control tree!

# Capturing Features with User Stories

The beginning of any project is critical for its ultimate success. Starting off on the right foot can give the team a tremendous boost in confidence and morale. To start off on the right foot, you need time with the product owner and/or customer to define the initial features that will make up the application. Remember, in an agile environment, this list is a fluid list and after each sprint there is an opportunity for the stakeholders to modify the list to better suit their needs. Think of this as a baseline, a line in the sand where the team can start from.

We will take these features and turn them into user stories. The user story becomes a contract between the team and the stakeholder that states that they will have a conversation about this user story at the appropriate time. The conversation allows the stakeholder to provide some initial feedback to the team and helps the team to better understand the domain so that they may provide value to the stakeholder through this feature.

Tim: *Okay, let's get on with capturing requirements.*

## Playing Blackjack Stories

Simon and the rest of the team meet to begin capturing the initial features of the project.

---

■**Tip** Finding enough uninterrupted time for both the team and the stakeholder can be challenging, so don't be afraid to have this meeting as many times as necessary to ascertain the needed initial features.

---

Tim: *Simon, there are a couple of us on the team that have never played blackjack or have played it so infrequently that we do not know all the rules. Since you are the domain expert, can you explain how to play blackjack? Once we have this domain knowledge, we can begin capturing requirements.*

Simon: *Not a problem. I will talk you through the basics. Well, as you will have gathered, blackjack is a card game, the aim of which is to get as close as possible to 21 without exceeding it, while ensuring that you are closer to 21 than the dealer. The game starts with all players placing bets on the outcome of the game. Once bets are placed, each player and the dealer receive two cards from the deck. Players' cards are placed face up. The dealer has one of his cards face down, also known as "in the hole." Each player makes a decision to either hit, which will provide another card, or stand, which will pass on another card. If a player hits and the extra card results in the player's total exceeding 21, then the player has bust and he is out. Once all players have either selected to stand or have busted, the dealer then reveals his second card. If the dealer is closer to 21 than any other player, then the dealer wins. Or, the dealer hits until either he is the closest to 21 or goes bust. If the dealer and a player tie, that is called a "push" and the player receives his bet back. Those are the basics to the game. Should I carry on?*

Tim: *That is a great overview of the game, Simon. It is vital for us that we understand the domain that we are going to be working in.*

Tyler: *Shall we begin dissecting that overview into features that we can capture as user stories?*

Tim: *Not yet. It's really important that Simon writes the stories out in a language that he understands. We can help him, but at the end of the day these are his requirements and he needs to have them in a language that makes sense to him.*

Simon: *Right. So how should I start?*

Tim: *We typically write stories from the perspective of a user of the system, following a simple template along the lines of: "In order to achieve something, I should be able to perform some action." To better explain this idea, how about we start by writing out our first user story. Sarah, would you like to tackle the first story?*

Sarah: *Sure, can do. Simon, you mentioned that in order to start a game of blackjack, a player has to make a bet. I will take that bit of domain knowledge and create an Initial Bet user story that both you and I can understand.*

Sarah writes the first story card, as shown in Figure 4-6.

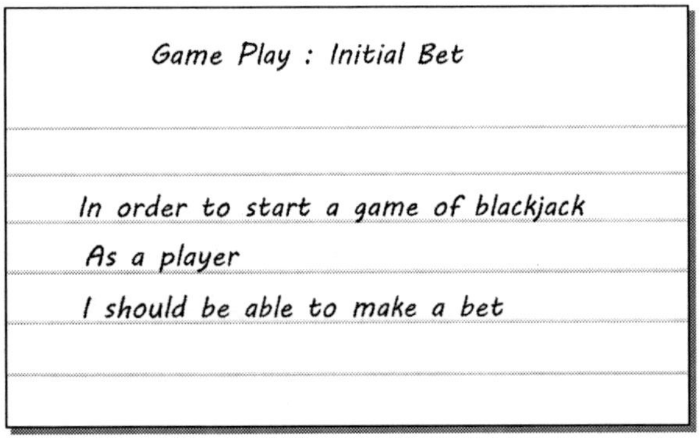

```
    Game Play : Initial Bet


    In order to start a game of blackjack
    As a player
    I should be able to make a bet


```

*Figure 4-6. Story card for placing a bet to start the game*

Simon: *Right. I see what you mean now. We are taking the domain knowledge and writing user stories in a way that both the developers and I can understand.*

Tim: *Simon, how about you try your hand at writing the next user story?*

Simon: *Okay. The next feature we need is one that has two cards dealt to each player as the next action after the bet has been placed. I supposed I can create a user story that captures that feature.*

Simon adds the Start Game story card, as shown in Figure 4-7.

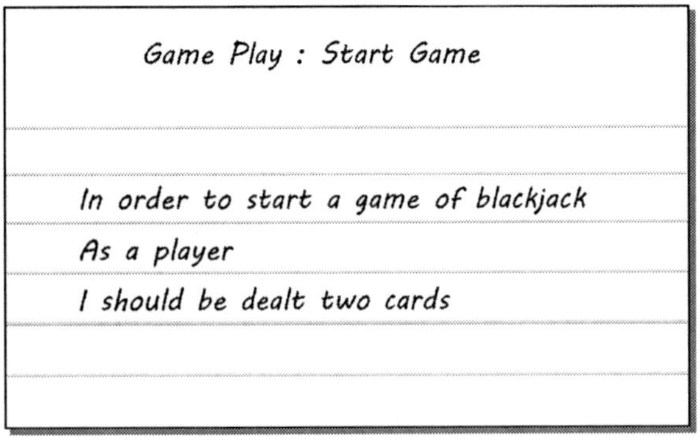

```
    Game Play : Start Game


    In order to start a game of blackjack
    As a player
    I should be dealt two cards


```

*Figure 4-7. Start Game user story*

Tyler: *Simon, is there any criteria that we need to cover when we work on this user story?*

Simon: *Yes, actually there is one. You need to make sure that when the game starts, only one of the dealer's cards is showing. We don't want to give the player an unfair advantage.*

Tyler: *Okay, that is a perfect example of acceptance criteria. It gives us an indication of when a user story is done. I will add this as a note to the back of the story that you have just written to remind me and the developers.*

Tyler flips over the Start Game story card and adds a note about the dealer showing only one of his two initially-dealt cards, as shown in Figure 4-8.

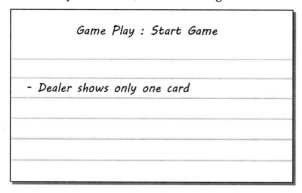

*Figure 4-8. Acceptance criteria on the Start Game story*

Tyler: *So we have talked about placing an initial bet and being dealt two cards, now I think we need to talk about how and what to do during the course of a game. Simon, how does a player get close to 21 again? I remember something about getting an additional card.*

Simon: *What you are describing, Tyler, is called a "hit." When a player has less than 21, she can request an additional card (hit) from the deck. That is definitely a feature we need.*

Simon grabs a new index card and writes out the next story, as shown in Figure 4-9.

```
            Game Play : Hit


   In order to achieve 21
   As a player
   I should be able to hit
   and receive an extra card from the pack
```

*Figure 4-9. Story card to capture hitting*

Simon: *And if a player doesn't want a hit or has finished hitting, he can "stand" and, thus, won't receive any additional cards. I will write that story out.*

The story card to stand is shown in Figure 4-10.

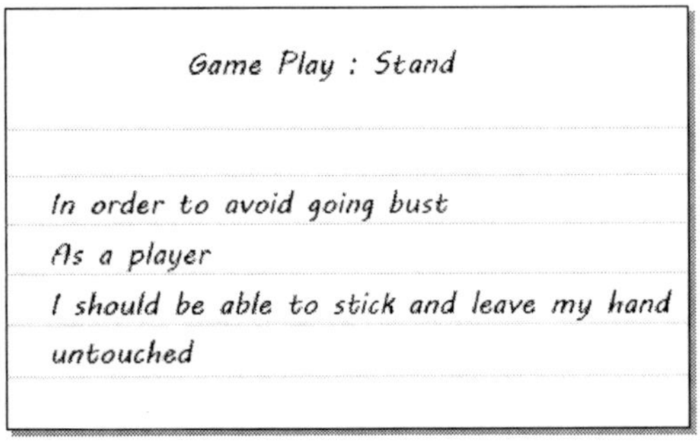

```
Game Play : Stand


In order to avoid going bust
As a player
I should be able to stick and leave my hand
untouched
```

*Figure 4-10. Story card to capture the feature of a player "standing"*

Sarah: *Okay, what's next?*

Simon: *Well, the next part of the game, once all the players have stopped getting additional cards, is to work out who has won. The winner is the player who is closest to 21 without going over.*

Tim: *Okay, Simon, can you turn that into a user story?*

Simon writes the story to capture the winning condition, shown in Figure 4-11.

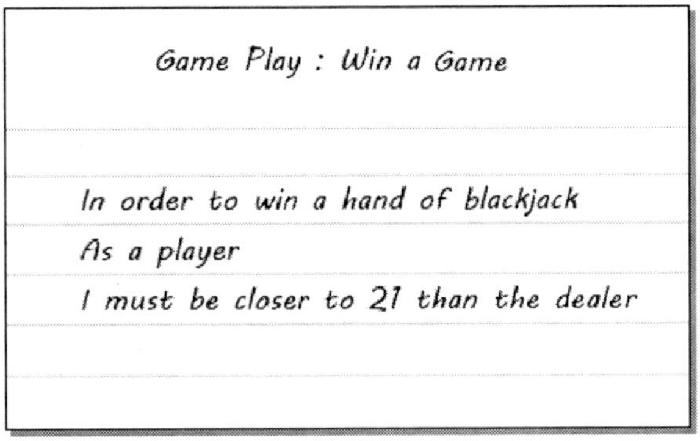

```
Game Play : Win a Game


In order to win a hand of blackjack
As a player
I must be closer to 21 than the dealer
```

*Figure 4-11. A story card to capture the blackjack winning condition*

Sarah: *So are kings, queens, and jacks worth 10 points? What is an ace worth?*

Simon: *Face cards are worth 10 and an ace can be 11 or 1.*

Sarah: *Since we are talking about the scoring of a game, I will add this information to the back of this user story. One thing to keep in mind is that this is a good spot to split this story into two cards, if the story becomes too large.*

In Figure 4-12, Sarah has added the worth of the aces and face cards to the back of the user story card.

*Figure 4-12.* Notes on the Win a Game story

Tyler: *So, it's possible to get 21 with the first two cards dealt if you get an ace and a face card?*

Simon: *Yes. This is what's known as "blackjack." If you get "blackjack," you will not be prompted to hit or stand, and automatically win your bet—because this is the best hand you can get.*

Sarah: *So what happens if a player and the dealer get 21 with two cards?*

Simon: *In that case, both have gotten "blackjack" and have tied. This is called a "push." In the event of a push, the player keeps his money. In fact, all cases of "push" end up with the player retaining his chips.*

Tyler: *Hang on a minute. It seems to me that all the dealer needs to do is wait and see what the player does before making a move.*

Simon: *Not quite. Dealers have certain rules that they must abide. They must hit until reaching at least 17 or bust by going over 21. In the event that the dealer goes over 21, all players who have not busted win their bets.*

Tyler: *So what happens if everyone busts?*

Simon: *If all players go bust, the house wins.*

Simon: *I will create a user story that encompasses the dealer's rules.*

Simon creates a story describing the dealer's rules, as shown in Figure 4-13.

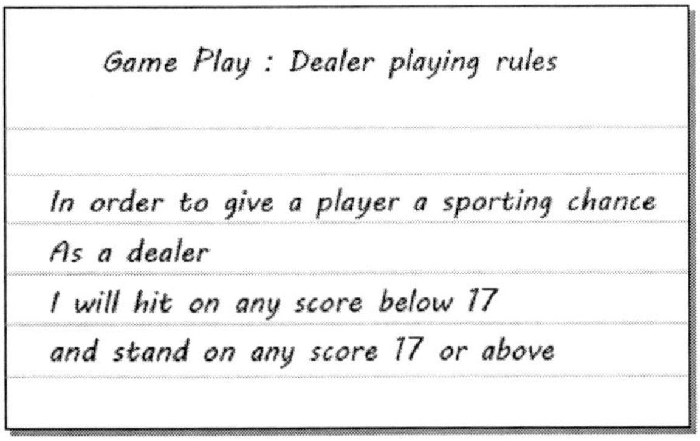

```
Game Play : Dealer playing rules


In order to give a player a sporting chance
As a dealer
I will hit on any score below 17
and stand on any score 17 or above
```

**Figure 4-13.** *A story to capture the playing rules of the dealer*

Simon: *There are a couple of things that I forgot to mention. First, you do not take turns to play. Each player has his turn until he stands, busts, or hits 21. Second, the payout for winning is your bet plus the same amount from the dealer. In a case when the player hits a "blackjack," the payout is his bet plus 1.5 times that amount from the dealer.*

*Okay, you have the basics covered, let's move to some of the advanced rules of the game specifically related to the gambling side. For instance, if your initial two cards add up to 9, 10, or 11, you will be offered the chance to "double down." If you choose to double down, your stake on the current hand is doubled, you are dealt only one more card, and your turn is over.*

Sarah: *What happens if you don't have enough money?*

Simon: *Then you won't be able to double down, or you will have to cash in to get more chips.*

Tyler: *Okay, so if your cards add up to 9, 10, or 11, you can double your bet, but you will only be allowed one more card.*

Simon: *Oh, one more thing.* [Simon does a poor impression of "Columbo."] *You cannot double down on an ace and a 10-value card, but you can double down with an ace and a 9 or an ace and an 8.*

Tyler: Let's capture this logic as the Double Down user story. [See Figure 4-14.]

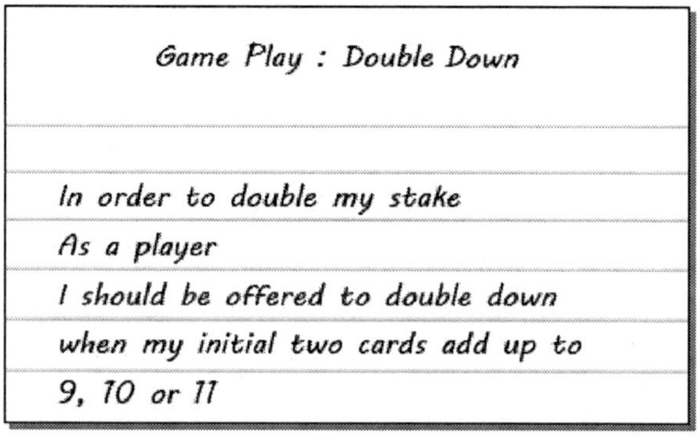

*Figure 4-14. A story to capture the double-down feature*

Sarah: *We had better make a note on the reverse of the card about making 11 with an ace and a 10 card.* [(See Figure 4-15)].

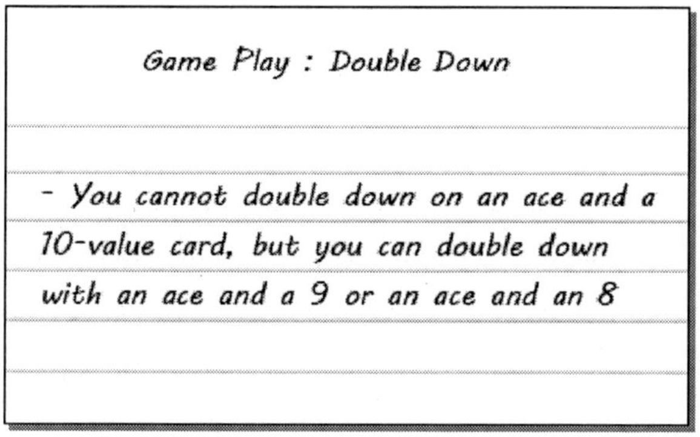

*Figure 4-15. Notes on the Double Down story*

Simon: *Another way to increase the stakes is to split your hand into two. You can only do this if your initial two cards are a pair. If you split, you will need to bet the same amount of chips on the new hand.*

Tyler: *Okay, so when you split do you get another two cards?*

Simon: *Yes, that's right. You will have two hands.*

Sarah: *So what happens if you get another pair, can you split again?*

Simon: *No, you can't split again and you can't achieve blackjack. For example, if you get to 21 with two cards this will not be blackjack, it will only be 21.*

Tyler: *Okay, you write the Split story and I will make a note of the acceptance criteria that we talked about on the back of the card.* [(See Figures 4-16 and 4-17)].

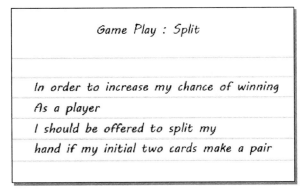

**Figure 4-16.** *A story to capture the split feature*

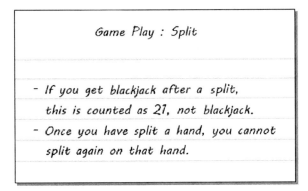

**Figure 4-17.** *Some acceptance criteria on the split story*

Sarah: *Are you allowed to double down after a split?*

Simon: *Yes, you can double down on either or both of the hands if you have a total of 9, 10, or 11.*

Sarah: *Are there any additional, game play options?*

Simon: *No, that's about it really. I suggest that we all sit down and play a couple of hands just for fun to ensure that we have captured all the requirements.*

Tyler: *Sounds like a good idea.*

As if by magic, a deck of cards appears from Simon's pocket and you play a few hands of blackjack to confirm that you understand the game.

## Playing for Money Stories

You have captured the features that describe playing a game of blackjack; now you can move onto the stories that describe playing blackjack for money.

Simon: *Alright team, now that you know how to play blackjack, let's move onto what the site is all about— playing for money. The basic idea is that a member will be able to cash in, which means buying some chips to use to bet with.*[1] *We have worked a good deal with PayPal*[2] *on fees, so I think we will be using them as the payment gateway.*

Sarah: *Okay, there seems to be a couple of features here. So let me ask you this, Simon: is it safe to assume that a player will need to create an account on the site before being able to play the game?*

Simon: *Yes, that's right. I will add a user story that contains the logic for registering a user on the site.* [(See Figure 4-18.)]

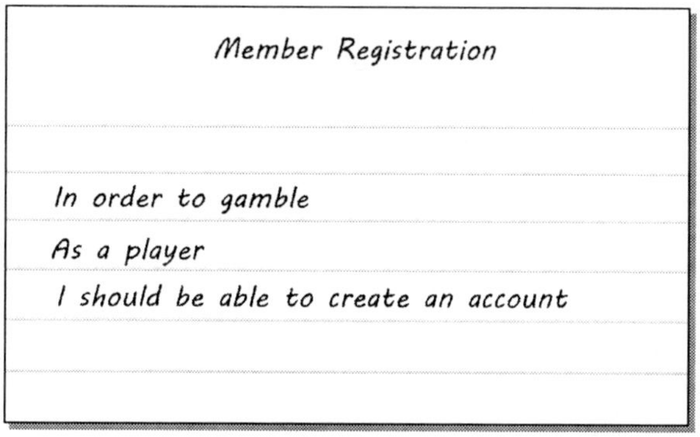

```
    Member Registration



  In order to gamble

  As a player

  I should be able to create an account


```

*Figure 4-18. A story about the feature of creating an account*

Tyler: *I guess the player will also want to manage her account so that she can update details such as e-mail address, password, etc.?*

Simon: *Yes that's correct. We won't need to store a lot of details—only name, e-mail, password, and the balance or the amount of money the player has in her account. I will create a user story that captures the ability of the player to manager her account.* [(See Figure 4-19.)]

---

[1] In blackjack, "cash in" means to buy and "cash out" means to sell.
[2] PayPal.com. "What Is PayPal?" https://www.paypal.com/us/cgi-bin/?cmd=xpt/Marketing/general/what-is-paypal-outside.

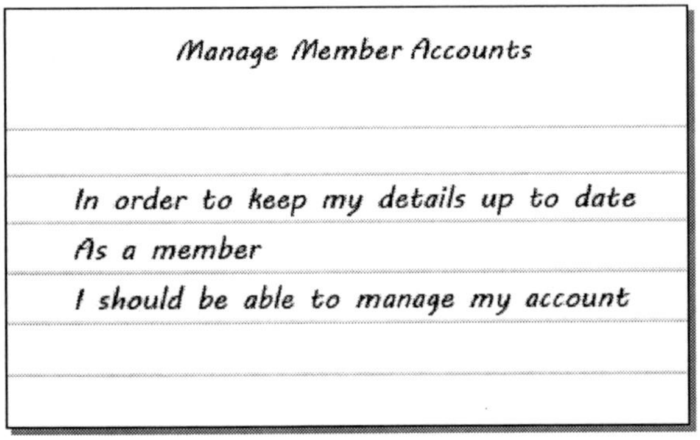

**Figure 4-19.** *A story on managing a user's account*

Tyler: *Okay, we have captured the features for membership. Now let's capture the feature of a member cashing in. Simon, can you write a user story that captures the feature of cashing in? [(See Figure 4-20.)]*

Simon: *Sure, no problem.*

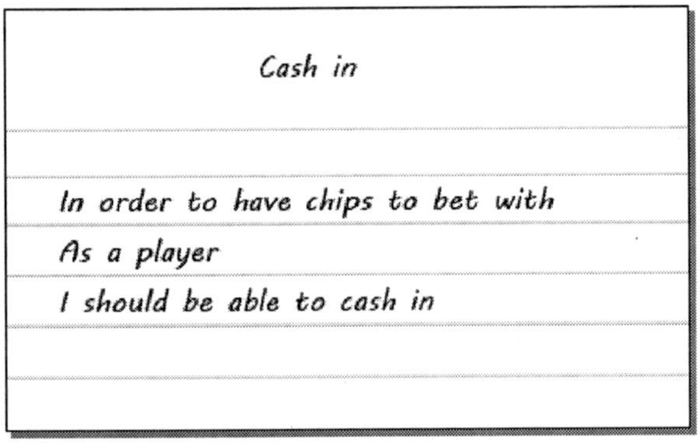

**Figure 4-20.** *A story on the feature of cashing in*

Sarah: *So, a registered member of the site has created an account and buys chips to bet with. Any limits on what she can bet per hand?*

Simon: *Yes, there is. In order to play, a member has to place a bet within the range of $5 to $20 for each hand she chooses. I will write a user story to account for this betting range. [(See Figure 4-21.)]*

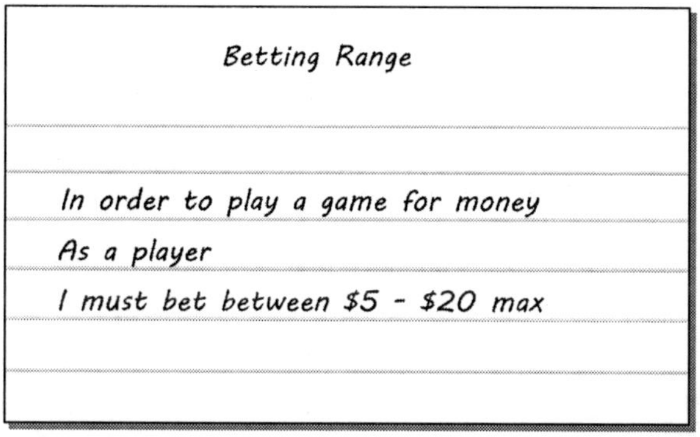

*Figure 4-21. A user story on the feature of a betting range*

Simon: *We also need to account for the fact that a player can play more than one hand in a game. In fact, he can play up to three. I will write a user story that captures playing multiple hands at once.* [(See Figure 4-22.)]

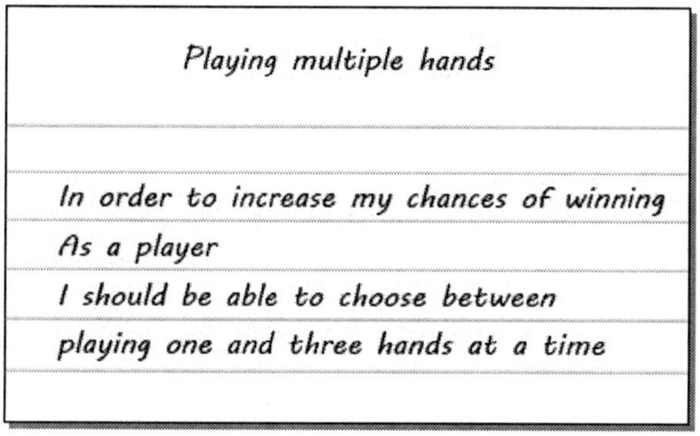

*Figure 4-22. A story on a player playing multiple hands*

Tyler: *Should we let the player know how much he has won or lost, so he doesn't get carried away with his betting?*

Simon: *Yes, we will want the player to be able to view some stats on how he has been playing. Sarah, can you write a user story on maintaining a player's betting history?*

Sarah: *Sure. I will write a user story to capture that.* [(See Figure 4-23.)]

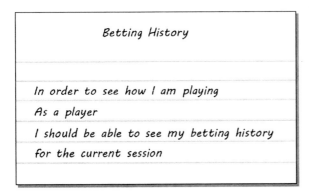

**Figure 4-23.** *A story on reporting a player's betting history*

Tyler: *So, we allow players to put money into the system, and it is only reasonable to allow them to remove money from the system when they are done. Simon, does this happen a lot and is it something that we need to account for?*

Simon: *Hopefully, players removing their money from the system won't happen too much! But when it does, then, yes, the member should be able to cash out her winnings. We need another user story to account for the player cashing out. [(See Figure 4-24.)]*

```
                     Cash out



        In order to spend my winnings
        As a player
        I should be able to cash out



```

**Figure 4-24.** *A story on a member cashing out*

Sarah: *Are there any other features that relate to the gambling side of this application that we need to concern ourselves with?*

Simon: *No, I believe that's it. You bring up a good question, though. What happens if, after the team got started, I realized that we missed a feature needed in the system? Would it be too late to get it in the project?*

Tim: *That's not a problem. Because we will be working in short time blocks, the project will be built in an iterative manner, meaning that every two weeks we are planning, developing, testing, and reviewing. At the end of those two weeks, we will show you what we have done and ask you to show us which items are the most important to complete in the upcoming sprint. Now, once a sprint starts, it's best not to change the features in that sprint because the team will be actively working on those items. You can add, edit, or delete a user story from the product backlog at any time. Basically, you will have full control over what goes into this application and what the team works on each sprint.*

Simon: *Brilliant!*

Sarah: *Okay, let's talk more about a member's account and what he can do with it.*

## Member Account Stories

Simon: *The member account section won't be that complex. I have already jotted down a story on managing an account and cashing in. The only other action I see is for a member to view statements on his balance.*

Tyler: *Can you write down the story about viewing statements? If you think of anything else, we can always add it to the product backlog later.* [(See Figure 4-25.)]

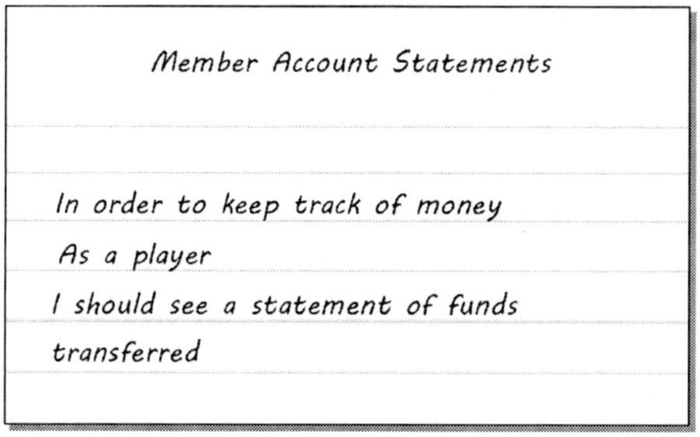

```
        Member Account Statements



  In order to keep track of money
  As a player
  I should see a statement of funds
  transferred
```

***Figure 4-25.*** *A story on member account statements*

Sarah: *Any other requirements for the system?*

Simon: *The only other features that we would like would be some reports on player registration and, of course, the balances across all players for our accounts.*

## Reporting Stories

Tyler: *Okay, let's capture those reporting features in two stories.*

Simon: *Right. So the first is for reporting on the financials of each account.* [(See Figure 4-26.)]

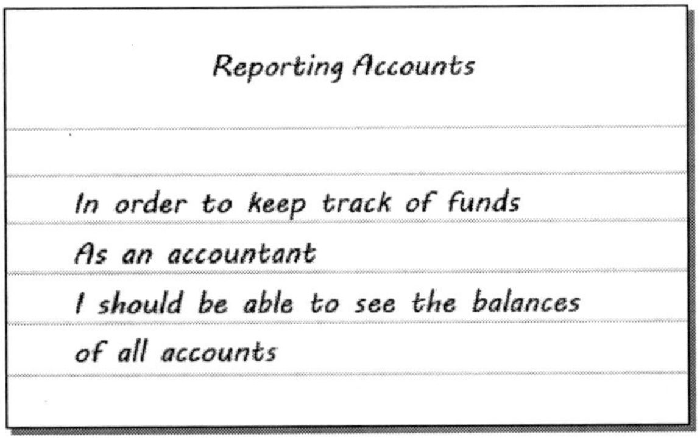

```
          Reporting Accounts


    In order to keep track of funds
    As an accountant
    I should be able to see the balances
    of all accounts
```

**Figure 4-26.** *A story on reporting account financials*

Simon: *And the second is for reporting member registration.*[(See Figure 4-27.)]

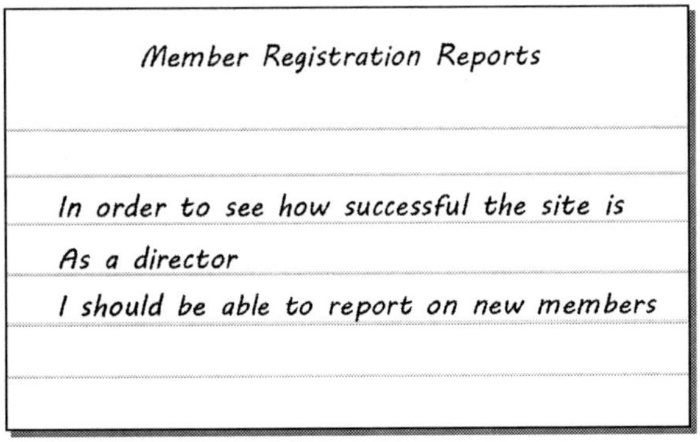

```
      Member Registration Reports


    In order to see how successful the site is
    As a director
    I should be able to report on new members
```

**Figure 4-27.** *A story on reporting of member registration*

## Technical Stories

Sarah: *As the game will be played online, how should we handle the event of a player losing connection mid-game?*

Simon: *Well, because blackjack is in essence a one-player game with an automated dealer, the player should be able to pick up where he left off, if he loses connection to the game for whatever reason.*

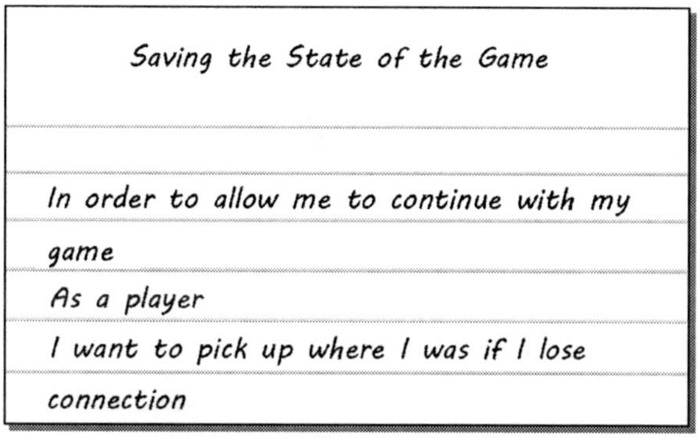

```
Saving the State of the Game

In order to allow me to continue with my
game
As a player
I want to pick up where I was if I lose
connection
```

*Figure 4-28. A story on saving the state of a game*

Tyler: *Brilliant. I can't think of anything else we need to cover, can you?*

Simon: *No, I think we have covered all of the features I had in mind.*

Tim: *Okay, well, if you do think of anything else, please let us know and we can add it to the product backlog of features.*

Simon: *So, what happens now?*

Tim: *Well, now that we have this list of user stories that will make up the application, it is time for us to compare them to one another to create an order of complexity. Once this comparison is done, we should have a general idea about which user stories may cause us trouble later on. Since we are only worried about comparing complexity between the different user stories, the system we will use to score the comparison will be T-shirt sizes—small or S, medium or M,, large or L, and extra-large or XL.*

Simon: *T-shirt sizes? I can't do anything with that.*

Tim: *Right. You will not be able to calculate delivery time from these in the beginning. That is the point. What we are trying to accomplish is to see which user stories are very complex, not how long it will take us to complete them all. You see, people are terrible at estimating how long it will take to get something done. However, anyone can compare two items, even if he doesn't understand the context for these items. Now, you will get some hard numbers, but not now. Later on in the process you will be able to derive how long it took us to do something from these shirt sizes and story points.*

Simon: *Okay, I am a little nervous, but I will give it a try. I'll let you get on with it then. When do we meet next?*

Tim: *How about we each look at our calendars and see what time works best for all of us? Thank you.*

# Initial Product Backlog

The stories shown in Table 4-2 form your initial product backlog of features. Keep in mind, this is not an exhaustive list, so don't be surprised if requirements change or are added or removed during the course of the project.

*Table 4-2. Initial Product Backlog of Features*

| Story Name | Story Description |
| --- | --- |
| Game Play: Initial Bet | In order to be in a game of blackjack<br>As a player<br>I should make a bet |
| Game Play: Start Game | In order to start a game of blackjack<br>As a player<br>I should be dealt two cards |
| Game Play: Hit | In order to achieve 21<br>As a player<br>I should be able to hit and receive an extra card from the pack |
| Game Play: Stand | In order to avoid going bust<br>As a player<br>I should be able to stand (keep your existing hand as it is) for each hand in turn |
| Game Play: Double | In order to double my stake<br>As a player<br>I should be offered to double down when my initial two cards add up to 9, 10, or 11 |
| Game Play: Split | In order to increase my chance of winning<br>As a player<br>I should be offered to split my hand if my initial two cards make a pair |
| Game Play: Win | In order to win a hand of blackjack<br>As a player<br>I must be closer to 21 than the dealer and not go bust |
| Game Play: Dealer Rules | In order to give a player a sporting chance<br>As a dealer<br>I will hit on any score below 17 and stand on any score above 17 |
| Member Registration | In order to gamble<br>As a player<br>I should be able to register my details |

| Story Name | Story Description |
|---|---|
| Manage Member Account | In order to keep my details up-to-date<br>As a member<br>I should be able to be able to manage my account |
| Cashing In | In order to get chips to play with<br>As a player<br>I should be able to cash in |
| Betting Range | In order to play a game for money<br>As a player<br>I must bet between $5.00 and $20.00 max |
| Playing Multiple Hands | In order to increase my chances of winning<br>As a player<br>I should be able to choose between playing one and five hands at a time |
| Game Betting History | In order to see how I am playing<br>As a player<br>I should be able to see my betting history for the current session |
| Cashing Out | In order to spend my winnings<br>As a player<br>I should be able to cash out |
| Member Account Statements | In order to keep track of money<br>As a player<br>I should see a statement of funds transferred |
| Reporting Accounts | In order to keep track of funds<br>As an account<br>I should be able to see all funds for all accounts |
| Reporting Registrations | In order to see how successful the site is<br>As a director<br>I should be able to see the number of member registrations |
| Saving Game State | In order to continue playing<br>As a player<br>I should pick up where I left off if I am disconnected from the internet |

# Planning Poker

Before we can plan the sprints that will make up the project, we need to understand the complexity of the work that is needed in the project. We will use Planning Poker as a tool to facilitate the conversation among the customer and the members of the team about the complexity of the user story. We are not concerned with how long it will take a developer to complete the user story. Those particular conversations take place further down in the individual sprints. What we are trying to accomplish with this is finding user stories that may be too large to complete in an individual sprint; the user stories that may cause us trouble later on.

Since this will be our initial Planning Poker session for this project, we will handle it slightly different from how we will handle them during our sprint-planning meeting. During this session we will generally compare the user stories to one another. To reflect this high-level comparison of complexity, we will use a different unit for measurement: T-shirt sizes (S, M, L, and XL). The understanding will be that if a user story is classified as XL, then that user story is flagged as one that potentially needs to be broken down.

Let's join our team as they start this initial Planning Poker session.

---

■ **Note** For the sake of brevity, the user stories themselves will not be duplicated during the complexity comparison. Please note, however, that the product owner will read aloud each story before the team estimates its complexity.

---

## Game Play: Initial Play

Tim: *Any thoughts on this user story?*

Sarah: *This one seems to be fairly simple. All we need to do is store the amount of chips that the player has waged on the hand.*

Tyler: *Hmmm. I'm not so sure it's that easy. We will need to have checks on whether the player has enough chips to make a bet. We will also need objects outside of the system to be to able to get to the point of actually running it.*

Sarah: *Yes, perhaps there is a little more to it. One key piece of logic we will need is to have the ability to update the player's balance according to the winnings or losings after a game is finished.*

Tyler: *So, what shall we set this at? I don't think it is a small user story. However, I also don't believe that this user story is large. How about we give it a "medium" size?*

Sarah: *I think I can go along with that. I vote medium, as well.*

The team decides a size of medium (M) for this user story. Let's move onto the next one.

## Game Play: Start Game

Tyler: *I think that this is much more complex than the last story. First off, we have to create the deck of cards to deal from. Second, we need to have logic in the system to handle which players have which cards at what time. Third, we need logic to keep track of which players in the game have busted.*

Sarah: *And, we need to create a dealer because the dealer also gets dealt two cards when the game starts. After looking at all of this, I have to say this is a story card that could give us some trouble. I vote this card an XL.*

Tyler: *I would have to agree with Sarah. This seems like a terribly large amount of work. Too much work for one sprint, I would surmise. I vote XL also.*

Tim: *Okay, so we flag this user story as one that is potentially troublesome. Since we are here, do you all have some ideas on how we could break up this extra-large story card into smaller cards?"*

Sarah: *What if we broke the user story along the lines of the cards? We create one user story about creating the deck of cards and place the remaining parts of the original user story into another one. Simon, do you have any feedback on this? Tyler, what are your thoughts?*

Tyler: *That idea makes sense to me. I have done something similar to creating a deck of cards in the past, so I could work on that part easily.*

Simon: *Since the deck of cards is a major linchpin of the whole system, it makes sense to me to break that off into its own user story. Since this is a vital piece, now that I think about it, we will need to make sure this user story gets done sooner rather than later. I will go ahead and write up another user story on creating the deck of cards.* [(See Figure 4-29.)]

```
┌─────────────────────────────────────┐
│                                     │
│    Game Play : Deck of Cards        │
│                                     │
│                                     │
│   In order to play a game of Blackjack │
│   As a dealer                       │
│   I should deal from a pack of cards │
│                                     │
│                                     │
└─────────────────────────────────────┘
```

*Figure 4-29. A user story on the creation of the deck of cards needed for the game*

Tyler: *Let's re-examine the two cards and compare them to the one we have already done. First, let's look at the Start Game user story minus the deck-of-cards piece. I change my vote from XL to M.*

Sarah: *I vote S.*

Tyler: *Sarah, why did you vote S? We still have to handle the logic for maintaining what everyone has throughout the game. I think it is more complicated than our baseline.*

Sarah: *I know. The reason I voted S is because I have handled logic like this before. It's maintaining where something is throughout a length of time. I can create a class that can handle that logic. Granted it is not a cake walk, but I think it is pretty close to an S.*

Tyler: *I am still a little unsure about that vote, but since you have experience in this, I will back you up and say S as well.*

## Game Play: Deck of Cards

Tim: *Now let's talk about the Deck of Cards user story.*

Sarah: *I am not sure. I think this user story is as complex as the Initial Bet user story. However, I am not that good with graphics, so it may be larger.*

Tim: *Sarah, what you must remember is that you are not estimating based on how quickly you could do this. You are simply comparing this user story to the user stories done before and seeing where it stacks up.*

Tyler: *I vote S.*

Sarah: *I forgot. Thanks, Tim, for reminding me. I vote S, as well.*

## Game Play: Hit

Sarah: *So after the initial cards have been dealt, the player can hit to get more cards. We will need to add some rules to check if the player goes bust.*

Tyler: *Okay, so all we are worried about here is giving a player more cards and checking that he hasn't gone bust. Sounds straightforward and on par with our baseline user story. Let's estimate.*

The team selects a size of S.

## Game Play: Stand

Tyler: *So, if a player hasn't bust but doesn't want to hit anymore, he can elect to stand—which basically means the player's turn is over?*

Sarah: *Yeah, we just need to end the player's turn and prevent her from doing anything else until the dealer has made his move. This should also be straightforward and on par with our baseline user story. Let's estimate the complexity.*

The team selects a size of S.

## Game Play: Win

Sarah: *This is the winning condition story. We need to add a check to work out who has the best hand based on a number of winning combinations.*

Tyler: *Among the players or just between the player and the dealer?*

Simon: *You will always compare the hands of an individual player to that of a dealer.*

Sarah: *What are the winning combinations? Simon, what are these conditions?*

Simon: *Well, as an ace can be 11 or 1, it means a score of 11 can be achieved in a variety of ways. Also if you get to 21 with three cards, then it beats a winning hand using more than three cards.*

Tyler: *It sounds like there are some more acceptance criteria for this user story. I will add these conditions to the back of the card. I think this is more complicated that the Hit or the Stand user stories, so I vote M.*

Sarah: *Sounds good, I vote M, too.*

## Game Play: Dealer Rules

Simon: *This feature deals with the dealer's game play. There are a few things to remember about the logic behind this. If a dealer has a score lower than 17, then he will continue to hit until he has more than 17 or goes bust.*

Sarah: *That's right. Regardless of what a player does, if the dealer is below 17, he will keep hitting until he goes bust or is above 17.*

Tyler: *Seems like that won't be too much trouble. But it seems to be more complex than a lot of the small ones.*

The team selects a size of M.

## Game Play: Double

Tyler: *Doubling is when you have a total card value of 9, 10, or 11.*

Sarah: *That's right. You get the chance to double your stake.*

Tyler: *If you have the chips to do so.*

Sarah: *Ah yes. If not, we need to give the player the option to buy some more.*

Tyler: *The state of the game will need to be persisted anyway, so if a player goes off mid-game to buy more chips, that shouldn't cause any issues.*

Sarah: *Yes, I was thinking the same thing.*

Tyler: *So all we need to do is check for a 9, 10, or 11, and offer the player to double up if he has enough chips?*

Sarah: *Yeah, seems that way.*

Tyler: *Okay, let's estimate.*

The team selects a size of M.

## Game Play: Split

Sarah: *Splitting is the option given to a player when his initial two cards are a pair. If he has a pair, he can make two separate hands. Again, he will need to have enough chips to cover the bet for the second hand.*

Tyler: *Yes, and after splitting blackjack cannot be achieved, neither can the player split again in the event he is dealt another pair.*

Sarah: *Although you can still double down.*

Tyler: *Yes, that's correct. Okay, this seems a little more complex than simply doubling down. Ready to estimate?*

Sarah: *Yep!*

The team selects a size of L.

## Member Registration

Sarah: *We've created a lot of membership registration systems in the past, so I think this one should be fairly easy.*

Tyler: *I agree. Plus there are a number of ready-made membership providers that we can use, so I don't think that this feature is going to be too complex.*

Sarah and Tyler select a size of S.

## Managing Member Accounts

Sarah: *This is, again, a bread-and-butter requirement. Just forms over data really. No real behavior to this at all.*

Tyler: *Yes I agree. This should be an easy one to estimate.*

Sarah and Tyler select size of S.

## Cashing In

Tyler: *Cashing in is the act of the player paying money in return for chips, right?*

Sarah: *Yes, that's right. We will need to code the workflow of buying chips and taking the player through the steps of paying.*

Tyler: *Okay, that sounds complex.*

Sarah: *I agree. It seems like a lot of items that need to be performed in order to consider this card done. I think this is another XL card.*

Tyler: *I think I would have to agree.*

Tim: *Okay, guys, since we have another XL card, do we want to try and break it up?*

Sarah: *No, not at the moment. We could do that when we look to implement this card in a sprint.*

Tyler and Sarah select a size of XL.

For the sake of brevity, we will skip over comparing the remaining user stories. This might be a good time for you to look at the remaining user stories and compare them to the ones we have already compared. See what you think about their complexity. The following is a list of user stories that need to be compared and assigned a T-shirt size:

- Betting Range
- Playing Multiple Hands
- Game Betting History
- Cashing Out
- Member Account Statements
- Reporting Accounts
- Reporting Registrations
- Saving Game State

## Prioritizing the Backlog

With the user stories compared to one another and given a T-shirt size, it is time for the product owner to prioritize this backlog for the first sprint, as shown in Table 4-3.

*Table 4-3. Updated Product Backlog of Features*

| Story | Size | Description |
| --- | --- | --- |
| Game Play: Initial Bet | M | In order to be in a game of blackjack<br>As a player<br>I should make a bet |
| Game Play: Start Game | S | In order to start a game of blackjack<br>As a player<br>I should be dealt two cards |
| Game Play: Deck of Cards | S | In order to play "blackjack"<br>As a player<br>I will need a deck of cards to play with |
| Game Play: Hit | S | In order to achieve 21<br>As a player<br>I should be able to Hit and receive an extra card from the pack |

| Story | Size | Description |
|---|---|---|
| Game Play: Stand | S | In order to avoid going bust<br>As a player<br>I should be able to stand (keep your existing hand as it is) for each hand in turn |
| Game Play: Double | M | In order to double my stake<br>As a player<br>I should be offered to double down when my initial two cards add up to 9, 10, or 11 |
| Game Play: Split | L | In order to increase my chance of winning<br>As a player<br>I should be offered to split my hand initial two cards make a pair |
| Game Play: Win | M | In order to win a hand of blackjack<br>As a player<br>I must be closer to 21 than the dealer and not go bust |
| Game Play: Dealer Rules | M | In order to give a player a sporting chance<br>As a dealer<br>I will hit on any score below 17 and stand on any score above 17 |
| Member Registration | S | In order to gamble<br>As a player<br>I should be able to register my details |
| Manage Member Account | S | In order to keep my details up to date<br>As a member<br>I should be able to be able to manage my account |
| Cashing In (XL) | XL | In order to get chips to play with<br>As a player<br>I should be able to cash in |
| Betting Range | S | In order to play a game for money<br>As a player<br>I must bet between $5.00 and $20.00 max |
| Playing Multiple Hands | L | In order to increase my chances of winning<br>As a player<br>I should be able to choose between playing one and five hands at a time |
| Game Betting History | L | In order to see how I am playing<br>As a player<br>I should be able to see my betting history for the current session |

| Story | Size | Description |
|---|---|---|
| Cashing Out (XL) | XL | In order to spend my winnings<br>As a player<br>I should be able to cash out |
| Member Account Statements (XL) | XL | In order to keep track of money<br>As a player<br>I should see a statement of funds transferred |
| Reporting Accounts | L | In order to keep track of funds<br>As an account<br>I should be able to see a all funds for all accounts |
| Reporting Registrations | L | In order to see how successful the site is<br>As a director<br>I should be able to see the number of member registrations |
| Saving Game State | L | In order to continue playing<br>As a player<br>I should pick up were I left off if I am disconnected from the internet |

# Committing to the First Sprint

Tim: *Simon, which user stories would you like for us to work on in the first sprint?*

Simon: *I have given it some thought and this is what I am thinking I will need in the first sprint. First, Game Play: Initial Bet. Second, Game Play: Start Game. Third, Game Play: Deck of Cards. Fourth, Game Play: Hit.*

Sarah: *That sounds all right, except for one thing. I am not confident that we can complete all that work in one sprint. Would you be open to dropping one of them? I feel we could get three user stories done, but I think adding a fourth right now would be pushing it.*

Tyler: *I agree with Sarah. Might as well pay for the stuff now and then use it when we need it.*

Simon: *I could let the "Game Play: Hit" user story slide to the following week. This is a critical piece of the application, so it has to be able to run on the computer.*

Tim: *It's official then: Tyler and Sarah will drop the Hit user story from the sprint backlog and will work on it next week.*

Table 4-4 shows the Sprint 1 backlog.

*Table 4-4. Sprint 1 Backlog*

| Story Heading | Shirt Size |
|---|---|
| Game Play: Initial Bet | M |
| Game Play: Deck of Cards | S |
| Game Play: Start Game | L |

## Summary

This chapter introduced you to the blackjack project that you will be creating over the next five chapters as part of our case study. You met the team, and with an understanding of the goal of the project (in the form of a mission statement), you set about capturing the features of the system with the product owner.

With a list of features forming a product backlog, you then used Planning Poker to assign relative complexity points to those stories. With the stories' complexity estimated, the product owner then prioritized the backlog.

One thing to keep in mind is that the product backlog is a fluid document and can change anytime. Just make sure you are communicating well with your team and your product owner so that you are sure you are working on the user stories that will bring the greatest value.

From this prioritized backlog, the product owner was able to pick the three user stories that he felt were the most important; these will be the focus of the first sprint.

In the next chapter you will start your first sprint and work through the tasks that you defined.

# CHAPTER 5

# Sprint 1: Starting a Game

It's time to begin writing features for Kojack Games! With our initial backlog created and prioritized, our development infrastructure established, and our initial product backlog prioritized, we are ready to start coding features! In this chapter we'll layout a plan on how to approach writing features using BDD and see it through to the code implementation. We'll go through the practice of a sprint planning session, the way daily stands-up work, and how to manage the task board and burn-down charts.

## Sprint Planning Meeting

The team has gathered in the conference room. Simon has brought in user stories for the team to work on and discuss.

Tim: *Good morning, team. Since this is our first feature-driven sprint, we'll discuss each user story and gather more information and acceptance criteria, so that as a team we know when we are done with a particular user story. Simon will give us an overview of the user story, we'll discuss acceptance criteria, and decide when this card is done, and then we'll size the user story to commit to during this sprint. First, let's define the theme of this sprint.*

## The Theme of the Sprint

Tim: *I wanted to take this opportunity to discuss with you all what the theme of this sprint is.*

Sarah: *Why do sprints need themes? We are just working on user stories for the customer.*

Tim: *A theme for the sprint gives us a chance to see what goal we are trying to accomplish with the sprint. It shows us the common purpose that all the user stories in the sprint are striving toward. By having a sprint theme, we have a way to make sure we are working on the items we need to be working on for that sprint. If you are working on something that doesn't reflect the theme of the current sprint, then you need to let us know so we can assess the situation and see what the right course of action is.*

*The theme for Sprint 1 is going to be "Starting a Game." The reason for this is because all the work being done in this sprint will lay the foundation for all future sprints. We can't work on cashing in unless we have a basic game to play. The stories in this sprint are in regards to the basic gameplay of the game. User stories in the remaining sprints will add onto the basic gameplay that will be implemented in this sprint.*

## Determining Availability and Capacity

Tim: *Since we are working in two-week sprints, we need to determine who will not be able to work on the project any time during this sprint. Since we don't have any holidays over the next two weeks and everyone is 100 percent allocated to this project, is anyone taking time off during the next two weeks?*

Sarah: *I'm still wrapping up my previous project with quick support questions, but other than that I'm fully available to this project.*

Tyler: *I'm fully dedicated to this project.*

Simon: *Me too.*

Tim: *Great, we are pretty much at full capacity! Capacity is the availability of everyone on the team for the sprint. As all of us know, life happens. Time away is inevitable so we need to account for that. If someone is going to be out any time during the sprint, it's best for the team to know early of the absence so that we can factor it into what we commit to for the sprint and re-adjust the schedule if we need to. Now that we have determined our availability for this sprint, let's get on with planning what user stories we want to commit to!*

## Planning Poker

Tim: *Simon, what user story do you want bring forward to the team first to size?*

Sarah: *Didn't we size this in the release planning meeting? Why do we need to size it again?*

Tim: *Yes, we did. In the release planning we sized it using T-shirt sizes so we could get a ballpark estimate of what it would take to develop the feature. Now that we are planning for the sprint, we want to get more detailed information on the story and play Planning Poker using a Fibonacci-like sequence: 1, 2, 3, 5, 8, 13, 20, 40, 60, 80, 100. While the numbers are similar to the Fibonacci sequence, they are not exactly the same. The intent is to not show a direct correlation between the numbers. If we've broken down the user stories correctly, estimates should be in the single digits. If we discover that we've missed complex functionality within the user story and it needs to be broken down further, we'll split the user story up, give it back to Simon, the product owner, and have him prioritize it. As with release planning, these estimates are arbitrary and relative in size. We will say that displaying a form over a database table is a 2-point story, in other words, the easiest thing you will do. You can use this to estimate the relative complexity of future stories. Simon, what's the first user story we need to discuss?*

Simon: *Let's begin with the Game Play: Initial Bet user story. [(See Figure 5-1.)] In release planning, we mentioned that a player will need to be able to make an initial bet and our T-shirt size for this story was M.*

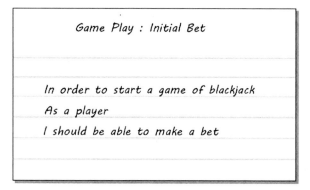

*Figure 5-1. User story: Initial Bet*

Tyler: *Yes, I remember Sarah brought up the idea of a game and player and determining whether or not the player has enough chips to play, as well as updating the player's balance.*

Simon turns over the user story says the acceptance criteria tells the team the following:
- The player must have navigated to the bet page.
- The player needs to have money in order to bet.

Tim: *Now that we've reviewed the acceptance criteria, does anyone have any additional questions?*

Sarah: *No, I think I have what I need.*

Tyler: *Me too.*

Tim: *Great, let's play Planning Poker! What level of effort do you believe this would be?*

Sarah: *I vote for an 8.*

Tyler: *I agree with Sarah. It's a lot more difficult than a form over a database table.*

Tim: *Great, 8 it is. Let's move on. Simon, the next user story?*

Simon: *The next user story is Game Play: Start Game.* (See Figure 5-2.)

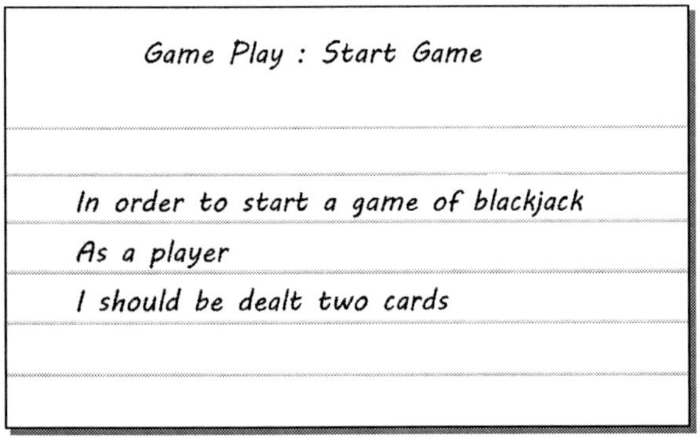

```
┌─────────────────────────────────────────────┐
│                                               │
│        Game Play : Start Game                 │
│                                               │
│  ─────────────────────────────────────────    │
│                                               │
│   In order to start a game of blackjack       │
│   As a player                                 │
│   I should be dealt two cards                 │
│                                               │
│                                               │
│                                               │
└─────────────────────────────────────────────┘
```

**Figure 5-2.** *User story: Start Game*

Sarah: *What are the acceptance criteria of this user story?*

Simon: *Good question.*

Simon flips over the card and tells the team the following:

- The player and the dealer must be dealt two cards.
- The player's cards will both be face up. The dealer will have one card face up, one card face down.
- A bet must be placed before the cards are dealt.

Sarah: *Didn't we talk about having a deck of cards user story?*

Tim: *Yes, we did. We can size this one under the assumption that the Deck of Cards user story is done. We know that there will be a dependency on that particular user story by this user story. While user stories should be independent of each other, oftentimes there is a dependency that cannot be worked around. In this case, the dealer cannot deal the cards unless there is a deck to deal from.*

Sarah: *Okay, that makes sense to me. So let me get this straight. Assuming that the Deck of Cards user story is done, we need to deal two cards each to the dealer and the player, with both cards face up to the player and one card face up and one card face down to the dealer?*

Simon: *That's correct.*

Tim: *Any more questions? If not, let's play Planning Poker on this user story.*

Tyler: *This doesn't seem to be as difficult as the initial bet, so I'll say a 3.*

Sarah: *I agree this one isn't too much more difficult than having a form over a database table. I'm comfortable with a 3.*

Tim: *A 3 it is. Let's move onto the next one. Right now, as a team, we have committed to 8 points. What do you all think about committing to another user story for this sprint?*

Tyler: *I don't see why not. Nothing that we have committed to so far seems overly complicated.*

Sarah: *I would agree. I think we can commit to one smaller one during this sprint and get them all done.*

Tim: *Okay. Let's do one, more, small feature, because we don't want to commit to work we can't accomplish.*

Simon: *The next user story in the backlog that the team deemed an S in the release planning is Game Play: Deck of Cards.* [(See Figure 5-3.)]

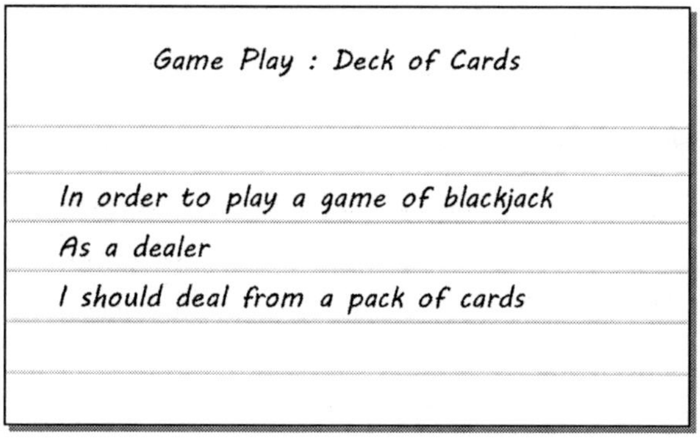

```
  Game Play : Deck of Cards



 In order to play a game of blackjack
 As a dealer
 I should deal from a pack of cards


```

**Figure 5-3.** *A user story on the creation of the deck of cards needed for the game*

Simon: *As part of this user story I have a list of acceptance criteria that will mark this user story as done.*

Simon tells the team the following:

1. Create a deck of cards

2. Add ability to deal cards from the dealer

3. Add ability to shuffle cards so each hand is unique

4. There has to be 52 unique cards in the deck

Tim: *Given the two user stories we've estimated, is the effort similar to either of those?*

Sarah: *I think this is similar to the Start Game user story, so I vote a 3.*

Tyler: *I vote a 5 because I think the graphics are a larger undertaking than I first thought.*

Sarah: *I vote a 3. I checked—we can use the graphics from a free, online site. That will allow us not to worry about the graphics and focus on the logic.*

Tyler: *Great, that seems like less effort.*

Tim: *Let's play another round.*

Sarah: *I vote 3.*

Tyler: *I still have concerns. The online site is unknown and will be a learning curve, so I'll go 4.*

Sarah: *So do I.*

Tim: *Great, we've sized this as a 4. If there's nothing else…*

Simon: *Wait, can we put one more story in?*

Tim: *Team, what do you think?*

Tyler: *I'm uncomfortable adding more stories. I think we have a solid amount of work. If we add more work, I'm afraid we won't be able to get it all done in time.*

Sarah: *I agree. I think adding more user stories will set us up for failure to get all the stories done on time.*

Simon: *Okay. I'd rather have fewer stories 100 percent completed than have more stories half completed.*

Tim: *Since this is our first sprint, we need to be cautious on our commitments until we are comfortable with the velocity of the team. Tyler and Sarah will work on getting these user stories done and we'll demo the completed user stories to make sure we are delivering value to the customer.*

Simon: *Sounds great. I'll be looking forward to seeing them!*

## Project Management/Feedback Progress

Tim: *Now that we have the stories sized, I want to share information on how we'll make our progress transparent for our team members and whoever would like to check on the progress. In order to keep track of our progress, we will use a simple, daily burn-down chart that will visually help us to understand if we are on course to deliver all of the stories that we committed to. There are a wide variety of open source, online, and integrated software solutions for managing the backlog of items on an agile project. Our project will be minimalistic, and use an Excel spreadsheet along with a task card wall to map progress.*

Figure 5-4 shows all the items that the team has on backlog for the current sprint. It's a good idea to have a physical board placed where the team can see it. It's also a great idea to allow pairs to select their own story to work on. You can also add the tasks to the board, but we prefer team members to work on a story from start to finish. If you have a pair of developers and no stories left, then you can break down stories that other teams are working on into tasks so that the workload can be shared. Alternatively, developers with no work can start to work on technical debt tasks or perhaps scope out the features for the next sprint.

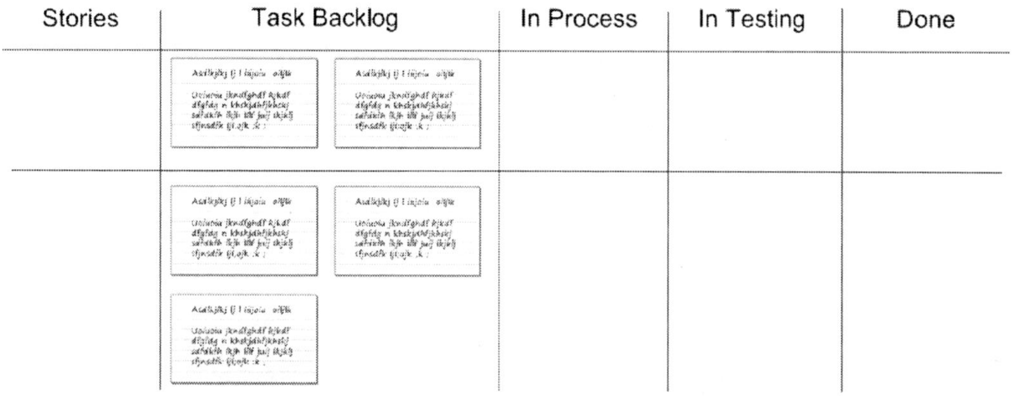

| Stories | Task Backlog | In Process | In Testing | Done |
|---------|-------------|------------|------------|------|
| | | | | |

*Figure 5-4. Task wall for Sprint 1*

Figure 5-5 shows the daily burn-down for the sprint. The bars along the bottom of the graph show the number of hours that have been burnt each day. The scale on the left-hand side is in ideal hours (6 hours/day). The straight line shows the "happy day" scenario when the sprint should be complete and the wavy line shows how much work there is left to complete. This daily burn-down chart is not essential for most Scrum teams, however, if you find that you are consistently unable to complete stories that you committed to, it's useful to see where your time has gone.

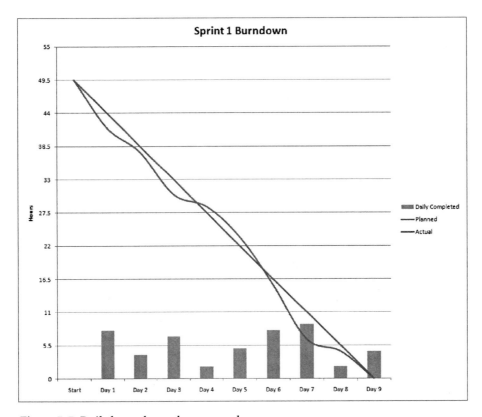

*Figure 5-5. Daily burn-down chart example*

Tim: *Now you know how we'll communicate our progress to others. Everyone should have enough information to get started on their user stories. Let's meet tomorrow morning at 9 AM for a quick, daily stand-up.*

## Sprint 1's Backlog

Table 5-1 reviews the user stories that team committed to for this iteration.

*Table 5-1. Sprint 1 Backlog*

| User Story Name | Initial Size |
| --- | --- |
| Game Play: Initial Bet | 8 |
| Game Play: Deck of Cards | 4 |
| Game Play: Start Game | 3 |

# Day 1

Welcome to the first day of the first sprint. As we enter this and every day, we will begin with a daily stand-up meeting where the team talks about what it did yesterday, as well as what everyone plans to do today and if there are any roadblocks that prevent us from accomplishing our work.

## Daily Stand-Up

Tim: *Hello everyone. I wanted to take some time here at the beginning and discuss with you what our daily stand-up meetings are. These meetings are a way for members of the team to bring issues or concerns to the forefront early in the process. These meetings will happen every day at the same time and should last no more than 10 to 15 minutes.*

Sarah: *Fifteen minutes? What do we plan to accomplish in a 15-minute meeting? Seems like a waste of time to me.*

Simon: *I agree. Shouldn't we be spending that time working on story cards for the customer?*

Tim: *These meetings are not a waste of time. They are meant to be short so the people in the meeting can get in, share the information they have for that day, and get out. With that goal in mind, the meeting will follow a pattern. Each team member will answer three questions in this meeting: One, what did you do yesterday? Two, what are you doing today? And three, is there anything blocking you from doing your work for today? This gives everyone on the team a chance to know what is going on with the work that the team has committed to. If someone is having an issue, then these meetings are a chance for you to notify either me or Simon of the problem, so that we can start working on a solution. It is better to find a problem at the beginning of the sprint, than to have it fester the entire sprint unbeknownst to anyone that could have solved it.*

Sarah: *How do we keep this to 10 to 15 minutes? We can get long-winded sometimes and sometimes we only need to discuss issues with a sub-set of the group, not the whole group.*

Tim: *If a team member needs to meet with another team member to discuss an issue that doesn't really benefit the whole team, then have a one-on-one "meeting after the meeting" to not take up everyone's time. Keep in mind, these daily stand-ups are merely quick, status meetings—they are not problem-solving sessions. It is the responsibility of the ScrumMaster to keep these meetings quick. As for the long-windedness, it is the team's responsibility to police themselves and each other so that we can all move on with our day.*

Tyler: *What about our customers or management? If we really are committed to a 15-minute meeting, then we better make sure not to invite them.*

Tim: *Everybody is invited to attend these meetings. In fact, we are going to have these meetings in the open area so there is no hiding what we are working on or discussing. That being said, just because everyone is invited to attend this meeting does not mean they can talk in these meetings. If you remember from earlier, about the story of the chicken and the pig, we members of the team are classified as the pigs. We have the larger stake in this project. Everyone else is classified as the chickens. They can attend, but they can only observe.*

Tyler: *What happens if one of these "chickens" tries to interrupt our meeting by talking about issues outside of the team's control?*

Tim: *Then it is the job of every member of this team to politely let the person know that this meeting is not the right venue for the discussion. If they are still having an issue with that, then I will pull them aside sometime later and explain it to them. If there are no further questions, how about we get this meeting started? Sarah, would you like to start?*

Sarah: *Let's see. Yesterday I worked with other members of the team and our customer to size the user stories we are doing for this sprint using a variation of the Fibonacci sequence. I plan on working on the highest priority story in the backlog and there is nothing at the moment that is blocking me from getting to work on the story.*

Tim: *Tyler, your turn.*

Tyler: *Well, yesterday I worked with Sarah and the customer on the backlog thing, like Sarah said. Today, I plan on working on a user story and I have no blocks.*

Simon: *Yesterday, worked with the customer on the product backlog. Today, I plan on spending some more time with the customer hashing out more of the remaining user stories in the backlog to make sure we are not missing any key piece of functionality. I have no blocks.*

Tim: *Great! So you can see, these meetings won't take long after this first one, and it will give us a chance to see how we are doing as a team.*

## Developing the First Story: The Initial Bet Feature

This is where we will start looking at the coding side of the project. With the Initial Bet user story, we will show you how to develop it from the ground up using test-driven development (TDD) and behavior-driven development (BDD). You will see how a pair of developers can create a stable feature from writing their tests first.

## Implementing the First Story

Sarah: *I'll take the Initial Bet feature. Tyler, do you want to pair with me?*

Tyler: *Sure, let's do it!*

Sarah moves the Initial Bet user story in the In Process swim lane to let people know that this user story is being work on. The first thing we need to do is to add our first SpecFlow feature.

## Adding the First SpecFlow Feature

Once SpecFlow has been installed, add a new feature to the Features folder named 001-BetAtTheStartOfAGame.feature. Once created, update the feature file so that it matches the feature shown in Figure 5-6.

*Figure 5-6. Bet feature with the first scenario*

If you run the tests, you will, of course, find that there are no step definitions set up for the steps in our first scenario. As described in Appendix B, SpecFlow outputs the skeleton code for us so that we can simply copy and paste it into our Steps folder. In order to organize steps, we will group them by function.

Add a new NavigationSteps class to the Steps folder and update with the following code definition:

```
using TechTalk.SpecFlow.

namespace KojackGames.Blackjack.Acceptance.Tests.Steps
{
    [Binding]
    public class NavigationSteps
    {
        [Given(@"I have navigated to the game play screen to play a hand")]
        public void GivenIAmOnTheGamePlayScreen()
        {
            SiteNavigator.go_to_bet_page();
        }
    }
}
```

Don't worry that the SiteNavigator class doesn't exist; this is merely a placeholder that tells us the type of behavior we want to provide in order to run our test. In other words, this step in our scenario describes a user navigating to the bet page, so we need an object that will do just that. We will get back to this class in just a moment, but before we do, we should press on and fill out the remaining step definitions.

Add a second class to the Steps folder named GamePlaySteps with the following definition:

```
using NUnit.Framework;
using TechTalk.SpecFlow;

namespace KojackGames.Blackjack.Acceptance.Tests.Steps
{
    [Binding]
    public class GamePlaySteps
    {
```

```
        [When(@"I click on the bet button")]
        public void WhenIClickOnTheBetButton()
        {
            BetOnHandPage.bet();
        }
    }
}
```

The GamePlaySteps class has methods that match the scenario steps with code that we have yet to write, which will confirm the existence of a Deal button and will also click the Bet button.

Again, the code within the step definitions for the GamePlaySteps doesn't yet exist; however, we are not concerned with that, we are more concerned with the behavior that the code is trying to portray. Even though this is only a test and not production code, it is still important to put the same effort into creating intention, revealing methods and classes.

The last step class that you will create deals with steps that assert on the view of the game. Add a new class to the Steps folder named GameDisplaySteps and update it as shown in the following code listing:

```
using NUnit.Framework;
using TechTalk.SpecFlow;

namespace KojackGames.Blackjack.Acceptance.Tests.Steps
{
    [Binding]
    public class GameDisplaySteps
    {
        [Then(@"I should see the deal button")]
        public void ThenIShouldSeeTheDealButton()
        {
            Assert.That(BetOnHandPage.Has_Deal_Button, Is.True);
        }
    }
}
```

Again, this code will not compile because the BetOnHandPage object does not exist.

## Interacting with the Browser Using WatiN

Now that we have all of the step definitions for our first scenario defined, we can start to add the code that will perform the actions of the steps, in other words, the code that is currently giving the compiler lots to moan about. The first piece of code that we will deal with is the non-existent SiteNavigator class that is used in the NavigationSteps class. The purpose of this class is to navigate to the blackjack site. In order for this class to operate, it will need to talk to the browser; so before we create the SiteNavigator class, let's create the browser.

The browser abstraction will use WatiN (see Appendix E) to interact with the web browser during testing, so go ahead and install this class along with the Cassini web server (also covered in Appendix E) that we will use when running acceptance tests. You should add these tools and libraries to the local project folder so that they are referenced locally and can be included when we check the source code in.

With the WatiN and Cassini libraries in place, add a reference to them from them Acceptance.Tests project and add a new class named WebBrowser to the Utilities folder with the following definition:

```csharp
using System.IO;
using Cassini;
using TechTalk.SpecFlow;
using WatiN.Core;

namespace KojackGames.Blackjack.Acceptance.Tests.Utilities
{
    public class WebBrowser
    {
        public const string RelativePath = @"KojackGames.Blackjack.Ui.Web";

        public const int Port = 14387;

        public static Browser Current
        {
            get
            {
                if (!ScenarioContext.Current.ContainsKey("browser"))
                    ScenarioContext.Current["browser"] = new IE();
                return (Browser)ScenarioContext.Current["browser"];
            }
        }


        public static void Stop()
        {
            if (ScenarioContext.Current.ContainsKey("browser"))
                Current.Close();
        }

        protected static Server WebServer { get; private set; }

        private static string GetPhysicalPath()
        {
            var dir = Directory.GetCurrentDirectory();

            var index = dir.LastIndexOf(
                    "KojackGames.Blackjack.Acceptance.Tests");

            dir = dir.Remove(index);

            return Path.Combine(dir, RelativePath);
        }

        public static void InitializeBrowser()
        {
            WebServer = new Server(Port, "/", GetPhysicalPath());

            WebServer.Start();
        }

        public static void ShutdownBrowser()
```

```
        {
            WebServer.Stop();
        }
    }
}
```

This class uses WatiN to interact with the browser and also uses the development web server to run the project. Again, the details of this class can be found in Appendix E, which covers WatiN.

With the WebBrowser class in place, we can now tackle the SiteNavigator that is referenced in the NavigationSteps class. The role of the SiteNavigator class is to make it easy to navigate the site and abstract away the details of interacting with the WebBrowser class.

Add a new class named SiteNavigator with the following definition. You will also need to include a using statement in the NavigationSteps class to leverage this class.

```
namespace KojackGames.Blackjack.Acceptance.Tests.Utilities
{
    public static class SiteNavigator
    {
        private static void go_to(string relativeUrl)
        {
            WebBrowser.Current.GoTo(
                string.Format("http://localhost:{0}/{1}",
                                WebBrowser.Port,relativeUrl));
        }

        public static void go_to_bet_page()
        {
            go_to("bet");
        }
    }
}
```

The SiteNavigator is very straightforward and provides a façade to navigate the site, hiding away the details of the URLs. This will make it easier to reuse this class throughout the project.

If you notice we have already made the first design decision of our application, in that the bet page will map to the URL site/bet.

We have failing tests and code that doesn't compile. Let's work on getting the code to compile.

## Interacting with Pages Using the Page Object Pattern

To structure our tests in order to enable easy maintenance as our acceptance test project grows, we will use the page object pattern.

The GamePlaySteps and GameDisplaySteps classes already use this non-existent class, so you already know what it's going to look like based on how we want to interact with it. This is a great design process; always create objects from the client's point of view, even if it's in the test code. Remember that your test code can still get just as messy as production code if it is not looked after.

Add the new BetOnHandPage to the PageObjects folder with the following definition:

```
using KojackGames.Blackjack.Acceptance.Tests.Utilities;

namespace KojackGames.Blackjack.Acceptance.Tests.PageObjects
{
```

```
public class BetOnHandPage
{
    public static void bet()
    {
        WebBrowser.Current.Button("btnBet").Click();
    }

    public static void deal()
    {
        WebBrowser.Current.Button("btnDeal").Click();
    }

    public static bool has_deal_button
    {
        get { return WebBrowser.Current.Button("btnDeal").Exists; }
    }
}
}
```

You will need to add a using statement to the GamePlaySteps and GameDisplaySteps class in order to satisfy the compiler. The BetOnHandPage simply wraps the calls to WatiN to interact with the page. As previously mentioned, this abstracts away the implementation of the view and provides a cleaner, more manageable class for clients to work against.

In order for the web server and browser to be in a clean state for each scenario, you will need to initialize the browser object and then shut down that browser object after each feature, and close the current instance of IE after each scenario has completed. SpecFlow has some bindings you can use to run code during these specific events. Add a new class named FeatureEvents to the Events folder with the following definition. The code should be self-explanatory.

```
using KojackGames.Blackjack.Acceptance.Tests.Utilities;
using TechTalk.SpecFlow;

namespace KojackGames.Blackjack.Acceptance.Tests.Events
{
    [Binding]
    public class FeatureEvents
    {
        [BeforeFeature]
        public static void BeforeFeature()
        {
            WebBrowser.InitializeBrowser();
        }

        [AfterFeature]
        public static void AfterFeature()
        {
            WebBrowser.ShutdownBrowser();
        }

        [AfterScenario]
        public void AfterScenario()
        {
```

```
                WebBrowser.Current.Close();
        }
    }
}
```

You should now be able to build your solution. However, before we run the tests we need to reference the `CassiniWebServer.exe` in the `Ui.Web` ASP.NET MVC project. Ensure that SQL 2008 R2 SQL Express is installed.

If you run the tests as is, you will receive an error. This is due to the fact that IE is not thread-safe, so in order to resolve the error you will need to configure NUnit to run in single thread state mode by adding a configuration file to the `Acceptance.Tests` project named `App.config` with the following mark-up:

```xml
<?xml version="1.0" encoding="utf-8"?>
<configuration>
  <configSections>
    <sectionGroup name="NUnit">
      <section name="TestRunner"
               type="System.Configuration.NameValueSectionHandler"/>
    </sectionGroup>
  </configSections>

  <NUnit>
    <TestRunner>
      <add key="ApartmentState" value="STA" />
    </TestRunner>
  </NUnit>

</configuration>
```

Once the `App.Config` file is in place, build the solution and run the acceptance tests. Once the tests have ran you will find that it compiles but fails due to the lack of any production code, as shown in Figure 5-7.

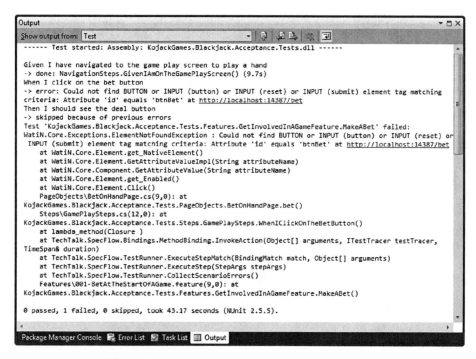

```
Output                                                                    ▼ □ ×
Show output from:  Test                              ▼ | 🔊 | 🔊 🔊 | 🔊 | 🔊
------ Test started: Assembly: KojackGames.Blackjack.Acceptance.Tests.dll ------

Given I have navigated to the game play screen to play a hand
-> done: NavigationSteps.GivenIAmOnTheGamePlayScreen() (9.7s)
When I click on the bet button
-> error: Could not find BUTTON or INPUT (button) or INPUT (reset) or INPUT (submit) element tag matching
criteria: Attribute 'id' equals 'btnBet' at http://localhost:14387/bet
Then I should see the deal button
-> skipped because of previous errors
Test 'KojackGames.Blackjack.Acceptance.Tests.Features.GetInvolvedInAGameFeature.MakeABet' failed:
WatiN.Core.Exceptions.ElementNotFoundException : Could not find BUTTON or INPUT (button) or INPUT (reset) or
 INPUT (submit) element tag matching criteria: Attribute 'id' equals 'btnBet' at http://localhost:14387/bet
    at WatiN.Core.Element.get_NativeElement()
    at WatiN.Core.Element.GetAttributeValueImpl(String attributeName)
    at WatiN.Core.Component.GetAttributeValue(String attributeName)
    at WatiN.Core.Element.get_Enabled()
    at WatiN.Core.Element.Click()
    PageObjects\BetOnHandPage.cs(9,0): at
KojackGames.Blackjack.Acceptance.Tests.PageObjects.BetOnHandPage.bet()
    Steps\GamePlaySteps.cs(12,0): at
KojackGames.Blackjack.Acceptance.Tests.Steps.GamePlaySteps.WhenIClickOnTheBetButton()
    at lambda_method(Closure )
    at TechTalk.SpecFlow.Bindings.MethodBinding.InvokeAction(Object[] arguments, ITestTracer testTracer,
TimeSpan& duration)
    at TechTalk.SpecFlow.TestRunner.ExecuteStepMatch(BindingMatch match, Object[] arguments)
    at TechTalk.SpecFlow.TestRunner.ExecuteStep(StepArgs stepArgs)
    at TechTalk.SpecFlow.TestRunner.CollectScenarioErrors()
    Features\001-BetAtTheStartOfAGame.feature(9,0): at
KojackGames.Blackjack.Acceptance.Tests.Features.GetInvolvedInAGameFeature.MakeABet()

0 passed, 1 failed, 0 skipped, took 43.17 seconds (NUnit 2.5.5).

Package Manager Console  🔊 Error List  🔊 Task List  🔊 Output
```

***Figure 5-7.*** *SpecFlow output from failing step*

At this stage, all we have are failing step definitions, but code that compiles. It's time to start development.

## Using Behavior-Driven Design to Drive the Feature Development

With the acceptance test project set up and with a good idea of what we need to develop, we can now jump into code. Following the "outside in" development process shown in Figure 5-8, we can start to discover all of the underlying classes that will form our application, without straying from the required behaviors of the system as laid out in the acceptance criteria scenario.

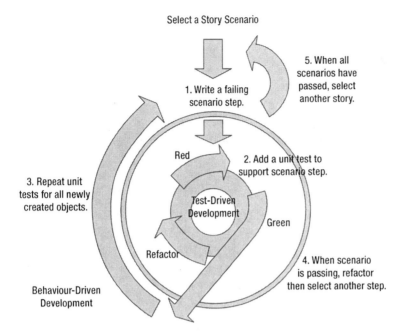

**Figure 5-8.** *The TDD/ BDD process*

The first failing step deals with navigating to the bet page, so it makes sense to write a test that confirms that the Url/bets URL results in an appropriate controller method being mapped to it.

We will use the MSpec framework (covered in Appendix B) to drive the design of the applications objects, so add the MSpec libraries to the Lib folder of the solution structure and add a reference to it from the Core.Tests project.

To keep our unit tests organized, add a new folder into the Core.Tests project named Controller_specs to store all of your controller tests. As you are going to be testing against the ASP.NET MVC framework, a great third-party framework to assist can be found within the MVC Contrib framework (http://mvccontrib.codeplex.com/) or by installing it using NuGet. Again, ensure you add the library to the Lib folder of your solution structure.

Now that you have MSpec and the MvcContrib library in place, you can add your first specification that will confirm the behavior of the route mapping. Add a new class to the Controller_Specs folder named route_mapping_specs, as shown in the following:

```
using System.Web.Routing;

using Machine.Specifications;
using MvcContrib.TestHelper;

namespace KojackGames.Blackjack.Core.Tests.Controller_specs
{
  [Subject(typeof(RouteMapper), "route mapper")]
  public class route_mapping_specs
  {
    private Establish context = () =>
    {
```

```
        var routes = RouteTable.Routes;
        routes.Clear();
        RouteMapper.add_mappings_to(routes);
    };

    private It should_map_to_the_bet_route = () =>
    {
        "~/bet/".Route().ShouldMapTo<BetController>();
    };
  }

}
```

You will notice that we have had to add a reference to the System.Web.Routing and System.Web.Mvc libraries in order to test the routing maps. Currently, the spec will not compile as the RouteMapper class that will contain the route mappings does not yet exist. Add this class to the root of the Ui.Web project with the following definition:

```
using System.Web.Mvc;
using System.Web.Routing;

namespace KojackGames.Blackjack.UI.Web
{
    public class RouteMapper
    {
        public static void add_mappings_to(RouteCollection routes)
        {
            routes.IgnoreRoute("{resource}.axd/{*pathInfo}");
            routes.IgnoreRoute("{*favicon}",
                new { favicon = @"(.*/)?favicon.ico(/.*)?" });

            routes.MapRoute(
                "Default", // Route name
                "{controller}/{action}/{id}", // URL with parameters
                new { controller = "Bet", action = "Bet",
                    id = UrlParameter.Optional } // Parameter defaults
            );
        }
    }
}
```

The other class to add is the missing BetController. Add this to the Ui.Web projects controllers folder as laid out in the following:

```
using System.Web.Mvc;

namespace KojackGames.Blackjack.UI.Web.Controllers
{
    public class BetController : Controller
    {

        public BetController()
        { }
```

```
        public ActionResult Bet()
        {
            return View();
        }
}
```

In order to get the BetController to compile, you will need to add a corresponding view. Right-click on the highlighted View method and select "add view without a master page." Add the following code to the view markup:

...

```
<body>
    using (Html.BeginForm())
    {%>
        <input id="btnBet" type="submit" value="Bet $5" />
    <%
    }%>
</body>
</html>
```

In order to register your route mappings with the ASP.NET MVC engine, you will need to add the following code snippet to the Global.asax file:

```
public static void RegisterRoutes(RouteCollection routes)
{
        RouteMapper.add_mappings_to(routes);
}
```

Finally, include a reference to the BetController and RouteMapper classes in your route_mapping_specs class.

You will now be able to run the acceptance test and you should find that the first two steps will pass, as seen in Figure 5-9.

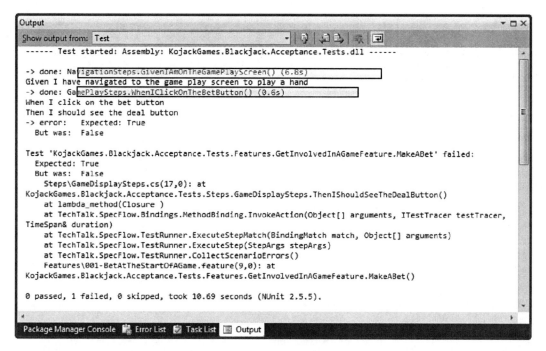

```
Output                                                                        ▾ □ ✕
Show output from:  Test                                      ▾  │ ⟳ │ ⧉ ⧉ │ ☰ │ ⤢ │
------ Test started: Assembly: KojackGames.Blackjack.Acceptance.Tests.dll ------

-> done: NavigationSteps.GivenIAmOnTheGamePlayScreen() (6.8s)
Given I have navigated to the game play screen to play a hand
-> done: GamePlaySteps.WhenIClickOnTheBetButton() (0.6s)
When I click on the bet button
Then I should see the deal button
-> error:   Expected: True
  But was: False

Test 'KojackGames.Blackjack.Acceptance.Tests.Features.GetInvolvedInAGameFeature.MakeABet' failed:
  Expected: True
  But was:  False
    Steps\GameDisplaySteps.cs(17,0): at
KojackGames.Blackjack.Acceptance.Tests.Steps.GameDisplaySteps.ThenIShouldSeeTheDealButton()
    at lambda_method(Closure )
    at TechTalk.SpecFlow.Bindings.MethodBinding.InvokeAction(Object[] arguments, ITestTracer testTracer,
TimeSpan& duration)
    at TechTalk.SpecFlow.TestRunner.ExecuteStepMatch(BindingMatch match, Object[] arguments)
    at TechTalk.SpecFlow.TestRunner.ExecuteStep(StepArgs stepArgs)
    at TechTalk.SpecFlow.TestRunner.CollectScenarioErrors()
    Features\001-BetAtTheStartOfAGame.feature(9,0): at
KojackGames.Blackjack.Acceptance.Tests.Features.GetInvolvedInAGameFeature.MakeABet()

0 passed, 1 failed, 0 skipped, took 10.69 seconds (NUnit 2.5.5).

Package Manager Console  🖳 Error List  📋 Task List  📃 Output
```

*Figure 5-9. SpecFlow showing two of the three steps passing*

## Discovering the Lower-Level Objects Using BDD

With the first two steps passing, we move onto the next failing step—which handles the registering of a bet and the display of a Deal button signifying to the player that the game is ready to begin.

To drive the design and focus on testing a single class at a time, we will use the RhinoMocks mocking engine. As with all other third-party libraries, remember to include and reference the library from the Libs folder so that it is available for other developers when they check the code out of source code.

Creating a plan of attack, we need to first see what we want to test. Starting with the behavior of the BetController reacting to a call to place a bet on a hand results in a to-do list, as shown in Figure 5-10, that will form the basis of the specification. This becomes our plan of attack.

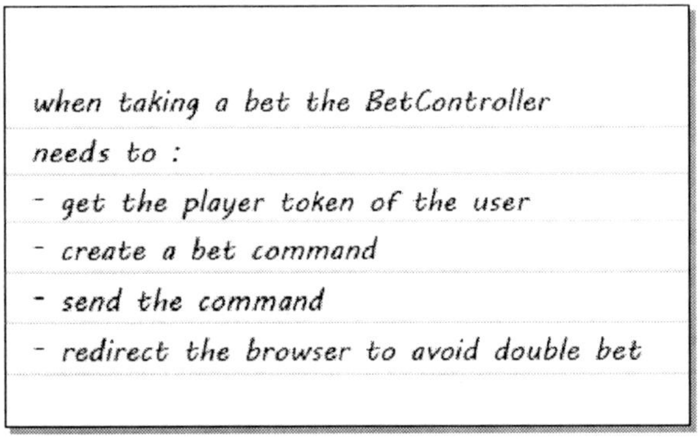

*Figure 5-10. Checklist for BetController Behaviors*

Add the following class into the Controller_Specs folder and name it when_betting_on_a_hand, that covers getting the players id. Note how the name of the specification closely matches our original note; it's important to have well-named specifications that reveal what you are asserting.

```
using Rhino.Mocks;
using KojackGames.Blackjack.Ui.Web.Controllers;
using Machine.Specifications;

namespace KojackGames.Blackjack.Core.Tests.Controller_specs
{
  [Subject(typeof(BetController), "BetController")]
  public class when_betting_on_a_hand
  {
    private Establish context = () =>
    {
      player_token = Guid.NewGuid();

      bet_on_hand_form = new BetOnHandForm() { bet = 5m};

      player_authenticator =
          MockRepository.GenerateStub<IPlayerAuthenticator>();
      player_authenticator.Stub(x =>
          x.get_player_token()).Return(player_token);

      SUT = new BetController(player_authenticator);
    };

    private Because of = () => SUT.Bet(bet_on_hand_form);

    private It should_ask_for_my_player_token = () =>
    {
      player_authenticator.AssertWasCalled(x =>
          x.get_player_token());
    };

    private static BetOnHandForm bet_on_hand_form;
```

```
        private static Guid player_token;
        protected static IPlayerAuthenticator player_authenticator;
        protected static BetController SUT;
    }
}
```

So let's take a look at what is going on in this specification. The action of posting a BetOnHandForm to
the BetController should result in a call to the IPlayerAuthenticator to obtain the player's identity
token. In order to use the IPlayerAuthenticator, we have elected to use constructor dependency
injection. This is logical because we need to identify the player when communicating with the server. To
get the spec to compile, create the IPlayerAuthenticator and put it in the Infrastructure project under
a folder named Authentication, as this is a non-domain concern..

```
using System;

namespace KojackGames.Blackjack.Infrastructure.Authentication
{
    public interface IPlayerAuthenticator
    {
        Guid get_player_token();
    }
}
```

Next, add a BetOnHandForm class to the Models folder of the Ui.Web project. This will be the object that
is created by the framework when we hit the Bet button and the form data is posted backed to the server.

```
namespace KojackGames.Blackjack.Ui.Web.Models
{
    public class BetOnHandForm
    {
        public decimal bet { get; set; }
    }
}
```

Finally, update the BetController to add a new action and to include the IPlayerAuthenticator as a
constructor parameter. Don't forget to make the call to the IPlayerAuthenticator from within the new
Bet action to obtain the player's token.

```
using System.Web.Mvc;
using KojackGames.Blackjack.Infrastructure.Authentication;
using KojackGames.Blackjack.Ui.Web.Models;

namespace KojackGames.Blackjack.Ui.Web.Controllers
{
    public class BetController : Controller
    {
        private readonly IPlayerAuthenticator _player_authenticator;

        public BetController(IPlayerAuthenticator player_authenticator)
        {
            _player_authenticator = player_authenticator;
        }

        public ActionResult Bet()
```

```
    {
        return View();
    }

    [HttpPost]
    public ActionResult Bet(BetOnHandForm bet_on_hand_form)
    {
        var player = _player_authenticator.get_player_token();

        return View();
    }
  }
}
```

You will need to reference the two new classes from within your when_betting_on_a_hand class by adding the following two using directives:

```
using KojackGames.Blackjack.Infrastructure.Authentication;
using KojackGames.Blackjack.Ui.Web.Models;
```

If you run the spec, it will pass as shown in Figure 5-11.

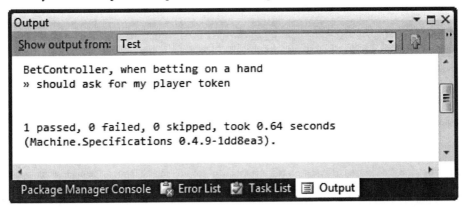

*Figure 5-11. Passing specification*

Because we are going to be writing a number of specifications against the BetController, it's a good idea to have a base class that sets up the BetController. Create a new class named with_a_BetController with the following definition:

```
using KojackGames.Blackjack.Infrastructure.Authentication;
using KojackGames.Blackjack.Ui.Web.Controllers;
using Rhino.Mocks;

namespace KojackGames.Blackjack.Core.Tests.Controller_specs
{
    public abstract class with_a_BetController
    {
        protected static IPlayerAuthenticator player_authenticator;
        protected static BetController SUT;

        public with_a_BetController()
        {
            player_authenticator =
                MockRepository.GenerateStub<IPlayerAuthenticator>();

            SUT = new BetController(player_authenticator);
        }
    }
}
```

You can now update the when_betting_on_a_hand class to inherit from the base class to simplify some of the setup code. This will help when the complexity of the BetController grows.

```
using System;
using KojackGames.Blackjack.Ui.Web.Models;
using KojackGames.Blackjack.Ui.Web.Controllers;
using Machine.Specifications;
using Rhino.Mocks;

namespace KojackGames.Blackjack.Core.Tests.Controller_specs
{
    [Subject(typeof(BetController))]
    public class when_betting_on_a_hand : with_a_BetController
    {
        private Establish context = () =>
        {
            player_token = Guid.NewGuid();
            bet_on_hand_form = new BetOnHandForm() { bet = 5m};
            player_authenticator.Stub(x =>
                    x.get_player_token()).Return(player_token);
        };

        private Because of = () => SUT.Bet(bet_on_hand_form);

        private It should_ask_for_my_player_token = () =>
        {
            player_authenticator.AssertWasCalled(x => x.get_player_token());
        };

        private static BetOnHandForm bet_on_hand_form;
        private static Guid player_token;
```

```
        }
}
```

After obtaining the id of the player, the next step in the betting process is to create a command to send. Add another assertion to the when_betting_on_a_hand class, as seen in the following code listng:

```
[Subject(typeof(BetController))]
public class when_betting_on_a_hand : with_a_BetController
{
    ...

    private It should_map_the_viewmodel_to_a_bet_command = () =>
    {
        bet_command_mapper.AssertWasCalled(x =>
                x.map_from(bet_on_hand_form, player_token));
    };

    ...

}
```

We will explain what the bet_command_mapper field is after you have updated the base class as listed in the following code snippet:

```
using KojackGames.Blackjack.Infrastructure.Authentication;
using KojackGames.Blackjack.Ui.Web.Controllers;
using KojackGames.Blackjack.Ui.Web.Models;
using Rhino.Mocks;

namespace KojackGames.Blackjack.Core.Tests.Controller_specs
{
    public abstract class with_a_BetController
    {
        protected static IPlayerAuthenticator player_authenticator;
        protected static BetController SUT;
        protected static ICommandMapper<BetCommand, BetOnHandForm>
                                                bet_command_mapper;

        public with_a_BetController()
        {
            player_authenticator =
                    MockRepository.GenerateStub<IPlayerAuthenticator>();
            bet_command_mapper = MockRepository
                .GenerateStub<ICommandMapper<BetCommand, BetOnHandForm>>();

            SUT = new BetController(player_authenticator,
                                    bet_command_mapper);
        }
    }
}
```

The job of the `ICommandMapper<BetCommand, BetOnHandForm>` is to convert a `BetOnHandForm` that is generated from the posted form data to a `BetCommand` that can be sent to the domain model for auctioning. Note also that the `BetController` requires the `ICommandMapper` to do its job, so we inject it via the constructor.

With an idea for the contract and the behavior of the `ICommandMapper` set, you can now implement it. As this interface is specific to the `Ui.Web` project, go ahead and add it to the `Models` folder of the `UI.Web` project, as shown in the following listing. Note how we have used generics to enable reuse of the contract throughout the application.

```
using System;

namespace KojackGames.Blackjack.UI.Web.Models
{
    public interface ICommandMapper<out TCommand, in TFrom>
    {
        TCommand map_from(TFrom view_model, Guid player_token);
    }
}
```

Next, add a `BetCommand` that will contain all of the information required to action the placing of a bet for a player; for example, the player's identifying token and the wager amount.

The `BetCommand` is part of the core domain, so it will live in the `Domain` project. Create a new folder structure within the `Domain` project starting with a context folder of `GamePlay` and then an artifact folder named `Commands`. When the folder structure is complete, add the `BetCommand` class to it, as defined in the following listing:

```
using System;

namespace KojackGames.Blackjack.Domain.GamePlay.Commands
{
    public class BetCommand
    {
        public decimal wager { get; set; }
        public Guid player_token { get; set; }
    }
}
```

All that remains to do in order for the specification to pass is to call the `ICommandMapper` from within the overloaded Bet method. Again, inject the `ICommandMapper` in via the constructor and call the `ICommandMapper` in the Bet Action, as seen in the following listing:

```
using System.Web.Mvc;
using KojackGames.Blackjack.Domain.GamePlay.Commands;
using KojackGames.Blackjack.Infrastructure.Authentication;
using KojackGames.Blackjack.Ui.Web.Models;

namespace KojackGames.Blackjack.Ui.Web.Controllers
{
    public class BetController : Controller
    {
        private readonly IPlayerAuthenticator _player_authenticator;
        private readonly ICommandMapper<BetCommand, BetOnHandForm>
                                            _bet_command_mapper;
```

113

```
    public BetController(IPlayerAuthenticator player_authenticator,
        ICommandMapper<BetCommand, BetOnHandForm> bet_command_mapper)
    {
        _player_authenticator = player_authenticator;
        _bet_command_mapper = bet_command_mapper;
    }

    public ActionResult Bet()
    {
        return View();
    }

    [HttpPost]
    public ActionResult Bet(BetOnHandForm bet_on_hand_form)
    {
        var bet_command = _bet_command_mapper.map_from(bet_on_hand_form,
                            _player_authenticator.get_player_token());

        return View();
    }
  }
}
```

The next specification to write is to assert that after the BetCommand is created, that it is sent via a bus to be auctioned. This follows the Command Query Responsibility Segregation architecture that we are following. The specification is shown in the following listing.

```
namespace KojackGames.Blackjack.Core.Tests.Controller_specs
{
    [Subject(typeof(BetController))]
    public class when_betting_on_a_hand : with_a_BetController
    {
        private Establish context = () =>
        {
            player_token = Guid.NewGuid();
            bet_on_hand_form = new BetOnHandForm() { bet = 5m};
            player_authenticator.Stub(x =>
                    x.get_player_token()).Return(player_token);

            bet_command = new BetCommand()
                    { wager = 5m, player_token = player_token };

            bet_command_mapper.Stub(x => x.map_from(bet_on_hand_form,
                        player_token)).Return(bet_command);
        };

            ...

        private It should_send_a_bet_command_to_the_bus = () =>
        {
            command_bus.AssertWasCalled(x => x.send(bet_command));
        };
```

```
        private static BetOnHandForm bet_on_hand_form;
        private static Guid player_token;
        private static BetCommand bet_command;
    }
}
```

Again, you will need to update the base class to provide the ICommandBus via the constructor.

```
namespace KojackGames.Blackjack.Core.Tests.Controller_specs
{
    public abstract class with_a_BetController
    {
        protected static IPlayerAuthenticator player_authenticator;
        protected static BetController SUT;
        protected static ICommandMapper<BetCommand, BetOnHandForm>
                                        bet_command_mapper;
        protected static ICommandBus command_bus;

        public with_a_BetController()
        {
            player_authenticator =
                MockRepository.GenerateStub<IPlayerAuthenticator>();
            bet_command_mapper = MockRepository
             .GenerateStub<ICommandMapper<BetCommand, BetOnHandForm>>();
            command_bus = MockRepository.GenerateStub<ICommandBus>();

            SUT = new BetController(player_authenticator,
                                bet_command_mapper, command_bus);
        }
    }
}
```

The ICommandBus forms part of the framework for our Command Query Responsibility Segregation (CQRS) architecture. It will live in the Infrastructure project under the folder structure of Cqrs/Command. The ICommandBus has a single method that accepts the BetCommand, as shown in the following code listing:

```
namespace KojackGames.Blackjack.Infrastructure.Cqrs.Command
{
    public interface ICommandBus
    {
        void send(BetCommand bet_command);
    }
}
```

115

There is an issue with this, though, as the job of the ICommandBus is to send all of the domain commands and not have a method for each. With this in mind, create a marker interface called ICommandBus. Again, add it to the Cqrs/Command folder with the following definition:

```
namespace KojackGames.Blackjack.Infrastructure.Cqrs.Command
{
    public interface ICommand
    {
    }
}
```

You can now update the ICommandBus interface to accept an ICommand rather than a BetCommand.

```
namespace KojackGames.Blackjack.Infrastructure.Cqrs.Command
{
    public interface ICommandBus
    {
        void send(ICommand bet_command);
    }
}
```

This means, of course, that now the BetCommand needs to implement the new ICommand marker interface; so go ahead and add this to the BetCommand.

```
using System;
using KojackGames.Blackjack.Infrastructure.Cqrs.Command;

namespace KojackGames.Blackjack.Domain.GamePlay.Commands
{
    public class BetCommand : ICommand
    {
        public decimal wager { get; set; }
        public Guid player_token { get; set; }
    }
}
```

To make the specification pass, you will again need to modify the BetController class as shown in the following listing.

```
using System.Web.Mvc;
using KojackGames.Blackjack.Domain.GamePlay.Commands;
using KojackGames.Blackjack.Infrastructure.Authentication;
using KojackGames.Blackjack.Infrastructure.Cqrs.Command;
using KojackGames.Blackjack.Ui.Web.Models;

namespace KojackGames.Blackjack.Ui.Web.Controllers
{
    public class BetController : Controller
    {
        private readonly IPlayerAuthenticator _player_authenticator;
        private readonly ICommandMapper<BetCommand, BetOnHandForm>
                                                _bet_command_mapper;
        private readonly ICommandBus _command_bus;
```

```
    public BetController(IPlayerAuthenticator player_authenticator,
      ICommandMapper<BetCommand, BetOnHandForm> bet_command_mapper,
                                        ICommandBus command_bus)
    {
        _player_authenticator = player_authenticator;
        _bet_command_mapper = bet_command_mapper;
        _command_bus = command_bus;
    }

    ...

    [HttpPost]
    public ActionResult Bet(BetOnHandForm bet_on_hand_form)
    {
        var bet_command =
          _bet_command_mapper.map_from(bet_on_hand_form,
                      _player_authenticator.get_player_token());

        _command_bus.send(bet_command);


        return View();
    }
  }
}
```

As you can see the ICommandBus is injected via the constructor and is passed into the BetCommand in the overloaded Bet method.

The final specification on our checklist is to ensure that the controller redirects the client back to the original Bet action in order to avoid the customer resubmitting by mistake. Also, the user will want to see confirmation of his action and so in a later specification the behavior to present the placed bet will be added to the original Bet method.

Update the when_betting_on_a_hand class to include the new specification assertion, as shown in the following listing:

```
...
using MvcContrib.TestHelper;

namespace KojackGames.Blackjack.Core.Tests.Controller_specs
{
    [Subject(typeof(BetController))]
    public class when_betting_on_a_hand : with_a_BetController
    {

        private Because of = () => result = SUT.Bet(bet_on_hand_form);

        ...

        private It should_return_a_redirect_to_display_the_bet_page = () =>
        {
            result.AssertActionRedirect().ToAction("Bet");
```

```
        };

        private static BetOnHandForm bet_on_hand_form;
        private static Guid player_token;
        private static BetCommand bet_command;
        private static ActionResult result;
    }
}
```

This assertion utilizes another helper from the Mvc Contrib library to test that the result of the controller method call is a RedirectToAction ActionResult.

There are no other supporting classes to create for this action, so go ahead and update the BetControllers Bet action to return RedirectToAction method back to the original Bet action, as seen in the following listing:

```
[HttpPost]
public ActionResult Bet(BetOnHandForm bet_on_hand_form)
{
    var bet_command = _bet_command_mapper.map_from(bet_on_hand_form,
                            _player_authenticator.get_player_token());

    _command_bus.send(bet_command);

    return RedirectToAction("Bet");
}
```

This completes the demonstration of how you can drive the design of you application via your acceptance criteria and then discover the lower-level object using behavior-driven design.

If you compare the checklist that we wrote in Figure 5-10 to the output from MSpec in Figure 5-12, you will see a very near match. Like we said before, it's a great idea to jot down what behaviors and what responsibilities you feel that the system under test has before you start to program.

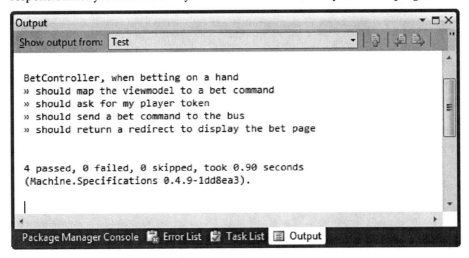

*Figure 5-12. Passing specifications for the BetController*

Now that we have implemented the first feature and we have confidence that it works, it's now ready for QA. We are sure you are wondering where the QA people are on the team. Well, the main QA for the project are the automated tests, with the developers handling the more hands on portions of testing of the application. To see the entire code, you can download from the Apress web site (www.apress.com).

# Day 4

At this point we are partway through the first half of our initial two-week sprint. Let's look in on the team to see where they are at with the user stories that they committed to for this sprint.

## Daily Stand-Up

Tim: *All right, everyone. Let's get the meeting started. Tyler, would you like to start us off?*

Tyler: *Sure, let's see. I continued my pairing with Sarah on the Initial Bet feature. We have finished coding the feature, and have all the Acceptance and WatiN tests passing, so now it is ready for one of us to give it a smoke test, and show Simon what we implemented. Today, I plan on taking the next card on the board, which I believe is the Deck of Cards feature, and working on it with Sarah. And, I have no blocks.*

Tim: *Sarah, you're next.*

Sarah: *Well, I worked with Tyler on the Initial Bet feature, and got it ready for testing like Tyler said. Today I plan on pairing up with Tyler on the next user story, and I have no blocks.*

Simon: *Okay, I guess it's my turn now. I spent some time answering questions from the developers on the user stories, as well as some time with the customer going over ordering of the user stories for future sprints. Today, I plan on getting with Tyler and/or Sarah to look over the user story they have completed. I have no blocks.*

Tim: *Okay. I wanted to share with you where we stand on the current sprint. From the looks of the burn-down chart, we are right on schedule with everything we planned for this sprint. [(See Figure 5-13)]. I also wanted to reiterate that I am here for you all. If there is something that is blocking you from doing your work, let me know and I will try my best to remove it.*

Tyler: *Well, now that you mention it, I am having an issue that is beginning to affect my productivity.*

Tim: *What is the problem?*

Tyler: *Well, I have been having issues running Visual Studio and the application on my machine. The same setup on Sarah's machine seems to run fine, but on mine it goes at a crawl. Upon further research, we found that Sarah's machine has 4GB of RAM whereas my machine only has 2GB of RAM. It's really beginning to affect how much I get done each day. I didn't think that was something you handled, so that's why I didn't bring it up.*

Tim: *No, anything that hinders your daily work should be brought to my attention so we can discuss it and see if we can fix it. Your machine definitely needs to match Sarah's machine when it comes to specs. I will get in touch with some people and see if I can get some more memory for you machine.*

Tyler: *Thanks!*

Tim: *Well, that's all for now. Everyone have a great day.*

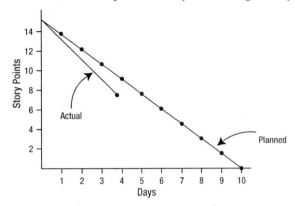

*Figure 5-13. Burn-down chart, Day 4 of Sprint 1*

# Working on the Next User Story: Deck of Cards

Sarah: *All right, Tyler. Let's get started on the Deck of Cards feature. Do you have some ideas on this one?*

Sarah moves the Deck of Cards user story to the In Process swim lane to let the team and anyone outside the team know what is currently being worked on. An updated shot of the task board is shown in Figure 5-14.

| Stories | Task Backlog | In Process | In Testing | Done |
|---------|--------------|------------|------------|------|
| | *card* | *card* | | |
| | | | *card* | |

*Figure 5-14. Updated task board*

Tyler: *No, not really, I think we should get Simon involved to make sure we are implementing what we need to be implementing. Do you think that we should get Tim involved, as well?*

Sarah: *I don't think so. If we have any questions, I am sure we can pull him into the meeting then. We should give this a shot by ourselves.*

Sarah and Tyler sit down with Simon to go over the user story and the acceptance criteria for the story. At the end of the conversation, the developers have a better understanding of what is required for this user story.

Sarah: *How about I drive for a while on this one?*

Tyler: *You drove a lot on the last feature. I would like to get some time at the keyboard. What if we did Ping-pong programming?*

Sarah: *What is that?*

Tyler: *It's a pair-programming style where one of the developers writes a test and then hands off the keyboard to the other developer so she can write the code to get the test to pass. This way, we both can have some time driving.*

Sarah: *That sounds like an interesting idea. Wouldn't that slow us down, though?*

Tyler: *Maybe at first, but as time goes on and we get better at it, the more efficient we'll get at it. I think the end improvements are worth the up-front cost.*

Sarah: *I think this is something that we should bounce off Tim.*

Sarah and Tyler find Tim where they explain their plan to him.

Tim: *I like the idea, try it out on this user story. Only do it for this user story in this sprint and at the end of the sprint, we can talk about using it long term.*

## Adding the SpecFlow Feature

To start off, add a new feature to the Features folder in the Acceptance.Tests project named 021-DeckOfCards.feature. Update the file to contain the feature we need for this user story, as shown in Figure 5-15.

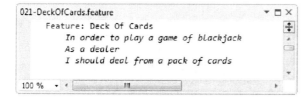

*Figure 5-15. Deck of Cards feature*

## Adding Scenarios

Now that we have added our feature file and feature to the system, let's add some scenarios to the feature.

Update the 021-DeckOfCards.feature with the following scenarios, see the Figure 5 -16.

```
021-DeckOfCards.feature                                              ▾ □ ×
    Feature: Deck Of Cards
        In order to play a game of Blackjack
        As a dealer
        I should deal from a pack of cards

  ⊟Scenario: Take a card from the deck
        Given I have a new deck of 52 cards
        When I take "1" cards
        Then I should have 51 cards left in the deck

  ⊟Scenario: Take cards from an ordered deck
        Given I have a new deck of 52 cards
        And I have taken the first card
        And that the card is a "Ace" of "Clubs"
        When I take "3" cards
        Then the last "3" cards taken should be equal to:
            | Suit  | Value |
            | Clubs | Two   |
            | Clubs | Three |
            | Clubs | Four  |

  ⊟Scenario: Shuffle the deck
        Given I have a new deck of 52 cards
        And I have taken the first card
        And that the card is a "Ace" of "Clubs"
        And I have shuffled the deck
        When I take "3" cards
        Then the last "3" cards taken should not be equal to:
            | Suit  | Value |
            | Clubs | Two   |
            | Clubs | Three |
            | Clubs | Four  |

  ⊟Scenario: check for 52 different cards
        Given I have a new deck of 52 cards
        When I take "52" cards
        Then I should have 52 unique cards
        And an empty deck
            |

100 %   ▾  ◂                                                        ▸
```

*Figure 5-16. Scenarios for the Deck of Cards feature*

---

■ **Note** Even though we have listed four scenarios in the feature file, for the sake of brevity, we are only going to go through one of the scenarios.

---

When you run the tests, you will see that there are no step definitions defined for the steps in the "check for 52 different cards" scenario. SpecFlow was nice enough to output the skeleton of these steps for us.

Add a new steps file to the Steps folder called CardDeckSteps.cs and update the file with the code skeleton that was generated by SpecFlow, as follows:

```
[Binding]
public class CardDeckSteps
{
    [Given(@"I have a new deck of 52 cards")]
    public void GivenIHaveANewDeckOf52Cards()
    {
        var deck = new Deck();
        deck.initialize();
```

```
        current_deck = deck;
    }

    [When(@"I take ""(.*)"" cards")]
    public void WhenITakeCards(int number_of_cards_to_take)
    {
        var deck = current_deck;

        int no_of_cards_left_to_take = number_of_cards_to_take;

        while(no_of_cards_left_to_take > 0)
        {
            cards_taken.Add(deck.take_card());
            no_of_cards_left_to_take --;
        }
    }

    [Then(@"I should have 52 unique cards")]
    public void ThenIShouldHave52UniqueCards()
    {
        var cards = cards_taken;

        Assert.That(cards.Count(), Is.EqualTo(52));

        foreach(var card in cards)
        {
            Assert.That(cards.Count(x => x.Equals(card)), Is.EqualTo(1));
        }
    }
```

```
[Then(@"an empty deck")]
public void ThenAnEmptyDeck()
{
    Assert.That(current_deck.no_of_cards_left_in_deck, Is.EqualTo(0));
}
}
```

## Implementing the "Check for 52 Different Cards" Scenario

Now that we have the steps we need to get the steps to compile, one thing you will notice is that we need to create a Deck object. To do this, go to the KojackGames.Blackjack.Domain project and create a new folder under the Model folder called CardDeck. This folder will house all the objects related to a deck of cards. Inside this folder create a new file called Deck.cs and update it with the following code:

```
public class Deck
{
    public Deck()
    {
    }
}
```

Remember, right now we are only concerned about getting the test to fail and to do that we only need to get it to compile.

Inside the Deck object we need to create an Initialize method. Add the following code to the Deck object:

```
public void initialize() {}
```

Now let's talk about the current_deck variable. This variable is part of the steps class and will be used to store the Deck object between tests. This is done because we are only testing against one Deck object. Add the following code to the CardDeckSteps.cs file:

```
public Deck current_deck
{
    get { return (Deck)ScenarioContext.Current["current_deck"]; }
    set { ScenarioContext.Current["current_deck"] = value; }
}
```

We also need to have a variable in the step class to store the cards already pulled from the deck. Add this property to the CardDeckSteps.cs file.

```
public List<Card> cards_taken
{
    get
    {
        if(!ScenarioContext .Current.ContainsKey("cards_taken"))
            ScenarioContext.Current["cards_taken"] = new List<Card>();
```

```
        return (List<Card>)ScenarioContext.Current["cards_taken"];
    }
    set { ScenarioContext.Current["cards_taken"] = value; }
}
```

Finally, to get this test to compile we need to add a take_card method as well as a property to tell us if there are any cards left in the deck. Add the following code to the Deck object.

```
public int no_of_cards_left_in_deck { get { return -1; }}
```

```
public Card take_card()
{
    return new Card();
}
```

This method should return a Card from the deck. We now need to add a Card object to the domain, as well. Add a new file to the KojackGames.Blackjack.Domain project under the Model\CardDeck folder called Card.cs.

We should have compiling tests that fail. Now we need to get them to pass. To get these tests to pass, we need to implement two pieces. We need to implement the take_card method as well as the no_of_cards_left_in_deck property on the Deck object. To implement them, we are going to need to add another object to the domain. We also need a way to keep track of the position of a card in the deck. To do that, we will create a DeckPosition object in the domain project to store that information.

```
public class DeckPosition
{
    public int position_in_pack { get; set; }
    public Card card { get; set; }
}
```

We will now create a private variable to house a list of these types of objects.

```
private IList<DeckPosition> _cards_in_deck;
```

With the private variable in place, we can implement the take_card method. Update the take_card method to look like the following.

```
public Card take_card()
{
    var card = _cards_in_deck.First();
    _cards_in_deck.RemoveAt(0);
    return card.card;
}
```

With that implementation, we have one passing test and one failing test. To get the remaining failing test to pass, we need to update the no_of_cards_left_in_deck property with the following code:

```
public int no_of_cards_left_in_deck { get { return _cards_in_deck.Count(); } }
```

With that we have finished the implementation of the scenario. The remaining scenarios are available for you to finish, or you can look at the finished results by downloading the code.

# Day 6

Entering the second week of the first sprint, the team starts to see some of the fruits of their labors.

## Daily Stand-Up

Tim: *All right, let's get going. Sarah, you have the honors.*

Sarah: *Well, I worked with Tyler to finish up the Deck of Cards feature. All the code is implemented and the tests are passing, so we are ready to show Simon the user story and handle the testing of it. One thing I want to add was that Tyler and I used a pair-programming style called "ping-pong programming" and it worked very well for us. If anyone wants to know more about it, I can stay after the meeting and answer questions. Today, I will start on the Start Game feature, and I have no blocks.*

Tim: *Sounds great! I love hearing how you two are trying different approaches to pair programming. Do you feel that this impacted your capacity for this sprint?*

Sarah: *No, we were a little slow at first, but towards the end of the implementation we were cranking out tests and code pretty quickly.*

Tim: *Okay, Tyler, you are next.*

Tyler: *Let's see. Like Sarah said, I worked with her on the Deck of Cards feature, and with that finished, I will probably pair up with Sarah again on the Start Game feature. I have no blocks.*

Simon: *I worked with the customer and answered questions from the developers. I also looked over the Initial Bet user story and I have signed off on it. I am planning on getting ready for the product demo and talking with the customer about the upcoming sprint. I have no blocks.*

Tim: *Awesome! We have our very first story done. Congratulations team! Everyone have a great day!*

## Final User Story of the Sprint: Start Game

Tyler: *Sarah, shall we start on the last user story?*

Tyler moves the Start Game user story to the In Process swim lane. An updated shot of the task board is shown in Figure 5-17.

| Stories | Task Backlog | In Process | In Testing | Done |
|---------|-------------|------------|------------|------|
| | | (card) | | |
| | | | (card) | (card) |

*Figure 5-17. Updated task board*

Sarah: *I am not sure at all about the domain aspects of this. We need to grab Simon for a little bit and hammer this out.*

Tyler: *Okay. Isn't it nice that we have this avenue for "real-time" communication with the customer on questions about the application? I mean, the old methodology we had told us to implement what was on the spec and if we had questions, to use our best guess. It feels refreshing to be able to get the questions answered up front so that we are creating what the customer needs.*

Sarah: *I would have to agree. In a way it takes a lot of guesswork out of our time.*

## Adding the SpecFlow Feature

Let's start by adding a new Feature file to the system. Create a new feature file called 002-DealCards.feature. Update the file to contain the feature we need for this user story ,as shown in Figure 5-18.

*Figure 5-18. Deal Cards feature*

## Adding Scenarios

Now that we have added our feature file and feature to the system, let's add some scenarios to the feature.

Update the 002-DealCards.feature with the scenario shown in Figure 5-19.

**Figure 5-19.** *Scenarios for the Deal Cards feature*

An interesting thing about this feature is that a large portion of the setup for this feature is already created by the previous features. For instance, navigating to the game play screen and placing a bet is already covered in the Initial Bet feature. To implement this feature, we will concentrate on the Deal button and the deck.

Go to the GameSetUpSteps.cs file and add the following step:

```
[Given(@"the deck contains the following cards:")]
public void GivenTheDeckContainsTheFollowingCards(Table table)
{
        var mapper = new TableObjectMapper();
        var game_builder = new GameBuilder().find_game_by_player_id(PlayerToken.player_id);

        int card_position = 1;
        foreach(var row in table.Rows)
        {
            game_builder.add_to_deck(mapper.create_deck_row_from(row, card_position));
            card_position++;
        }

        var game = game_builder.build();

        DataBaseHelper.save_or_add<BlackJackTableRow>(game);
```

```
}
```

What this step is going to do is verify that the deck contains the cards we requested in the scenario. In this step we are also introducing a new object called TableObjectMapper. This object is a utility object that is only used in testing, and would not be shipped out with production code. What this object does is take the table parameter that is passed into the step method and converts it to a collection of a new type called a DeckRow object.

```
public class TableObjectMapper
{
    public DeckRow create_deck_row_from(TableRow row, int card_position)
    {
        DeckRow deckRow = new DeckRow();

        var suit = EnumParser.parse_enum<Suit>(row["Suit"]);
        var value = EnumParser.parse_enum<CardValue>(row["Value"]);

        deckRow.suit = (int)suit;
        deckRow.card_value = (int)value;
        deckRow.position_in_pack = card_position;

        return deckRow;
    }
}
```

The DeckRow object is another utility object that easily stores the card information for use later in the test.

Now, with the Deal button, you have a lot of the same infrastructure as in the Initial Bet feature. Instead of duplicating code here, we wanted to give you an overview of what you are testing and implementing. You will be testing the interaction of the web page with their related controllers as before. You can see the finished result in the code available for this book.

# Day 10

Congratulations, you've made it through your first sprint! Today, the team has its sprint retrospective and performs a sprint demo for the customer.

## Sprint 1 Retrospective

Tim: *Well, team, you made it through your first sprint. Congratulations. Now it's time for us to have the retrospective meeting. The retrospective is a meeting in which the team gets together and reflects on the sprint that was. We look at the things that went right in the sprint and the things that went wrong in the sprint.*

Sarah: *Why would we want to do that?*

Tim: *We want to have these meetings so that we can be proud of the things we as a team accomplished. This positive reinforcement will strengthen our resolve to continue to do the right thing even when the easier thing to do would be to revert back to the old way of doing. Just as we want to be proud of the things we accomplished, we also need to address the things we did not do so well.*

*Scrum and agile as a whole are about iterative change. We may not get it right the first time out. If we don't, then we try something else and we keep trying something new until we find the solution to our problem. Other members of the team might not know that a person is having a problem. The problems could range from the technical side, like "the test suite we are using is causing major performance problems" to "I don't feel like we are getting enough direction from the product owner or the customer." The sooner we know these issues, the sooner we as a team can start working on solutions.*

Sarah: *What is the format for these meetings? How are we going to feel comfortable enough to talk about the problems we are having?*

Tim: *The format of the meeting can vary from sprint to sprint. We keep it changing so we don't get stuck in a rut of using the same structure to produce the same comments. This time I'd like to do the following. When each person comes into the room, they will get a set of Post-it notes in three different colors: red, blue, and green. At the start of the meeting someone will set a timer for three to five minutes. When the timer starts, everyone will have that time to write their thoughts on the Post-it notes. There will be no talking at this time, so there cannot be any influence on your thoughts from anyone else.*

Tyler: *What do the different color Post-it notes mean?*

Tim: *On the green Post-its, jot down your opinions on things that went well during the sprint. Use the blue Post-its to note your thoughts on things that were confusing during the sprint. Finally, on the red Post-its, write your thoughts on things that went wrong or caused trouble during the sprint. The colors give everyone a visual impression of any major issues during the sprint.*

*Once the time is up, we will gather everyone's notes and put them on the board. As the ScrumMaster, I, along with one other person, will try to group all the notes into general categories. Once we have done the grouping, we will read aloud the notes from each group and discuss them. We will try to generate any action items from the blue and red notes. We will keep doing this until we have gone over all the categories. If there are no further questions, let's get started.*

The timer buzzes after five minutes.

Tim: *Okay, time is up. Sarah, will you help me gather up all the notes and group them into general categories?*

Sarah: *Sure.*

Tim and Sarah organize the Post-its into three categories for this retrospective. They are as follows:

- Testing
- Process
- Team Dynamics

Tim: *Let's start with the Testing category. We seem to have a lot of the green, or "good things," notes here so let's read off a few.*

Tim reads the following comments:

- "Testing showing bugs earlier in the process."

- "Confident in refactoring code due to having tests wrapped around the code in question."

- "Unit tests rock!"

Tim: *Since there are not any blue or red notes in the Testing category, which is great, let's move on to the next category, which is Team Dynamics. Let's read the positive notes before we address any problem notes.*

Tim reads the following positive comments:

- "With acceptance criteria we know when something is really done."

- "Daily stand-ups giving us an opportunity to address roadblocks as soon as possible."

- "Ping-pong programming was great!"

Tim: *There's a red Post-it, or a critical note, saying that the build is breaking regularly.*

Sarah: *I wrote the red Post-it. While I was working on my feature, I would update the latest but learned that the build was breaking regularly. I have no way of easily knowing that the build was broken and every time I got latest or tried to run the tests locally, I would get errors that were causing me real headaches. I think we need a way to notify the team that the build is broken. That way, while it is broken, they know not to check in or get the latest version of the code until the build is working again.*

Tim: *How about we set up the e-mail notification on CruiseControl.* [(See Appendix G.)] *That way, when the build breaks, CruiseControl will send out an e-mail to all of us to let us know.*

Sarah: *Sounds like a good idea. If it's all right with everyone, I would like to take this action item. I want to know more about the inner workings of CruiseControl and this would be as good of a time as any.*

Tim: *Consider it yours. Let's move onto the Process category. This category had one critical point and one "uncertain" point. The red note states, "Daily stand-ups seem to be long." The blue note reads, "I'm being pulled away to another project too often."*

Tyler: *I put the red card up. The daily stand-ups seem to be over-running the intentional 10 minutes because we like to go into problem-solving sessions. This causes issues because not everyone needs to be concerned with what is being discussed. I'd rather go back and continue my work.*

Tim: *Good point, Tyler. As a reminder, daily stand-ups are only to be used to answer the following questions: what did you do yesterday, what are you doing today, and do you have any roadblocks preventing you from getting your work done. So as a team we need to be aware of that. If there are additional discussions or problem-solving sessions that need to happen, which is very likely, bring the needed people aside after the stand-up and have a "meeting after the meeting." The purpose of the "meeting after the meeting" is for a targeted group of people to discuss issues while the other team members return to working. As ScrumMaster, I'll take this is as an action item to keep everyone on track to ensure that the stand-ups are effective and not overly long. Let's move on to the blue card, which reads, "I'm being pulled away to another project too often."*

Sarah: *I wrote this card. It's very frustrating because the expectation was that I would spend the majority of my time on this project while wrapping up some loose ends on my previous project. During this past sprint, the project manager for the other project kept pulling me off this project to fix issues, although I'm not the only person capable of handling them. This takes time away from me working on this project.*

Tim: *This is definitely a roadblock and sounds like an action item. I know the project manager you're referring to. I'll talk with him and see what kind of solution we can come up with. We need you on this project, so I'll handle this and follow up with him.*

Sarah: *Thanks. I don't want to get anyone in trouble, but that's surely an issue.*

Tim: *No worries. That took courage to bring up. Thanks for informing me. I'll follow up with you once I've talking to the project manager.*

Sarah: *Great, thanks.*

Tim: *Looks like we have discussed all the categories of the retrospective and we are done with the retrospective. Let's recap the action items from this meeting.*

Tim states that action items from the sprint are as follows:

- Set up an e-mail notification on CruiseControl to alert team members when the build is broken. This is assigned to Sarah to handle.

- Keep everyone on focused so that the team can have short, yet effective daily stand-ups. This is assigned to Tim.

- Speak with the project manager on Sarah's previous project regarding her capacity on this current project. Tim also takes this action item.

Tim: *Thanks, everyone, for your time. This ends our first retrospective!*

## Product Demo

At the end of each sprint, the team will sit down with the customer, at a time that is convenient for the customer, to demonstrate all the user stories that were completed in the sprint. This product demo adds a layer of transparency to the project. The development team no longer remains closed off without communicating until the end of the project—when they ultimately deliver a product that isn't what the customer wanted. The team also gets feedback from the customer during these demo meetings to clarify that they are working on the items the customer deems most important.

Let's look in on the team as they sit down with Bill, the customer and senior sponsor, and Simon to show what they have accomplished in this iteration.

Tim: *Bill, we wanted to take this time to show you all that the team accomplished in this sprint. This is also a chance for you to give us feedback on what we did. Taking a look at the screen, is it what you envisioned? Are there things you would like us to add to features going forward? Or are there things that you see now that you don't need? Let us know things of that nature. Simon has already seen these features and has given us some good feedback on them. This is your chance to look over the features and give us the final OK on them. If you do want any changes, we can address them as user stories in the upcoming sprints.*

Bill: *That sounds great. I would very much like to see the progress being made. It helps me feel more confident that the project is moving along and the team is creating what Kojack Games really wants. I was wondering, is this code for real? What I mean is, can we use this code at any time?"*

Tim: *Bill, one of the main points of Scrum is that the team creates potentially releaseable code at the end of every sprint. What this means is that if you ever wanted us to push code to production at the end of a sprint, we would be able to do that without hesitation. I can't stress this enough. Though we want your feedback on what we are about to show you. I want to make sure that the team is delivering what you want this application to be. If we're not, then tell us and we can make the necessary changes to give you what you need and want.*

*If there are no further questions, let's begin with the demo. One of the first things the team completed was the Initial Bet feature. With this story complete, the player can click on the Bet button to place his initial wager. Once the user clicks on the button, he will also see the Deal button and the wager that he placed. [(See Figure 5-20.)] The code generated from the story passed all the acceptance criteria and we now consider this story done. Bill, what are your thoughts on this piece?*

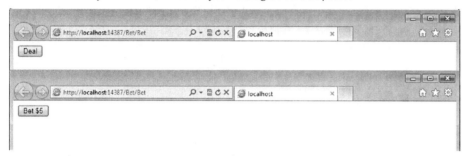

*Figure 5-20. The result of clicking the Bet $5 button*

Bill: *I think it looks good. It does everything we need it to do when the user is placing an initial bet. Now that I see it firsthand, I don't see anything I would like to change. I hope we can build on this, but for now keep it as it is. What else do you have to show me?*

Due to the size of this application and for the sake of readability, we have elected to skip over the remaining parts of the product demo. The customer, Bill, was shown every feature that was completed by the team and his feedback on it was positive. There were, however, a few minor changes in the product from Simon's perspective.

# Summary

This was your first glimpse into the Blackjack project. While going through this chapter you may have asked yourself why there weren't any discussions about the baseline architecture or load or stress testing. The reason is that we wanted to concentrate on the team dynamics first and the code second.

Through witnessing how team dynamics evolve, you learn a vital lesson. You learn how communication is key in software development and how Scrum facilitates conversations. This is done through the different types of meetings, such as daily stand-ups, sprint planning, sprint retrospectives, and sprint demo meetings. These meetings give the team and the customer avenues where they can discuss the project and any ideas or concerns they may have about it. The developers are front and center in these discussions with the customer.

Communication is key. We cannot stress this enough. If team members and customers aren't talking, then no one is certain that what is being developed and delivered is accurate.

You also saw how the team broke down a user story to create testable working code using BDD and TDD practices. By starting with a set of behaviors that the customer wanted the feature to have, the developers were able to generate a test bed. Once the tests were written, they generated the code to get the tests to pass. This is also known as "red-green-refactor." By starting with behavior that the customer wants, we are more in line with producing something the customer needs. Another nice part about this is that we are not writing as much bloat code into our system. We are only writing the bare minimum of code needed to get the test to pass—nothing more, nothing less.

A side effect of this minimalist approach on code generation is that our technical debt should be kept to a minimum as we move forward into the project.

If you would like a more in-depth look at the framework that is driving this application, check out the appendices at the end of this book. If you would like to have a deeper dive into the code itself, skip to Chapter 9, which reviews the baseline architecture.

Finally, you saw a glimpse of a product demo and the team's transparency with showing the customer what was accomplished in the sprint. This presented an avenue for discussion on the customer's needs. By getting the customer involved early in the process, you can be sure that you are producing customer value.

In the next chapter the team takes the action items from this sprint's retrospective, as well as the customer feedback to plan and layout Sprint 2.

# CHAPTER 6

# Sprint 2: Playing a Basic Game

With our first development sprint under our belt, we are learning what Scrum activities occur during a sprint. These include sprint planning, daily stand-ups, keeping track of user stories using a task board, and having a sprint retrospective.

## Sprint Planning Meeting

The team has gathered in the conference room. Simon has brought in user stories for the team to work on, discuss, and size.

Tim: *Good morning, team. We had a great Sprint 1. For this sprint, we'll do like we did in Sprint 1: size the stories and work with Simon on what needs to be done for this sprint. Before we begin, I would like to go ahead and define the theme for this sprint.*

### The Theme of the Sprint

Tim: *The theme for Sprint 2 is going to be "Playing a Basic Game." The reason for this is that in the last sprint, we were able to implement what was needed to start a game. Now, building on that success, the next thing we want to be able to do is play a game. Again, I want to reiterate that a theme is a way to show a common purpose of all the user stories we do in a sprint, and if you find yourself working on items that don't reflect the theme of the current sprint, let me or Simon know so we can address the situation.*

### Determining Availability and Capacity

Tim: *Now it is time for us to determine any availability issues that may crop up this sprint. Sarah, as a follow-up to our last sprint retrospective meeting, I spoke with your project manager regarding your availability for this project. He agreed that he could get another developer involved, so he should stop pulling you away from this project. Starting with this sprint, your availability should be greater than it was in the previous sprint.*

Sarah: *Thanks, Tim, for following up. I'm excited to have more availability for this project. I will keep you apprised of changes.*

Tim: *Thanks Sarah. Please do keep me apprised. Looking at the calendar, there are no holidays during this next sprint. Is anyone taking time off during the next two weeks?*

Sarah: *No, I should be here.*

Tyler: *Me too.*

Simon: *Me three.*

Tim: *Great. Everyone should be here the entire the sprint. Well, based on the last sprint, we were able to complete 15 points. By using that as a basis, we have a capacity of 15 points. With that being said, let's get on with planning the user stories we decide to commit to!*

# Planning Poker

Simon: *All right gang, here is the first user story. We are going to start with the Game Play: Hit user story. [(See Figure 6-1.)] When this user story came up in the release planning, we mentioned that a player will need the ability to receive an additional card from the deck if they ask for it. The T-shirt size for this user story is an S.*

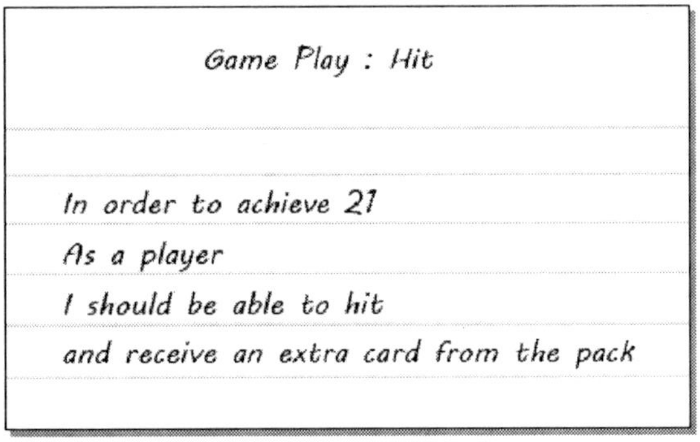

```
Game Play : Hit


In order to achieve 21
As a player
I should be able to hit
and receive an extra card from the pack

```

**Figure 6-1.** *User story: Hit*

Tyler: *Simon, what can you tell us about this story?*

Simon: *Well, the basics of this user story are to give the player the chance to get closer to 21 by giving her another card from the deck. There are guidelines for giving the player the card.*

Tyler: *What are these guidelines? Can we turn these guidelines into the acceptance criteria?*

Simon: *Yes, that's a good idea to turn these into the acceptance criteria.*

Simon tells the team the following guidelines for this user story:

- There must be a game in progress before this functionality is available to the player.
- The card dealt to the player from the dealer must be face up.
- The player can receive an additional card until he either reaches a score of 21 or he goes over 21.

Tim: *If there are no further questions, please vote on the level of complexity.*

Tyler: *I vote a 5.*

Sarah: *I vote an 8.*

Tim: *Sarah, why did you vote an 8?*

Sarah: *I choose an 8 because I think there will be a large amount of work involved with getting the game in a state that we can implement the hit.*

Tyler: *Actually, Sarah, it won't be that bad at all. Most of the framework to get us to that point is already implemented.*

Sarah: *Ah, I didn't realize that.*

Tim: *All right, round two of voting.*

Tyler and Sarah: *Five.*

Tim: *We have a 5. Next!*

Simon: *The next user story is Game Play: Stand.* [(See Figure 6-2.)] *This user story gives the player the ability to stand on her hand. What I mean by this is the player has the ability to say, "I don't want any more cards; this is the hand I am using against the dealer." In the release planning, this user story was sized as an S.*

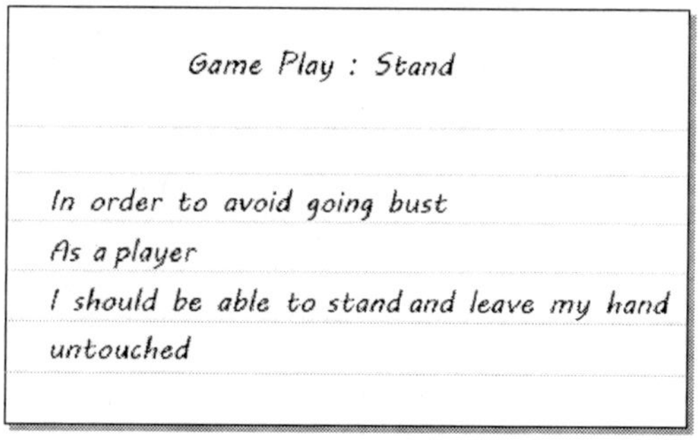

```
Game Play : Stand



In order to avoid going bust
As a player
I should be able to stand and leave my hand
untouched

```

*Figure 6-2. User story: Stand*

Tyler: *What are the acceptance criteria for this user story?*

Simon: *Currently, it looks like there are no acceptance criteria.*

Sarah: *How about we work on some? How many times can a player stand during a hand?*

Simon: *Well, once a player stands, his hand is done. So a player can only stand once per game.*

Tyler: *Okay, I have another question. At what point can the player stand during the game?*

Simon: *Well, the player can stand at any point during the game, except in the following two scenarios: the player has a score of 21, at which point he can no longer play. Or, the player goes bust, at which point he has lost his hand.*

Sarah: *So, let's sum it up.*

Sarah lists the following as the acceptance criteria:

- A player can only stand once per hand.
- A player cannot stand once he has hit 21.
- A player cannot stand once he has gone over 21.

Simon: *That sounds great! Let's go with that.*

Tim: *If there are no questions, place your votes.*

Tyler: *There is a lot in common with this user story and the Hit user story. I would almost consider this an add-on to that story. With that in mind, I vote a 3 for this user story.*

Sarah: *I agree with Tyler on this. I vote a 3 as well.*

Tim: *All right, 3 it is. Simon, what is next?*

Simon: *Winning. The next user story is defining how to win a game.  [(See Figure 6-3.)] In order for a player to win a hand of blackjack, he must be closer to 21 than the dealer, without going bust—or over 21. If the player goes over 21, then he has lost the hand. So let's discuss this one and determine acceptance criteria and how we can determine when it is finished.*

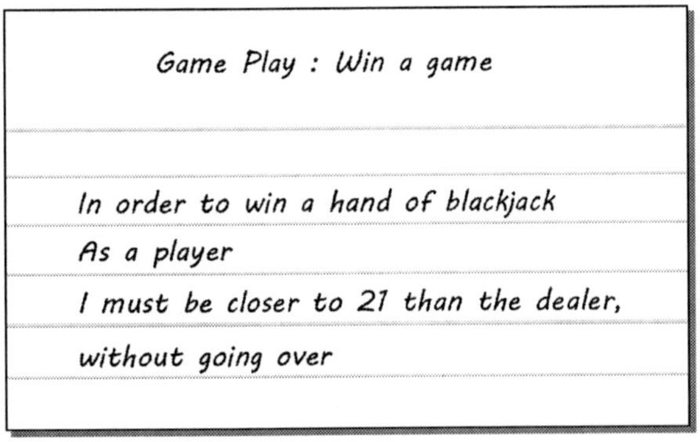

```
Game Play : Win a game


In order to win a hand of blackjack

As a player

I must be closer to 21 than the dealer,

without going over
```

*Figure 6-3. User story: Win*

Tyler: *I have been reading through this user story and there are three scenarios that I would like to ask you about, Simon.*

Simon: *Tyler, what is the first scenario?*

Tyler: *How does a player win the game when both she and the dealer finish under 21?*

Simon: *In that scenario the person closest to 21 is the winner.*

Tyler: *Okay. Next scenario: what happens if either the player or the dealer finishes the game over 21? Can both player and dealer go bust in the same hand?*

Simon: *I will answer your second question first. No, both the player and the dealer cannot go bust in the same hand. The reason for that is the answer to your first question. Since the player goes first, if she goes bust—ends up over 21—then she automatically loses to the dealer. Now here is the confusing part: there can be multiple players and hands at a table. When a hand busts, that hand loses to the dealer and the dealer takes the bet. If a hand does not go bust, the dealer has to play its hand, which could end up going bust. In this scenario, the dealer loses to the players that have stopped over 21 and wins the hands where the players went bust.*

Sarah: *So, we should look at this scenario on a hand-by-hand basis?*

Simon: *That is correct. What is the third scenario you had questions about, Tyler?*

Tyler: *What happens if the player and the dealer finish the game tied?*

Simon: *That scenario is called a draw or push. In the event of a push, the player gets back the money he bet. The player and the dealer neither win nor lose the game. Is there anything else in question here?*

Sarah: *It sounds like we could break this user story up into multiple user stories. Should we do that?*

Tyler: *I don't think we need to. I think we can get this all done within the sprint. However, if we get behind, I think these scenarios give us a good place to break up the user story into multiple user stories that are vertical slices through the system.*

Simon: *I would agree with Tyler on this. The customer really needs this user story, and if we can get it done in the sprint, I don't see why we need to break it up. If we can't get it done in the sprint, then, yes, we should break it up so that I have something to show the customer after each sprint.*

Sarah: *Sounds like a sound plan. I have nothing further.*

Tim: *If there are no further questions, let's vote.*

Tyler: *Based on the different scenarios we have to account for and handling on a hand-by-hand basis, this seems a little more complicated than the previous user stories that we've covered in this meeting. So, I vote an 8.*

Sarah: *I would agree with Tyler and vote 8 as well.*

Tim: *So, I will mark this one down as an 8. Does the team feel they can tackle any more user stories for this sprint?*

Sarah: *I feel comfortable committing to this amount of work. Any more and I would worry about not getting it done in this sprint.*

Tyler: *I second that.*

Tim: *Well, then I guess that wraps up the sprint planning meeting. I will see you all at the stand-up meeting tomorrow.*

## Sprint 2's Backlog

Let's review what the team committed to for this iteration. The team committed to the user stories shown in Table 6-1 for a total of 16 points, which is the team's capacity for this sprint.

*Table 6-1. Sprint 2 Sized Backlog*

| User Story Name | Initial Size |
|-----------------|--------------|
| Game Play: Hit | 5 |
| Game Play: Stand | 3 |
| Game Play: Win | 8 |

# Day 1

We'll start Day 1 with the daily stand-up and continue on working with the user story. One advantage of Scrum is a consistent, predictable pattern of how the days in a sprint play out.

## Daily Stand-Up

Tim: *Good to see everyone here. Let's get the meeting started. Simon, would you like to start us off?*

Simon: *Yesterday, I worked with the customer on the product backlog. I was also involved in the sprint planning meeting where I worked with the other members of the team to hash out the work for this sprint. Today, I plan on being available for questions from the team, as well as working with the customer to hash some more user stories. I have no blocks.*

Tyler: *Okay, I am going to go next. Yesterday, I worked with the team to size the user stories that we have agreed to do for this sprint. I plan on pairing with Sarah starting today to work on the Game Play: Hit user story. I have no blocks.*

Sarah: *Yesterday, I also worked with the team to size the user stories for the sprint. Today, I plan on pairing with Tyler on the Game Play: Hit user story. I have no blocks.*

Tim: *All right, guys and gals, that is all for now.*

## Developing the User Story: Hit

Tyler: *Sarah, want to get started on the Hit feature?*

Sarah: *Sure. Let's get started.*

Tyler moves the Hit user story into the In Process swim lane to notify the team that the story is currently being worked on.  Tyler and Sarah begin by talking to Simon to clarify all the acceptance criteria.

Sarah: *Hey Simon. Got a moment?*

Simon: *Sure. What's up?*

Tyler: *We have looked over the information for the Game Play: Hit user story and believe we have come up with all the behaviors of the user story. Would you mind looking at it and make sure we covered it all?*

Simon: *No problem.*

Sarah: *Here is what we have.*

Sarah and Tyler show Simon two scenarios for the Hit user story, as shown in Figures 6-4 and 6-5.

```
Scenario: Option to Hit
    Given that I have the following cards:
    | Suit   | Value  |
    | Hearts | Two    |
    | Clubs  | Six    |
    And the dealers hand contains the following cards:
    | Suit   | Value  |
    | Hearts | Ten    |
    | Hearts | Three  |
    Then I should given the option to hit
```

*Figure 6-4. Option to Hit scenario*

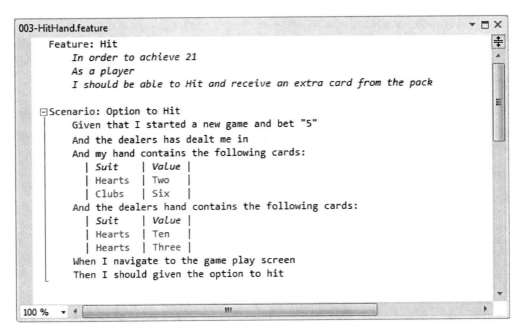

**Figure 6-5.** *Hit scenario*

Simon: *It looks pretty good. I can't think of anything else we need to cover.*

Tyler: *Thanks!*

## Adding the SpecFlow Feature

Now that we have the acceptance criteria for the Hit user story completed, it is time to start coding.

Start by adding a new feature to the Features folder named 003-HitHand.feature. Once the file is created, update the contents of it to match the feature shown in Figure 6-6.

Scenario: Hit
    Given that I have the following cards:
    | Suit    | Value |
    | Hearts  | Two   |
    | Clubs   | Six   |
    And the dealers hand contains the following cards:
    | Suit    | Value |
    | Hearts  | Ten   |
    | Hearts  | Three |
    And the deck contains the following cards:
    | Suit    | Value |
    | Hearts  | Four  |
    | Hearts  | Five  |
    When I hit
    Then my hand should show the following cards:

    | card            |
    | Two of Hearts   |
    | Six of Clubs    |
    | Four of Hearts  |

***Figure 6-6.*** *Hit SpecFlow feature option to Hit scenario*

You will notice that it is more verbose than the initial scenarios that the developers went through with the product owner, because of the steps required to set up the game state. It is still important, however, that it is written in a language that the product owner understands so that he is able to confirm the completed feature.

If you run your `Acceptance.Tests` project, you will be presented with the following missing step definition:

```
[Then(@"I should given the option to hit")]
public void ThenIShouldGivenTheOptionToHit()
{
    ScenarioContext.Current.Pending();
}
```

Tyler: *It looks like the only action we need to verify is that the Hit button displayed. Am I missing something or is that it?*

Sarah: *You're right. That's it.*

Now we need to update the step definition so that it will actually do something. Update the step to contain the following code:

```
[Then(@"I should given the option to hit")]
public void ThenIShouldGivenTheOptionToHit()
{
    Assert.That(BetOnHandPage.has_hit_button, Is.True);
}
```

The next step is to add a new property called `has_hit_button` to the `BetOnHandPage` class to keep the compiler from complaining. This property will return whether the web page contains the Hit button at the correct time.

```
namespace KojackGames.Blackjack.Acceptance.Tests.PageObjects
{
```

```
public class BetOnHandPage
{

    . . .

    public static bool has_hit_button
    {
        get { return WebBrowser.Current.Button("btnHit").Exists; }
    }
}
}
```

With the last compiler error corrected, run all the acceptance tests. When you run these tests, they should all run and fail. We know we hate failing tests and assume that you do, too. Let's get some green on the screen.

# Using BDD to Drive the Feature Development

Tyler: *Okay, so we have our acceptance test working, but failing. I say we jump into a test. Where should we start?*

Sarah: *Well, there really isn't any test we can do in the controller because the query service will just return a domain view, which will have to update in a minute.*

Tyler: *Okay, so we should just jump into the domain model and write a test that checks for a hit option after the hands have been dealt?*

Sarah: *Yeah. I will write a specification for exactly that.*

Add a new test class named when_hitting_the_players_hand to the DealerAction_Specs/HitHand folder of the Core.Tests project with the following definition:

```
namespace KojackGames.Blackjack.Core.Tests.Domain_Specs.DealerAction_Specs.HitHand
{
    [Subject(typeof(Domain.GamePlay.Model.Dealer.Actions.HitHand), "Hit")]
    public class when_hitting_the_players_hand : with_a_hit_hand_action
    {
        private Establish context = () =>
        {
        };

        Because of = () => SUT.action_to_perform(playing_positions, card_shoe, player);

        private It should_take_a_card_from_the_card_shoe = () =>
        {
        };

        private It should_add_a_card_to_the_players_hand = () =>
        {
        };
    }
}
```

What you want to make sure is that you are asserting that some kind of specification class is called at the start of the hit action, like so:

```
private It should_take_a_card_from_the_card_shoe = () =>
{
    card_shoe.AssertWasCalled(x => x.take_card());
};
```

What this does is assert that when the Hit button is pressed, the card will be removed from the card shoe. The next thing you could assert is that the card that was removed from the card shoe shows up in the player's hand, as follows:

```
private It should_add_a_card_to_the_players_hand = () =>
{
    players_hand.AssertWasCalled(x => x.add(Arg<Card>.Is.Anything));
};
```

This specification can be added to the base `with_a_hit_hand_action` class in a roundabout way. What you can do is add objects that will be adversely affected by this, namely the `IHandStatusFactory` and `IPlayDealersHand` interfaces, as follows:

```
namespace KojackGames.Blackjack.Core.Tests.Domain_Specs.DealerAction_Specs.HitHand
{
    public abstract class with_a_hit_hand_action
    {
        protected static Domain.GamePlay.Model.Dealer.Actions.HitHand SUT;
        protected static IAnnouceWinnerAction annouce_winner_action;
        protected static IHandStatusFactory hand_status_factory;
        protected static IPlayDealersHand player_dealers_hand;

        public with_a_hit_hand_action()
        {
            hand_status_factory = MockRepository.GenerateStub<IHandStatusFactory>();

            annouce_winner_action = MockRepository.GenerateStub<IAnnouceWinnerAction>();
            player_dealers_hand = MockRepository.GenerateStub<IPlayDealersHand>();

            SUT = new Domain.GamePlay.Model.Dealer.Actions.HitHand(hand_status_factory,
player_dealers_hand, annouce_winner_action);
        }
    }
}
```

From this point on, you need to work from the outside in. You will implement the `HitHand` class, as well as the methods behind the process of removing a card from the shoe and adding it to the player's collection of cards for the game. Please see the source code available at www.apress.com if you have any questions.

# Day 4

As we move a few days into this sprint, we come to our team starting their daily stand-up and discussing a roadblock.

## Daily Stand-Up

Tim: *Tyler, start us off.*

Tyler: *Well, I worked with Sarah on the Hit feature. We have hit numerous roadblocks. Unfortunately, Simon is not around. We hope to find out soon where he is and talk to him about this user story.*

Sarah: *Ditto for me on the Hit user story and with Simon. I have e-mails out to him, but until we hear back, we will work on the next user story.*

Tim: *Okay. I will try to reach Simon myself and see if I can get some kind of response for you guys. How much is Simon's absence hampering your time in this sprint?*

Tyler: *If we don't get some answers from Simon soon, we risk not getting user stories completed this iteration. It's getting frustrating because we are fairly close to getting this particular user story done.*

Sarah: *I agree. It's not an emergency yet, but a couple more days and it will be.*

Tim: *Okay. I will try to contact Simon right after this meeting and see what I can find out. Thank you all for the update. I wanted to share with you where we stand on the current sprint. From the looks of the things, we are on schedule.* [(See Figure 6-7.)] *However, the roadblock on the Hit user story has me concerned. I will let you know when I hear something from Simon. If you hear something from him before that, please let me know.*

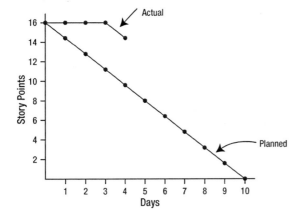

*Figure 6-7. Burn-down chart, Day 4 of Sprint 2*

# Working on the User Story: Stand

Sarah: *While we are waiting on Simon, let's start on the Stand user story.*

Sarah moves the Stand user story to the In Process swim lane, as shown in Figure 6-8.

| Stories | Task Backlog | In Process | In Testing | Done |
|---------|--------------|------------|------------|------|
| | *Asdikjlkj lj l liijoiu oiljlk*<br>*Uoiwoiu jkndlghaf kjkdf dfgfdg n khskjdhfjkhdkj sdfskfh lkjh lilf juij lkjklj tljndsflk ljlkjlk k ;* | *Asdikjlkj lj l liijoiu oiljlk*<br>*Uoiwoiu jkndlghaf kjkdf dfgfdg n khskjdhfjkhdkj sdfskfh lkjh lilf juij lkjklj tljndsflk ljlkjlk k ;* | | |
| | | *Asdikjlkj lj l liijoiu oiljlk*<br>*Uoiwoiu jkndlghaf kjkdf dfgfdg n khskjdhfjkhdkj sdfskfh lkjh lilf juij lkjklj tljndsflk ljlkjlk k ;* | | |

*Figure 6-8. Updated task board*

Tyler: *Okay, I think I have an understanding of what we need to do with this one. Shall we begin?*

Sarah: *Sure.*

## Adding the SpecFlow Feature

To begin this user story, add the new feature to the system. Create a new file called 004-StandHand.feature. Update the file to contain the feature we need for the user story, as shown in Figure 6-9.

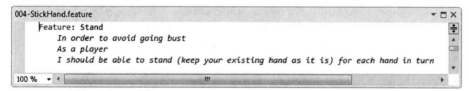

*Figure 6-9. Stand feature*

## Add Scenario

As before, now that we have the feature file and feature added to the system, we need to add a scenario to that feature.

Update the StandHand.feature user story file with the scenario shown in Figure 6-10.

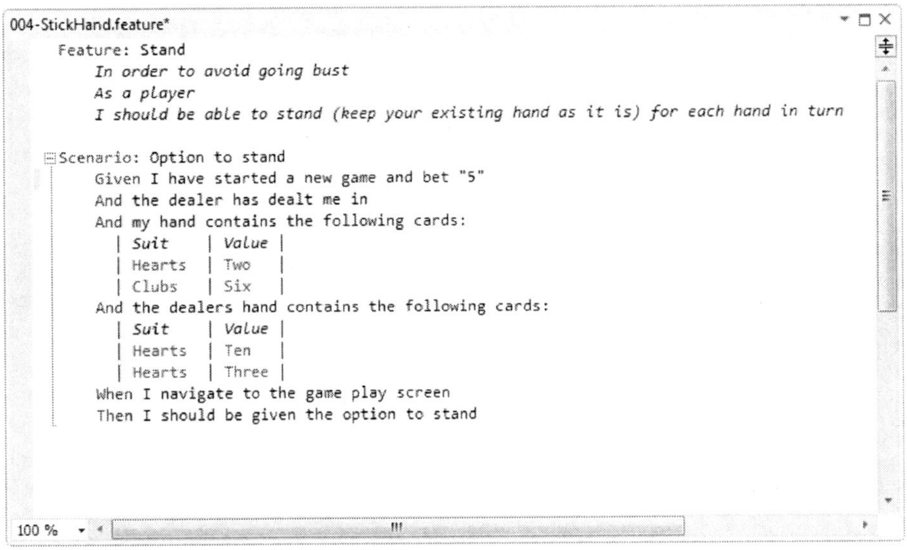

```
004-StickHand.feature*                                              ▼ □ ×
    Feature: Stand
        In order to avoid going bust
        As a player
        I should be able to stand (keep your existing hand as it is) for each hand in turn

 ⊟Scenario: Option to stand
        Given I have started a new game and bet "5"
        And the dealer has dealt me in
        And my hand contains the following cards:
          | Suit   | Value |
          | Hearts | Two   |
          | Clubs  | Six   |
        And the dealers hand contains the following cards:
          | Suit   | Value |
          | Hearts | Ten   |
          | Hearts | Three |
        When I navigate to the game play screen
        Then I should be given the option to stand



100 %  ▼ ◄                           III                         ►
```

*Figure 6-10. Scenario for the Stand feature*

One thing you will notice is that as we move further along into this application, more of the basic foundation of the app is already written. Each new user story just extends the existing architecture. With that information at hand, you know that navigating to the game play screen, placing a bet, and dealing the cards is already covered and implemented by previous user stories and tests. One additional thing you will notice is how most of the And conditions are already implemented. This reusability of setup code between tests can improve the efficiency and productivity of a team. From the Hit user story, we know that the "my hand contains the following cards" and "the dealer's hand contains the following cards" steps are already implemented. We only need to concern ourselves with the act of standing on a hand, which in this case is the Then part of the scenario.

When you run the feature, you will notice that you are missing just one of the steps of the scenario. Go to the GameDisplaySteps.cs file located in the Steps folder. Once in there, add a new method to the class called TheIShouldGivenTheOptionToStick. Rerun the tests and you will notice that you have a failure. Update the method with the following code:

```
namespace KojackGames.Blackjack.Acceptance.Tests.Steps
{
    [Binding]
    public class GameDisplaySteps
    {
        . . .

        [Then(@"I should given the option to stick")]
        public void ThenIShouldGivenTheOptionToStick()
        {
            Assert.That(BetOnHandPage.has_stick_button, Is.True);
        }
    }
}
```

From here you see that you need to add properties and methods to the `BetOnHandPage` class to get this test to pass. This process is very similar to the previous user stories in that regard, so we will not duplicate it here.

# Day 6

We have skipped ahead to Day 6 to check on our team and see how they are doing.

## Daily Stand-Up

Tim: *Let's get this started. Who wants to start?*

Tyler: *I will. Sarah and I continued to pair to finish up the Stand user story. We have all the code and tests done for it, so we are ready to show Simon and get his approval. Today, I plan on pairing with Sarah on the remaining user story in the sprint. And, I have no blocks.*

Sarah: *Let's see. A lot of what Tyler said applies to me. I will pair with Tyler today on the Game Play: Win user story. I have no blocks.*

Tim: *Is there an update on the Hit user story?*

Sarah: *Yes, we were finally able to get in touch with Simon and get the answers to the questions we had. With the information from Simon, we were able to complete the code and tests for the user story. The user story is ready to show Simon and get his approval on it.*

Tim: *Okay. We need to get with Simon soon to get approval for these user stories. If we end up with numerous user stories blocked waiting on his approval, then we will need to come up with another solution to get them out the door. It's better to have a couple of user stories completed and out the door than numerous user stories in various stages of incompleteness. Well, that is all for now. Everyone have a great day.*

## Final User Story of the Sprint: Win

Tyler: *Sarah, I am ready to start on the last user story whenever you are.*

Tyler moves the Game Play: Win user story to the In Process swim lane. Figure 6-11 shows what the task board currently looks like.

| Stories | Task Backlog | In Process | In Testing | Done |
|---------|--------------|------------|------------|------|
| | | Asdlikjfkj lj I lifjoiw aslfjik<br>Uoiuoiu jlxvdfjghdlf kjkdf rlfgfdg n lxhskjsbhfjkbskj zdfkfefn fkjh llfl jwij fkjklj sfjnsdfk fjl;asjk ;k ; | Asdikjfkj lj I lifjoiw aslfjik<br>Uoiuoiu jlxvdfjghdlf kjkdf rlfgfdg n lxhskjsbhfjkbskj zdfkfefn fkjh llfl jwij fkjklj sfjnsdfk fjl;asjk ;k ; | |
| | | | Asdikjfkj lj I lifjoiw aslfjik<br>Uoiuoiu jlxvdfjghdlf kjkdf rlfgfdg n lxhskjsbhfjkbskj zdfkfefn fkjh llfl jwij fkjklj sfjnsdfk fjl;asjk ;k ; | |

*Figure 6-11. Updated task board*

Sarah: *There seems to be more complexity to this one than previous ones.*

Tyler: *I would agree. I get the feeling that there is more involved on the business-rules side. Let's find Simon to see if he is free for some questions.*

Simon: *Hi guys. What can I do for you?*

Sarah: *We're starting on the Game Play: Win user story and have some questions. We know the basics are that if a player is closer to 21 than the dealer, without going over, the player is the winner. We've talked about the scoring of each card and things of that sort. Could you explain to us again exactly what a "push" is?*

Simon: *Sure. A push is when a dealer and a player end the game with the same point total. When this happens, the player receives back his bet and the game is over. Neither the player nor the dealer wins or loses the game. Do you guys remember the scenarios we talked about for this card during the planning meeting?*

Sarah: *Yes, we do. The first scenario is when both dealer and player stand on a point total less than 21. The second scenario is when either the player or the dealer goes bust. And the third scenario is when the player and the dealer tie or push. Tyler and I understand the other scenarios, but were a little hazy on the push scenario. Thank you, Simon. That should be all we need.*

Simon: *Anytime.*

## Adding the SpecFlow Feature

We begin by adding a new feature file to the Features folder called 005-WinGame.feature. Update it with the feature definition shown in Figure 6-12.

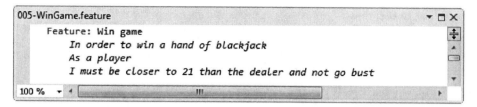

**Figure 6-12.** *User story feature, Win game*

The thing about this feature is that there are numerous scenarios that we will need to test. We need to think of all the ways that a player could win and lose a game, and write scenarios about them. Some of the ways a player could win or lose include the following:

- Player has blackjack with first two cards dealt. Player wins.

- Dealer has blackjack with first two cards dealt. Player loses.

- Player and the dealer have blackjack with first two cards dealt or any time both finish with the same point total. Player pushes.

- Player ends up with a point total higher than the dealer. Player wins.

- Player ends up with a point total lower than the dealer. Player loses.

- Player stands on a hand and the dealer busts. Player wins.

## Adding Scenarios

Let's start with the first one on the list. Update the feature file with the scenario shown in Figure 6-13.

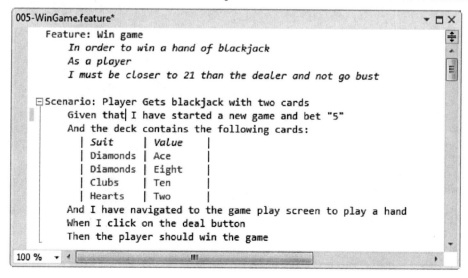

**Figure 6-13.** *Win Game feature updated with a scenario*

As per the previous user stories, most, if not all, of the Given and When steps for this scenario are already implemented by previous user stories. We only need to concern ourselves with the Then in this scenario.

Go to the GameDisplaySteps.cs file and add a method called ThenThePlayerShouldLoseTheGame. You will need to update the method, as shown in Figure 6-14.

```
[Then(@"the player should win the game")]
public void ThenThePlayerShouldWinTheGame()
{
    Assert.That(GameDisplayPage.player_status_message, Is.EqualTo("Won"));
}
```

With this method in place, you can continue trying to get this test to pass by adding functionality to the GameDisplayPage class.

The next scenario in the list is very similar to the previous scenario. Update the feature to look like Figure 6-14.

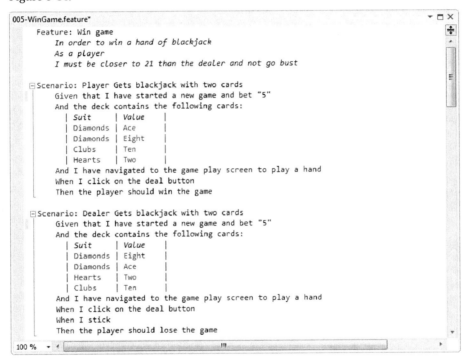

*Figure 6-14. Win Game feature updated with a scenario*

In the previous scenario the player won the game, now the player will lose the game. Add the following method to the GameDisplaySteps.cs file:

```
[Then(@"the player should lose the game")]
public void ThenThePlayerShouldLoseTheGame()
{
    Assert.That(GameDisplayPage.player_status_message, Is.EqualTo("Lost"));
}
```

```
}
```

For the push scenario, add the following method to the same class:

```
[Then(@"the game should be drawn")]
public void ThenTheGameShouldBeDrawn()
{
    Assert.That(GameDisplayPage.player_status_message, Is.EqualTo("Push"));
}
```

The scenarios about the player scoring more or less than the dealer have a couple more steps in them. Update the feature to include the scenario in Figure 6-15.

*Figure 6-15. Win Game feature updated with an additional scenario*

Now, everything in this scenario is implemented except for the When step.

To implement the When step, we need to add the step skeleton generated for us to the GamePlaySteps.cs file. Update this file to contain the following method:

```
[When(@"I stick")]
public void WhenIStick()
{
    GameDisplayPage.stick();
}
```

What you see is that you need to implement a `stick` method on the `GameDisplayPage`. The `Then` is the same `Then` step that we have already implemented in the previous scenarios, so nothing more is required here except to add the necessary functionality to get the test to pass. The finished result is available at `www.apress.com`.

# Day 10

Congratulations, you've made it through your second sprint! As this is the second full sprint, we hope that a consistent and predictable pattern is starting to emerge from this Scrum process. Since this is the last day of our sprint, we'll do a retrospective to see how we can improve the process. We'll also do a sprint demo with the customer.

## Sprint 2 Retrospective

Tim: *Congratulations, team! You've made it through Sprint 2. I hope as we are introducing Scrum and XP that you've seen common themes from these past two sprints. While agile consistently looks at how to improve process, it also aims to become consistent and predictable. We want to remain consistent in developing quality, maintainable code and predictable by delivering the features the team commits to. In the last sprint, our primary action item was assigned to Sarah to set up an e-mail notification on CruiseControl to let other members of the team know when the build is broken. Sarah, how did that go?*

Sarah: *It went well. I was able to learn more about the inner workings of CruiseControl, plus add value to the team. I discovered that CruiseControl is configured through an XML file and that we can set up e-mail notifications from within the cc.config file. If anyone wants to know more about it, I'm happy to share with you. Just contact me after our meeting. I also discovered the CCTray, which a system client can download. It's an icon that sits beside your system clock and changes color based on the status of the build.*

Sarah explains that the CCTray icon works as follows:

- Red : the build broke
- Yellow : the build is currently running
- Green : the last build was successful

Sarah: *I set this up on my machine. If you'd like to know how to do this, let me know and I can walk you through it.*

Tyler: *Yes, Sarah showed me the CCTray and it's pretty neat! I can show anyone that would like this, too.*

Tim: *Fantastic! Thanks for completing that action item, Sarah. Let's review the work that was accomplished over this sprint. The board says that the following stories were completed during this sprint. Is this correct?*

Tim points to the status of completed user stories, as shown Table 6-2.

*Table 6-2. Sprint 2 Completed User Stories*

| User Story Name | Initial Size |
|---|---|
| Game Play: Hit | 5 |
| Game Play: Stand | 3 |
| Game Play: Win | 8 |

Tyler: *Yes, that's correct by my account.*

Sarah: *Same here. That's what we got accomplished this week.*

Tim: *Great. That means, adding up the user story points, we have a velocity of 16 points. Does this workload seem sustainable to you, or did we plan a sufficient amount of work for the sprint?*
Tyler: *For me, this was a sufficient amount of work.*

Sarah: *Same here. I wasn't sitting around twiddling my thumbs all day waiting for something to do. We had enough user stories in the backlog to continue to work on and get things done.*

Tim: *We will take this into account during our next sprint. With each sprint retrospective, one item we need to monitor is the amount of work we get done, which is measured as velocity compared to what we planned for. This sprint, it seemed we planned for a sufficient amount of work and all this work was completed in a sustainable manner. Now let's move onto this week's retrospective activity. Similar to the last retrospective, please take a few of the red, blue, and green Post-its. Do you remember what each stood for?*

Tyler: *No, I forget. What do they stand for again?*

Sarah: *I remember. Red stands for things that went badly during the sprint, blue is for the confusing parts of the sprint, and green represents things that went well.*

Tim: *That's right, Sarah! Good job! I'm going to put three minutes on the buzzer. Jot down your feedback on the appropriate Post-it notes.*

Three minutes pass.

Tim: *Time's up. Let's gather the Post-its. Tyler, would you help me arrange them into three categories?*

Tyler: *Sure.*

Tim: *It looks like we have only two categories for this iteration: Testing and Process. Process is the larger category, so let's start with that one. We seem to have a lot of good things in the Process.*

Tim states that the positive Process feedback is as follows:

- "Working together, pair programming"
- "Having work laid out for us to work on"

- "Daily stand-up and the "meeting after the meeting"

Tim then states that the only negative feedback is the following:

- "Domain knowledge—product owner was out"

Tim: *Let's talk about the negative item.*

Sarah: *I wrote this note. Simon was out at a show and the customer wasn't available. Tyler and I had a number of questions and clarifications on specifically how the Hit feature was supposed to work, but unfortunately, we didn't think of these questions until we started working on it. No one was available to answer these questions, so that was a roadblock. So we started another story instead, but that held us up. What happens when neither Simon nor the customer is available?*

Simon: *As I informed the team at one of our daily stand-ups, I was going to be out for part of this sprint. I hoped the team would work around me.*

Tim: *I have a suggestion. The next time Simon is out, Simon needs to inform Bill of his absence and verify that Bill will be available if the team has any further domain-related questions. When Simon is unavailable, there is a problem with getting domain knowledge from the domain expert. If the team has an issue where they need to get domain questions answered, the team should brainstorm to see if they can collectively come up with a working solution based on their collective knowledge. Once that occurs, Bill can be brought in and the proposed solution will be presented and worked through with Bill. Once Simon has returned, Bill will check with Simon about the information he's given to the team so that everyone continues to be on the same page and so the team is not held up due to Simon's absence.*

Simon: *I'm okay with that. I will coordinate with Bill whenever I'll be unavailable for a few days. I'll tell him that he'll need to serve as the liaison in my absence, but that the team will first try and work through the question themselves. If the team sees fit to bring Bill in, they will do so.*

Tim: *Sarah, Tyler, does that sound good to you?*

Sarah: *Yes, it sounds like we still have someone available to ask questions when we need to and we'll get answers instead of hitting roadblocks.*

Tyler: *Sounds good to me too.*

Tim: *If the team has domain questions, the team will collectively come up with a proposed solution first and present it to Bill. Bill will work with the team and inform Simon when he returns, of what he conveyed to the team. Simon, we'll assign this action item to you since you'll inform Bill of this process. Now, let's move on to the Testing category.*

Tim says that the Testing category has one blue note, which means a "confusing issue" comment. The note read as follows:

- "We spend so many more hours per user story writing tests vs. just cranking out code."

Tyler: *I wrote this card. Before agile and this project, I just spent time cranking out code and not worrying about writing a lot of tests. With this agile thing, it seems as if I'm spending more time writing test code than production code. It's frustrating because I just want to develop features and not worry about the tests.*

Tim: *Tyler, I understand where you are coming from, but when you only spent time "cranking out code," how many bugs did you have to fix once that code was released—and did you ever see the same bug twice?*

Tyler: *Sometimes we'd have to make a large number of bug fixes and, I'll have to admit, I have seen the same bug twice. It typically happens when someone checked in changes over another team member's changes or didn't get the latest, or someone implemented a new feature and introduced the same bug again.*

Tim: *Exactly! One goal we want to achieve is a sustainable working pace. In past projects you've worked on, did you hurry to get the code out the door, but then had to work a bunch of overtime to fix a ton of bugs that you didn't know you had?*

Tyler: *Yes, I must admit, I've worked a lot of overtime at the end of projects just to fix bugs.*

Tim: *We don't want that to happen on this project. The reason we provide potentially shippable code at the end of each sprint is because when we say something is done, we don't want to have to do the same thing or fix the same thing over again. With the CI server in place, we know that a third-party tool is doing our builds. The work we've done in Sprint 0 enables us to compile and deploy much more quickly. That way, you guys know within minutes if someone checked in changes or didn't get the latest. Plus, because we have already written our automated tests, we have a level of confidence that we never had before. Having a good automated test suite that is derived from the acceptance criteria allows us to call something done, actually done. Let me ask you this, how many projects have you worked on where you were trying to integrate a new feature into an existing system without automated tests? You developed the new feature only to find out that you broke other features further into the system, which you didn't even know existed and didn't even find out about until later in the process?*

Tyler: *Yes, I must admit that that has happened to me. It's frustrating when you think you have a simple change but, in reality, it breaks three other things down the line. Think of rock climbing, it's better to inch up a cliff slowly and carefully, driving pitons and cutting footholds, than to race up hastily and wind up dead at the foot of the cliff because you slipped. You even reach the top sooner because dead people can't climb very quickly.*

Tim: *So the reason we are spending all this time writing automated tests and developing from "the outside in" is because we want to minimize bugs, and if bugs exist, we want to know sooner than later—using the CI server. Automated testing also allows traceability between the requirements and the code, and because we are only developing enough code to make the test pass, this ensures that we develop each card based on the requirements, and that each card, once developed, stays developed. Also, we need to develop for the next developer that's going to work on this code. Later, the customer will want features added to this code base and another developer will have to come in and develop that feature. With a solid set of tests, that other developer will know what he broke when implementing a new feature. These automated tests bring value to the customer over the entire software development lifecycle because it creates a tighter feedback loop between the code and the developer, who now has the ability to quickly add features without risk to the existing features. Does that help, Tyler?*

Tyler: *Yes, I understand better now. We want to deliver a solid product and be able to develop for this code base's posterity. We build in automated tests now so the code can outlive the business requirements.*

Tim: *You got it. Tyler, I've run across other business users who don't understand the importance of unit testing and TDD. I think it would be helpful if someone would do a short, 15-minute presentation on unit testing and TDD, and how it relates to the business. Mostly discussing what we just discussed. Would you be willing to prepare a short presentation and present the case of unit testing and TDD to the business?*

Tyler: *Sure, I think that sounds like a good idea. Sometimes when you need to explain a topic to other people you understand it better. I would be willing to do that.*

Tim: *Great, thank you. Let me know if you have any questions. I can help you out if you need, but I think you have the general idea.*

Sarah: *I have a question, but it's not related to these notes. Is now a good time to ask?*

Tim: *Sure, we have a few minutes left before the discussion portion is over. What's up?*

Sarah: *We've discussed all these user stories, but I haven't seen a user story about how the site should look. We've spent most of our time getting the functionality down. Is there a story about the UI and how the site should look?*

Tim: *Good question. Simon do you have that in the backlog?*

Simon: *No, that is a good question. I'll meet with the customer during this sprint and we will get that ironed out. Thanks for bringing that to our attention.*

Tim: *Great. Sounds like another action item. If that's all, let's recap our action items.*
    Tim lists the action items as follows:

- Whenever he is to be unavailable, Simon needs to coordinate with Bill, who will serve as the domain expert in Simon's absence. If the team has a domain question during Simon's absence, the team will collectively first try to solve it and then work with Bill. Bill will touch base with Simon on his return to ensure everyone is on the same page. This item is assigned to Simon.

- Tyler will do a 15-minute presentation to business users on the value of unit testing and TDD.

- Simon will determine, with the customer, how the site should look and then meet with the developers to plan the UI for the site.

Tim: *This concludes our retrospective. Everyone, thanks for your feedback!*

## Product Demo

Now it's show-and-tell time. It's important for the customer to be present and involved in the product demo and it's important that everyone, customer and team, have agreed to the definition of the product being "done," which is the same as the acceptance criteria, before the product demo. The purpose of the product demo is to show the customer what the team has done over the course of the sprint.
    Agile brings transparency, being open and honest with what the team has accomplished; eliminating the concept of developers hiding in a room while the customer hopes to get something desirable after a period of months. We want to remain consistently transparent to the customer, showing them, in small increments, what the team has accomplished or not accomplished. This level of transparency has a way of openly exposing the risks to a project. These risks need to be identified sooner than later so that a plan can be put in place to mitigate them. The product demo also provides the chance to allow the customer to share with the team any political changes, and for both the customer and the team to communicate over a working piece of software.
    Sarah is meeting with Bill and Tim for this product demo.

Sarah: *We wanted to show you what the team has accomplished in this sprint. As you know, the team committed to and, I'm pleased to announce, accomplished getting the following three stories done: Game Play: Hit, Game Play: Stand, and Game Play: Win. This product demo will allow you to see the functionality the team added to the software as it relates to these stories. In the Game Play: Hit user story, the player can click the Hit button and the player will receive another card.*

Bill: *I think this looks fine. Can we put different images on the back of the cards that a user could choose from?*

Tim: *Yes, we can do that. However, since that wasn't part of either this story or an existing user story, we can write a user story for that additional functionality and get it worked into the backlog. If you and the customer decide that it's important enough to develop that functionality, we can add it into a release. If you think it needs to be done sooner, we can work that into an upcoming sprint, but in exchange, we will have to remove a user story that's planned in this release.*

Bill: *Okay, that sounds good. I agree it wasn't part of this user story. It's another idea I just came up with while looking at the demo that I think could be useful. I'll talk to the customer about adding that functionality and if deemed important, we'll replace another user story of a similar size with this one in a future sprint. The functionality, as it currently is, does meet what we determined by our definition of done. Good job, team! I am really enjoying the transparency of this process. In previous projects, I never knew what the developers were working on because we never saw anything until the end. I like seeing what the team has been working on. It gives me confidence that we are moving forward, creating value, and delivering a quality product. Let's move on to the next user story.*

As before, due to the size of this application and for the sake of readability, we have elected to skip the remaining parts of the product demo. The customer, Bill, was also shown every feature completed by the team and his feedback was good. There were no changes needed to the product from Bill's perspective.

## Summary

As we worked on our second sprint, we learned some important lessons. They included the following:

- The team realized the importance of having an available product owner or customer. When either of these two cannot be reached or the developers are not confident about what they should be implementing, confusion arises and becomes a roadblock to development.

- We also learned that although we spend time with release planning and user stories, items come up that were either forgotten or not previously considered. Using agile and the retrospective, we caught an item early. Sarah brought to our attention that the UI had not yet been discussed, which resulted in an action item for Simon to go over with the client. Tight feedback loops are extremely important so that any weaknesses can be exposed and fixed early in the process. Larger issues at the end of a project are avoided.

# CHAPTER 7

# Sprint 3: Changing the Game

Now that we have a couple of sprints under our belt, we want to shake things up a little bit. In this shake-up, we are going to change the dynamics of the team by adding a new developer to the mix. Keep an eye on the team in this sprint and see how this additional person affects them.

## Sprint Planning Meeting

The team has gathered in the conference room. Simon has brought in user stories for the team to work on, discuss, and size. Tim enters the room with someone new close behind.

Tim: *Good morning, team. With two sprints under our belts, things should be getting to be a routine. Today we are going to size the user stories that Simon has brought to the meeting and see what we can commit to in this sprint. I also wanted to let you know that there is a new person joining the team. Say hello to Joe.*

All: *Hello Joe!*

Joe: *Hello everybody. I'm excited to be joining this team. I have heard good things about you, so I'm really excited to get up to speed and contribute what I can to this project.*

Tyler: *First of all, I would like to say welcome aboard, Joe. Second, Tim, why are we adding a developer to the team at this point in the project?*

Tim: *That's a great question, Tyler. The main reason is to give people outside our original team some exposure to Scrum and agile. The ultimate goal is to branch out and use these methodologies and practices in other teams. Second, while I know that adding people to a project will not get work done sooner—it will actually take longer initially—after an initial drop in velocity, we will start to see an increase as Joe becomes more comfortable with the team, the product, and the process.*

Sarah: *No offense to Joe, but are we sure this is the right idea? We are coming up on a release soon and with our velocity and capacity plummeting, it will limit what is ultimately in that release. Is the customer okay with this?*

Simon: *I have talked to the stakeholders and they have come to a consensus that exposing Scrum and agile to the rest of the company is beneficial. Now is the time to begin rebuilding our company infrastructure through an agile lens. We do this by involving other developers in the process, even if that means a drop in velocity. This should be looked at as an investment in the company and, Joe in particular, and not as a drain to our velocity.*

Tyler: *Wow, that is a first!*

Simon: *Yeah, it took a lot of convincing on my part and Tim's, but we were able to show the potential upswing on this—and the business agreed.*

Tim: *All right, guys. I will go ahead and define the theme for this sprint.*

## The Theme of the Sprint

Tim: *The theme for Sprint 3 is going to be "Changing the Game." The reason for this is because the user stories that we need to do in this sprint are all related to changing the basic game of blackjack. Once again, I would like to reiterate that a theme is a way to show the team a common purpose to all the user stories done in this sprint. Continually ask yourself if what you are working on reflects the theme of the sprint. If not, then please let me or Simon know so that we can address it.*

## Determining Availability and Capacity

Tim: *Do any of you know if you are going to be out for an extended period during this sprint?*

Joe: *I will be here the whole time.*

Tyler: *I will not be available the entire sprint. I received notice that I have jury duty. It's only for a couple of days, so it should not be a major impact, but it will have some impact, nonetheless.*

Tim: *Okay, well that is going to hurt us some in our capacity this sprint, but we will plan accordingly. Thank you, Tyler, for the heads up.*

Sarah: *I will be here the entire sprint. Just make sure they don't put you on trial, Tyler!*

Simon: *We have been forewarned. I will be available the entire sprint.*

Tim: *All right. During the last sprint, our velocity was 16 points. Considering that Tyler is going to be out a couple of days and that we're bringing on Joe, we need to consider a lower capacity. Let's move on to planning.*

## Planning Poker

Tim: *Simon, please take it away.*

Simon: *All right, gang, I would like to bring up the first user story. We are going to start with the Game Play: Dealer Rules user story. [(See Figure 7-1.)] When this particular user story came up in the release planning meeting, we stated that its purpose is to give the blackjack dealer certain rules to play by. The T-shirt size for this user story is an M.*

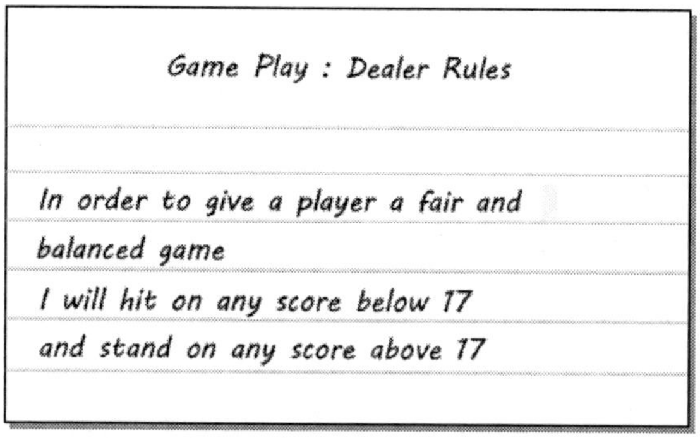

**Figure 7-1.** *User story: Dealer Rules*

Simon: *Are there any questions?*

Tyler: *Can you refresh our memories and tell us what the business rules are?*

Simon tells everyone the rules are as follows:

- The dealer must continue to hit on its hand until reaching at least 17.
- Once the dealer reaches at least 17 it must stay.
- If the dealer goes over 21, it goes bust.

Simon: *You must remember that this user story is the logic that the dealer needs when playing the game so they know what to do. Without this we could have many, many unhappy customers.*

Sarah: *So, can we safely assume that these are the acceptance criteria for this user story and once they are implemented, we can count this user story done?*

Simon: *That is correct.*

Tim: *If there are no further questions, let's vote.*

Sarah: *I vote 5.*

Tyler: *I vote 3.*

Tim: *Joe, do you have a feeling about this yet?*

Joe: *Not yet, since I'm new and just observing for now to get a sense of what this agile thing is about.*

Tim: *All right. Tyler, why did you vote a 3?*

Tyler: *Well, the framework is already there. We can hit and stay on a player, and the dealer is nothing more than a type of player. The only thing we have to do is factor in these rules when programmatically deciding to hit or stay.*

Sarah: *That is a great point, Tyler! I was overlooking some of that and didn't realize how simple this is.*

Tim: *Sarah, do you care to discuss why you voted a 5 or shall we go ahead with the next round of voting?*

Sarah: *I am ready to vote.*

Tim: *All right, round two in voting.*

All: *Three.*

Tim: *Let's mark it as a 3 and move on. What's next?*

Simon: *The next user story is Game Play: Double. [(See Figure 7-2.)] This user story gives the player the ability to double the player's stake in the current and be dealt exactly one more card, under certain circumstances. The T-shirt size on this user story is an M.*

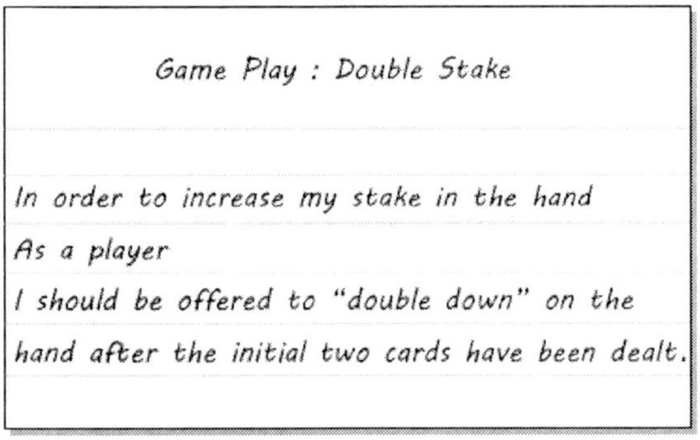

```
Game Play : Double Stake


In order to increase my stake in the hand
As a player
I should be offered to "double down" on the
hand after the initial two cards have been dealt.
```

*Figure 7-2. User story: Double Stake*

Tyler: *Simon, can you give us an example of this? We need to know what the acceptance criteria are for this user story.*

Simon: *Sure, to double down is a way a player can increase his initial bet on a hand. There is a catch to it, though. By giving a player the option to increase his bet, he must commit to stand after receiving exactly one more card. This option is only available on the initial two cards that are dealt to the player that total 9, 10, or 11. There is one additional rule: double down does not apply to the dealer. The dealer's rules trump any playing rules like this in the system.*

Sarah asks if the acceptance criteria for this user story are as follows:

- The option can only be given to the player once the first two cards are dealt and before he "hits" or "stands."
- The option can only be given to the player if the initial two cards total 9, 10, or 11.
- The player must "stand" after taking one additional card.

Simon: *That is correct.*

Sarah: *That's good to know, Simon. I am ready to vote.*

Tim: *Sounds good to me. All right, people, what are your numbers?*

All: *Five.*

Tim: *Five sounds good. Next.*

Simon: *Next up is the user story, Game Play: Insurance. [(See Figure 7-3.)] Now this user story was not one that was in the initial product backlog, so there is no T-shirt size on this one. This user story gives the player the ability to make an insurance bet if the dealer's first card that was dealt face up is an ace.*

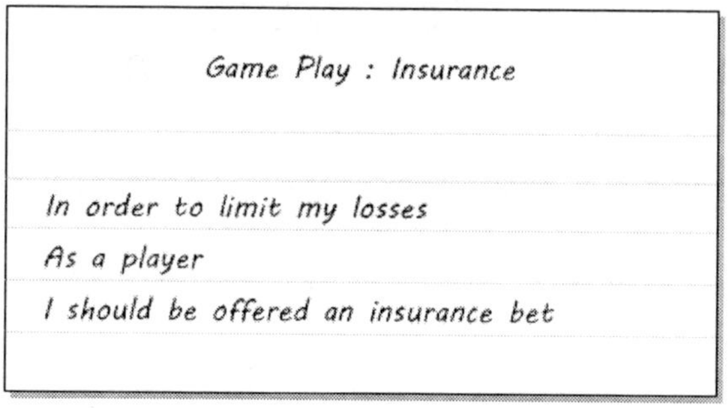

```
Game Play : Insurance



In order to limit my losses
As a player
I should be offered an insurance bet
```

**Figure 7-3.** *User story: Insurance*

Joe: *If this was not in the initial list of work, how can we work on it? This sounds like scope creep and I thought agile was supposed to hinder scope creep from coming into a project.*

Tim: *Good question, Joe. This is not scope creep because the list is always in motion. The customer and Simon are always prioritizing the backlog. With them constantly prioritizing the backlog, there is no scope creep because we are always working on the most important features for the customer. Does that answer your question?*

Joe: *Yes it does, thank you.*

Sarah: *So what is insurance and what does it do?*

Simon: *An insurance bet is a completely separate bet. What the player is betting on is whether the dealer has blackjack or not. This bet is not dependent on the outcome of a player's hand. The amount of an insurance bet is fixed at half the original bet of each hand the player is currently playing.*

Tyler: *What happens if the dealer does not have blackjack? Is the game over at that point?*

Simon: *No. If the dealer does not have blackjack, the player loses the insurance bet, but she can continue to play the hands she has on the table. If the dealer does have blackjack, then the player will win the insurance bet, but lose the hands she was playing in that game.*

Tim: *Okay, let's vote on this one.*

Tyler: *Five.*

Sarah: *Three.*

Tim: *Okay, Sarah, why did you vote a 3?*

Sarah: *I voted a 3 because the logic for this user story is very similar to the Double Down user story. The framework for this user story is already there. We are only talking about adding to an existing functionality.*

Tim: *Sounds good. Tyler, why did you vote a 5?*

Tyler: *I voted a 5 because I thought it was going to be the same level of complexity as the Double Down user story. I didn't realize that since most of the work would be done with the other user story that this one will be less complex.*

Tim: *How about another round of voting?*

Sarah and Tyler: *Three.*

Tim: *Looks like we have a 3 on this user story. Simon, do you have any more user stories that you would like us to look at?*

Simon: *I have one more. This next user story is Saving Game State. [(See Figure 7-4.)] It is a little more technical in nature than ones we have done in the past, but is still a high priority for the customer. This user story is needed to add functionality to the system in the event that the player happens to lose his internet connection or something like that, mid-game. In the initial planning, this user story had a T-shirt size of L.*

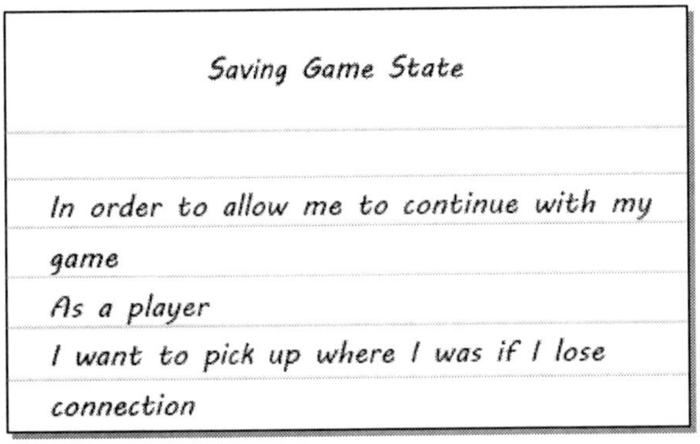

Figure 7-4. *User story: Saving Game State*

Tyler: *How should this work?*

Simon: *Well, since blackjack is in essence a one player game, this user story should give the player ability to pick up where he left off if he loses connection.*

Sarah: *So, it sounds like we need to maintain some kind of "state of the game." That way, if the player loses his connection to the game, when he reconnects, we can see that there is a game in progress and reload that game. Simon, how often should we save the state of the game?*

Simon: *There is no definite information on that. I am comfortable letting you all decide how often to save.*

Tyler: *How many games should we save at one time for the player?*

Simon: *I would say one game at a time.*

Tim: *All right, it is time for a vote.*

Tyler: *It does not sound that complicated. Three.*

Sarah: *I would agree with Tyler.*

Tim: *Looks like the 3s have it. Simon is there anything more for this sprint?*

Simon: *No, that is all I have.*

Tim: *Are there any questions about the amount of work that we have? Do we, as a team, feel comfortable committing to this sprint?*

Sarah: *It is less than what we have been producing the last couple of sprints, but with Tyler being out for jury duty, I feel we can handle it.*

Tyler: *I would agree. I am not expecting my time on jury duty to be more than a few days. Taking that into consideration, I think this amount is enough for the team.*

Joe: *This being my first time planning with the team, I have to defer to my teammates.*

Tim: *Well, then, I guess this is it for the planning meeting. I will see you all at the stand-up meeting tomorrow.*

## Sprint 3's Backlog

Let's review what the team committed to for this iteration. The team committed to the user stories shown in Table 7-1 for a total of 14 points. This is the team's capacity for Sprint 3 and you will notice that it is less than the previous sprints. This is a reflection of the scheduled absences of team members.

*Table 7-1. Sprint 3 Sized Backlog*

| User Story Name | Initial Size |
|---|---|
| Game Play: Dealer Rules | 3 |
| Game Play: Double Stake | 5 |
| Game Play: Insurance | 3 |

| Saving Game State | 3 |
| --- | --- |

# Day 1

As we enter the start of the sprint, we have our first daily stand-up to get a sense of what the team will be tackling first in this sprint.

## Daily Stand-Up

Tim: *Good morning, everyone. Joe, this will be your first stand-up experience. You'll quickly get the hang of it, but we want to concisely answer the following three questions: What did you do yesterday? What are you doing today? What roadblocks are you experiencing, if any?*

Joe: *Great, sounds easy enough.*

Tim: *Okay Joe, how about you start us off?*

Joe: *Yesterday I attended my first-ever sprint planning meeting. Today, I'm not sure what I'll be doing, so I guess that's a roadblock I have right now.*

Sarah: *Same as Joe, I attended the sprint planning meeting yesterday. Today I plan to tackle the Dealer Rules story. Joe, you can pair with me and I can begin to show you how we develop software since it's a bit different than what you might be used to. Simon, will you be available this morning to go over the Dealer Rules story?*

Simon: *I have some free time right after this meeting, but that is it for me. I am busy all day.*

Tyler: *Yesterday, I attended the sprint planning meeting. Today, I guess I'll plan to pick up the Double Stake user story. My goal is to begin sketching out tests and I'll review those tests with Sarah and Joe before I begin to implement them. That way, Sarah can still be in the loop on this user story and it will also expose Joe to some tests on a different user story.*

Tim: *Yes, it might be a challenge having an odd number of developers because the pair programming isn't so "pair," but I think you guys can handle it. Tyler, thanks for being flexible and starting on the tests with the Double Stake user story, and Sarah, thanks for showing Joe the ropes. Joe, these guys are top-notch. I'm sure they'll be able to bring you up to speed quickly. Thanks everyone!*

## Developing the User Story: Dealer Rules

Joe: *Shall we get started, Sarah?*

Sarah: *Let's get to it.*

Sarah moves the Dealer Rules user story into the In Process swim lane to notify the team that the user story is currently being worked on.

Sarah: *Hey Simon. You ready to look over what we have in the way of behavior for this user story?*

Simon: *Sure, I would be happy to.*

Sarah shows Simon the Dealer Rules scenario, as shown in Figure 7-5.

```
Scenario: Dealer plays until he gets over 17
    Given I have started a new game and bet "5"
    And the dealer has dealt me in
    And my hand contains the following cards:
        | Suit     | Value    |
        | Hearts   | Ten      |
        | Clubs    | Jack     |
    And the dealers hand contains the following cards:
        | Suit     | Value    |
        | Spades   | Five     |
        | Hearts   | Six      |
    And the deck contains the following cards:
        | Suit     | Value    |
        | Diamonds | Two      |
        | Diamonds | Four     |
        | Clubs    | Two      |
        | Diamonds | Seven    |
    And I have navigated to the game play screen to play a hand
    When I stand
    Then the dealers hand should show the following cards:
        | card             |
        | Five of Spades   |
        | Six of Hearts    |
        | Two of Diamonds  |
        | Four of Diamonds |
```

***Figure 7-5.*** *Dealer Rules scenario*

Simon: *That looks about enough to cover it. I'd say to move ahead with it.*

Joe: *Great. Thanks Simon!*

# Adding the SpecFlow Feature

Now that we have the acceptance criteria for the user story, we can start writing the tests that we need.

Start by adding a new feature object to the **Features** folder named **006-DealerPlayingRules.feature**. Once the file is created, update the file contents to match the feature shown in Figure 7-6.

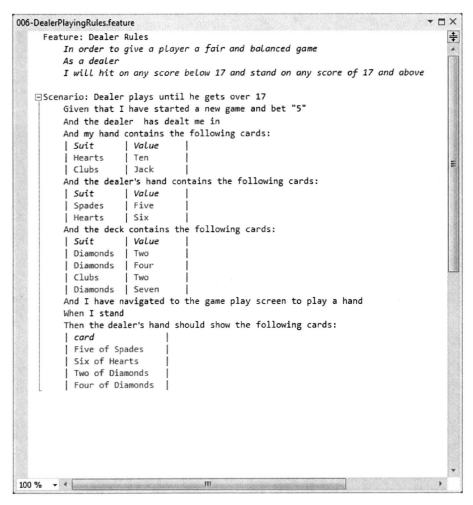

**Figure 7-6.** *Dealer Rules SpecFlow feature*

When you run the `Acceptance.Tests` project, you will notice that there are no missing step definitions. All of the steps have already been defined from previous user stories.

Sarah: *This is fortunate. It looks like everything is defined for this test. All we need to do is modify the logic of the code for this user story and make sure our tests pass.*

Joe: *Is this a common thing?*

Sarah: *By using TDD and BDD, the further into the project we get, the more the foundation for our user stories are completed.*

Since there are no compile errors when you write this feature, your next step is to handle the failing tests. To do that, you need to look at the `CanHitDealer` object that is located in the `Domain.GamePlay.Model.Dealer.Actions` namespace. This object will contain the logic that says if the dealer can hit or stand. In the same namespace, the object called `PlayDealersHand` will contain the action that hits on the dealer's hand if the logic is true. Look at the companion code for an example of how this is done.

# Day 4

Day 4 brings the completion of one user story and the start of another.

## Daily Stand-Up

Tim: *Joe, how about you start today?*

Joe: *Sure. Well, I have been pairing with Sarah on the Dealer Rules user story and I have been learning a tremendous amount from her about testing and Scrum. Today, I plan on working with Sarah and Simon on acceptance criteria and scenarios for other user stories in this sprint.*

Sarah: *Yesterday I worked with Joe on the Dealer Rules user story and today I plan on working with Tyler on the next user story. I have been talking with Tyler, and I may have a block, but I will let Tyler discuss this first.*

Tyler: *Well, I was stuck in jury duty for the last couple of days, but that is over with now. Today, I plan on working with Sarah on the Double Stake user story. However, I have been feeling under the weather the last couple of hours. I am not getting any better, so I may end up going home by lunchtime.*

Tim: *How is that going to affect you, Sarah?*

Sarah: *Well, Tyler has been doing some of the preliminary work on that user story, so if he ends up going home, I will not be able to work with him and I won't have the information that he has.*

Tim: *What if we did a knowledge dump between you and Tyler right after this meeting to see if we can get you both on the same page in case he goes home?*

Tyler: *I am up for that.*

Sarah: *It's better than nothing.*

Tim: *Good. We will have an after-meeting after the stand-up. Next.*

Simon: *I have been working with the customer on getting the backlog prioritized and hashing out the user stories at the top of the list for the next sprint. Today, I plan on continuing to work with the customer on that, as well as provide any support that is needed to the team.*

Tim: *Great. Guys, thank you for the updates. I want to share with you where we stand on the current sprint. From the looks of things, we are starting off a little slow. We are only averaging 0.75 points completed each day. I am not completely worried yet, but we all need to keep an eye on this.*
[(See Figure 7-7.)]

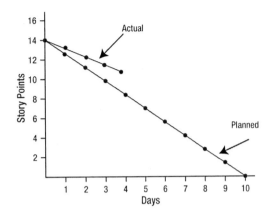

**Figure 7-7.** *Burn-down chart, Day 4 of Sprint 3*

# Working on the User Story: Double Stake

Sarah: *Shall we get started?*

Tyler: *I'm sorry, Sarah, but I am still feeling terrible, so I am going to head home.*

Sarah: *I'm sorry to hear that. Well, go home and don't keep infecting us with your germs. Tim, what should I do?*

Tim: *Did you have the knowledge transfer with Tyler?*

Sarah: *Yes.*

Tim: *Okay, I would suggest that you bring Joe on board with this.*

Sarah: *Okay. Joe, you want to pair with me on this user story?*

Joe: *Sure.*

Sarah: *Great. We are starting to work on the Double Stake user story.* [(See Figure 7-8.)]

*Game Play : Double*

In order to double my stake

As a player

I should be offered to double down

when my initial two cards add up to

9, 10 or 11

*Figure 7-8. User story; Double Stake*

Sarah: *Before we start work, let's have a chat with Simon and come up with some acceptance criteria for this story.*

Sarah and Joe locate Simon.

Sarah: *Hey Simon. We are working on the Double Stake game play story and we have come up with acceptance criteria based on our meetings. Could you take a look to see if we have captured all of the behaviors of this feature?* [(See Figure 7-9)].

Simon: *Sure. I only have a few minutes to spare before my next meeting, so we need to make this quick.*

```
Scenario: Offer to double
Given I that I have been dealt the following cards:
    | Suit      | Value    |
    | Diamonds  | Eight    |
    | Hearts    | Two      |
Then I should be offered to double my stake

Scenario: Can't double on ace and 10
Given I that I have been dealt the following cards:
    | Suit      | Value    |
    | Diamonds  | Jack     |
    | Hearts    | Ace      |
Then I will not be offered to double down again
```

*Figure 7-9. Double Stake user story feature*

Simon: *What if a player doesn't have the funds to double down?*

Sarah: *Could we just hide the option to double down?*

Simon: *Not quite. Remember, we want players to spend money with us, so we should give them the option to cash in and get more funds —and return to the game to double down.*

Sarah: *Well, we have a user story currently in the product backlog that talks about allowing the user to cash into the system. Should this scenario be added to that user story? I am afraid if we add it to this user story, it will become too large to complete in this sprint.*

Simon: *I would love to have it as part of this user story, but I also want something instead of potentially nothing this sprint, so I am okay with adding this to the Cashing In user story and getting it done later. Other than that, I think you have it covered.*

## Adding the Double Stake SpecFlow Feature

Sarah: *Okay, now that we have gathered the initial acceptance criteria for the Double Stake story, it's time to fire up Visual Studio and start coding the new feature.*

To begin, add the new feature to the system. Create a new file called `007-DoubleStake` to the `Features` folder of the `Acceptance.Tests`. Once created, update the feature file so that it matches the feature, as shown in Figure 7-10.

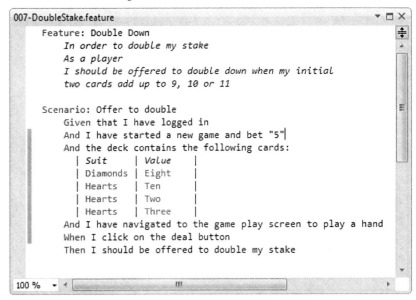

*Figure 7-10. Double Down SpecFlow feature offer to double scenario*

You will notice that it is more verbose than the initial scenarios that the developers went through with the product owner. This is due to the steps required to set the game state up. It is still important, however, that it is written in a language that the product owner understands in order for him to be able to confirm the completed feature.

If you run your `Acceptance.Tests` project, you will be presented with the following missing step definition:

```
[Then(@"I should be offered to double my stake")]
public void ThenIShouldBeOfferedToDoubleMyStake()
{
```

```
        ScenarioContext.Current.Pending();
    }
```

To create these missing step definitions, the only action is to verify that the Double button is displayed.

```
namespace KojackGames.Blackjack.Acceptance.Tests.Steps
{
    [Binding]
    public class GameDisplaySteps
    {
        [Then(@"I should be offered to double my stake")]
        public void ThenIShouldBeOfferedToDoubleMyStake()
        {
            Assert.That(GameDisplayPage.has_double_button, Is.True);
        }

        ...
    }
}
```

To stop the compiler from complaining, we will need to update the `GameDisplayPage` with the new `has_double_button` property.

```
namespace KojackGames.Blackjack.Acceptance.Tests.PageObjects
{
    public class GameDisplayPage
    {
        public static bool has_double_button
        {
            get { return WebBrowser.Current.Button("btnDouble").Exists; }
        }

        ...
    }
}
```

Sarah: *Let's run the suite of acceptance tests to ensure that we haven't broken anything and to confirm our failing scenario.*

If you run the acceptance tests, all should pass—apart from the Double Stake scenario that you have just created.

## Using BDD to Drive the Feature Development

Sarah: *We have our acceptance test working, but failing. I say we jump into a test, but where should we start?*

Joe: *I don't understand. Do you mean "working, but failing" in regards to our tests?*

Sarah: *What I mean is that our tests are now compiling and the system is running them. However, the test itself is currently failing. The test runs, but it is passing at this moment. Well, there really isn't any test we can do in the controller, as the query service will just return a domain view, which will have to update in a minute. What I am thinking we do is jump into the domain model and write a test that checks for a double option after the hands have been dealt.*

Joe: *Sounds good to me. I will write up a specification for exactly that.*

Sarah: *Okay. Let's make a note of exactly what we want to happen.* [(See Figure 7-11.)]

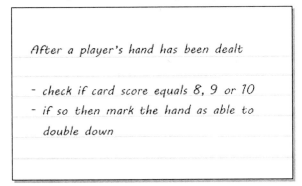

After a player's hand has been dealt

- check if card score equals 8, 9 or 10
- if so then mark the hand as able to
  double down

**Figure 7-11.** *Notes on expected behavior*

Sarah: *With that in place, let's write the skeleton of the tests.*

Add a new test class named when_a_players_hand_meets_the_criteria_to_double_after_dealing to the DealerAction_Specs/DealCardsIn folder of the Core.Tests project with the following definition:

```
namespace KojackGames.Blackjack.Core.Tests
                   .Domain_Specs.DealerAction_Specs.DealCardsIn
{
    [Subject(typeof(Domain.GamePlay.Model.Dealer.Actions.DealCardsIn))]
    public class
        when_a_players_hand_meets_the_criteria_to_double_after_dealing
                                    : with_a_deal_in_cards_action
    {
        private Establish context = () =>
        {

        };

        Because of = () => SUT.perform_on(positions, card_shoe);

        It should_check_the_players_hand_for_a_double = () => { };

        It should_mark_the_players_hand_as_being_able_to_double_down =
                                               () => { };

    }
}
```

Ideally, you want to be able to assert that some kind of specification class is called after the hands are dealt.

```
It should_check_the_players_hand_for_a_double = () =>
{
    double_down_spec.AssertWasCalled(x => x.is_satisfied_by(players_hand));
};
```

Let's add this specification to the base with_a_deal_in_cards_action class and include it as a constructor parameter to the DealCardsIn class that's under test.

```
namespace KojackGames.Blackjack.Core.Tests.Domain_Specs.DealerAction_Specs.DealCardsIn
{
    public abstract class with_a_deal_in_cards_action
    {
        ...

        protected static ICanDoubleDown can_double_down_spec;

        public with_a_deal_in_cards_action()
        {
            can_double_down_spec =
                MockRepository.GenerateStub<ICanDoubleDown>();

            ...

            SUT = new Domain.GamePlay.Model.Dealer.Actions.DealCardsIn(
                                        hand_status_factory,
                                        annouce_winner_action,
                                        can_double_down_spec);
        }
    }
}
```

Now add the new interface and put it with the other Dealer observation specifications.

Add the ICanDoubleDown to the GamePlay/Model/Dealer/Observations folder of the Domain project with the following definition:

```
using KojackGames.Blackjack.Domain.GamePlay.Model.PlayingPosition.Hands;
using KojackGames.Blackjack.Infrastructure.Domain;

namespace KojackGames.Blackjack.Domain.GamePlay.Model.Dealer.Observations
{
    public interface ICanDoubleDown : ISpecification<IHand>
    {
    }
}
```

To stop the compiler from complaining, include the ICanDoubleDown specification as a new constructor parameter. Add a new method within the perform_on to check if a player's hand can double down.

```
namespace KojackGames.Blackjack.Domain.GamePlay.Model.Dealer.Actions
{
```

```
public class DealCardsIn : IDealerAction
{
    ...

    private readonly ICanDoubleDown _double_down_spec;

    public DealCardsIn(IHandStatusFactory hand_status_factory,
                       IAnnouceWinnerAction annouce_winner_action,
                       ICanDoubleDown double_down_spec)
    {
        _hand_status_factory = hand_status_factory;
        _annouce_winner_action = annouce_winner_action;
        _double_down_spec = double_down_spec;
    }

    ...

    public void perform_on(IPlayingPositions hands, ICardShoe card_shoe)
    {
        if (can_perform_on(hands))
        {
            deal_two_cards_to_each_hand_in(hands, card_shoe);

            update_the_status_of_each_hand_in(hands);

            if (hands.contain_a_hand_with_blackjack())
                _annouce_winner_action.determine_winner_from(hands);

            check_if_player_can_double_down(hands);

            hands.mark_cards_as_dealt();
        }
        else
            throw new IllegalMoveException();
    }

    private void check_if_player_can_double_down(IPlayingPositions hands)
    {
        _double_down_spec.is_satisfied_by(hands.players_hand);
    }

    ...
    }
}
```

Joe: *Should we add a new property or method on the player's hand to be updated with the result of the call to see if the hand satisfies the criteria for double down?*

Sarah: *No, this test is just asserting that the specification is called. Don't think of these as tests, think of them more along the lines of design scaffolding. By writing tests first we can drive the design of the system from the behaviors we want it to portray. Right now, build and run the test.*

The test passes. Now we can test the behavior of the player's hand being told that it can double down. Update the second test to assert that the player's hand has a method named mark_as_able_to_double_down and that it was called.

```
It should_mark_the_players_hand_as_being_able_to_double_down = () =>
{
    players_hand.AssertWasCalled(x => x.mark_as_able_to_double_down());
};
```

We will need to add the new method to the IPlayersHand interface and PlayersHand class.

```
namespace KojackGames.Blackjack.Domain.GamePlay.Model.PlayingPosition.Hands.Player
{
    public interface IPlayersHand: IHand
    {
        Bet wager { get; }
        void mark_as_able_to_double_down();
    }
}
```

Joe: *So why didn't we just expose a Boolean property instead of a method?*

Sarah: *The answer lies in the question, young one...*

Joe: *Huh?*

Sarah: *We don't want to expose anything about the data structure of our classes, only expose behaviors. By making it a method, we can control the logic of how a hand will be marked as having the ability to be doubled down without letting the user know how we do it.*

Update the PlayersHand and have it implement the new mark_as_able_to_double_down method and privately update an internal field.

```
namespace KojackGames.Blackjack.Domain.GamePlay.Model.PlayingPosition.Hands.Player
{
    public class PlayersHand : Hand, IPlayersHand
    {
        private bool _can_double_down;

        public PlayersHand(Bet bet_amount, IBlackJackTable black_jack_table)
            : base(black_jack_table)
        {
            wager = bet_amount;
        }

        protected PlayersHand() : base()
        { }

        public Bet wager { get; private set; }

        public void mark_as_able_to_double_down()
        {
            _can_double_down = true;
```

```
        }

        public override void add(Card card)
        {
            card.show();
            base._cards.Add(card);
        }
    }
}
```

Sarah: *Now if we just update the class under test so that it calls the player's hand, we should be able to get the test to pass.*

```
namespace KojackGames.Blackjack.Domain.GamePlay.Model.Dealer.Actions
{
    public class DealCardsIn : IDealerAction
    {
        ...

        private void check_if_player_can_double_down(IPlayingPositions hands)
        {
            if (_double_down_spec.is_satisfied_by(hands.players_hand))
                hands.players_hand.mark_as_able_to_double_down();
        }

        ...
    }
}
```

Joe: *Oh, that's odd, the test failed.*

Sarah: *Ah, that's because you didn't set the expected return value of the double down specification.*

Tell the stub to return true when asked if the player's hand satisfies its criteria.

```
private Establish context = () =>
{
    double_down_spec.Stub(x => x.is_satisfied_by(players_hand)).Return(true);
};
```

Sarah: *Brilliant. Two new tests passing and no broken tests!*

Figure 7-12 shows the two passing tests.

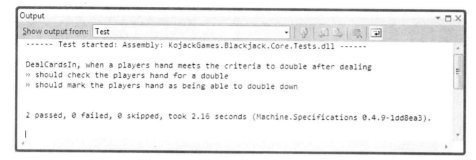

*Figure 7-12. Two new passing tests*

Joe: *Next, I suppose we had better create the double down specification.*

Sarah: *Good idea. I guess we need a couple of tests to prove that a hand with a score that is between and inclusive of 8 and 10 with the first two cards meets the specification criteria, and a hand without does not. We will also need a test to confirm that you can't double down with an ace and a 10. Let's create those tests.*

Add a new folder to the Core.Tests project named DoubleDownSpecification within DomainSpecs/HandObservations_Specs. Add new class to the folder named when_checking_if_a_hand_with_a_score_of_8_can_double_down.

```
using KojackGames.Blackjack.Domain.GamePlay
                        .Model.Dealer.Observations;
using KojackGames.Blackjack.Domain.GamePlay
                        .Model.PlayingPosition.Hands.Player;
using Machine.Specifications;
using NUnit.Framework;
using Rhino.Mocks;

namespace
KojackGames.Blackjack.Core.Tests.Domain_Specs.HandObservations_Specs.DoubleDownSpecification
{
    [Subject(typeof(CanDoubleDown))]
    public class when_checking_if_a_hand_with_a_score_of_8_can_double_down
    {
        private Establish context = () =>
        {
            SUT = new CanDoubleDown();
            players_hand = MockRepository.GenerateStub<IPlayersHand>();
            players_hand.Stub(x => x.score).Return(8);
            players_hand.Stub(x => x.number_of_cards).Return(2);
        };

        private Because of = () => result =
                        SUT.is_satisfied_by(players_hand);

        It should_be_able_to_double_down = () =>
        {
            Assert.That(result, Is.True);
```

```
        };

        private static CanDoubleDown SUT;
        private static IPlayersHand players_hand;
        private static bool result;
    }
}
```

After a few minutes and a couple of extra tests, the developers come up with the following definition for the CanDoubleDown. Add this class to the GamePlay/Model/Dealer/Observations folder of the Domain project.

```
using KojackGames.Blackjack.Domain.GamePlay.Model.PlayingPosition.Hands;

namespace KojackGames.Blackjack.Domain.GamePlay.Model.Dealer.Observations
{
    public class CanDoubleDown : ICanDoubleDown
    {
        public bool is_satisfied_by(IHand hand)
        {
            if (hand.number_of_cards == 2)
            {
                if (hand.score > 7 && hand.score < 11 ||
                    hand.score == 11 && hand.number_of_aces == 0)
                {
                    return true;
                }
            }

            return false;
        }
    }
}
```

That's all the cases for the CanDoubleDown specification covered, as seen in Figure 7-13.

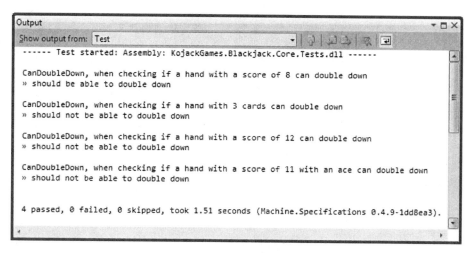

*Figure 7-13. The CanDoubleDown specification passing tests*

## Wiring Up and Getting the Scenario to Pass

Let's wire up the code and get this scenario to pass. The first thing we need to do is add a new column to the Hands table to store the field on the PlayersHand that signifies that a player can double down, as seen in Figure 7-14. Remember to allow nulls, as this table also stores, the dealer's hands won't have a value for it.

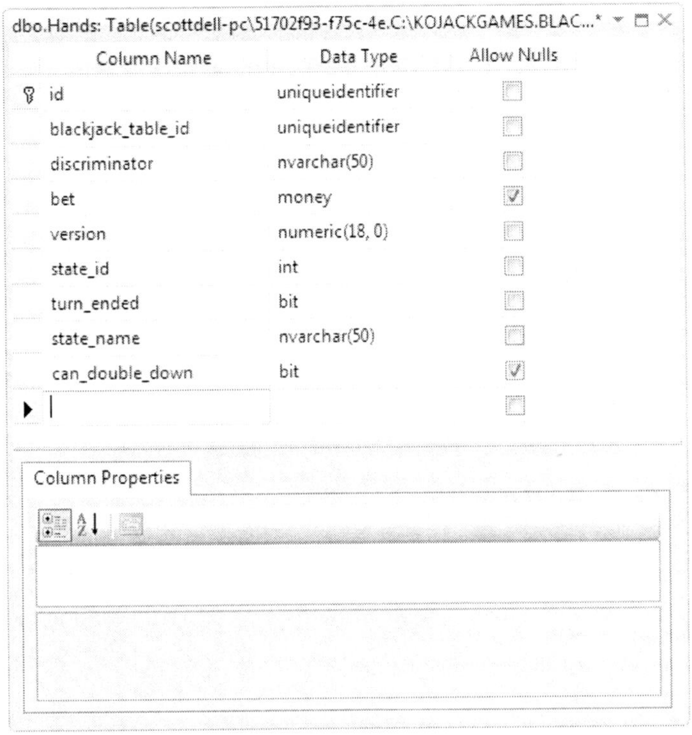

*Figure 7-14. The new can_double_down column on the Hands table*

Now we need to update the NHibernate mapping mark up so that it will write up the `PlayersHand` to store and retrieve the `_can_double_down` field.

```xml
<?xml version="1.0" encoding="utf-8" ?>
<hibernate-mapping xmlns="urn:nhibernate-mapping-2.2"
    namespace="KojackGames.Blackjack.Domain.GamePlay.Model.PlayingPosition.Hands"
        assembly="KojackGames.Blackjack.Domain">
  <class name="Hand" table="Hands" lazy="false" >

    ....

    <subclass
name="KojackGames.Blackjack.Domain.GamePlay.Model.PlayingPosition.Hands.Player.PlayersHand"
discriminator-value="Player" lazy="false">

      <property name="_can_double_down" access="field"
              column="can_double_down"/>

      <component name="wager"
class="KojackGames.Blackjack.Domain.GamePlay.Model.PlayingPosition.Hands.Player.Bet">
        <property name="value" column="bet"/>
      </component>
```

```
        </subclass>

        <subclass
name="KojackGames.Blackjack.Domain.GamePlay.Model.PlayingPosition.Hands.Dealer.DealersHand"
discriminator-value="Dealer" lazy="false">
        </subclass>

    </class>
</hibernate-mapping>
```

We added a new parameter to the DealCardsIn class, so we will have to update the StructureMap registry so that it knows about it at runtime.

Joe: *Okay good point, I will update that now.*

```
namespace KojackGames.Blackjack.UI.Web
{
    public class BootStrapper
    {
        public static void ConfigureDependencies()
        {
            ObjectFactory.Initialize(x =>
            {
                x.AddRegistry<ControllerRegistry>();
                x.AddRegistry<CommandHandlerRegistry>();
                x.AddRegistry<CommandMappersRegistry>();
                x.AddRegistry<DomainRegistry>();
            });
        }

        ...

        public class DomainRegistry : Registry
        {
            public DomainRegistry()
            {
                ...

                For<ICanHitDealerSpecification>().Use<CanHitDealer>();
            }
        }

    }
}
```

Now we need to update the query side of the CQRS architecture. Go ahead and add a new can_double_down property to the PlayerHandView.

```
namespace KojackGames.Blackjack.Domain.GamePlay.DomainViews.InPlayView
{
    public class PlayersHandView : HandView
```

```
    {
        public bool turn_ended { get; set; }
        public decimal wager { get; set; }
        public bool can_double_down { get; set; }
    }
}
```

We will also need to update the markup so that NHibernate can rehydrate it for us.

```xml
<?xml version="1.0" encoding="utf-8" ?>
<hibernate-mapping xmlns="urn:nhibernate-mapping-2.2"
    namespace="KojackGames.Blackjack.Domain.GamePlay.DomainViews.InPlayView"
        assembly="KojackGames.Blackjack.Domain">

  <class name="HandView" table="Hands" mutable="false" lazy="false">

    ...

    <subclass name="PlayersHandView" discriminator-value="Player"
            lazy="false">
        <property name="wager" column="bet"/>
        <property name="turn_ended" column="turn_ended"/>
        <property name="can_double_down" column="can_double_down"/>
    </subclass>

    <subclass name="DealersHandView" discriminator-value="Dealer"
            lazy="false">
    </subclass>

  </class>
</hibernate-mapping>
```

Finally, we need to update view to show a Double button if the hand.

```aspx
<%@ Page Language="C#"
Inherits="System.Web.Mvc.ViewPage<KojackGames.Blackjack.Domain.GamePlay.DomainViews.InPlayView
.BlackJackTableView>" %>
    ...

<body>
    ....
      <%
          if (!hand.turn_ended)
          {
              using (Html.BeginForm("Index", "Stick"))
              { %><input id="btnStick" type="submit" value="Stick" /> <% }

              using (Html.BeginForm("HitActiveHand", "Hit"))
              {%> <input id="btnHit" type="submit" value="Hit" /> <% }

              if (hand.can_double_down)
              {%> <input id="btnDouble" type="submit" value="Double" /> <% }
          }
```

```
    }%>
    </p>

    ...

</body>
</html>
```

Sarah: *Right. Now let's run the acceptance tests, core unit tests to see if all is good.*

Joe: *Bingo! All pass.*

Figure 7-15 shows the passing of the Double Stake user story acceptance tests.

*Figure 7-15. The passing double acceptance test*

# Day 6

## Daily Stand-Up

Tim: *Good morning, team. Who wants to go first?*

Joe: *I will. I worked with Sarah yesterday on the Game Play: Double Stake user story. Today, I plan on working with Tyler on the Game Play: Insurance user story. And I don't have any blocks.*

Sarah: *Let's see. Yesterday I started looking into the Saving Game State user story. This user story is looking to be a bit more complex than we originally estimated, but I'm going to work on that today and also answer any questions Joe or Tyler may have. The complexity of this user story and the fact that we have been short-handed the last couple of days makes me worry that we will not get this user story done in time.*

Tim: *Is there something that Joe or Tyler can help you with to help you get it done sooner?*

Sarah: *No. I'm still figuring out what pieces need implementing from a development perspective. Once we have that, then either Tyler or Joe can help, but right now, in my opinion, I'd rather have Tyler and Joe pairing together to get the Insurance user story done.*

Tim: *Okay, we'll keep an eye on the Saving Game State user story. The worst-case scenario is that we don't get it done and we'll have to tell the customer, but continue working on it because we know it's a priority and will add value. Tyler?*

Tyler: *I have been out of the office randomly the last few days. I am still not feeling 100 percent, but I feel like every day is better. Like Joe said, we finished up the Double Stake user story yesterday and I'll be pairing with him, to work on the Insurance user story today.*

Tim: *Well, that is all for now. Everyone have a great day!*

## User Story: Game Play Insurance

Tyler: *Joe, I am ready to start on the Insurance user story whenever you are.*

Joe: *I'll be right over. I'll go ahead and move the Insurance user story card to the In Progress swim lane.*

Figure 7-16 shows the current task board.

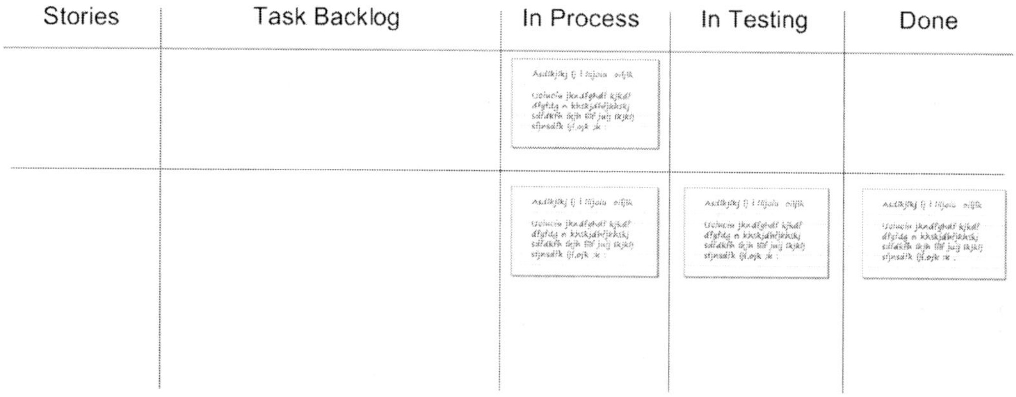

| Stories | Task Backlog | In Process | In Testing | Done |
|---------|--------------|------------|------------|------|
|         |              | *[card]*   |            |      |
|         |              | *[card]*   | *[card]*   | *[card]* |

*Figure 7-16. Updated task board*

Tyler: *Let's first review the Game Play: Insurance user story and acceptance criteria.* [(See Figure 7-17)].

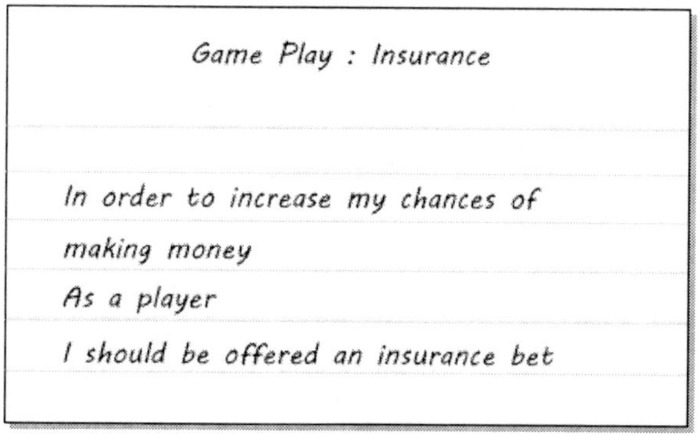

Game Play : Insurance

In order to increase my chances of
making money
As a player
I should be offered an insurance bet

*Figure 7-17. Game Play: Insurance*

Tyler flips the card over and reviews the acceptance criteria, as shown in Figure 7-18.

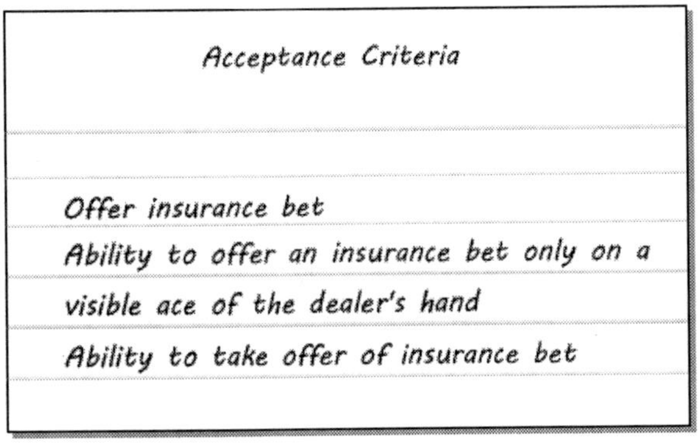

**Figure 7-18.** *Acceptance criteria*

Joe: *How about we start developing the ability to offer an insurance bet? I'll get into the code and begin making the changes.*

Tyler: *Hang on a second, Joe. We begin with writing out specs and different scenarios with SpecFlow. We develop from the outside in. Rather than the traditional way of developing from the database out, we create scenarios that a business user can understand and we develop from those scenarios. The first thing we want to do is to add this feature to our project.*

## Adding the SpecFlow Feature

We will begin as usual. Add a new feature file to the `Features` folder called `009-Insurance.feature` and update it with the following feature definition:

```
Feature: Insurance
        In order to increases my chances of making money
        As a player
        I should be offered an insurance bet
```

The thing about this feature is that there are numerous scenarios that we will need to test for. Based on the acceptance criteria, we need to think of different ways that the Insurance feature can be offered and used. Since we have good acceptance criteria, we can translate those into our different testing scenarios.

Joe: *How do we translate the acceptance criteria into a usable scenario?*

Tyler: *Let's look at the first acceptance criterion. We need to offer an insurance bet.*

Tyler explains that to offer an insurance bet, the following needs to happen:

- Start a new game
- Check the deck for specific cards

- Click the deal button, which should give the player an option for insurance

Joe: *Okay, that makes a bit more sense as we are laying out the steps we need to do to develop the functionality, but shouldn't we need to log in or something?*

Tyler: *As of right now, the system doesn't have that functionality. We only need to develop what is associated with the acceptance criteria and nothing more. We don't want to get into a scope creep situation, so we stick to what the business wants. That may be a user story for later, but for now we're focusing on Insurance. So let's walk through how we turn these steps into a scenario we can run.*

## Adding Scenarios

Let's start with the first scenario on the list, offering an insurance bet. Update the feature file with the scenario shown in Figure 7-19.

```
Scenario: Offer insurance bet
Given I have started a new game and bet "10"
And the deck contains the following cards:
    | Suit     | Value |
    | Diamonds | Eight |
    | Hearts   | Ace   |
    | Hearts   | Two   |
    | Hearts   | Three |
And I have navigated to the game play screen to play a hand
When I click on the deal button
Then I should be given the option for insurance
```

*Figure 7-19. Offer insurance bet scenario*

As per the previous user stories, most if not all of the "Given" and "When" steps for this scenario are already implemented from previous user stories. We only need to concern ourselves with the "Then" in this scenario. Go to the `GameDisplaySteps.cs` file and add a method called `ThenIShouldBeGivenTheOptionForInsurance`, as with the following code snippet:

```
[Then(@"I should be given the option for insurance")]
public void ThenIShouldBeGivenTheOptionForInsurance()
{
    Assert.That(GameDisplayPage.has_insurance_button, Is.True);
}
```

With this method in place, you can continue trying to get this test to pass by adding functionality to the `GameDisplayPage` class.

The next scenario should deal with the next item in the acceptance, the ability to offer an insurance bet—but only on a visible ace. Most of this was implemented in the previous scenario; we will add just one bit of functionality. The scenario will look like Figure 7-20.

```
Scenario: Offer insurance bet only on visible ace
Given I have started a new game and bet "10"
And the deck contains the following cards:
    | Suit      | Value     |
    | Diamonds  | Eight     |
    | Hearts    | Two       |
    | Hearts    | Three     |
    | Hearts    | Ace       |
And I have navigated to the game play screen to play a hand
When I click on the deal button
Then I should not be given the option for insurance
```

*Figure 7-20. Offer insurance bet, scenario 2*

As with the previous scenario, the "Then" piece is the only one we need to implement. Back in the GameDisplaySteps.cs file, you'll need to update it with the following:

```
[Then(@"I should not be given the option for insurance")]
public void ThenIShouldNotBeGivenTheOptionForInsurance()
{
    Assert.That(GameDisplayPage.does_not_have_insurance_button, Is.True);
}
```

With the test scenario in place, you can add functionality to the GameDisplayPage class.

Tyler: *Since we've done two different scenarios, is this starting to make sense?*

Joe: *I'm confused as to why we use a certain card state and it still seems to me that this is a lot of overhead to implement a feature, although I can see how the text in the scenarios would be helpful to a business user or someone who isn't a developer.*

Tyler: *In order to test, we need to have an expected input with an expected output. We can't leave it to chance, so we set up the deck with a certain configuration to get a desired outcome. You want to take a look at the next scenario, taking the offer of insurance?*

Joe: *Sure. Seems like the steps would be similar to the others, but we need to build into the test, "When I click 'take insurance,'" then something should happen. Is that right?*

Tyler: *You're on the right track.*

The scenario should look like Figure 7-21.

```
Scenario: Take offer of insurance
Given I have started a new game and bet "10"
And I have "100" dollars in my pot
And the deck contains the following cards:
    | Suit      | Value     |
    | Diamonds  | Eight     |
    | Hearts    | Ace       |
    | Hearts    | Two       |
    | Hearts    | Three     |
And I have navigated to the game play screen to play a hand
When I click on the deal button
Then I should be given the option for insurance
When I click on take insurance
Then my pot should show "$95.00" dollars
```

*Figure 7-21. Insurance taken scenario*

The only thing we need to add is another "Then" to specify the result. Since we've implemented the rest of the scenario, we just need to focus on the following code:

```
When I click on take insurance
```

The following code will go in the GamePlaySteps.cs file, as it is a step in the game:

```
[When(@"I click on take insurance")]
public void WhenIClickOnTakeInsurance()
{
    GameDisplayPage.take_insurance();
}
```

With the test scenario in place, you can add functionality to the GameDisplayPage class.

Joe: *These scenarios are good, but what about when the dealer does not get blackjack and the player loses?*

Tyler: *Good point. That scenario wasn't specifically laid out in the acceptance criteria, but we do need to account for it.* [(See Figure 7-22.)]

```
Scenario: Take offer of insurance with dealer not getting blackjack and player losing
Given I have started a new game and bet "10"
And I have "100" dollars in my pot
And the deck contains the following cards:
    | Suit     | Value   |
    | Diamonds | Eight   |
    | Hearts   | Ace     |
    | Hearts   | Two     |
    | Hearts   | Two     |
    | Hearts   | Seven   |
And I have navigated to the game play screen to play a hand
When I click on the deal button
When I click on take insurance
Then my pot should show "$95.00" dollars
When I stand
Then my pot should show "$95.00" dollars
```

*Figure 7-22. Insurance taken, no dealer blackjack scenario*

Tyler: *I can't think of any other scenario. Can you think of any other scenario, Joe?*

Joe: *Well, we just wrote a scenario for the dealer not getting blackjack, but what about if the dealer does get blackjack? I think we need to test for that scenario.*

Tyler: *True, didn't think of that one. That will be written very similar to the last one but with a couple tweaks.* [(See Figure 7-23)].

```
Scenario: Take offer of insurance with dealer getting blackjack and player losing
Given I have started a new game and bet "10"
And I have "100" dollars in my pot
And the deck contains the following cards:
    | Suit     | Value   |
    | Diamonds | Eight   |
    | Hearts   | Ace     |
    | Hearts   | Two     |
    | Hearts   | Jack    |
And I have navigated to the game play screen to play a hand
When I click on the deal button
When I click on take insurance
Then my pot should show "$95.00" dollars
When I stand
Then my pot should show "$110.00" dollars
```

*Figure 7-23. Insurance taken, dealer blackjack scenario*

Joe: *That looks good. Besides that scenario, I can't think of any other scenarios. I think we have it covered.*

Tyler: *Yes, I'd agree. Let's test-drive and implement these, and we should be done with this feature.*

Joe: *Great. Let's do it.*
Download the latest code from www.apress.com to see all the implementation details.

# Day 10

As with all sprints, we continue to do the product demo and the retrospective to verify that we are on the right track with the customer and to improve customer confidence.

## Product Demo

Once again, it's time for the product demo, the show-and-tell for the customer that demonstrates the features implemented throughout this past sprint. We do this after each sprint to maintain transparency and accountability with the customer and to increase team moral because they should continue to be proud of the work they've accomplished.

Since Joe joined the team during this sprint, he'll get his first exposure to a product demo. Tyler volunteered to drive this demo.

Tyler: *As we wrap up another sprint, we want to take this opportunity to demo the new features that we added to the system. Let's recap the features that the team took on during this sprint. They were Game Play: Dealer Rules, Game Play: Double Stake, Game Play: Insurance, and Saving Game State. The team was able to finish up the first three stories, but as Sarah mentioned in stand-up, the Saving Game State seemed to be more complex than we originally thought. I think we grossly underestimated it. I also think the team was overly optimistic about what we could accomplish this sprint. Tim mentioned that bringing on and mentoring another developer would decrease our velocity, but I don't think the team realized how dramatically it would reduce our velocity. This is not a reflection of Joe, it's a reflection of the team and our zealousness for velocity. Also, I was out a couple more days than planned due to illness. The other potential jurors must have had some bad germs! But, it will be up to Simon and Bill to determine if we need to continue working on this during the next sprint. Again, we did complete the Dealer Rules, the Double Stake, and the Insurance user stories.*

Simon: *You said Sarah mentioned that the one user story was more complex than originally thought. Why was it more complex than expected?*

Sarah: *Originally, I thought that it was little effort, but after digging into the code and learning NHibernate—which is a good tool but there is a learning curve to deal with—it was taking more time than I had thought. I think if we had to do it over again, we should have done a research spike so we could learn and become familiar with NHibernate before committing to this story. It is true that with Tyler being out, I also had less time to focus on this user story.*

Simon: *Research spike? What's that?*

Tim: *A spike is where we put in a time block on research and put it into the sprint planning session. The goal is, like Sarah said, to become familiar with a new tool or process. The goal of the time block is to come away with enough information to better estimate a user story that uses a new tool or process.*

Simon: *Okay, well, if it's not done, it's not done, but it is still a priority. Can we continue it during the next sprint?*

Tim: *Sure, even though Sarah didn't get the user story done, I'm sure she came away with enough information to come up with a better estimate during the next sprint. Would you say that's correct Sarah?*

Sarah: *Yes, unfortunately the time spent during this sprint was more or less learning the tool. I'm much more familiar with the tool now and I believe we can get it done during the next sprint.*

Simon: *Okay. Tyler mentioned the team did finish some stories this sprint. I'm anxious to see them!*

Tyler: *Let's start with the Dealer Rules user story.*

Tyler navigates to the application and demos the Dealer Rules user story. He plays a couple games and is able to show how the system hits on a score below 17 and stands on a score above 17.

Simon: *That looks pretty straightforward. Seventeen is the magic number, so this will come in very useful.*

Tyler: *Let's move onto the next user story, the Double Stake.*

Again, Tyler navigates to the application and demos the Double Stake user story. While he needs to play a few games to get the right configuration, he is able to demo the Double Stake feature and explain how it works.

Simon: *When you guys test this, you don't rely on chance to test it, do you? Seems like it would take a while to test and get the result you want.*

Tyler: *Luckily, no! We have a testing strategy where we can pre-determine and set up the cards in a certain way so that we can target specific test scenarios. When we demo it to you, we obviously want to demo it from the perspective of the user. That's why there isn't a way to pre-determine the cards dealt.*

Simon: *Oh, okay! Whew, good! This looks good and is what we had agreed to.*

Tyler: *We used this same testing framework for the next user story we'd like to demo, the Insurance user story.*

Tyler loads up the application and runs through a few games to demo the Insurance feature and how the Insurance feature works.

Simon: *What about when the player gets blackjack and the dealer loses? I didn't see that.*

Tyler: *We did account for that, but we may have to work through a few random games to get to that point. We can either keep playing by chance, or I can show you the test we wrote to account for that scenario, or you can take our word for it.*

Simon: *You guys have been doing good work. I'll take your word for it.*

Tyler: *Okay, but if you ever want to dig in and look at the tests we've written, you're more than welcome to.*

Simon: *Okay, thanks for the offer.*

Tyler: *That concludes the demo for this sprint. Thanks for your time, Simon.*

Simon: *Thank you guys, too. While we weren't able to get the Saving Game State feature completed, the other user stories look like they are complete. Hopefully we'll be able to see the Saving Game State feature at the end of the next sprint.*

Tim: *That's the plan. I think that wraps it up. Thanks for your time everyone.*

## Retrospective

As we want to continue to work on, refine, and make our team more efficient through process, it's time for a retrospective. As we've done this for the past few sprints, hopefully the team is prepared for the retrospective, ready to talk about key points on how to improve the next sprint.

Tim: *Welcome to another retrospective, team. In order to keep things fresh and feedback valuable, we are going to try a different game today called "The Soup." As before, we'll have three colors of Post-it notes: red for things that went poorly, blue for things that were confusing, and green for things that went well. The difference in this activity, however, is that instead of dividing the Post-its by category, we are going to split them up into three new categories.* [(*See Figure* 7-24.)]

Tim explains "The Soup" categories, as follows:

- *Team Control*: Post-it notes go in this circle if the item is under the direct control of the team.

- *Team Influences*: Represents items that the team can influence, but not take total ownership of. These include items in which your influence may affect others or items that you can make suggestions on, but you are unable to directly make the change.

- *The Soup*: These are suggestions items. Think of this as a company suggestion box in which the team can make a suggestion, but cannot directly influence the outcome.

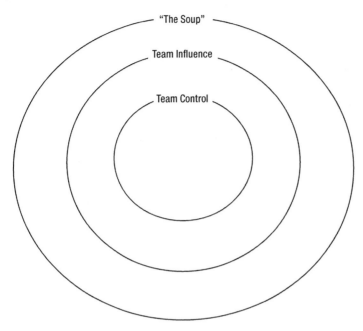

**Figure 7-24.** *The Soup*

There are many different ways to run a retrospective, but one thing to remain consistent on is that we always want fresh feedback. To get stale defeats a retrospective's usefulness, so one way to remain fresh is by doing different activities to gather the data needed to provide useful feedback and useful, value-added action items *Agile Retrospectives* by Diana Larsen and Esther Derby is, again, a great resource on ways to run a retrospective.

Tim: *Teams sometime get stuck blaming others, but may not realize it. This exercise will show us how much we can influence. This is a different way of organizing our thoughts, in order to get a different perspective on things. As with the last sprint, we have three minutes to write down our feedback on the appropriate Post-it notes. Does anyone have any questions?*

Sarah: *No, seems pretty straightforward. I like that we are doing something a bit different.*

Tyler: *None here.*

Tim: *Okay. Let's get started. The timer is set for three minutes. Go!*
    Tick, tock...

Tim: *Time's up. I'll come around and collect the Post-its and place them in the circles.*
    Tim places the Post-its notes in the appropriate circles. The result looks similar to Figure 7-25.

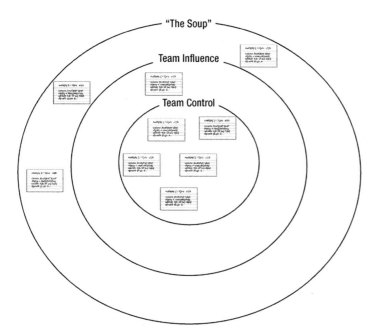

**Figure 7-25.** *Results of the retrospective*

Tim: *Let's talk about The Soup first.*

Tim reads the following three items in this category:

- A green Post-it said "adding a new member"

- A red Post-it said "adding a new member affected our velocity"

- Another green Post-it said "the company's commitment to the agile process"

Tim: *I'll time block us for ten minutes to discuss the topics in The Soup. Remember, the items in The Soup are ones that you can make suggestions on, but not directly contribute to. The primary topic for The Soup is adding a new team member. This topic fits in this category because the team didn't decide to bring in a new team member nor had influence in making the decision. So, who would like to start?*

Tyler: *I used the red Post-it for adding a new member. While I like Joe and enjoyed pairing with him, bringing on a new person to a fairly new team, I thought, affected our velocity poorly. No offense to Joe, but because he didn't know how this team or the agile process works, there was a lot of time spent mentoring him and bringing him up to speed, and it impacted the amount of work done at the end of the sprint.*

Sarah *I agree with Tyler that this affected our velocity, but I'm glad to have Joe on our team and it gives us a chance to mentor and bring him up to speed on this new development process. Our velocity initially decreased, but the hope is that once Joe is up to speed, he can contribute more and our velocity will go up. I wrote the green Post-it about the company's commitment to the agile process. For me, it's encouraging to see that there is support from upper-management to be committed to this process by investing another resource in it. It shows that the company is serious in its agile approach.*

Tim: *Yes, Sarah, that was the thinking. We knew that this sprint's velocity may have ended up a bit lower than normal by bringing in a new team member, however, we needed to bring on a new person for a couple reasons: one, we wanted to bring him on to expose Joe to the agile process and to the agile way of engineering software, but also, Joe is a seasoned developer, and we thought he could help us develop more features faster after a couple of sprints.*

Joe: *I must admit, developing the "agile" way in terms of behavior-driven design and writing code from the outside in, is a different mindset than I'm used to. It's a struggle to develop this way, but the concept of pairing and mentorship is helping me gain more experience and have the ability to catch on quicker. Hopefully, there's more of that in the next sprint.*

Tim: *Sounds like an action item! While the team didn't have any influence or control over adding a new team member, the team can now decide how it's going to react. How about we pair Joe with Tyler more in this next sprint since he spent a lot of time with Sarah last sprint. He'll get different perspectives.*

Sarah: *Sounds good to me. Tyler, Joe, let me know if I can help out.*

Joe: *Thanks for your help, Sarah. Will do.*

Tyler: *You bet I'll tap your shoulder if we need help.*

Tim: *What's next? Let's look at Team Influence, which are items that are under our influence. Looks like there is one blue Post-it that says the team didn't have any control of who the new team member was nor were asked about having a new team member.*

Tyler: *I thought one advantage of this agile process was that the team is supposed to be self-managing and have a "control your own destiny" philosophy. If that's the case, how come the team couldn't decide if and when a new team member joined us?*

Tim: *That's a good point Tyler. Agile teams are meant to be self-organizing. Unfortunately, some things still remain out of our control, so we work with what we have. Agile has built-in feedback loops in order to remain transparent. It was transparent to upper management that our velocity would decrease during this mentoring time. While we can and should remain transparent, this doesn't mean that we always get our way. An advantage of being transparent is to shine the proverbial flashing light to alert of roadblocks ahead, but it's not necessarily within our power to go around the roadblocks. Sometimes we will be slowed down by things outside of our control, but communication and expectations are important that when something unexpected happens, in our case adding a team member, a reasonable result is an initially lowered velocity. As ScrumMaster, I will push back the next time this happens and fight for the team to determine any decision about adding a new team member. While in the future we hope we can influence this, this is not always under our direct control.*

Tyler: *Okay. Sometimes it's frustrating when we are told that the team owns its own destiny and then something like this happens. Thanks for explaining and hopefully next time will be different.*

Tim: *The third and final category is Team Control. These are items that we directly have control of. Wow, a lot of red Post-its!*

Tim reads aloud the comments in the Team Control category:

- A red Post-it says "the team didn't complete what we committed to"

- A red Post-it says "the demo didn't go well since we didn't get everything done"

- A red Post-it says "Tyler unexpectedly being out for a couple more days"

- A red Post-it says "that poor estimation on the Saving Game State user story"

- A green Post-it says "mentoring Joe"

Sarah: *I put one of those red notes up. I was frustrated that we didn't correctly estimate the amount of effort for completing the Saving Game State user story. I personally didn't think it was much effort, but between learning the tool and incorporating that into the application, it was more complex than I thought.*

Joe: *I didn't have any experience in NHibernate to lend you some knowledge, or else I would have. How can we better estimate the next time something like this happens?*

Sarah: *The next time we have a situation like this, specifically when we need to incorporate some new tool or technology, we should do a spike. Tim, I was reading about agile and it mentioned something called a spike. If I remember correctly, a spike is used as a time block to research a new tool or technology before the team estimates and commits to a user story during a sprint. The purpose of the spike is to gain enough knowledge to more accurately estimate the user story using the new tool or technology. Is that right?*

Tim: *That's right Sarah. Next time, I agree that, even if we think it's small, we should take a spike to research that new tool before we commit to completing that user story for a particular sprint. That sounds like another action item: before we try to incorporate a new tool or technology, create a spike to perform research and plan it prior to the sprint. I'll assign that action item to me so I can be sure to ask the proper questions to determine if we should have a spike.*

Tyler: *That sounds good. I, for one, didn't really enjoy going into that demo having not completed all the work we committed to.*

Sarah: *Yes. That didn't make me proud to even show off what we did.*

Joe: *Since this is my first sprint, I'm guessing it isn't always like this?*

Tyler: *No, it isn't. Typically we get everything we committed to finished. We just had too much going on this sprint. Unfortunately, I was out a couple more days than expected, but people get sick and sometimes there's just nothing you can do about it.*

Sarah: *On the plus side, I enjoyed working with and mentoring Joe and bringing him up to speed.*

Joe: *Thanks Sarah, likewise. This agile thing is a mental shift from the way we used to do things, but I'm starting to see the value in it. The quicker feedback loops definitely cuts down on wasted development effort and we are much more confident that what we are working on is something of value and not just "busy work." I highly value that. I enjoy delivering value, not busy work. Re-prioritizing every sprint and the way that we develop code shows that we are delivering value and building a product that is meant to last.*

Tim: *Joe, sounds like you've learned a lot over the course of the sprint. Tyler, I think you're right. In retrospective, I think we just took on too much, but this is a lesson learned and can be applied in the future. And, then with Tyler being out, unfortunately unforeseen things happen. With this retrospective activity, we see a lot of red in the middle, which, on a positive note, is a good thing because we can directly affect the outcome—it's not out of our control. Let's work on things that we do have control over and make this team an even better team! Does anyone have anything else?*

Silence.

Tim: *Okay, I think that wraps it up today. Let's review our action items.*

Tim lists the action items, as follows:

- Use spikes for new tools/technology before estimating and committing to getting a user story done. This is assigned to Tim.

- Tyler and Joe will pair more in the next sprint to give Joe a better understanding of agile and to get a different perspective by pairing with another developer. This is assigned to Joe.

- Push back when upper management wants to add a new team member and let the team make this decision, rather than having it forced on them. This is assigned to Tim if and when it comes up again.

Tim: *Thanks for your time today, team! I believe with these lessons learned, the next sprint will be better!*

# Summary

This chapter, our third sprint, introduced the impact of adding a new team member. Joe was added to the team to provide an opportunity for the team to teach a developer the agile methodology and engineering practices. Adding a team member to a team mid-way through a project incurs risk because the team needs to take the time to teach the new team member. The payoff is worth the risk, however, because once a new team member like Joe has learned the agile framework and engineering practices of BDD, he can teach someone else. As the organization makes this investment in team members, the agile framework permeates throughout the organization.

This chapter implemented the following user stories of the Kojack blackjack game:

- Dealer Rules

- Double Stake

- Insurance

Although the team finished these three stories, this sprint demonstrated the result of over-committing by not completing the Saving Game State story. In the retrospective, the team admitted that they had taken on too much with training Joe, trying to conquer a new technology, and having Tyler out for a few expected and unexpected days. The team learned that adding a team member and coaching that team member with Scrum and XP practices was a bigger investment than originally thought.

Throughout the sprint, the team kept Tim, the ScrumMaster, and Simon, the product owner, apprised of the situation so there were no surprises at the end when the team didn't finish what it committed to; Tim and Simon could plan appropriately. Obviously, having the team not complete its commitments is not ideal, but it does happen at times. Whenever it is a possibility, communication is important.

In the next chapter, we'll continue developing new features to the Kojack game, and at the end of that sprint, talk about the first release of the software.

# CHAPTER 8

# Sprint 4: The Release

Over the last three sprints you have seen how a team goes about working on user stories for a customer. While most real-world projects have more than four sprints, we've limited this case study to four to make it manageable and readable. As we enter the last sprint, you will see how everything comes together to produce a finished product that is released to the customer.

## Sprint Planning Meeting

With the team gathered in the conference room, Simon and Tim enter with user stories for the team to work on, discuss, and size.

Tim: *Good morning, all. Welcome to the final sprint before our first release. In case you haven't heard, we are planning to take what we have completed for the blackjack application and release it to users at the end of this sprint.*

### The Theme of the Sprint

Tim: *The theme for Sprint 4 is going to be "The Release," since we are releasing all that we have completed at the end of this sprint. Once again I want to stress that a theme is a way to show a common purpose in our stories for this sprint. If you find yourself working on something that doesn't reflect this theme, let either me or Simon know and we will do what we can to address it.*

### Determining Availability and Capacity

Tim: *What about the availability for this sprint? Do any of you know that you are not going to be here for an extended period of this sprint?*

Sarah: *I should be here the whole time. However, I may have something coming up towards the end of the sprint. When I know more for sure, I will let you know.*

Joe: *I have no vacation coming up, so I will be here the entire sprint.*

Tyler: *I wouldn't miss the release for anything. I will be here with bells on for the entire sprint!*

Simon: *I will be here the entire sprint. Will someone remind me to bring headphones in tomorrow so I don't have to listen to the bells?*

Tim: *Let's hope Tyler doesn't actually do that. Anyway, it looks like we should be at full capacity for most of the sprint. It's good to have the team back after absences in the last sprint! If no one has questions, I would like to start Planning Poker.*

# Planning Poker

Simon: *All right, guys and gals, I have the list of user stories I would like us to look at for this sprint. As an update, we have one user story that did not get done in the last sprint. The user story is the Saving Game State. I spoke with the customer to tell him that the story was placed back into the product backlog and would need to be prioritized in relation to everything else currently in the backlog. The customer decided that the Saving Game State user story is the top priority of this sprint and placed it at the top of the product backlog. So, let's go ahead and discuss this user story again. [(See Figure 8-1.)] When we originally started talking about Saving Game State, we said that we wanted to give the user the ability to pick up where she left off in her game in the event she lost her internet connection for any reason. We originally sized this story as a 3 and the T-shirt size for it was an L. Just to clarify, the 3 and the L are not compatible with each other. These are estimates that were derived from two different planning meetings. The L is a high-level estimate, whereas the 3 is a lower-level estimate determined after we discussed more of the details.*

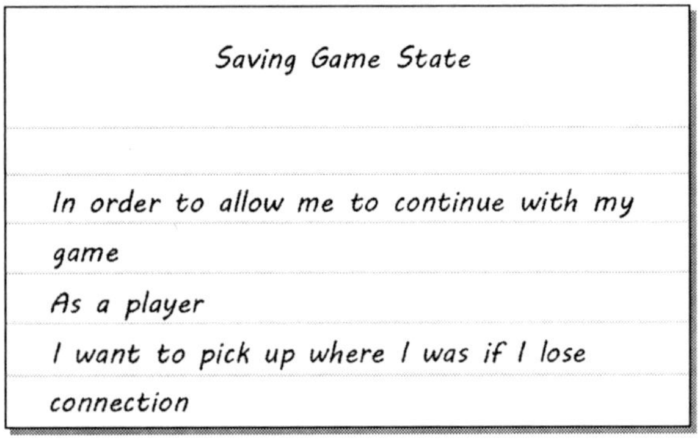

> Saving Game State
>
> In order to allow me to continue with my game
>
> As a player
>
> I want to pick up where I was if I lose connection

**Figure 8-1.** *User story: Saving Game State*

Simon: *Now where do we stand on this?*

Sarah: *Yeah, I wasn't able to get this done last sprint. Since I spent the time I had on this card learning NHibernate, I'm much more comfortable estimating this now. After looking into NHibernate and looking at how we'll need to integrate it into our current code base, I believe this user story is more complex than we originally anticipated. I think we underestimated it.*

Tim: *All right, everyone give me a number on the amount of work it will take to complete this card.*

Sarah: *I would give it a 5.*

Joe: *I looked over what Sarah was researching and I think it will be easier than that. I would vote 3.*

Tyler: *I don't think it is as easy as Joe says. I am more comfortable betting a 5 than a 3.*

Tim: *Joe, it looks like the majority of the team wants the user story to be a 5. Is this something you are comfortable with? If not, please explain to use why you feel strongly that it is a 3.*

Joe: *I am comfortable with calling it a 5.*

Tim: *All right then. We have decided the Saving Game State user story is a 5. Simon, what is next?*

Simon: *The next user story was added by the customer after our last product demo. This user story is Paying Out.* [(See Figure 8-2.)] *This user story gives the player the ability to actually receive his winnings at the end of a hand. This user story will take whatever amount of money the player has won in the hand and move it to his gambling pot, so the player can actually receive his winnings.*

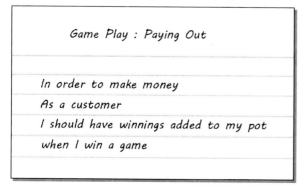

Game Play : Paying Out

In order to make money

As a customer

I should have winnings added to my pot

when I win a game

**Figure 8-2.** *User story: Paying Out*

Tyler: *This seems pretty straightforward.*

Sarah: *Yes, this one seems pretty simple. Most of the groundwork for this user story is done by culmination of finishing other user stories, so we just need to tie it all together with this one.*

Tim: *Let's vote.*

The Team: *Three.*

Tim: *A 3 it is then. Next.*

Simon: *Certainly. The next user story is Member Registration.* [(See Figure 8-3.)] *This user story gives the player the ability to register as a member on the site. The goal is to require users to enter membership registration information only once so they don't have the bother of repeatedly entering it every time they come to the web site to play. In the initial product backlog, this was an S.*

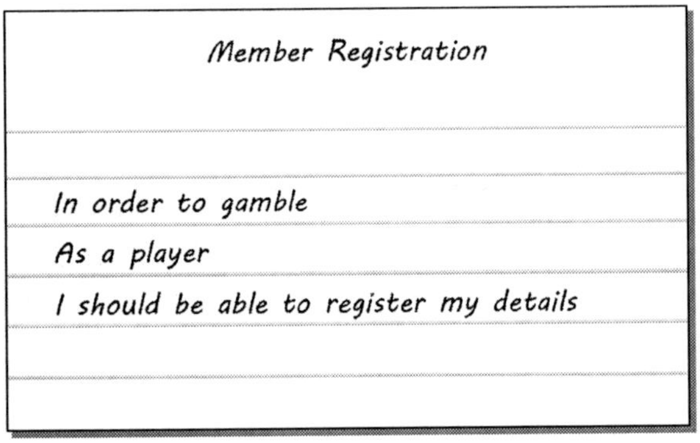

```
┌──────────────────────────────────────────────────────────┐
│ ┌──────────────────────────────────────────────────────┐ │
│ │                Member Registration                   │ │
│ │                                                      │ │
│ │  In order to gamble                                  │ │
│ │  As a player                                         │ │
│ │  I should be able to register my details             │ │
│ │                                                      │ │
│ │                                                      │ │
│ └──────────────────────────────────────────────────────┘ │
└──────────────────────────────────────────────────────────┘
```

**Figure 8-3.** *User story: Member Registration*

Tyler: *What are the acceptance criteria for this? How far down this rabbit hole to we need to go?*

Simon: *Well, users will need the ability to sign into the site with a username and password. Once on the site, they need the option to save information like name and address on the site so that they do not have to re-enter it the next time they sign in.*

Sarah: *So what you are saying is that you are asking for a simple way to store this information?*

Simon: *That is correct. For now, we just need to keep it simple.*

Tim: *If there are no additional questions, we will go ahead and vote.*

Joe: *Three.*

Tyler: *Three.*

Sarah: *Three.*

Tim: *A 3 it is. Next!*

Simon: *I have one more card, but before I present it, I want to know if the team is confident that they can take on another user story for this sprint?*

Tim: *Looking at the numbers, we currently have three user stories that we estimate for a total of 11 points. As a comparison, our last sprint's velocity was 11 points.*

Sarah: *Given the numbers and that the entire team expects to be available for most of the sprint, I feel pretty confident that we have some spare capacity in this sprint. I am comfortable taking on another one.*

Joe: *I'm getting more up to speed each and every day. I'm comfortable that we can take on an additional user story this sprint.*

Tyler: *I have some hesitations. I know that our history shows that we can take on the additional user story, but I am concerned that we might be taking on too much this sprint.*

Sarah: *Good point, Tyler. I guess I have a reservation or two, as well. I have an idea, what if we made it a stretch goal?*

Simon: *Stretch goal? I haven't heard of that. What is that?*

Sarah: *A stretch goal is like a fallback user story. We discuss it and size it, but we only work on it if we have finished the other user stories in the sprint. The team does not commit to getting this done, so the expectation from a customer perspective is that it could possibly get done, but the feature is secondary in this sprint. You can think of it as a prioritized backlog. The high-priority user stories are the ones that the team commits to, whereas the "stretch goal" user stories are ones we work on when the top priority ones are completed.*

Simon: *How do we account for this user story in the velocity and capacity for this sprint?*

Tim: *If we work on the user story, it will be counted towards our velocity of the sprint. Since we did not commit to the user story here, it will not be counted towards our capacity. If we finish everything this sprint, it will show that we completed more user stories that we committed to. Simon, is this all right with you?*

Simon: *Yes, I think so. I really need this user story this sprint, however, it is not more important than the other ones we have discussed so far. So, let's give this a try. This next user story is Cashing In. [(See Figure 8-4.)] The purpose of this user story is to give the user the ability to deposit money into the system so that he has chips for the game. The user can select a way to supply the money to the system, whether through PayPal or credit card. He will also have the ability to specify how much he wants to deposit. In the initial product backlog, this user story was rated an XL.*

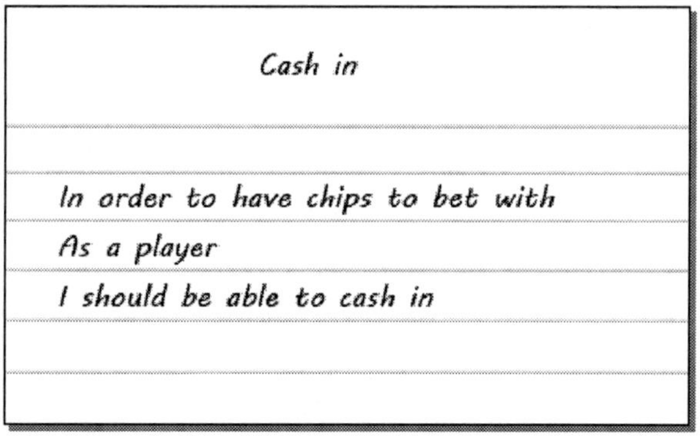

Cash in

In order to have chips to bet with

As a player

I should be able to cash in

*Figure 8-4. User Story: Cashing In*

Tyler: *This sounds like something that's going to be involved. Do we have expertise with using the PayPal system?*

Simon: *The customer has used PayPal on numerous other projects, so there are some references that we can tap into when working on that piece.*

Joe: *On a previous project, I worked with handling credit card transactions, so I have some technical knowledge. Plus, I have some contacts that I can hit up with any questions that we have.*

Tim: *Are we ready to size this? If so, please give me some numbers.*

Tyler: *I vote an 8.*

Sarah: *I vote a 3.*

Joe: *I vote a 3.*

Tim: *All right. Tyler, would you care to discuss why you voted an 8 on this user story?*

Tyler: *I voted an 8 due to the amount of work that is involved with handling credit card transactions. I feel there is a lot of work involved in working with encryption and things like that.*

Tim: *Okay. Sarah, please discuss why you voted a 3.*

Sarah: *I voted a 3 because we had Joe join our team since we originally put a T-shirt size on this user story. Joe has experience in this area, whereas beforehand, we didn't have someone with experience. I know some of this stuff is covered in other aspects of the system. Besides, we now seem to have the resources, whether it is Joe and/or the code samples, at our disposal if we run into any issues.*

Tim: *Okay, let's vote again.*

Joe: *Three.*

Sarah: *Three.*

Tyler: *Five.*

Tim: *Tyler, would you be satisfied with a 3?*

Tyler: *Yes, that's fine. While my experience would say that it's higher, I have confidence in Joe and Sarah since they have much more direct experience than I do.*

Tim: *Okay, 3 it is. Simon, am I safe in saying that this is all for this sprint?*

Simon: *Yes.*

Tim: *I guess that wraps up the planning meeting for this sprint. I will see you all at our stand-ups.*

## Sprint 4's Backlog

For Sprint 4, the team committed to user stories with a total of 11 points (as shown in Table 8-1), which is their capacity for this sprint. The team selected the Cashing In user story as a stretch goal for this sprint, with an initial size of 3 points. This means is that the team could have maximum velocity of 14 points for this sprint.

*Table 8-1. Sprint 4 Sized Backlog*

| User Story Name | Initial Size |
| --- | --- |
| Saving Game State | 5 |
| Paying Out | 3 |
| Member Registration | 3 |

# Day 1

As we enter Day 1 of the sprint, we begin with the daily stand-up. By now these meetings are routine so the team should be able to go through them quickly.

## Daily Stand-up

Tim: *All right, ladies and gents, it is time for the stand-up. Joe, would you care to do the honors?*

Joe: *No problem. Let's see, yesterday I attended the planning meeting for the sprint and helped sized the workload for this sprint. Today, I plan on pairing with Sarah and finishing up the Saving Game State user story.*

Tim: *Thank you, Joe. Tyler, you're up.*

Tyler: *Yesterday, I was in the planning meeting for the sprint. Today, I plan on working on the Member Registration user story.*

Simon: *Yesterday, like all of you, I attended the planning meeting for the sprint. Today I plan on working with the customer on getting everything ready for the release. I will also be available for any questions you all may have.*

Sarah: *I was in the planning meeting with everyone else. Today, I plan on pairing with Joe and we hope to finish the Saving Game State user story.*

Tim: *Great. Thanks all. If there is nothing else, then I say that is all for now.*

# Day 4

Mid-sprint, we will be developing the next user story and attending the stand-up. Again, if there are any issues or concerns, the team needs to bring it up in the stand-up.

## Daily Stand-up

Sarah: *Since Tim seems to be running late, Tyler, can you start us off?*

Tyler: *Sure. Let's see, I have been working on the Member Registration user story and I will have it completed and ready for acceptance testing today. After that, I plan on pairing with Sarah on the next user story. I have no blocks.*

Tim: *Sorry, that I'm late. I'm glad that you all started without me.*

Sarah: *No problem. I have been working with Joe on the Saving Game State user story. I think we have it about done. I will let Joe talk about the specifics. Today I plan on pairing with Tyler on the next user story. I have no blocks.*

Simon: *I have been working with the customer about the upcoming release and I will continue to do so throughout the sprint. I will also be available for questions or clarifications if the need arises. I have no blocks.*

Joe: *I was working with Sarah on the Saving Game State user story. It is about finished. I am writing a few more tests and refactoring the implementation. Today, I'm planning on finishing the refactoring and completing the Saving Game State user story.*

Tim: *Great! Talk to you all later.*

## Developing a Feature: Paying Out

Sarah: *Let's tackle the Paying Out feature. What do you say?*

Tyler: *Yes, good idea. Let's tackle it.*

Tyler selects the Paying Out user story card, shown in Figure 8-5, on the task board and moves it into the In Process swim lane.

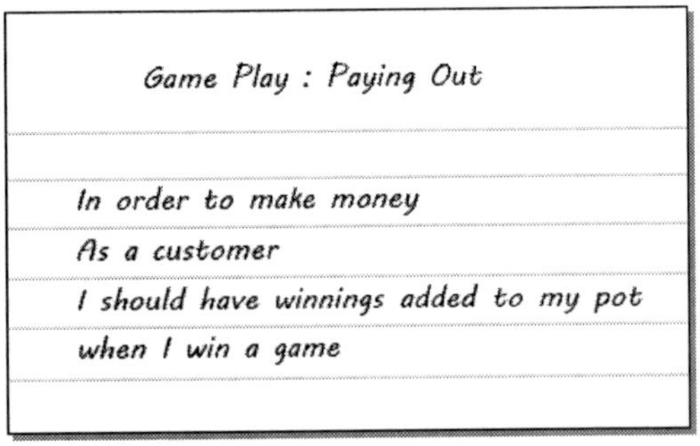

**Figure 8-5.** *User story: Paying Out*

Sarah: *Let's review the acceptance criteria.*

Tyler: *This one is simple. The only acceptance criteria is if the player wins a hand, then the winnings from the hand should be added to the player's pot. In other words, the player's pot should increase in amount equal to the amount of the winnings.*

Sarah: *That seems simple enough. Let's get started. We need to come up with scenarios that handle the different possibilities. Do you have any ideas?*

Tyler: I have a couple. First, we have a scenario for a player winning. [(See Figure 8-6.)]

```
Scenario: Player gets Blackjack and beats Dealer
Given I have started a new game and bet "10"
And I have "10" dollars in my pot
And the deck contains the following cards:
    | Suit       | Value   |
    | Diamonds   | Ace     |
    | Diamonds   | Eight   |
    | Clubs      | Ten     |
    | Hearts     | Two     |
When I click on the deal button
Then I should get Blackjack and win the game
And my pot should show "$35.00" dollars
```

*Figure 8-6. Player winning scenario*

Tyler: *Then, there is a scenario for a tie or push.* [(See Figure 8-7.)]

```
Scenario: Both player and dealer get blackjack so game ends in draw
Given I have started a new game and bet "5"
And I have "10" dollars in my pot
And the deck contains the following cards:
    | Suit      | Value   |
    | Hearts    | Ace     |
    | Spades    | Ten     |
    | Hearts    | Ten     |
    | Clubs     | Ace     |
And I have navigated to the game play screen to play a hand
When I click on the deal button
Then my pot should show "$15.00" dollars
```

*Figure 8-7. Player push scenario*

Tyler: *A scenario for losing without insurance.* [(See Figure 8-8.)]

```
Scenario: Player loses
Given I have started a new game and bet "5"
And I have "10" dollars in my pot
And the deck contains the following cards:
    | Suit       | Value     |
    | Diamonds   | Eight     |
    | Diamonds   | Ace       |
    | Hearts     | Two       |
    | Clubs      | Ten       |
And I have navigated to the game play screen to play a hand
When I click on the deal button
Then my pot should show "$10.00" dollars
```

*Figure 8-8. Player loses, no insurance scenario*

Tyler: *And a scenario for losing with insurance.* [(See Figure 8-9.)]

```
Scenario: Player loses but has taken insurance
Given I have started a new game and bet "5"
And I have "10" dollars in my pot
And the deck contains the following cards:
    | Suit       | Value     |
    | Diamonds   | Eight     |
    | Diamonds   | Ace       |
    | Hearts     | Ten       |
    | Clubs      | Ten       |
And I have navigated to the game play screen to play a hand
And I have "10" dollars in my pot
When I click on the deal button
When I click on take insurance
When I stick
Then my pot should show "$15.00" dollars
```

*Figure 8-9. Player loses, has insurance scenario*

Tyler: *And finally, a scenario for winning after doubling down.* [(See Figure 8-10.)]

```
Scenario: Double Down and win
Given I have started a new game and bet "10"
And I have "30" dollars in my pot
And the deck contains the following cards:
    | Suit     | Value   |
    | Diamonds | Eight   |
    | Hearts   | Ten     |
    | Clubs    | Two     |
    | Hearts   | Three   |
    | Hearts   | Two     |
    | Hearts   | Jack    |
    | Hearts   | King    |
And I have navigated to the game play screen to play a hand
When I click on the deal button
When I click on the double button
Then my pot should show "$70.00" dollars
```

*Figure 8-10. Player wins by double down scenario*

Sarah: *What about scenarios that cover the winning variants when the player has split?*

Tyler: *Ah yes, good point. We didn't take that into consideration when we wrote these because we hadn't started working on the Split feature. Let's get those acceptance criteria down before we start to work.*

Tyler adds all the variants to cover checking the pot amounts when winning, losing, and drawing with a split pair.

## Refactoring and Technical Debt

Sarah: *Great. I think we have all the bases covered.*

Tyler: *Well, all the bases that we can think of at the moment.*

Sarah: *Good point. Okay, let's move on with the first feature…*

Download the source code and you'll find a feature in the Features folder of the Acceptance.Tests project named 014-PayingOut.feature. You'll see the feature file matches the feature shown in Figure 8-11.

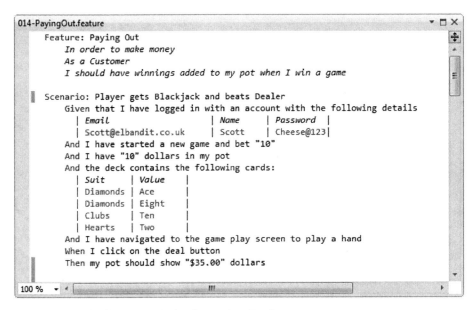

**Figure 8-11.** *The first scenario for the Paying Out feature*

Sarah: *We already have all the steps defined for this scenario, so we can go ahead and run the acceptance tests straight off the bat.*

Tyler: *Rather unsurprisingly, the acceptance tests fail. Why do we need to bother?*

Sarah: *Ah, young Padawan. What would have happened if they had passed? Remember, red, green, refactor. We need to start with a failing scenario so you know the state of the code base before you develop.*

Tyler: *Fair enough. Okay, then, I suppose we drop into the code and discover what objects are going to be responsible for paying out any winning chips to the player?*

Sarah: *You got it.*

This scenario deals with the scenario of a player getting blackjack from the deal, so we should take a look at the DealCardsIn class to see where the paying out behavior should fit in. The unit test was made to handle the context of a player achieving blackjack from the deal in, so let's add another assertion to check that some kind of chip allocator will be used in the event of a player achieving blackjack.

Sarah updates the specification as shown in the following code with the extra assertion highlighted in bold.

```
using Machine.Specifications;
using Rhino.Mocks;

namespace KojackGames.Blackjack.Core.Tests
                    .Domain_Specs.DealerAction_Specs.DealCardsIn
{
    [Subject(typeof(Domain.GamePlay.Model.Dealer.Actions.DealCardsIn),
```

```
                                                          "Dealer")]
    public class when_dealing_in_the_hands_and_one_achieves_blackjack :
                                            with_a_deal_in_cards_action
    {
        private Establish context = () =>
        {
            positions.Stub(x => x.player_has_blackjack()).Return(true);
        };

        Because of = () => SUT.perform_on(positions, card_shoe, player);

        It should_check_if_a_hand_has_blackjack =
            () => positions.AssertWasCalled(x => x.player_has_blackjack());

        It should_determine_the_winning_hands =
            () => playing_hands_end_game_status_decider
                    .AssertWasCalled(x =>
                        x.decide_end_game_status_for_hands_in(positions));

        It should_pay_out_any_winnings_to_the_player =
            () => chip_allocator.AssertWasCalled(
                    x => x.allocate_chips_to_winnings_hands_in(positions));
    }
}
```

Now we need to set up the dependency in the with_a_deal_in_cards_action base class. Take a look at the base class, which is displayed in the following listing.

...

```
namespace KojackGames.Blackjack.Core.Tests.Domain_Specs.DealerAction_Specs.DealCardsIn
{
    public abstract class with_a_deal_in_cards_action
    {
        protected static Domain.GamePlay.Model.Dealer.Actions.DealCardsIn
                                                                    SUT;
        protected static IPlayingHandsEndGameStatusDecider
                                    playing_hands_end_game_status_decider;
        protected static IHandStatusFactory hand_status_factory;

        protected static IPlayingPositions positions;
        protected static IPlayersHand players_hand;
        protected static IDealersHand dealers_hand;
        protected static List<IHand> hands;
        protected static IHand hand;
        protected static ICardShoe card_shoe;
        protected static ICanDoubleDown double_down_spec;
        protected static ICanSplit split_spec;
        protected static ICanTakeInsurance insurance_spec;
```

```
        public with_a_deal_in_cards_action()

        {
            double_down_spec = MockRepository.GenerateStub<ICanDoubleDown>();
            split_spec = MockRepository.GenerateStub<ICanSplit>();
            insurance_spec =
                        MockRepository.GenerateStub<ICanTakeInsurance>();

            card_shoe = MockRepository.GenerateStub<ICardShoe>();
            positions = MockRepository.GenerateStub<IPlayingPositions>();

            players_hand = MockRepository.GenerateStub<IPlayersHand>();
            positions.Stub(x => x.players_active_hand).Return(players_hand);
            dealers_hand = MockRepository.GenerateStub<IDealersHand>();
            positions.Stub(x => x.dealers_hand).Return(dealers_hand);

            hand = MockRepository.GenerateStub<IHand>();
            hands = new List<IHand>() { hand };
            positions.Stub(x => x.all_hands).Return(hands);

            hand_status_factory = MockRepository
                        .GenerateStub<IHandStatusFactory>();
            playing_hands_end_game_status_decider = MockRepository
                        .GenerateStub<IPlayingHandsEndGameStatusDecider>();

            SUT = new Domain.GamePlay.Model.Dealer
                    .Actions.DealCardsIn(hand_status_factory,
                        playing_hands_end_game_status_decider,
                                        double_down_spec,
                                            split_spec,
                                    insurance_spec);
        }
    }
}
```

There seems to be a lot of dependencies. Let's take a quick look at the DealCardsIn class before we start adding to it to see if we can't clear things up a little.

```
using KojackGames.Blackjack.Domain.GamePlay.Model.Dealer.Observations;
using KojackGames.Blackjack.Domain.GamePlay.Model.PlayingPosition;
using KojackGames.Blackjack.Domain.GamePlay.Model
                                    .PlayingPosition.Hands.Status;
using KojackGames.Blackjack.Domain.Membership.Model;

namespace KojackGames.Blackjack.Domain.GamePlay.Model.Dealer.Actions
{
    public class DealCardsIn : IDealerAction
    {
        private readonly IHandStatusFactory _hand_status_factory;
        private readonly IPlayingHandsEndGameStatusDecider
                            _playing_hands_end_game_status_decider;
        private readonly ICanDoubleDown _double_down_spec;
```

```
private readonly ICanSplit _split_spec;
private readonly ICanTakeInsurance _insurance_spec;

public DealCardsIn(IHandStatusFactory hand_status_factory,
                   IPlayingHandsEndGameStatusDecider
                       playing_hands_end_game_status_decider,
                   ICanDoubleDown double_down_spec,
                   ICanSplit split_spec,
                   ICanTakeInsurance insurance_spec)
{
    _hand_status_factory = hand_status_factory;
    _playing_hands_end_game_status_decider =
                   playing_hands_end_game_status_decider;
    _double_down_spec = double_down_spec;
    _split_spec = split_spec;
    _insurance_spec = insurance_spec;
}


private void deal_two_cards_to_each_hand_in(IPlayingPositions hands,
                                            ICardShoe card_shoe)
{
    int no_of_cards_to_deal = 2;

    while (no_of_cards_to_deal > 0)
    {
        hands.players_active_hand.add(card_shoe.take_card());
        hands.dealers_hand.add(card_shoe.take_card());

        no_of_cards_to_deal--;
    };
}

public void perform_on(IPlayingPositions playing_positions,
                       ICardShoe card_shoe, IPlayer player)
{

    raise_illegal_move_if_action_cannot_be_made_on(playing_positions);

    deal_two_cards_to_each_hand_in(playing_positions, card_shoe);

    update_the_status_of_each_hand_in(playing_positions);

    if (playing_positions.player_has_blackjack())
    {
        _playing_hands_end_game_status_decider
            .decide_end_game_status_for_hands_in(playing_positions);
    }
    else
    {
        check_if_player_can_double_down(playing_positions);
```

```
            check_if_player_can_split(playing_positions);

            check_if_player_can_take_insurance(playing_positions);
        }

        playing_positions.mark_cards_as_dealt();

        playing_positions.update_active_hand();
    }

    private void check_if_player_can_take_insurance(
                            IPlayingPositions playing_positions)
    {
        if (_insurance_spec.is_satisfied_by(
                            playing_positions.dealers_hand))
            playing_positions.players_active_hand
                            .mark_as_able_to_take_insurance();
    }

    public void raise_illegal_move_if_action_cannot_be_made_on(
                            IPlayingPositions playing_positions)
    {
        if (playing_positions.have_cards_been_dealt())
            throw new IllegalMoveException(
                    "Cannot stick hand as your turn has ended.");
    }

    private void check_if_player_can_split(
                            IPlayingPositions playing_positions)
    {
        if (_split_spec.is_satisfied_by(
                        playing_positions.players_active_hand))
            playing_positions.players_active_hand
                            .mark_as_able_to_split();
    }

    private void check_if_player_can_double_down(
                            IPlayingPositions playing_positions)
    {
        if (_double_down_spec.is_satisfied_by(
                        playing_positions.players_active_hand))
            playing_positions.players_active_hand
                            .mark_as_able_to_double_down();
    }

    protected void update_the_status_of_each_hand_in(
                            IPlayingPositions playing_positions)
    {
        foreach (var hand in playing_positions.all_hands)
            _hand_status_factory.set_status_for(hand);
    }
```

```
        }
    }
```

The `DealCardIn` class is breaking the Single Responsibility Principle and is doing far more than it ought.

Tyler: *Okay, so how do we sort out the responsibility explosion?*

Sarah: *Refactor, dear boy, refactor.*

When faced with a large refactoring, it is helpful to make a sketch of all of the objects in the class and their relationships to each other. Michael Feathers' *Working Effectively with Legacy Code* (Prentice Hall, 2004) is a good book to read more on this.

The three specification classes can be logically grouped together under options available to the player. The status update method can be moved onto the `HandStatusFactory` and we can also extract the code that actually deals cards to better align the level of abstraction in the class. It's fine to break the Single Responsibility Principle initially because we have tests wrapped around this piece of code. Since we have tests wrapped around it, we can safely refactor. If we refactor incorrectly, the tests that will fail as a result of our refactoring will tell us that something is wrong and we need to correct it. The tests serve as a safety net for refactoring. Also, Visual Studio 2010 has some neat built-in refactoring capabilities that we can utilize to ease the burden.

Tyler: *Okay, let's refactor the code before we continue with adding the new feature for allocating chips. I will comment out the new assertion for the time being.*

```
[Subject(typeof(Domain.GamePlay.Model.Dealer.Actions.DealCardsIn), "Dealer")]
public class when_dealing_in_the_hands_and_one_achieves_blackjack :
with_a_deal_in_cards_action
{
    private Establish context = () =>
    {
        positions.Stub(x => x.player_has_blackjack()).Return(true);
    };

    Because of = () => SUT.perform_on(positions, card_shoe, player);

    It should_check_if_a_hand_has_blackjack =
        () => positions.AssertWasCalled(x => x.player_has_blackjack());

    It should_determine_the_winning_hands =
        () => playing_hands_end_game_status_decider.AssertWasCalled(
                x => x.decide_end_game_status_for_hands_in(positions));

    //It should_pay_out_any_winnings_to_the_player =
    //    () => chip_allocator.AssertWasCalled(x =>
    //        x.allocate_chips_to_winnings_hands_in(positions));
}
```

Tyler: *Let's start to clean up this mess. We can perform an extract class refactor to start to move the options that are available to a player after the initial deal into a class of its own.*

Sarah: *Hand me the keyboard.*

Sarah creates the OptionsAvailableToPlayerAfterDealing class, as follows:

```
namespace KojackGames.Blackjack.Domain.GamePlay.Model.Dealer.Observations
{
    public class OptionsAvailableToPlayerAfterDealing
    {
        public void set_for_hands_in(IPlayingPositions playing_positions)
        {

        }
    }
}
```

Now we need to create an instance of the OptionsAvailableToPlayerAfterDealing class within the DealCardsIn class and call the method to set the options for the player's hands.

```
namespace KojackGames.Blackjack.Domain.GamePlay.Model.Dealer.Actions
{
    public class DealCardsIn : IDealerAction
    {
        ...
        private readonly OptionsAvailableToPlayerAfterDealing
                            _options_available_to_player_after_dealing;

        public DealCardsIn(IHandStatusFactory hand_status_factory,
                        IPlayingHandsEndGameStatusDecider
                            playing_hands_end_game_status_decider,
                        ICanDoubleDown double_down_spec,
                        ICanSplit split_spec,
                        ICanTakeInsurance insurance_spec)
        {
           ...

            _options_available_to_player_after_dealing = new
                            OptionsAvailableToPlayerAfterDealing();

        }

         ...

        public void perform_on(IPlayingPositions playing_positions,
                        ICardShoe card_shoe, IPlayer player)
        {

           raise_illegal_move_if_action_cannot_be_made_on(playing_positions);

           deal_two_cards_to_each_hand_in(playing_positions, card_shoe);

           update_the_status_of_each_hand_in(playing_positions);

           if (playing_positions.player_has_blackjack())
```

```
        {
            _playing_hands_end_game_status_decider
                    .decide_end_game_status_for_hands_in(playing_positions);
        }
        else
        {
            _options_available_to_player_after_dealing
                            .set_for_hands_in(playing_positions);

            check_if_player_can_double_down(playing_positions);

            check_if_player_can_split(playing_positions);

            check_if_player_can_take_insurance(playing_positions);
        }

        playing_positions.mark_cards_as_dealt();

        playing_positions.update_active_hand();
    }

    ...

    }
}
```

Sarah: *Let's just run the tests to see if we have broken anything... Nope, good stuff.*

Now we can perform a move method refactor to move the double down check from the DealCardsIn class to the OptionsAvailableToPlayerAfterDealing class.

```
public class OptionsAvailableToPlayerAfterDealing
{
    private readonly ICanDoubleDown _double_down_spec;

    public OptionsAvailableToPlayerAfterDealing(
                                ICanDoubleDown double_down_spec)
    {
        _double_down_spec = double_down_spec;
    }

    public void set_for_hands_in(IPlayingPositions playing_positions)
    {
        if (_double_down_spec.is_satisfied_by(
                            playing_positions.players_active_hand))
            playing_positions.players_active_hand
                            .mark_as_able_to_double_down();
    }
}
```

Now remove the call to the check_if_player_can_double_down method from within the DealCardsIn.

Sarah: *Okay, let's run the tests again before we make any more modifications to ensure we haven't changed any behavior.*

Tyler: *Ah, we broke a test.*

The when_a_players_hand_meets_the_criteria_to_double_after_dealing test broke because it assumes that a call will be made to the CanDoubleDown specification class from within the DealCardsIn class. Tyler points out that they have changed the behavior, so now it occurs within the OptionsAvailableToPlayerAfterDealing class.

Sarah: *Okay, let's update that class so that the test is performing against the new class.*

```
using KojackGames.Blackjack.Domain.GamePlay.Model.Dealer.Observations;
using KojackGames.Blackjack.Domain.GamePlay.Model.PlayingPosition;
using KojackGames.Blackjack.Domain.GamePlay.Model.PlayingPosition.Hands.Dealer;
using KojackGames.Blackjack.Domain.GamePlay.Model.PlayingPosition.Hands.Player;
using Machine.Specifications;
using Rhino.Mocks;

namespace KojackGames.Blackjack.Core.Tests.Domain_Specs.DealerAction_Specs
                                                        .DealCardsIn
{
    [Subject(typeof(OptionsAvailableToPlayerAfterDealing))]
    public class when_a_players_hand_meets_the_criteria_to_double_after_dealing :
                                    with_OptionsAvailableToPlayerAfterDealing
    {
        private Establish context = () =>
        {
            playing_positions = MockRepository.GenerateStub<IPlayingPositions>();
            playing_hand = MockRepository.GenerateStub<IPlayersHand>();
            playing_positions.Stub(
                    x => x.players_active_hand).Return(playing_hand);

            double_down_spec.Stub(
                    x => x.is_satisfied_by(playing_hand)).Return(true);
        };

        private Because of = () => SUT.set_for_hands_in(playing_positions);

        It should_check_the_players_hand_for_a_double = () =>
        {
            double_down_spec.AssertWasCalled(
                        x => x.is_satisfied_by(playing_hand));
        };

        It should_mark_the_players_hand_as_being_able_to_double_down = () =>
        {
            playing_hand.AssertWasCalled(x => x.mark_as_able_to_double_down());
        };

        private static IPlayingPositions playing_positions;
        private static IPlayersHand playing_hand;
```

```
    }
}
```

The base class will set up the `OptionsAvailableToPlayerAfterDealing` class with all of its dependencies, as we will be adding the insurance and split specifications to this later.

```
using KojackGames.Blackjack.Domain.GamePlay.Model.Dealer.Observations;
using Rhino.Mocks;

namespace KojackGames.Blackjack.Core.Tests.Domain_Specs.DealerAction_Specs
                                                           .DealCardsIn
{
    public abstract class with_OptionsAvailableToPlayerAfterDealing
    {
        protected static ICanDoubleDown double_down_spec;
        protected static ICanSplit split_spec;
        protected static ICanTakeInsurance insurance_spec;
        protected static OptionsAvailableToPlayerAfterDealing SUT;

        public with_OptionsAvailableToPlayerAfterDealing()
        {
            double_down_spec = MockRepository.GenerateStub<ICanDoubleDown>();

            SUT = new OptionsAvailableToPlayerAfterDealing(double_down_spec);
        }
    }
}
```

Sarah: *Now that test was updated, we should be able to run all of our unit tests to prove that we have not changed the behavior of the system.*

Tyler: *Brilliant. All tests are passing. Now let's perform the move methods refactors and updates to the existing test for the split and insurance checks.*

Tyler and Sarah repeat the steps made for moving the `CanDoubleDown` specification, and make the `CanSplit` and `CanTakeInsurance` checks, resulting in the update to the `OptionsAvailableToPlayerAfterDealing` class, as shown in the following listing:

```
public class OptionsAvailableToPlayerAfterDealing
{
    private readonly ICanDoubleDown _double_down_spec;
    private readonly ICanSplit _split_spec;
    private readonly ICanTakeInsurance _insurance_spec;

    public OptionsAvailableToPlayerAfterDealing(
                        ICanDoubleDown double_down_spec,
                        ICanSplit split_spec,
                        ICanTakeInsurance insurance_spec)
    {
        _double_down_spec = double_down_spec;
        _insurance_spec = insurance_spec;
        _split_spec = split_spec;
```

```
    }

    public void set_for_hands_in(IPlayingPositions playing_positions)
    {
        if (_double_down_spec.is_satisfied_by(
                            playing_positions.players_active_hand))
            playing_positions.players_active_hand
                            .mark_as_able_to_double_down();

        if (_split_spec.is_satisfied_by(
                            playing_positions.players_active_hand))
            playing_positions.players_active_hand.mark_as_able_to_split();

        if (_insurance_spec.is_satisfied_by(playing_positions.dealers_hand))
            playing_positions.players_active_hand
                            .mark_as_able_to_take_insurance();
    }
}
```

The DealCardsIn class is also updated to remove all calls to the internal method in favor of delegating to the OptionsAvailableToPlayerAfterDealing class, as shown in the following listing:

```
public class DealCardsIn : IDealerAction
{
    private readonly IHandStatusFactory _hand_status_factory;
    private readonly IPlayingHandsEndGameStatusDecider
                        _playing_hands_end_game_status_decider;
    private readonly OptionsAvailableToPlayerAfterDealing
                        _options_available_to_player_after_dealing;

    public DealCardsIn(IHandStatusFactory hand_status_factory,
                    IPlayingHandsEndGameStatusDecider
                                playing_hands_end_game_status_decider,
                    ICanDoubleDown double_down_spec,
                    ICanSplit split_spec,
                    ICanTakeInsurance insurance_spec)
    {
        _hand_status_factory = hand_status_factory;
        _playing_hands_end_game_status_decider =
                    playing_hands_end_game_status_decider;
        _options_available_to_player_after_dealing =
                    new OptionsAvailableToPlayerAfterDealing(double_down_spec,
                                                            split_spec,
                                                            insurance_spec);

    }

    private void deal_two_cards_to_each_hand_in(
                            IPlayingPositions hands, ICardShoe card_shoe)
    {
        int no_of_cards_to_deal = 2;
```

```
        while (no_of_cards_to_deal > 0)
        {
            hands.players_active_hand.add(card_shoe.take_card());
            hands.dealers_hand.add(card_shoe.take_card());

            no_of_cards_to_deal--;
        };
    }

    public void perform_on(IPlayingPositions playing_positions,
                           ICardShoe card_shoe, IPlayer player)
    {
        raise_illegal_move_if_action_cannot_be_made_on(playing_positions);

        deal_two_cards_to_each_hand_in(playing_positions, card_shoe);

        update_the_status_of_each_hand_in(playing_positions);

        if (playing_positions.player_has_blackjack())
        {
            _playing_hands_end_game_status_decider
                    .decide_end_game_status_for_hands_in(playing_positions);
        }
        else
            _options_available_to_player_after_dealing
                    .set_for_hands_in(playing_positions);

        playing_positions.mark_cards_as_dealt();

        playing_positions.update_active_hand();
    }

    public void raise_illegal_move_if_action_cannot_be_made_on(
                                    IPlayingPositions playing_positions)
    {
        if (playing_positions.have_cards_been_dealt())
            throw new IllegalMoveException(
                        "Cannot stick hand as your turn has ended.");
    }

    protected void update_the_status_of_each_hand_in(
                                    IPlayingPositions playing_positions)
    {
        foreach (var hand in playing_positions.all_hands)
            _hand_status_factory.set_status_for(hand);
    }
}
```

We have removed one of the four responsibilities. Now let's take a look at the update_the_status_of_each_hand_in method. This really belongs on the HandStatusFactory class. Let's perform a move method refactor to replace it.

```
namespace KojackGames.Blackjack.Domain.GamePlay.Model.PlayingPosition
                                                      .Hands.Status
{
    public class HandStatusFactory : IHandStatusFactory
    {
        private readonly IHasBlackjackSpecification _has_blackjack_spec;
        private readonly IHasBustedSpecification _has_bust_spec;
        private readonly IHasSoftBlackJackSpecification
                                        _has_soft_blackjack_spec;

        public HandStatusFactory(
                        IHasBlackjackSpecification has_blackjack_spec,
                        IHasBustedSpecification has_bust_spec,
                        IHasSoftBlackJackSpecification
                                        has_soft_blackjack_spec)
        {
            _has_blackjack_spec = has_blackjack_spec;
            _has_soft_blackjack_spec = has_soft_blackjack_spec;
            _has_bust_spec = has_bust_spec;
        }

        public void set_status_for(IHand hand)
        {
            if (_has_blackjack_spec.is_satisfied_by(hand))
                hand.change_state_to(HandStatus.blackjack);

            if (_has_bust_spec.is_satisfied_by(hand))
                hand.change_state_to(HandStatus.bust);

            if (_has_soft_blackjack_spec.is_satisfied_by(hand))
                hand.change_state_to(HandStatus.soft_blackjack);
        }

        public void update_the_status_of_each_hand_in(
                            IPlayingPositions playing_positions)
        {
            foreach (var hand in playing_positions.all_hands)
                set_status_for(hand);
        }
    }
}
```

We'll also need to push the method up onto the IHandStatusFactory interface.

```
namespace KojackGames.Blackjack.Domain.GamePlay.Model.PlayingPosition
                                                      .Hands.Status
{
    public interface IHandStatusFactory
    {
        void set_status_for(IHand hand);
        void update_the_status_of_each_hand_in(
                            IPlayingPositions playing_positions);
```

```
        }
}
```

Tyler: *Great let's run the tests and see where we are at.*

Sarah: *All passing!*

Let's take a look at the DealCardsIn class now that we removed the extra method and deleted to the IHandStatusFactory.

```
public class DealCardsIn : IDealerAction
{
    private readonly IHandStatusFactory _hand_status_factory;
    private readonly IPlayingHandsEndGameStatusDecider
                        _playing_hands_end_game_status_decider;
    private readonly OptionsAvailableToPlayerAfterDealing
                _options_available_to_player_after_dealing;

    public DealCardsIn(IHandStatusFactory hand_status_factory,
                        IPlayingHandsEndGameStatusDecider
                         playing_hands_end_game_status_decider,
                        ICanDoubleDown double_down_spec,
                        ICanSplit split_spec,
                        ICanTakeInsurance insurance_spec)
    {
        _hand_status_factory = hand_status_factory;
        _playing_hands_end_game_status_decider =
                            playing_hands_end_game_status_decider;
        _options_available_to_player_after_dealing =
            new OptionsAvailableToPlayerAfterDealing(double_down_spec,
                                                     split_spec,
                                                     insurance_spec);

    }

    private void deal_two_cards_to_each_hand_in(IPlayingPositions hands,
                                                ICardShoe card_shoe)
    {
        int no_of_cards_to_deal = 2;

        while (no_of_cards_to_deal > 0)
        {
            hands.players_active_hand.add(card_shoe.take_card());
            hands.dealers_hand.add(card_shoe.take_card());

            no_of_cards_to_deal--;
        };
    }

    public void perform_on(IPlayingPositions playing_positions,
                        ICardShoe card_shoe, IPlayer player)
    {
```

```
            raise_illegal_move_if_action_cannot_be_made_on(playing_positions);

            deal_two_cards_to_each_hand_in(playing_positions, card_shoe);

            _hand_status_factory
                        .update_the_status_of_each_hand_in(playing_positions);

            if (playing_positions.player_has_blackjack())
            {
                _playing_hands_end_game_status_decider
                        .decide_end_game_status_for_hands_in(playing_positions);
            }
            else
                _options_available_to_player_after_dealing
                                    .set_for_hands_in(playing_positions);

            playing_positions.mark_cards_as_dealt();

            playing_positions.update_active_hand();
        }

        public void raise_illegal_move_if_action_cannot_be_made_on(
                                        IPlayingPositions playing_positions)
        {
            if (playing_positions.have_cards_been_dealt())
                throw new IllegalMoveException(
                            "Cannot stick hand as your turn has ended.");
        }
    }
}
```

We are left with two methods that are aimed at two different levels of abstraction. The perform_on method coordinates the logic of the dealing in and the deal_two_cards_to_each_hand_in actually does the work of dealing the cards. This is another extract class refactor. Let's create a CardDealer class to be responsible for the actual dealing out of the cards.

```
using KojackGames.Blackjack.Domain.GamePlay.Model.PlayingPosition;

namespace KojackGames.Blackjack.Domain.GamePlay.Model.Dealer.Actions
{
    public class CardDealer
    {
        public void deal_two_cards_to_each_hand_in(IPlayingPositions hands,
                                                    ICardShoe card_shoe)
        {
            int no_of_cards_to_deal = 2;

            while (no_of_cards_to_deal > 0)
            {
                hands.players_active_hand.add(card_shoe.take_card());
                hands.dealers_hand.add(card_shoe.take_card());

                no_of_cards_to_deal--;
```

```
        };
    }
}
}
```

Now we can remove the method from the DealCardsIn class and simply delegate.

```
public class DealCardsIn : IDealerAction
{
    private readonly IHandStatusFactory _hand_status_factory;
    private readonly IPlayingHandsEndGameStatusDecider
                        _playing_hands_end_game_status_decider;
    private readonly OptionsAvailableToPlayerAfterDealing
                    _options_available_to_player_after_dealing;
    private CardDealer _card_dealer;

    public DealCardsIn(IHandStatusFactory hand_status_factory,
                        IPlayingHandsEndGameStatusDecider
                            playing_hands_end_game_status_decider,
                        ICanDoubleDown double_down_spec,
                        ICanSplit split_spec,
                        ICanTakeInsurance insurance_spec)
    {
        _hand_status_factory = hand_status_factory;
        _playing_hands_end_game_status_decider =
                    playing_hands_end_game_status_decider;
        _options_available_to_player_after_dealing =
            new OptionsAvailableToPlayerAfterDealing(double_down_spec,
                                                     split_spec,
                                                     insurance_spec);
        _card_dealer = new CardDealer();

    }

    public void perform_on(IPlayingPositions playing_positions,
                            ICardShoe card_shoe, IPlayer player)
    {
        raise_illegal_move_if_action_cannot_be_made_on(playing_positions);

        _card_dealer
            .deal_two_cards_to_each_hand_in(playing_positions, card_shoe);

        _hand_status_factory
            .update_the_status_of_each_hand_in(playing_positions);

        if (playing_positions.player_has_blackjack())
            _playing_hands_end_game_status_decider
            .decide_end_game_status_for_hands_in(playing_positions);
        else
            _options_available_to_player_after_dealing
                            .set_for_hands_in(playing_positions);

        playing_positions.mark_cards_as_dealt();
```

```
            playing_positions.update_active_hand();
    }

    public void raise_illegal_move_if_action_cannot_be_made_on(
                                IPlayingPositions playing_positions)
    {
        if (playing_positions.have_cards_been_dealt())
            throw new IllegalMoveException(
                        "Cannot stick hand as your turn has ended.");
    }
}
```

The DealCardsIn class is now much cleaner, more cohesive, and better adheres to a single responsibility.

Tyler: *Yes, the tests pass!*

Sarah: *Awesome. Now let's move on to developing the payout feature.*

## Developing the Payout Feature

First, we can uncomment the assertion we created in the
when_dealing_in_the_hands_and_the_player_achieves_blackjack class.

```
[Subject(typeof(Domain.GamePlay.Model.Dealer.Actions.DealCardsIn), "Dealer")]
public class when_dealing_in_the_hands_and_the_player_achieves_blackjack :
                                                with_a_deal_in_cards_action
{
    private Establish context = () =>
    {
        positions.Stub(x => x.player_has_blackjack()).Return(true);
    };

    Because of = () => SUT.perform_on(positions, card_shoe, player);

    It should_check_if_a_hand_has_blackjack =
        () => positions.AssertWasCalled(x => x.player_has_blackjack());

    It should_determine_the_winning_hands =
        () => playing_hands_end_game_status_decider.AssertWasCalled(
                x => x.decide_end_game_status_for_hands_in(positions));

    It should_pay_out_any_winnings_to_the_player =
        () => chip_allocator.AssertWasCalled(
                x => x.allocate_chips_to_winnings_hands_in(positions));
}
```

Then we should update the with_a_deal_in_cards_action base class to expect the new collaborator.

```
public abstract class with_a_deal_in_cards_action
{
```

```
...
protected static IChipAllocator chip_allocator;

public with_a_deal_in_cards_action()
{
   ...
   chip_allocator = MockRepository.GenerateStub<IChipAllocator>();

   SUT = new Domain.GamePlay.Model.Dealer.Actions
                            .DealCardsIn(hand_status_factory,
                      playing_hands_end_game_status_decider,
                                        after_dealing_options,
                                             chip_allocator);
}
}
```

Tyler: *Better add the contract for the chip allocator as well to stop the complier complaining.*

```
using KojackGames.Blackjack.Domain.GamePlay.Model.PlayingPosition;

namespace KojackGames.Blackjack.Domain.GamePlay.Model.Dealer.Actions
{
    public interface IChipAllocator
    {
        void allocate_chips_to_winnings_hands_in(
            IPlayingPositions positions);
    }
}
```

Sarah: *With the compiler much happier, let's run the new unit test.*

Tyler: *Sweet. It's passing.* [(See Figure 8-12.)]

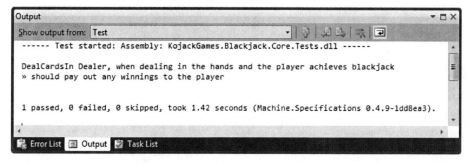

*Figure 8-12. Verifying test passed*

Now we need to add some tests to drive the design of the ChipAllocator itself. We want to check that a player who wins, gets winnings of 2 to 3 plus his original stake. So an initial bet of $5.00 would result in the player getting $7.50 in winnings, plus his original stake of $5.00, making the total $12.50.

```csharp
using System.Collections.Generic;
using KojackGames.Blackjack.Domain.GamePlay.Model.Dealer.Actions;
using KojackGames.Blackjack.Domain.GamePlay.Model.PlayingPosition;
using KojackGames.Blackjack.Domain.GamePlay.Model.PlayingPosition
                                              .Hands.Player;
using KojackGames.Blackjack.Domain.GamePlay.Model.PlayingPosition
                                              .Hands.Status;
using KojackGames.Blackjack.Domain.Membership.Model;
using Machine.Specifications;
using Rhino.Mocks;

namespace KojackGames.Blackjack.Core.Tests.Domain_Specs
                                  .DealerAction_Specs.PayingOut
{
    [Subject(typeof(ChipAllocator))]
    public class when_paying_a_winning_hand_with_a_bet_of_5_dollars
    {
        private Establish context = () =>
        {
            chips_that_the_player_should_win = new Chips(12.50m);
            var chips_bet = new Chips(5m);

            SUT = new ChipAllocator();
            playing_positions =
                    MockRepository.GenerateStub<IPlayingPositions>();
            var players_hands = new List<IPlayersHand>();
            var playing_hand = MockRepository.GenerateStub<IPlayersHand>();
            playing_hand.Stub(
                        x => x.has_status_of(HandStatus.won)).Return(true);
            playing_hand.Stub(x => x.wager).Return(chips_bet);
            players_hands.Add(playing_hand);
            playing_positions.Stub(
                        x => x.players_hands()).Return(players_hands);

            player = MockRepository.GenerateStub<IPlayer>();
        };

        private Because of = () =>
                    SUT.allocate_chips_to_player_for_winnings_hands_in(
                                        playing_positions, player);

        private It should_increase_players_pot_by_12_dollars_and_50_cents =
            () => player.AssertWasCalled( x => x.increase_pot_by(
                Arg<Chips>.Is.Equal(chips_that_the_player_should_win)));

        private static ChipAllocator SUT;
        private static IPlayingPositions playing_positions;
        private static IPlayer player;
        private static Chips chips_that_the_player_should_win;
    }
}
```

Now let's create the ChipAllocator class.

```
using KojackGames.Blackjack.Domain.GamePlay.Model.PlayingPosition;
using KojackGames.Blackjack.Domain.GamePlay.Model.PlayingPosition
                                            .Hands.Player;
using KojackGames.Blackjack.Domain.GamePlay.Model.PlayingPosition
                                            .Hands.Status;
using KojackGames.Blackjack.Domain.Membership.Model;

namespace KojackGames.Blackjack.Domain.GamePlay.Model.Dealer.Actions
{
    public class ChipAllocator : IChipAllocator
    {
        public void allocate_chips_to_player_for_winnings_hands_in(
                        IPlayingPositions positions, IPlayer player)
        {
            foreach(var players_hand in positions.players_hands())
            {
                var chips_to_give_to_player = new Chips(0m);

                if (players_hand.has_status_of(HandStatus.won))
                {
                    chips_to_give_to_player = chips_to_give_to_player.add(
                            players_hand.wager.multiple_by_odds_of(3, 2)
                                            .add(players_hand.wager));
                    player.increase_pot_by(chips_to_give_to_player);
                }
            }
        }
    }
}
```

Although this is how we want the class to work, the compiler is complaining about the lack of a multiple_by_odds_of method on the Chips class. We need to comment out the call to the non-existent method of the Chips class and then create a test.

```
using KojackGames.Blackjack.Domain.GamePlay.Model.PlayingPosition
                                            .Hands.Player;
using Machine.Specifications;
using NUnit.Framework;

namespace KojackGames.Blackjack.Core.Tests.Domain_Specs.Chip_Specs
{
    [Subject(typeof(Chips))]
    public class
            when_calculating_a_players_winnings_of_3_to_2_on_a_5_dollar_wager
    {
        private Establish context = () =>
        {
            SUT = new Chips(5m);
        };
```

```
            private Because of = () => result = SUT.multiple_by_odds_of(3, 2);

            private It should_create_chips_with_a_value_of_7_dollars_and_50_cents
                = () =>
            {
                Assert.That(result.value, Is.EqualTo(7.50m));
            };

            private static Chips SUT;
            private static Chips result;
        }
    }
```

Now we can create the new method on the Chips class.

```
using System;

namespace KojackGames.Blackjack.Domain.GamePlay.Model.PlayingPosition
                                                        .Hands.Player
{
    public class Chips
    {
        public Chips(decimal amount)
        {
            value = amount;
        }

        private Chips()
        { }

        public decimal value { get; private set; }

        public Chips halved()
        {
            return new Chips(value/2);
        }

        public override string ToString()
        {
            return string.Format("${0:0.00}", value);
        }

        public Chips multiple_by_odds_of(int you_receive_back,
                                int for_every_dollar_bet)
        {
            var result = (value/for_every_dollar_bet)*you_receive_back;

            return new Chips(result);
        }

        public Chips add(Chips wager)
```

```
    {
        return new Chips(wager.value + value);
    }

    public Chips double_stake()
    {
        return new Chips(value * 2);
    }

    public bool contains_chips()
    {
        return this.value > 0;
    }

    public bool Equals(Chips other)
    {
        if (ReferenceEquals(null, other)) return false;
        if (ReferenceEquals(this, other)) return true;
        return other.value == value;
    }

    public override bool Equals(object obj)
    {
        if (ReferenceEquals(null, obj)) return false;
        if (ReferenceEquals(this, obj)) return true;
        if (obj.GetType() != typeof (Chips)) return false;
        return Equals((Chips) obj);
    }

    public override int GetHashCode()
    {
        return value.GetHashCode();
    }
  }
}
```

Uncomment the call to the ChipAllocator and run the test.

Tyler: *Passing. Brilliant! Let's run the acceptance test to see if we have completed the scenario.*

Sarah: *Cool. All passing. On to the next scenario.*

# Day 6

As we enter the last part of the current sprint, we find the team completing the three user stories that they committed to. Now they will look at the Cashing In user story in the stretch goals for work to do.

## Daily Stand-up

Tim: *Who's up?*

Simon: *I will start. I have been working with the customer on the upcoming release and it looks like we have everything in place. As a side note, I just wanted to let you all know that the customer is really excited about the release.*

Tim: *That is great to hear! With their feedback throughout this process, they should be getting exactly what they want, within reason.* [Tim winks.] *Next.*

Joe: *I will go. I finished up the implementation of the Saving Game State user story. Today, I plan on pairing with Tyler on Cashing In, the user story we have in the stretch goal area. I have no blocks.*

Tyler: *I have been working with Sarah on the Paying Out user story and we are nearly complete. Today I plan on switching up and working with Joe on the stretch goal user story. I have no blocks.*

Sarah: *I have been working with Tyler on the Paying Out user story. At this point I am finishing up the user story. Today I plan on finishing up this user story . When I have this done, since we have tests around everything, I plan on tackling some technical debt that we have. Joe, just as a heads up, technical debt is anything that we can improve on specifically in the source code. For example, this can be refactoring an existing module in order to gain better test coverage or cleaning up some code that is no longer needed.*

Tim: *That's great, anytime we can take the time to improve our quality of code is a good thing. Well, that's all for now.*

# Day 10

Today is the last day of the sprint. As with all sprints, we continue to do the product demo and the retrospective to verify that we are on the right track with the customer and to improve customer confidence.

## Product Demo

Once again, it's time for the product demo to show the customer the features implemented throughout this past sprint in order to maintain transparency and accountability, and to increase team morale.

Since Joe joined the team during the last sprint and has seen how a demo works, Joe will lead this demo and show off what the team has done.

Joe: *As we wrap up another sprint, we want to take this opportunity to demo the new features we've added to the system. Let's recap the features that the team took on during this sprint. They were Saving Game State, Paying Out, Member Registration, and Cashing In. The team was able to finish up the Saving Game State story that was, unfortunately, left over from the last sprint because it was such a large undertaking. Since Simon said it is still a high priority with the customer, the team committed to getting this story finished during this sprint. We also worked on the Paying Out user story—which hopefully doesn't happen very often for Kojack—and we were able to accomplish the Member Registration and the Cashing In user stories.*

Sarah: *Joe, let's show the Member Registration feature first.*

Joe navigates to the application and demos the Member Registration to Simon. In the upper-right corner of the screen, there's a link to register. Joe shows Simon how the system now collects three pieces of user login information—name, e-mail address, and password—and clicks the Register button.

Joe: *What do you think, Simon? Do you agree that this meets all the acceptance criteria laid out in the sprint planning session?*

Simon: *It does. Good work! I was wondering, could we add a birthday field to the user registration so that we can send users a promotional e-mail on their birthdays?*

Joe: *Uh, I suppose so. That wasn't discussed in this user story.*

Simon: *It shouldn't be a lot of work, would it? Just adding that one field?*

Sarah: *We can add the field, but since it wasn't a part of this story, we can create another user story and put it in the backlog to be sized and implemented appropriately.*

Joe: *That's right. We can do that, it just wasn't a part of the requirements for this story.*

Simon: *Okay, that's fine. I agree that it wasn't a part of this user story, but I thought if it didn't take too much time, we could just slip it in there.*

Tim: *I'm guessing it wouldn't take a long time to implement, but Sarah's right. We need to create another user story and implement this feature.*

Simon: *I like this agile process, but it seems that there's a lot of overhead to implement one field. You mean, I have to create another user story for this one field?*

Tim: *Yes. We only do this for transparency to you and the customer. We always want to make sure we are providing the highest value and if we just slip one thing in here or there, that time adds up and that time needs to be spent on delivering high-value to the customer. If you and the customer deem this a high enough priority, we can certainly put it in the backlog and implement that feature.*

Simon: *Okay, I understand. I must agree that having gone through this process so far, things have gone relatively smoothly and the communication is much better than in other projects I have been apart of. I'll talk with the customer and see if it's a high priority or if something else can be swapped for this functionality. If it can, we'll swap it and if it can't, then it must not be that high of a priority and can be implemented once other items are out of the way. The Member Registration looks fine, the UI looks very intuitive, and we can collect the agreed-upon information. I'd agree that it's done. What's next?*

Joe: *Thanks! The next one we want to demo is the Saving Game State. This one was a bit trickier than originally expected and we underestimated it, but we were able to get it done during this sprint. This one is a little harder to demo, but we'll demo it by unplugging the network cable and plugging it back in to simulate a loss of network connectivity.*

Joe navigates to the application, logs in, and while playing a game, unplugs the network cable, waits a few seconds, and plugs it back in. The system wants him to log in again, but then the game can be picked up where it was left off.

Simon: *So, a player can continue his game play if he loses internet connectivity?*

Joe: *Yep. That way he doesn't have to restart the game—and hopefully he loses so you don't have to pay out.*

Simon: *Hah, true. Good work. What's next?*

Joe: *The last user story we want to demo is the Paying Out feature. Sarah and Tyler primarily worked on this feature and it looks as if they've done a great job.*

Joe navigates to the application, logs in as the user that he demoed during the Member Registration user story, and quickly plays a game to demonstrate that the player has her winnings added to the pot when she wins a game.

Simon: *I like how the team implemented that feature. It captures the acceptance criteria that we laid out at the beginning. Good work!*
Joe: *That's all we have for this sprint. What did you think overall?*

Simon: *I think the team is doing a great job. Thanks, Joe, for leading the demo this sprint.*

Joe: *You bet! Glad to do it. Thanks to Sarah, too, for helping me out for the first time.*

Sarah: *You bet!*

Tim: *Thanks everyone for your time!*

# Retrospective

We want to continue to work on, refine, and make our team more efficient through process, so it's time for a retrospective. We are doing this one differently, too, because we want the retrospectives to remain fresh in order to best go over ideas and issues. Instead of having a three-minute time block to write thoughts on Post-its, we'll vocally capture the feedback.

Tim: *Welcome to another retrospective team. During this retrospective we are going to gather our feedback in a different way. Instead of filling out Post-it notes within a private time box, we are going to share our feedback in a more public way. Throughout these last four sprints, I think we've grown together and have gained courage as a team to the point where we can comfortably give constructive criticism to each other and openly discuss issues. I'm going to set the timer for ten minutes. During these ten minutes, let's openly discuss things that went well during the sprint as well as the things that we need to change.*

Tim tells the team that the discussion will be based on the chart shown in Figure 8-13.

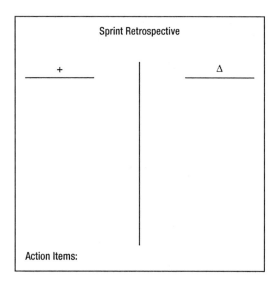

*Figure 8-13. Sprint retrospective*

Tim: *The timer is set. Go!*

Sarah: *I think the demo seemed to go well. I'm glad that as a team we have matured and have grown to have enough courage to push back with Simon to say that even little items that weren't originally considered still need to go through the process so that we continue to implement the greatest value for the customer.*

Simon: *Yes, Sarah, I agree. Sometimes as customers or product owners we get excited when we actually see what developers have produced, and then we hope to "'sneak in" additional features because we think they're small. Thanks for pushing back on the birthday feature. I'll check with the customer to see if it's of value relative to the other stories we have on our plate.*

Joe: *Yeah, as a new guy leading the demo, your request was a bit awkward for me, but it was a good conversation to have there rather than later. Simon, thanks for your understanding.*

Simon: *No problem!*

Tyler: *One thing I wanted to bring up was that I noticed that Joe broke the build a number of times this sprint and had to go back and fix code. Is there a particular reason that was consistent?*

Joe: *Since I'm new to this agile thing and new to writing test-first code, I keep falling back into the "old" way of thinking, where I just want to jump in and develop code. I learned that that doesn't work because there are numerous tests that run to ensure we have a solid code base. Be patient with me, I'm learning. Would it be possible for me to pair more with you or Sarah to keep me focused? I know we paired some during this sprint, but I'd like to pair more so I can develop this new way of thinking with this test-first mentality.*

Sarah: *That's a great idea, just swing on over, I'll pair with you any time. We want to make sure that the code base stays solid and easy to maintain, that's why we spend so much time testing and developing from tests. I was like you and wanted to just jump right in, but eventually learned that test-first is more efficient because it has saved me numerous times when I've changed code and it inadvertently affected something that I didn't expect—but the test caught it. This way I could fix it before it went into the QA process. The more bugs we can find and fix, the less costly it is and the better the team looks because we are developing dependable code.*

Tyler: *Yeah, I'm with Sarah. Don't be afraid to tell us when you don't know something or need help with something. If you need to pair, roll your chair over and tell me. I have no problems with that. We're a team, we're here to develop a quality product, but also to raise each other up so when we see that you consistently break builds. We don't want to shake a blaming finger at you, we want to figure out the root issue and mentor you. Next time, swing by, we'll take care of it with you.*

Joe: *Thanks! I really like this team spirit and teamwork. I used to develop in a vacuum, so it's a bit of a cultural shift to ask for help from other developers. I'll be sure to swing by next time and make sure I get the latest code and run the tests locally before I check in, to ensure I don't break the build.*

Tim: *Sounds like we have an action item. Joe needs to pair more with either Tyler or Sarah. We'll assign this action to Joe because he's responsible for reaching out for help, but Tyler, Sarah, you know you need to work on mentoring him.*

Sarah: *Sounds good. I'm in!*

Tyler: *Me too!*

Joe: *Thanks guys!*

Tim: *We have a few minutes left. Anything else to discuss?*

Sarah: *Since we've finished up the last sprint in our release, we did have some issues releasing the code into the production environment.*

Tyler: *I agree. This was the first time we sent out the code in a releasable state. We packaged up everything and deployed it to the production server, but the site wasn't running as expected. We were getting different types of errors. After a bit of research, we discovered that the server didn't have the right version of IIS. We installed the correct version of IIS and it worked. Once we had the right version of IIS, we deployed our packaged code and it worked without a hitch! It was just environment issues. I'm glad that we did that initial work when setting up the CI server. Since the CI server compiles the DLLs, it's nice to know that we have very few dependencies there and we can package up the code fairly quickly and deploy the code easily.*

Sarah: *Yep, we'll know for next time!*

Tim: *Sounds like a learning experience! Glad you guys got that resolved. Anything else?*

Bzzzz! The timer buzzes time's up...

Tim: *That's all the time we have. Joe, you have an action item to pair with Sarah and/or Tyler for at least four hours every day during the next sprint to build up your test-first skills. Thanks for your time today, team!*

# Summary

We have now completed our fourth sprint and released our first version of the app. This release was the culmination of four sprints' worth of work. A final point to remember from this sprint is that when you get a team to buy into the agile methodology, you begin to see the team take ownership of their process. In Sprint 4, you saw a daily stand-up start without the ScrumMaster present. The team understood the importance of keeping the daily stand-up meeting in tact whether the ScrumMaster was there or not.

From the product demo and the retrospective, we learned valuable lessons from the following situations:

- Joe's admitting his natural reaction to go back to "the old way" of just cranking out code. This is a common reaction. It's human nature to fight change. Oftentimes we want to return to the "safe" way of doing things. The team needs to hold each other accountable and raise each other up. In our example, we did this by having Joe spend more time pair programming with Sarah and Tyler. This will allow Sarah and Tyler to mentor Joe rather than tear him down by complaining that he doesn't get it. Building up fellow team members is crucial to a successful team.

- The team pushing back with Simon when he wanted to add just one, little field to the Member Registration. The team explained that they could add the feature, but that a user story would first need to be written. This user story will still need to go through the process (prioritized, estimated, and put in a sprint). The reason for this time and effort is to deliver the highest value to the customer. Don't struggle between delivering the highest value and scope creep. Scope creep will win every time. The goal is to stop that slippery slope before it ever occurs.

# CHAPTER 9

# Code Review

This chapter acts as a code review for the work achieved in the case study project. We recommend that you download the complete application from www.apress.com as you read through the review.

In order to give you a better understanding of the Kojack Games Blackjack application, you will learn how all the projects in the solution fit together to satisfy the features included in the case study. It's a good idea to have a copy of the source code open while you read this chapter so that you can flip between the code and the text.

Code snippets that we feel demonstrate an important concept in the application have been included in this chapter. It would have been ideal to list the application's source code in its entirety, but that would have made for a very large book. Instead, we felt it better to not scrimp on the code and to deliver you an application that you can study in conjunction with the book in order to give you the most realistic view of how an agile process can deliver a fully-working application.

## Solution Overview

Before we dig deeper into the architecture, let's review the implementation model we'll follow. Then we'll look at the Visual Studio Solution file and a high-level purpose of each project within the solution.

The implementation model chosen for this project is the Command and Query Responsibility Segregation (CQRS) implementation. The term *command query separation* was coined by Bertrand Meyer in his book *Object-Oriented Software Construction*, Second Edition (Prentice Hall, 2000). Fundamentally, CQRS divides an object's methods into two categories, as follows:

- Queries that return a result and do not change the observable state of the system. In other words, queries free from side effects.

- Commands that change the state of the system, but do not return a value.

Next, let's take a look at the Visual Studio Solution and discuss each of the following six projects at a high level:

- *Infrastructure Project*: This project contains all of the supporting framework for the domain model and CQRS implementation.

- *Domain Project*: This is the heart of the application, featuring all of the behaviors of the blackjack game. The project is split into the following sections: command handlers, commands, domain views, and the model.

- *Acceptance Tests*: This project contains all of our code to run our automated, front-end, web test suite to perform end-to-end testing.

- *Core Tests*: This project is our automated, unit testing suite that tests code directly beneath the UI.

- *NHibernate Infrastructure Project*: This project implements a generic repository class and serves as the implementation of the IQueryService, which forms the query side of the CQRS architecture.

- *Web Project*: This is the UI piece of the application that is implemented as a web application using the Model View Controller (MVC) pattern.

As you've seen, each project serves a primary purpose and acts as separate pieces to a larger puzzle. We intentionally did not put the entire application into one project. Splitting projects out has its advantages. For example, the NHibernate project focuses on implementing the repository logic and database persistence. If, in the future, there was a requirement to change our ORM layer to another ORM tool like ADO.NET Entity Framework (EF) for example, we have the ability to do that more easily because of this isolated structure than if it were compiled all in the same assembly within one project. Look at the domain project. This project contains the meat of the application, the core functionality. Because this contains the primary business logic, we could reuse this project and potentially implement a UI other than a web interface—perhaps a WPF or Silverlight application.

Splitting out testing projects is advantageous for scalability reasons. There exists a logical separation between your core tests and your acceptance tests that you can take advantage of. When you first start out, you will run both sets of tests on every check in. As you continue to add more and more tests to both projects, you will see that acceptance tests are going to run slower than your core tests. This is because the core tests test individual methods and the acceptance tests test vertical slices through the application. Dividing these into two test projects will allow the flexibility of running the core tests more frequent than the acceptance tests. It cuts down the build times on your CI server and gets the feedback needed to the developers that much sooner. This is a simple thing to do as long as there is forethought in splitting out the test projects.

## Infrastructure Project

The infrastructure project contains all of the supporting framework for the domain model and the CQRS implementation. Let's take a look at the implementation for the ICommandBus that you created earlier in the book.

The class that follows is the implementation of the ICommandBus, which depends on a ICommandHandlerRegistry to find a handler for a given command.

```
namespace KojackGames.Blackjack.Infrastructure.Cqrs.Command
{
    public class InProcessCommandBus : ICommandBus
    {
        private readonly ICommandHandlerRegistry _command_handler_registry;

        public InProcessCommandBus(ICommandHandlerRegistry
                                             command_handler_registry)
        {
            _command_handler_registry = command_handler_registry;
        }

        public void send<TCommand>(TCommand command)
                                             where TCommand : ICommand
        {
```

```
                _command_handler_registry
                        .find_handler_for(command).handle(command);
        }
    }
}
```

Later in this chapter, you'll see an example of an ICommandHandler.

Another class of note is the StructureMapCommandHandlerRegistry, which is an implementation of the ICommandHandlerRegistry. StructureMap is an Inversion of Control container.

```
using StructureMap;

namespace KojackGames.Blackjack.Infrastructure.Cqrs.Command
{
    public class StructureMapCommandHandlerRegistry : ICommandHandlerRegistry
    {
        public ICommandHandler<TCommand> find_handler_for<TCommand>
                                (TCommand command) where TCommand : ICommand
        {
            return ObjectFactory.TryGetInstance<ICommandHandler<TCommand>>();
        }
    }
}
```

Yet another class of note is the DomainBase class, which acts as a supertype to all of the entities contained in the domain project. All of the entities have an identifier and are compared on their type and identity. This base class provides this default behavior for all of the entity classes.

```
using System;

namespace KojackGames.Blackjack.Infrastructure.Domain
{
    public abstract class DomainBase<TEntityType> where TEntityType : IEntity
    {
        public Guid id
        {
            get; protected set;
        }

        public int version_id { get; private set; }

        public bool Equals(TEntityType other)
        {
            if (ReferenceEquals(null, other)) return false;
            if (ReferenceEquals(this, other)) return true;
            return other.id.Equals(id);
        }

        public override bool Equals(object obj)
        {
            if (ReferenceEquals(null, obj)) return false;
            if (ReferenceEquals(this, obj)) return true;
            if (obj.GetType() != typeof(TEntityType)) return false;
```

```
            return Equals((TEntityType)obj);
        }

        public override int GetHashCode()
        {
            return id.GetHashCode();
        }
    }
}
```

This `Domain` class allows base functionality from inherited classes and lets us check for equality.

This wraps up the discussion of the infrastructure project. Let's turn our attention to the domain project.

# Domain Project

The domain project contains the heart of the application, featuring all of the behaviors of the blackjack game. The project is split into the following sections:

- *Command Handlers*: This section of the `GamePlay` domain contains all of the handlers that perform the actions described by the commands.

- *Commands*: The commands folder contains the data transfer objects that represent actions performed in the context of a game.

- *Domain Views*: The domain views folder contains flat views of the domain. It is used to present a contextual view of the domain for presentation purposes.

- *Model*: The model contains the behavior of the system and is used to perform the state transitions based on the exposed commands. The model follows a domain-driven design approach in order to capture the rich logic of the blackjack card game.

We will explore each of these sections in more detail.

## Commands and Command Handlers

All of the commands of the application implement the `ICommand` interface. Take a look at the following code listing for the `DealCommand`. It contains a single property that is used to identify the player

```
using System;
using KojackGames.Blackjack.Infrastructure.Cqrs.Command;

namespace KojackGames.Blackjack.Domain.GamePlay.Commands
{
    public class DealCommand : ICommand
    {
        public Guid player_token { get; set; }
    }
```

}

A matching DealHandler exists to handle the DealAction when it is sent via the bus. The DealHandler simply pulls the blackjack table game from the repository and calls the deal_in_hands_by_asking method, passing a Dealer object that represents a blackjack game dealer. The Dealer object is stateless and is used to inject behavior into the system that fits naturally on any other entity.

```
using System;
using KojackGames.Blackjack.Domain.GamePlay.Commands;
using KojackGames.Blackjack.Domain.GamePlay.Model;
using KojackGames.Blackjack.Domain.GamePlay.Model.Dealing;
using KojackGames.Blackjack.Infrastructure;
using KojackGames.Blackjack.Infrastructure.Cqrs.Command;
using KojackGames.Blackjack.Infrastructure.Domain;

namespace KojackGames.Blackjack.Domain.GamePlay.CommandHandlers
{
    public class DealHandler : ICommandHandler<DealCommand>
    {
        private readonly IUnitOfWorkFactory _unit_of_work_factory;
        private readonly IDealer _dealer;
        private readonly IRepository<IBlackJackTable> _table_repository;

        public DealHandler(IUnitOfWorkFactory unit_of_work_factory,
                           IDealer dealer,
                           IRepository<IBlackJackTable> table_repository)
        {
            _unit_of_work_factory = unit_of_work_factory;
            _dealer = dealer;
            _table_repository = table_repository;
        }

        public void handle(DealCommand controlling_hand_command)
        {
            using (_unit_of_work_factory.create())
            {
                var table = _table_repository
                            .query_for_single(x =>
                    x.player == controlling_hand_command.player_token);

                if (table != null)
                {
                    table.deal_in_hands_by_asking(_dealer);
                    _table_repository.save(table);
                }
            }
        }
    }
}
```

A full list of command and command handler classes can be seen in Figure 9-1.

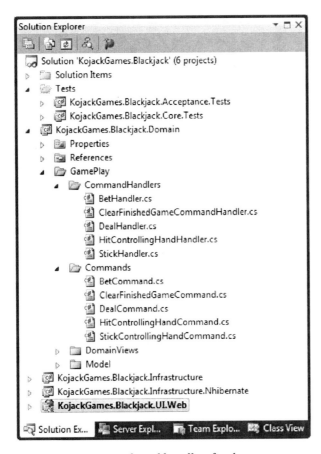

*Figure 9-1. Commands and handlers for the game*

## Model

The domain model is a conceptual model of the GamePlay context of the application. The model contains relationships, entities, and objects that represent concerns in the game of blackjack.

The BlackJackTable entity, as shown in Figure 9-2, acts as the root to the aggregate of objects that represents the blackjack game play. All interaction with the game, which comes in the form of command handlers, is performed through the BlackJackTable entity. Accessing only through the aggregate root ensures consistency and a consistently valid state.

The BlackJackTable entity contains an ICardShoe and an IHandCollection. The ICardShoe instance represents the card shoe in the game of blackjack and this holds the state of the deck of cards. The IHandCollection represents all hands in play during the game—that is the players' and the dealer's hands. As you can see from Figure 9-2, both the dealers' and players' hands inherit from a Hand base class that exposes the common behavior of a hand.

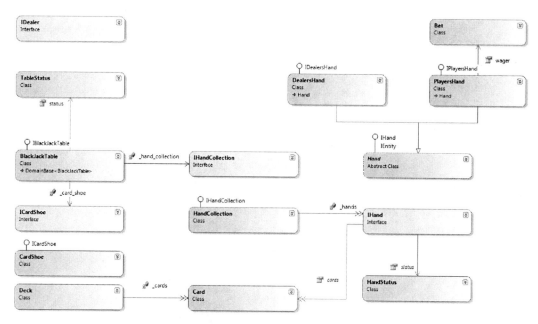

***Figure 9-2.*** *Class diagram for the blackjack game play*

Both the BlackJackTable and the Hand leverage the state pattern in the form of a TableStatus and HandStatus respectively, which can be seen in Figures 9-3 and 9-4. These objects encapsulate the state of each entity and enable the classes to focus on behavior only.

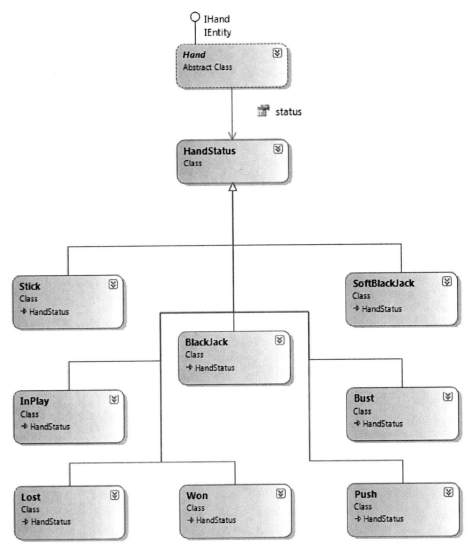

*Figure 9-3. Class diagram showing the state pattern for the Hand class*

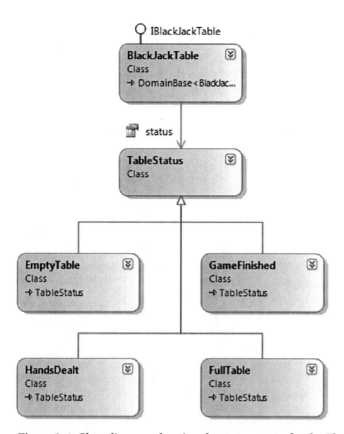

*Figure 9-4. Class diagram showing the state pattern for the BlackJackTable class*

The only other interface of note is that of the IDealer, which follows the Domain Service pattern in that it has no state but instead represents a concern and behavior that doesn't naturally fit anywhere else within the domain model. The BlackJackTable entity uses the double dispatch pattern to take an instance of the IDealer to act upon the entity, rather than exposing any of its internal collections.

Let's take a look at the workflow that is used to deal in the cards for the players. This section of code follows on from the DealHandler class that you saw in the last section.

The following code snippet is taken from the BlackJackTable class. The method shown is called directly from the DealHandler. First the status is checked to see if the deal action can take place; if so, a hand is created for the dealer and the collection of hands and the card shoe are passed to the dealer. After the cards have been dealt, the status of the table is changed to hands_dealt and a check is made to see if the game has finished. The check is made due to the fact that either the player or the dealer can achieve blackjack with the first two cards.

```
namespace KojackGames.Blackjack.Domain.GamePlay.Model
{
    public class BlackJackTable : DomainBase<BlackJackTable>, IBlackJackTable
    {
        ....
```

```
    public void deal_in_hands_by_asking(IDealer dealer)
    {
        if (status.can_deal)
        {
            _hand_collection.create_dealers_hand_for(this);

            dealer.deal_in(_hand_collection, _card_shoe);

            change_state_to(TableStatus.hands_dealt);

            check_if_game_finished();
        }
    }
    ...
    }
}
```

The Dealer class used in the previous code snippet can be seen in the following code snippet. Here the dealer delegates the act of dealing to a specific dealing action. After the cards are dealt, a check is made to see if any of the hands have achieved blackjack; if so, then the winner calculator determines the winner.

```
namespace KojackGames.Blackjack.Domain.GamePlay.Model.Dealing
{
    public class Dealer : IDealer
    {
    ....

        public void deal_in(IHandCollection hands, ICardShoe card_shoe)
        {
            _dealing_in_action.deal_cards_in(hands, card_shoe);

            if (hands.contain_a_hand_with_blackjack())
                _winner_calculator.determine_winner_from(hands);
        }

        ...
    }
}
```

If we take a look at the DealingInAction itself, we can see again that it is a very simple class that gives each hand two cards and then updates the status of the hand.

```
namespace KojackGames.Blackjack.Domain.GamePlay.Model.Dealing.Actions
{
    public class DealingInAction : BaseAction, IDealingInAction
    {
    ...

        public void deal_cards_in(IHandCollection hands, ICardShoe card_shoe)
        {
            deal_two_cards_to_each_hand_in(hands, card_shoe);

            update_the_status_of_each_hand_in(hands);
```

```
        }

        private void deal_two_cards_to_each_hand_in(IHandCollection hands,
                                                    ICardShoe card_shoe)
        {
            int no_of_cards_to_deal = 2;

            while (no_of_cards_to_deal > 0)
            {
                foreach(var hand in hands.get_all_hands())
                    hand.add(card_shoe.take_card());

                no_of_cards_to_deal--;
            };
        }
    }
}
```

The method to update the status of each hand comes from the BaseAction class, which acts as a supertype for all of the dealer's actions and can be seen in the following code snippet.

```
namespace KojackGames.Blackjack.Domain.GamePlay.Model.Dealing.Actions
{
    public abstract class BaseAction
    {
        private readonly IHandStatusFactory _hand_status_factory;

        public BaseAction(IHandStatusFactory hand_status_factory)
        {
            _hand_status_factory = hand_status_factory;
        }

        protected void update_the_status_of_each_hand_in(
                                        IHandCollection hands)
        {
            foreach(var hand in hands.get_all_hands())
            {
                hand.change_state_to(
                    _hand_status_factory.get_status_for(hand));
            }
        }

        ...

    }
}
```

The overriding theme within the domain project is of lots of small and concise classes working together to form the behavior of the application. The single responsibility principle has been adhered to in order to ensure that methods and classes have only one responsibility and one reason to change.

The rest of the domain project is made up of supporting classes that represents small units of behavior in the game play, as shown in Figure 9-5.

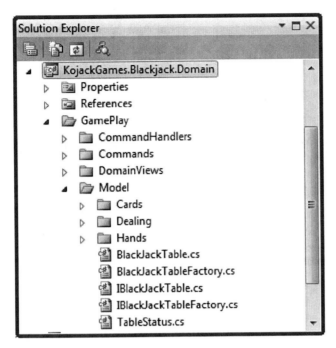

*Figure 9-5. The BlackJackTable section of the domain project*

Much of the logic is captured as specification objects; as an example, take a look at the following code snippet that shows the HasBlackJack class.

```
using KojackGames.Blackjack.Domain.GamePlay.Model.Dealing;

namespace KojackGames.Blackjack.Domain.GamePlay.Model.Hands.Status
{
    public class HasBlackJack : IHasBlackjackSpecification
    {
        private int blackjack_total = 21;
        private readonly IHandScorer _hand_scorer;

        public HasBlackJack(IHandScorer hand_scorer)
        {
            _hand_scorer = hand_scorer;
        }

        public bool is_satisfied_by(IHand hand)
        {
            bool has_blackjack = false;

            if (hand.number_of_cards == 2)
            {
                has_blackjack = (_hand_scorer.calculate_score_for(hand)
                                                == blackjack_total);
```

```
            }

        return has_blackjack;
        }
    }
}
```

Here the logic to determine a score of blackjack is kept out of the hand class, and instead, the hand, be it a dealer's or a player's, is passed in to see if it satisfies the criteria for reaching blackjack.

Also in the domain project are sections for the Cards in a blackjack game (Figure 9-6), The Dealing of a blackjack game (Figure 9-7), and a section on the Hands in the blackjack game (Figure 9-8).

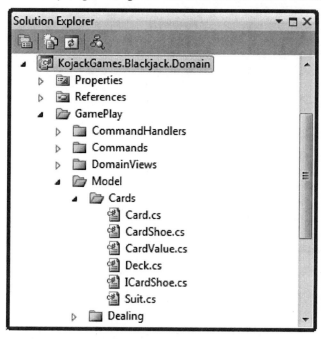

*Figure 9-6. The Cards section of the domain project*

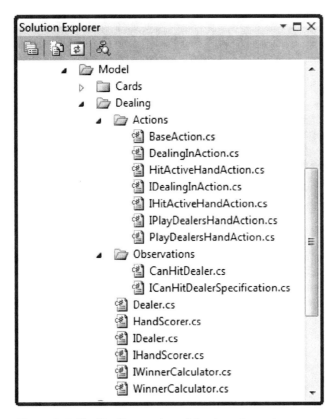

*Figure 9-7. The Dealing section of the domain project*

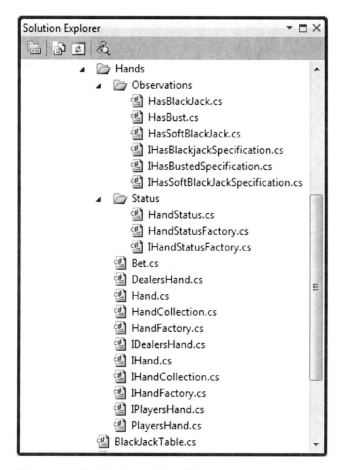

*Figure 9-8. The Hands section of the domain project*

## Domain Views

The domain views folder contains all of the flat views of the application and is used to present the state of the game. The objects themselves are very simple data transfer objects. The full list of domain views can be seen in Figure 9-9.

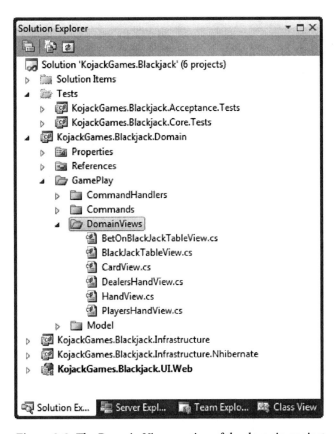

*Figure 9-9. The Domain Views section of the domain project*

The supporting data model to hold the state of the game can be seen in Figure 9-10. The data model is used both by the query service (the query side of the CQRS architecture) and to hold the state of the domain (the command side of the CQRS architecture). This data could be split up and stored separately, but that would increase the complexity of the application at this stage and would not return any benefit. As you can see from Figure 9-10, the data tables map clearly to the main entities in the domain model.

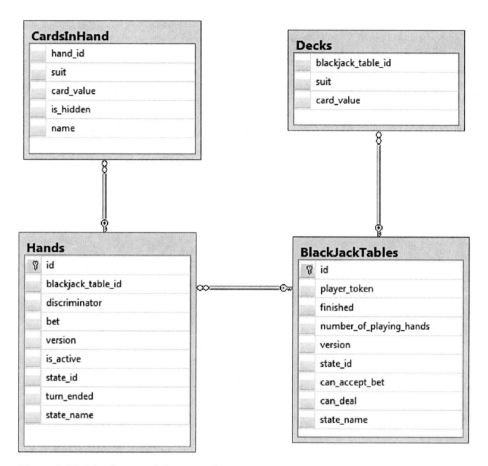

*Figure 9-10. The data model to store the game state*

## Acceptance Test Project

The acceptance test project builds upon the exercise you completed earlier in this chapter. As you can see from Figure 9-11, the Features folder contains a SpecFlow feature file for each of the user stories. You will also note that within the Utilities folder there are some NHibernate mapping files. These mapping files, along with the GameBuilder class, is the framework for a fluent interface that allows the tests to set up state in the database prior to running an acceptance testing scenario.

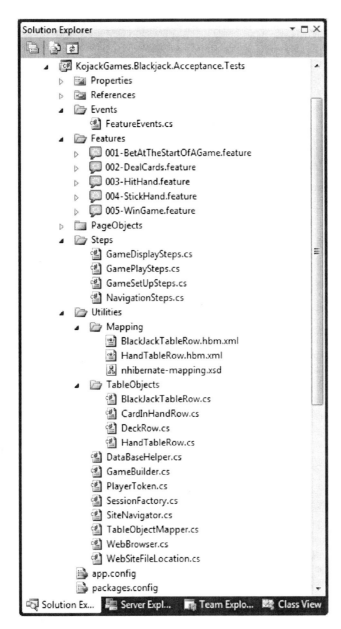

*Figure 9-11. The acceptance testing project*

# Fluent Game State Builder

The GameBuilder class is a fluent interface that allows the acceptance tests to set up the state of a game. Figure 9-12 shows the SpecFlow acceptance test scenario around the feature of the player winning a game when the dealer busts.

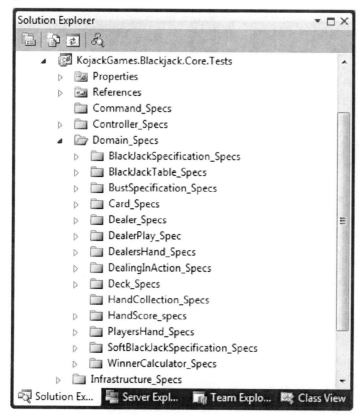

*Figure 9-12. WinGame feature scenario*

You can see in the scenario that the state of the player's hand, the dealer's hand, and the deck are set up in a given context so that when an action occurs, the outcome can be predicted. This is all achieved by setting up the state of the game directly in the database.

Take a look at the step definitions for the scenario in the following code listing.

```
[Binding]
public class GameSetUpSteps
{
    [Given(@"the deck contains the following cards:")]
    public void GivenTheDeckContainsTheFollowingCards(Table table)
    {
        var game_builder = new GameBuilder()
            .find_game_by_player_id(PlayerToken.player_id);
```

```
        foreach(var row in table.Rows)
            game_builder
              .add_to_deck(TableObjectMapper.create_deck_row_from(row));

        var game = game_builder.build();

        DataBaseHelper.save(game);
    }

    [Given(@"I have started a new game and bet ""(.*)""")]
    public void GivenIHaveStartedANewGameAndBet(decimal bet_amount)
    {
        var game = new GameBuilder()
                        .create_for(PlayerToken.player_id)
                        .add_hand_with_bet_of(bet_amount)
                            .with_status_of(HandStatus.in_play)
                            .set_as_active()
                            .build()
                        .set_number_of_playing_positions_as(1)
                        .set_game_state_to(TableStatus.full_table)
                        .build();

        DataBaseHelper.add(game);
    }

    [Given(@"my hand contains the following cards:")]
    public void GivenMyHandContainsTheFollowingCards(Table table)
    {
        var game_builder = new GameBuilder()
                            .find_game_by_player_id(PlayerToken.player_id);

        var cards = new List<CardInHandRow>();
        foreach(var row in table.Rows)
            cards.Add(TableObjectMapper.create_card_in_hand_row_from(row));

        game_builder.for_players_hand()
                    .add_cards(cards);

        var game = game_builder.build();

        DataBaseHelper.save(game);
    }


    [Given(@"the dealers hand contains the following cards:")]
    public void GivenTheDealersHandContainsTheFollowingCards(Table table)
    {
        var game_builder = new GameBuilder()
                            .find_game_by_player_id(PlayerToken.player_id);
```

```
    var cards = new List<CardInHandRow>();

    foreach (var row in table.Rows)
        cards.Add(TableObjectMapper.create_card_in_hand_row_from(row));

    game_builder.add_cards_to_dealers_hand(cards);

    var game = game_builder.build();

    DataBaseHelper.save(game);
}

    ...

}
```

You can see from the code snippet that the GameBuilder class is used to create the state of the game using a fluent builder and then given to the database helper, which in turn uses NHibernate to persist the game state.

The GameBuilder class, part of which is shown in the following code snippet, is very simple in that it returns a reference to itself after each method call so that methods can be chained together. The only exception to this is the Build method, which returns a BlackJackTableRow that maps directly to the data relational model.

```
public class GameBuilder
{
    private BlackJackTableRow _blackjacktablerow;

    public GameBuilder create_for(Guid player_id)
    {
        _blackjacktablerow = new BlackJackTableRow();
        _blackjacktablerow.id = Guid.NewGuid();
        _blackjacktablerow.hand_rows = new List<HandTableRow>();
        _blackjacktablerow.deck_rows = new List<DeckRow>();
        _blackjacktablerow.player_token = player_id;

        return this;
    }

    public BlackJackTableRow build()
    {
        return _blackjacktablerow;
    }

    public GameBuilder find_game_by_player_id(Guid player_id)
    {
        using (var session = SessionFactory.GetNewSession())
        {
            _blackjacktablerow = session
                                     .Query<BlackJackTableRow>()
                        .Where(x => x.player_token == player_id)
                                            .SingleOrDefault();
        }
```

```
        return this;
    }

    public GameBuilder add_to_deck(DeckRow card)
    {
        card.blackjacktable_id = _blackjacktablerow.id;
        _blackjacktablerow.deck_rows.Add(card);

        return this;
    }

    public GameBuilder set_game_state_to(TableStatus table_status)
    {
        _blackjacktablerow.can_accept_bet = table_status.can_accept_bet;
        _blackjacktablerow.can_deal = table_status.can_deal;
        _blackjacktablerow.state_id = table_status.id;
        _blackjacktablerow.state_name = table_status.name;

        return this;
    }

    ...

  }
}
```

## Core Test Project

As with the Acceptance.Tests project, the Core.Tests project follows on from the exercise that you completed earlier in the chapter. Figure 9-13 shows the breadth of features that the tests cover. The whole application was built in a test-first manner and with an inside-out method that allowed the underlying objects to be discovered by driving the design of the system from the acceptance tests.

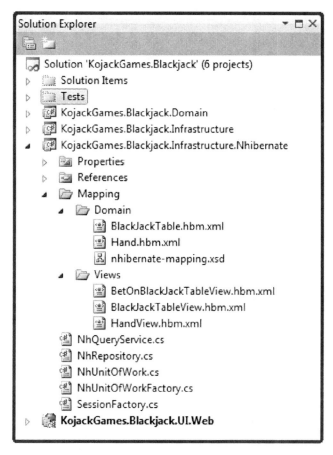

*Figure 9-13. The core unit test project*

## NHibernate Infrastructure Project

For the database relationship between the application and the database, we chose to use NHibernate, an open source object-relational mapping (ORM) tool that is widely used in the industry. Another ORM tool option is Entity Framework (EF).

The NHibernate project, as shown in Figure 9-14, is a fairly standard setup with separate mappings for the view and domain model classes. Both mappings map to the same tables, but the views only take a specific context view of the domain and map directly to the domain views, as can be seen in the domain project.

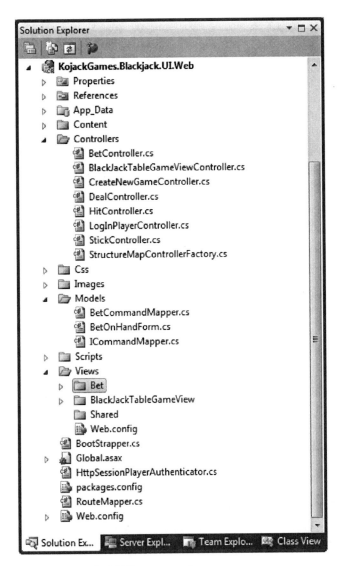

*Figure 9-14. The NHibernate project*

The NHibernate project has a generic repository class, as shown in the following code listing, which satisfies the needs of persisting the BlackJackTable entity.

```
namespace KojackGames.Blackjack.Infrastructure.Nhibernate
{
    public class NhRepository<T> : IRepository<T> where T : IEntity
    {
        private readonly ISession _session;
```

```
        public NhRepository(ISession session)
        {
            _session = session;
        }

        public T find_by(Guid id)
        {
            return _session.Get<T>(id);
        }

        public IEnumerable<T> find_all()
        {
            return new List<T>();
        }

        public void save(T entity)
        {
            _session.SaveOrUpdate(entity);
        }

        public T query_for_single(Func<T, bool> func)
        {
            return _session.Query<T>().Where(func).SingleOrDefault();
        }

        public void remove(T entity)
        {
            _session.Delete(entity);
        }
    }
}
```

The only other real class of note is the NhQueryService, an implementation of the IQueryService, which forms the query side of the CQRS architecture and can be seen in the following code listing.

```
namespace KojackGames.Blackjack.Infrastructure.Nhibernate
{
    public class NhQueryService : IQueryService
    {
        public T query_for_single<T>(Func<T, bool> query)
        {
            using (var session = SessionFactory.GetNewSession())
            {
                return session.Query<T>().Where(query).FirstOrDefault();
            }
        }
    }
}
```

# Web Project

The final project in the application is the web project, shown in full in Figure 9-15.

All of the controllers work in the same way shown in the exercise earlier in the chapter. They are created per UI task or concern to keep them thin. Controllers that deal with displaying the state of the game utilize the IQueryService as can be seen in the BlackJackTableGameViewController controller, shown in the following code listing.

```
namespace KojackGames.Blackjack.UI.Web.Controllers
{
    public class BlackJackTableGameViewController : Controller
    {
        private readonly IPlayerAuthenticator _player_authenticator;
        private readonly IQueryService _query_service;

        public BlackJackTableGameViewController(
                                    IPlayerAuthenticator player_authenticator,
                                            IQueryService query_service)
        {
            _player_authenticator = player_authenticator;
            _query_service = query_service;
        }

        public ActionResult display()
        {
            var game_summary =
                _query_service.query_for_single<BlackJackTableView>(
                    x => x.player_token ==
                            _player_authenticator.get_player_token());

            return View(game_summary);
        }
    }
}
```

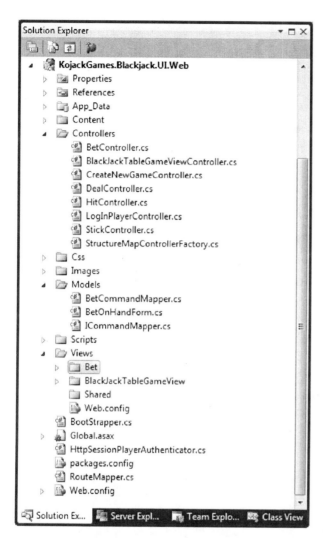

*Figure 9-15. KojackGames.Blackjack.UI.Web project*

# StructureMap

StructureMap is used to tie all of the dependencies together and build a collection of ICommandMapper and ICommandHandlers, as seen in the BootStrapper class.

```
namespace KojackGames.Blackjack.UI.Web
{
    public class BootStrapper
    {
        public static void ConfigureDependencies()
        {
```

```
        ObjectFactory.Initialize(x =>
        {
            x.AddRegistry<ControllerRegistry>();
            x.AddRegistry<CommandHandlerRegistry>();
            x.AddRegistry<CommandMappersRegistry>();
        });
    }

    public class CommandMappersRegistry : Registry
    {
        public CommandMappersRegistry()
        {
            Scan(s =>
            {
                s.TheCallingAssembly();
                s.ConnectImplementationsToTypesClosing(
                            typeof(ICommandMapper<,>));
            });
        }
    }

    public class CommandHandlerRegistry : Registry
    {
        public CommandHandlerRegistry()
        {
            Scan(s =>
            {
                s.Assembly("KojackGames.Blackjack.Domain");
                s.ConnectImplementationsToTypesClosing(
                            typeof(ICommandHandler<>));
            });
        }
    }

    public class ControllerRegistry : Registry
    {
        public ControllerRegistry()
        {
            For<IDealer>().Use<Dealer>();
            For<IHandScorer>().Use<HandScorer>();
            For<IDealingInAction>().Use<DealingInAction>();
            For<IPlayDealersHandAction>().Use<PlayDealersHandAction>();
            For<IHandStatusFactory>().Use<HandStatusFactory>();
            ...
        }
    }
}
}
```

This wraps up the key points and projects in the Kojack Games Blackjack application and the architecture that was built to build the features.

# Summary

This chapter walked you through a code review and a review of the architecture that the `Kojack.Blackjack` solution implements. For the sake of brevity, all the code is not printed in the book, so we encourage you to download the code located at `www.apress.com` and study the code in conjunction with the book. In this chapter, we covered the following topics:

- Discussed the solution architecture of the `Kojack.Blackjack` solution and the CQS pattern that was implemented

- Broke out the way projects were laid out and the reason for the logical breaking of projects

- Reviewed the third-party tools that were used, including `StructureMap` for Dependency Inversion and NHibernate as our ORM

Throughout the chapter, class diagrams were represented to show the plan and review the code in the solution. As we walked through the architecture, there tended to be at least one more layer needed to get the application up to that domain in the domain-driven design. This helps to improve communication with the business.

In the next chapter, we'll take a look at how the release went in the review session and cover what we've learned throughout the case study.

# What's Ahead for You and Scrum?

You made it!

You read about the drawbacks of plan-driven development, also known as the "waterfall" development method. With plan-driven development, we were not providing value to our customers or being transparent with our customers about what we were doing and what they needed. We needed to improve our way of developing software. We needed to get away from 400-page design documents as the solution to a problem. We needed to put our customer back into the forefront of our efforts.

You read about value-driven development and its champion, Agile. You learned what Scrum is all about and what defines eXtreme Programming. You saw an example of how agile can be used in the real world. You learned how to take the idea of agile from paper and apply it to your team. You may be asking yourself, where do we go from here? Well, first, let's look at where we have been.

## Scrum

Scrum's framework is a healthy framework, both from a cultural and software development standpoint, to use for guiding a development team. Scrum is about the accountability and transparency of a team. Scrum identifies problems earlier in the process; however, it will not fix the problems. Scrum does not teach you what frameworks to use or which source control to use or how to develop. It doesn't show you how to do your job; it provides you ways to better do your job. Scrum holds true to the values of the Agile Manifesto, which are as follows:

- Individuals and interactions over processes and tools

- Working software over comprehensive documentation

- Customer collaboration over contract negotiation

- Responding to change over following a plan

Throughout this case study, our process and, hopefully, we as individuals, have evolved. We started with understandable criticism. Why do we use all these Post-it notes? What are the swim lanes on the Kanban board for? Why are we having a meeting every, single, work day? Why do we have to write user stories in a certain format? And, for Pete's sake, why are we spending so much time on creating automated tests? I just want to crank out code! We're *software developers* and we are managing items with *Post-it notes and a board*? How could this ever be efficient? It seems as if we've taken a step back in time!

Yet over time, we came to appreciate that the Post-it notes and the swim lanes serve as great ways to capture manageable, measurable pieces of work that keep everyone updated on the team's progress. These tools allow us to create big, visible charts (BVCs), such as burn-down charts, to allow both team members and people outside the team a quick overview of how the project is progressing. We write user stories in a certain way to help capture what the business tells us it needs; and this consistency also helps to form and translate these requirements into interactive features.

Automated testing is important because developers can work with the business and with testers to determine the clear definition of requirements by writing our tests first and then writing the code to get those tests to pass; as opposed to writing code first from a piece of paper. Although this guarantees that the code does what it was written to do, it may not correspond to what the users want. This is where regular communication with the customer comes in. Automated testing also aids in producing robust and shippable code to verify that the tests work and that the code is what the business wants.

Scrum is a big advocate of a quick feedback loop for improving our process. As the team from the case study went through multiple sprints, they came to value this quick feedback loop. Feedback loops come in a few different varieties. From a "people" point-of-view, there are daily stand-ups, product demos, and retrospectives. From the code perspective, there is the continuous integration (CI) server.

The daily stand-ups are quick, simple, and effective. With everyone announcing what they did yesterday, what they are doing today, and what roadblocks they are experiencing, they are being transparent about their progress to the rest of the team. No one is able to hide from the team. No one can stay in his cube without anyone knowing what he is doing. Everyday everyone must stand up with their peers and tell what they did. This is one time where peer pressure is good.

It's important to note what we have not seen. In traditional methodologies, project managers or bosses would often come up to a developer and ask for a status update. At the extreme, these happen several times a day. Unfortunately, this wrecks a developer's train of thought when he is focused on getting something done. Context switching is a very costly exercise and it happens often in a "traditional" environment. With the daily stand-up, the project managers, the bosses, or any individuals that "need to know" come to this meeting to get information. Because the daily stand-up is quick and at a consistent time, it's easy to become a daily routine.

## Product Demos

Product demos are key to improving customer confidence and transparency. Through the sprint planning, the team commits to accomplishing a certain number of features for the sprint. When the product demos occur at the end of the sprint, the team shows the customer everything accomplished for that sprint. It provides transparency and confidence for the customer, and a sense of satisfaction for the team. Sitting with your customer to show them what you've done and listen to their comments about it is very valuable. It gives back to the customer in a way that was never done before. Developers are no longer allowed to go into a black hole while the customers pray that they get what they want at the end of three to six months. As shown in the case study, every two weeks the development team meets with the customer to show what the team is working on—and everyone is glad that they met.

Creating software is just that, creating software. In agile, it's the primary measure of progress as a team. It's creating something that oftentimes people have not seen before. When the team does a "show-and-tell" for the customer, that piece is already built and there's something concrete that the team and the customer can discuss. As with our case study, often the product demos will spark inspiration for new ideas from the team or the customer. This innovation and inspiration is a fruitful result of the collaboration between the team and the customer. While this innovation and inspiration is highly encouraged, the team and the customer need to understand that the definition of "done" that they decided beforehand is still in effect. Any new ideas need to be groomed and their priority determined before working on them. A great idea one day may become lowest-priority idea another day.

# Retrospectives

The sprint retrospectives have proved very efficient throughout this case study. At the end of each sprint, the team discusses what went right and wrong and decides how to improve these items for the next sprint. Having the team own its own process within a framework is ideal because each team member is a part of something and is not forced to do anything unwillingly.

Creating a safe, trustworthy environment for team members to speak is crucial. You may notice that certain people will want to constantly speak on things and others will simply blend into the background. To create a trustworthy environment, the ScrumMaster or team members need to notice when someone is taking control of a meeting and halt it so that others can speak. As for those who prefer to blend in the background, it is up to the team to encourage them to speak. Be an advocate for them to speak their minds. You may notice that the quiet ones have profound views on things.

Retrospectives are worthless if team members don't feel as if they can speak up or they don't have confidence that things will change as roadblocks are uncovered. Good, safe, clear communication is key to evolving a team and evolving any process. There needs to be good facilitation skills present to help with this. Normally, you can find these skills in the ScrumMaster or Agile coach, but it does not have to be limited to them. Team members can also bring these skills to the table. Retrospectives are a fantastic way to have the team own and improve their own process.

There were milestone action items that came from retrospectives, including the importance of pair programming and the importance of having an available customer and/or product owner. Be sure to occasionally change your activities on how to conduct a retrospective. You saw that the team started doing the retrospective one way and then switched to the retrospective game "The Soup" to get a better understanding of the issues the team was dealing with. As with anything, repeatedly doing the same thing gets dull and you may not see a problem unless it's presented from a different angle. If retrospectives get dull, they are no longer useful and you may as well discontinue having them because they become a waste of time. While not advised, teams have skipped a retrospective because they didn't think it was useful. Some times it may be more fruitful to not have a retrospective, as long as the team has an effective retrospective at the end of the following sprint.

Be prepared, have a variety of different activities to gather what went well and what didn't go so well during the sprint. You don't have to change how you run retrospectives at every sprint, but try something new and give it time to work. If it doesn't, then throw it out and try something else. If you are a ScrumMaster on a team, check out books or blogs on retrospectives. For example, the book *Agile Retrospectives* by Esther Derby and Diana Larsen (Pragmatic Bookshelf, 2006) is a great resource for discovering different ways of running a retrospective. These sources can yield a plethora of ideas on how to run your retrospectives. This keeps the team members alert and alert team members are more willing to give constructive feedback. That's what we want!

Also, make sure that the action items that come out of the retrospective get acted upon and resolved quickly. If the same painful action items appear week after week, there's nothing more damaging to a team's morale than to see that nothing is being done to update or resolve these matters. Have each action item assigned to one person on the team, even if the action item concerns the entire team. It's that person's responsibility to follow up and make sure the action item is getting handled.

If an action item gets carried over from sprint to sprint, throw it out. It obviously wasn't important enough to work on or it would have been completed. A truly important item will come back again.

By completing action items, the team gets a sense of accomplishment and confidence in the process. Presenting ways to improve a process and seeing nothing come of it is death to a team. Eventually team members become disconnected from the entire process. Without the team working together, you might as well go back to the old way of doing things. Remember, agile is excellent at bringing the weaknesses to the forefront, but solving them is *your* job—make sure you solve problems quickly to build team moral!

# Continuous Integration

A continuous integration (CI) server is the feedback loop from the code's perspective. This feedback is crucial to the whole team and, yes, the code does speak. It says things like the following:

- I can't build because there are build errors or reference issues.

- My automated tests are failing.

- Tests are taking a while to complete, better start organizing these tests into different groups that run at different times; some after every build and some at certain times of the day.

The CI server aids in development by saving developers time. Instead of the "old school" way of everyone checking in code after days or weeks of development, and dealing with merge conflicts, and having no way of knowing if changes broke an existing piece of functionality, how about allowing everyone to work off one branch of the code base, set up a CI server to run after every check in, and deal with any merge conflicts on a much smaller level. The CI server can also verify that the new functionality did not break existing functionality by running a set of automated tests against the code. Quickly providing this feedback to the developers instills confidence—and you will start seeing these developers checking in multiple times per day. Because the feedback loop is tighter, a lot of the merge conflicts disappear because everyone is working in and checking into the same code base at more frequent intervals.

By running the automated tests after every check in, you get the added benefit of having a stable environment that has already been smoke-tested. The code is ready for the team members that are testing to begin without first having to do regression testing to make sure the new functionality did not break the existing functionality.

# Plan-Do-Study-Act

Throughout the case study, we followed the Deming Cycle, which is the widely-recognized, four-step process for continual improvement, also known as PDSA or Plan-Do-Study-Act.

- *Plan*: With each sprint, there was a planning session on what the team wanted to accomplish. User stories were written and estimated; and acceptance criteria was written so the team and the customer knew the rules to determine if a feature was done.

- *Do*: This is the sprint. During the sprint, the features were developed.

- *Study*: At the conclusion of every sprint, the team conducted a retrospective to study what it just did and derive ways to improve the process. The team asked themselves, how can we improve, how can we become more efficient, and how can we improve our process? As a result of this study, action items were noted and assigned to be handled.

- *Act*: These were the action items that came from the retrospective. The team had great influence on the process. Taking the action items from the retrospective, the team acted to improve the process.

This cycle repeats for every sprint and even on a daily basis as the team evolves. The team proves it can handle greater tasks as its process evolves. The team becomes more efficient, and knowing that, they decide their own destiny.

# eXtreme Programming

While Scrum is the project management and process side of a project, eXtreme Programming (XP) is the process or methodology for developing features and is a tool for doing the work. Let's look at XP's five values and discuss how they were played out among the case study.

- *Communication*: The success or failure of a team largely depends on communication. As was determined early in the case study, Sarah became a bottleneck in the process due to her domain knowledge. This was communicated by Tyler since he spoke up and informed the group he couldn't finish a story due to waiting on Sarah. This proved to be constructive criticism as they needed to share domain knowledge. The spreading of domain knowledge across the team was accomplished through pair programming.

  The daily stand-ups also served to bridge this communication gap between the team. By facilitating the flow of communication among and outside the team, they could determine issues and roadblocks early, move them out of the way, and continue on the path of developing value-added software to the customer.

- *Simplicity*: Since both Sarah and Tyler, and even Joe later on, were good software developers, they were able to communicate and brainstorm together; the outcome resulted in a simple solution. Good solutions evolve and are typically not the result of the first thought. With pair programming, programmers can consult each other instantaneously to quickly produce a simpler solution. Simplicity makes a product more maintainable in the future. You noticed that code was written only when it was needed. The team started with a framework architecture (MVC, NHibernate, etc.) that the team decided upon based on the known, high-level requirements. The first few features were spent proving and building confidence that the architecture the team built worked. Over time, the architecture emerged from the team to become an architecture that was used when needed, not a "plan" for something that didn't even happen. The Agile Manifesto says "Simplicity—the art of maximizing the amount of work not done—is essential."

- *Feedback*: Feedback came from the time and effort the developers spent writing tests so as not to break anything. The feedback loop from a code perspective using a CI server can save countless hours by providing you quick feedback as opposed to trying to fix a build a week after five developers checked different things in over the course of time.

- *Courage*: The team needed courage to communicate that some of the customer's ideas on features that were out of scope. Instead of quietly going back and developing these features or gold-plating some functionality, the team had the courage to communicate to the customer that the new ideas were fantastic, but needed to be worked in because they were not part of the story. This proved the importance of determining the definition of "done" before a feature is written, so that everyone has the same expectation.

- *Respect*: While respect can come in many different ways, one example comes from team members breaking the build. Tyler had an issue with that early on; and while the team did not yell at him, they did bring it to his attention. Tyler began to pay closer attention, broke fewer builds, and became more respectful of the team. This openness and willingness to accept constructive criticism lead to a respectful team that could focus on work and not drama.

We started the case study with Sarah and Tyler in silos, each developing on their own. We soon discovered through daily stand-ups and retrospectives that this was not a sustainable path to continue; their different domain knowledge became roadblocks. But, through XP, two great minds came together and worked through the fear of using new tools and newly spelled-out features. This ended the self-made silos and the team began to work more efficiently. Sarah and Tyler worked with other team members to implement features and write scenarios. XP served to improve both their skill sets as they learned new tools, and also created a greater sense of team camaraderie and trust, which ultimately contributed to a more solid and efficient team.

XP also encourages automated testing. As this case study has shown, with behavior-driven development (BDD) there is a large amount of work that can be done through automated tests. Developing from the outside-in aligns the developers more closely with the business. BDD aids in bridging the communication gap between developers and the business by using SpecFlow; in this case, a business person could read the feature and the scenarios and understand what that feature is doing. That's what we want! We want to develop a code base that will stand the test of business time and not the test of code-smell/code-rot time. We can ensure this by bringing the language closer to the business, as we have through BDD and SpecFlow and, from this create automated tests so we know that when we change something, it doesn't break something else. Simplicity and reliability are attributes of code maintainability. We know that with pair programming, our process evolves to a simpler state than with a single developer. Code is more reliable due to automated tests. The cost of later adding a feature is dramatically reduced because the next developer can be confident that when he changes an existing feature or adds a new feature, he won't break existing functionality.

# Where to Go from Here

As you move forward and onto your next agile project, the following are things to remember:

*Agile is iterative.* Don't try to do it all at once. Rome was not built in a day and changing a team to becoming more agile is not very different. People change and changing the habits of people takes time and sensitivity. Do small chunks over and over as a way to build the confidence of the team. You can build off these small successes, which lead to greater rewards.

*You won't get it right the first time.* You are going underestimate a user story. You are going to select a tool that does not solve the problem. You are going to fail; however, don't be afraid to fail. Don't be afraid to try something and have it not work. When that happens, throw it out and try something else. Something will work eventually; you just need to find it. Work to set up an environment where failure is okay. Success comes from knowledge and knowledge comes from failure. As Sir Winston Churchill said, "To improve is to change; to be perfect is to change often."

*When you find something that doesn't fail, don't be afraid to improve it.* Don't become stagnant. Always strive to improve the process and yourself. Seek out new ways of doing things.

*No matter what you hear, there is no cookie-cutter approach to agile.* What tools work for this team may not work for that team, and that is okay. Agile is a framework that exposes our problems, but won't fix them. It is up to us to decide what we do with them. We just can't hide from them anymore. Each situation you encounter is different. Strive to find the tool that works for your team, not the hottest new tool out there. Don't be afraid to learn from the experience of others. Although you often have to do that kind of learning, you can't start from scratch every time or discover everything yourself.

*There are going to be tough times for you and your team.* See it through. Hell, you might even have a team member interrupt a meeting so they can point a finger and place blame on someone. Work through it. Communication is the key. No matter what, keep the lines of communication open among the team. Share your frustrations, have your "Kumbaya" moments, but talk about the frustrations that the team is having. More importantly work on ways, with your team, to improve the problem and relieve some stress. When that happens, you can laugh about that ridiculous time the team member interrupted a meeting to point a finger at another team member to blame him for something trivial. Trust us; we know. If you find it hard to work through these frustrations, consider inviting someone onto your team who already has experience and success of delivering at least one agile project.

*Testing is key.* Without testing you are doing yourself and your customer a serious injustice.

*Treat your test code the same way you treat your production code.* The code smell that comes from production code can just as easily come from the test code. You may not ship the test code to customers, but it is vital to the longevity of the application. Regularly re-factor and clean up your tests. It lends itself to making it that much easier to extend functionality in the application.

*Always seek out the smarter way to do things.* Use, engage, and never be afraid to ask your fellow developers questions. The team owns its destiny, be sure to build a team where you're excited to come to work every day to solve complex problems and create awesome software!

As software developers, we encourage you to make your mark on this infant industry. It is your duty as a software craftsman (or craftswoman) to engage and help evolve and mature our industry. Write or blog about your passions in software development. Talk about it with your peers. Find out what they know. We as a community need you to be passionate about this. Get out there and be vocal.

Finally, have fun!

# TDD Primer with NUnit

What tools do you use for testing in .NET? This is a question many new developers who come to the land of TDD have for experienced developers. New developers are often not sure which testing framework is the best one to use.

NUnit is a testing framework that has become the standard for testing in .NET. NUnit is a member of the XUnit family of testing languages, and as such is an open-source tool. There are other testing frameworks out there; however, none have had the level adoption that NUnit has. We plan on showing you how to install NUnit, either through the NUnit web site or through NuGet. We will finish this with a TDD primer to whet your appetite for using NUnit in the case-study chapters.

## Installation

NUnit can be installed in two ways: through the NUnit web site and through NuGet.

## Web Page Installation

To install NUnit you will need the following:

- Visual Studio (any version)

- The latest version of NUnit located at www.nunit.org/index.php?p=download

    - Please note that in order to get the NUnit client to run, you need to have .NET Framework 2.0 installed. It won't matter if you are using a different version of the framework for your development.

You will need to go the NUnit web site and download the latest version of the tool from the download tab, as shown in Figure A-1.

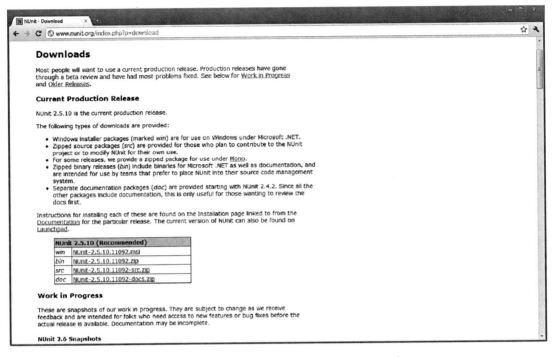

*Figure A-1. The download page at nunit.org*

Clicking the downloaded .msi file will launch the usual install wizard. We recommend that you select the Complete setup type, as shown in Figure A-2.

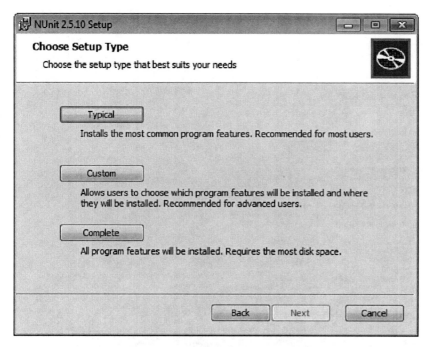

*Figure A-2. Selecting setup type while installing NUnit from .msi file*

As part of the installation, the NUnit client will also be installed on your system. We will show you how to use this tool in a moment. Once the installation is complete, the NUnit DLL is registered on your machine and available to be used in your testing projects.

## NuGet Installation

Another and more convenient option for installing NUnit is through the NuGet Package Manager. NuGet is an open-source development tool that integrates into Visual Studio and gives you a simpler way of adding libraries into your project. If you are a Ruby developer or familiar with the Ruby language, you can think of NuGet as the .NET equivalent to Ruby Gems.

Installing NuGet is very simple. NuGet is available through the Extension Manager that is a part of Visual Studio, as shown in Figure A-3. If you do not see it listed, you have the option to search for it in the search bar in the upper-right corner of the window. Simply click the Download button, and when the download is complete, restart Visual Studio. You are done.

*Figure A-3. The Extension Manager window in Visual Studio*

Once NuGet is installed, you can access the Package Manager Console; this is where you will interact with NuGet. To get to the Package Manager Console, navigate to View   Other Windows   Package Manager Console, as shown in Figure A-4.

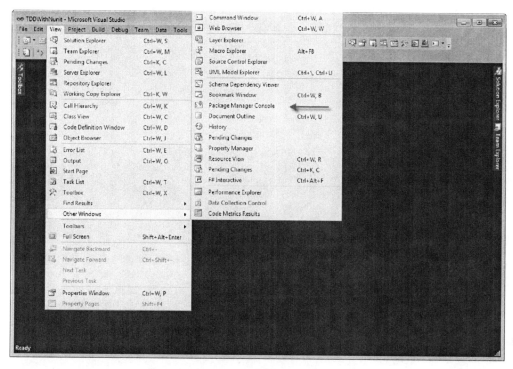

*Figure A-4. Navigating to the Package Manager console*

To install the NUnit package, first you need to have a solution open. For the TDD aspects of this, we created a solution called TDDWithNunit. We will talk more about this solution and the projects that make up the solution in a moment. From inside the Package Management Console window, run the following command:

```
PM> Install-Package NUnit
```

What this command does is go to the web and pull the latest version of NUnit that NuGet knows of and installs it in the project that is listed in the Default Project drop-down. NuGet will not install NUnit on the system. As part of installing NUnit into the project, NuGet will add references to NUnit to the project. To verify that the install was successful, run the following command to see which packages are installed on a project, as shown in Figure A-5.

```
PM> Get-Package
```

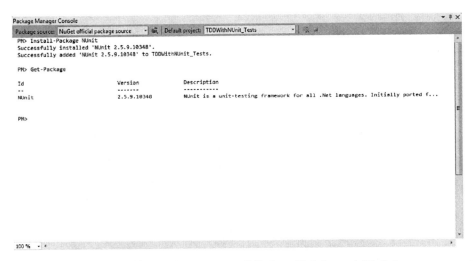

*Figure A-5. Checking that NUnit was successfully installed through NuGet*

---

■ **Note** If you install NUnit through NuGet, you do not get the NUnit client installed. There are multiple tools that you can use to run NUnit tests, including TestDriven.NET and ReSharper. If you want to use the NUnit client to run your tests, then install NUnit through the .msi file on the NUnit web site.

---

# TDD Walk-through

Now that you have NUnit installed, you can begin to write code using test-driven development (TDD). This is a software development practice in which the developer writes tests before code. Once the tests are written, the developer will write just enough code to get the tests to pass. Once the tests pass, the developer can be certain that the code does what the customer wanted it to do because the tests are based on acceptance criteria provided by the customer.

A common pattern in TDD is red-green-refactor. You start off with failed tests (red). You then write enough code to get them to pass (green). Then you refactor the code so that it is more manageable before moving on to the next step (refactor).

---

■ **Note** NuGet may not always have the latest version of a DLL, but you can update the DLL that you have for your project through NuGet. As of this writing, for example, the latest version of NUnit from its web site is 2.5.10.11092. NuGet, however, installs version 2.5.9.10348.

---

In this walk-through, we are going to write a simple math class that will handle multiplying two numbers. We will use TDD to write our tests and then write the code in the math class that will get the tests to pass. First, create a new console application and call it TDDWithNUnit. Once the solution is created, we need to do the following to write the first test:

1.  Add a new class library project to the solution. This new project should have the following naming convention *ProjectUnderTest*.Tests, where *ProjectUnderTest* is the name of the project that contains the methods you will be writing the tests against. For our walk-through, you will see that Figure A-6 contains a project called TDDWithNunit that contains the math class that we will be testing and a project called TDDWithNunit_Tests that will contain the tests.

2.  If you installed NUnit from the .msi file instead of through NuGet, you will need to add a reference to the NUnit DLL (nunit.framework) to the test project, as shown in Figure A-7. If you used NuGet to install NUnit, then you should already have the reference.

3.  Add a reference to TDDWithNunit to the test project TDDWithNunit_Tests.

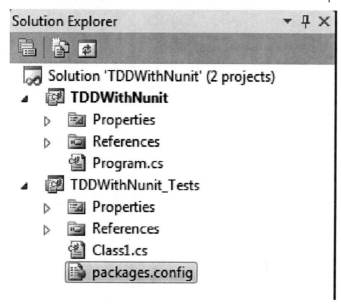

*Figure A-6. Folder structure*

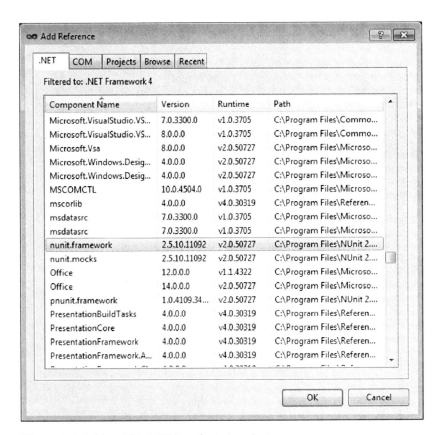

*Figure A-7. Adding NUnit DLL to the test project*

Once NUnit is set up, we can write our first tests. Create a class under the TDDWithNunit.Tests project called tddMathSpec.cs. You can go ahead and delete the file called Class1.cs but it is not mandatory. To be able to use the NUnit framework as well as access the tddMath class that contains our production code (we will talk about this file later), we need to add the following using statements to the tddMathSpec class:

```
using NUnit.Framework;
using TDDWithNunit;
```

Now we need to let NUnit know that this class contains tests that need to be run. To do this we mark the class tddMathSpec with the attribute TestFixture.

```
using NUnit.Framework;
using TDDWithNunit;

namespace TDDWithNUnit_Tests
{
    [TestFixture]
    public class tddMathSpec
    {
```

```
      }
}
```

Now, let's add the test method AddTwoNumbers_returns_3_when_given_1_and_2. (we always like to name our test methods this way so that we know what method they are testing, as well as what the expected inputs and outputs are). Once we add this method, we need to add the attribute Test to it so that NUnit knows that this is a test to be run.

```
[Test]
public void Add_returns_3_when_given_1_and_2()
{
}
```

---

▒ **Note** All test methods should be void methods.

---

To test the method, we need to set up the object to get it to a state that we can test the method in question. Next, add a new method to the class called Setup() and place the attribute Setup above this. What this attribute does is tell NUnit to run this method before each test that is run in the class. We use this method to set up everything we need to test the method. All that's left is to call the method with our two inputs and assert that the result from the method is what we expect.

```
using NUnit.Framework;
using NUnitTutorial;

namespace TDDWithNUnit_Tests
{
  [TestFixture]
  public class tddMathSpec
  {
        tddMath tMath;
        decimal expected = 3;

        [SetUp]
        public void setup()
        {
            tMath = new tddMath();
        }

        [Test]
        public void Add_returns_3_when_given_1_and_2()
        {
            Assert.That(tMath.Add(1, 2) == expected);
        }
  }
}
```

What this test simply does is call the Add method on the tddMath class, giving it a 1 and a 2, and asserts that result given back is a 3. When you try to build the solution, you will get compile errors saying that tddMath does not exist. We need to fix each compile error before we can get the tests to pass. To fix the compiler errors, you need to do the following:

- Add a new class called tddMath.cs to the TDDWithNunit project. Make sure it is marked as public.

- Add a new method to the tddMath class called Add. This method will take two decimal parameters and return a decimal, as well.

Now remember, at this point our goal is just to get the code to compile. We are not trying to get any tests to pass. We need them to first fail before we can pass them. Once the bulleted items are done, the tddMath class should look like the following:

```
namespace TDDWithNunit
{
    public class tddMath
    {
        public decimal Add(decimal num1, decimal num2)
        {
            return decimal.MinValue;
        }
    }
}
```

## Running NUnit

There are two ways that you can run the NUnit tests. Through the NUnit client or through a Visual Studio plugin like TestDriven.Net that allows you to run the tests from inside Visual Studio. If you had installed NUnit from NuGet, you will need to download and install a test runner like TestDriven.Net (www.testdriven.net/). If you did not install from NuGet, you should have the NUnit client already installed on your machine. Feel free to use whichever runner you prefer, but for this primer, we will stick with the NUnit client.

Start up the NUnit client by going to Program Files  NUnit2.5.9.10348  NUnit. Once it is up and running, click File  Open Project and navigate to where the DLLs generated from the test project are located, as shown in Figure A-8. You want to load the test project DLL into NUnit. Once the DLL is loaded, it will show you the tests that are in that DLL, as shown in Figure A-9. From here all you need to do is click the Run button and NUnit will run your tests and output the results, as shown in Figure A-10.

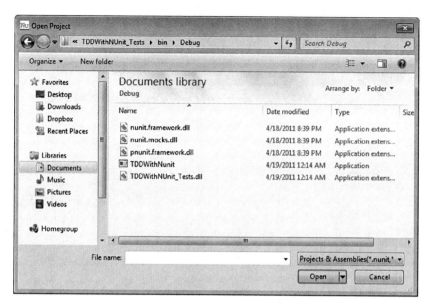

*Figure A-8. NUnit client open project dialog*

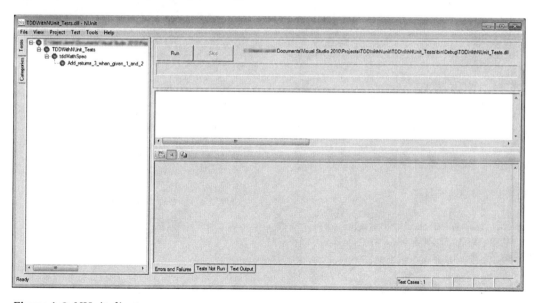

*Figure A-9. NUnit client*

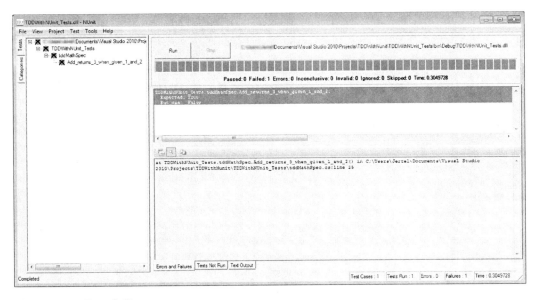

**Figure A-10.** *Tests failing*

Now that we have a failing test, we need to add code to the `tddMath` class and in particular the `Add` method to get this test to pass. To do this, let's look at the `Add` method.

```
public decimal Add(decimal num1, decimal num2)
{
    return decimal.MinValue;
}
```

What we see is that the method simply returns the decimal `MinValue`. Let's write this method so that it will take the two parameters and add them together and return that result. When finished, the method should look like the following:

```
public decimal Add(decimal num1, decimal num2)
{
    return num1 + num2;
}
```

With this change, we can build the solution and run the test again from the NUnit client. What we see now is that the tests pass, as shown in Figure A-11. With a passing test, we are finished with this piece and can move on to the next test.

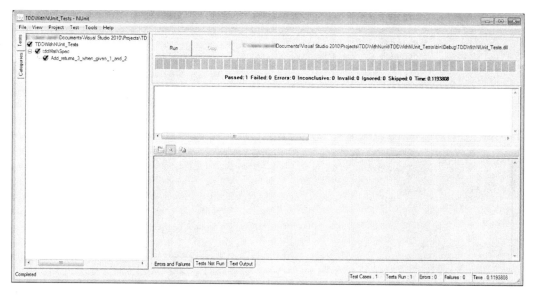

*Figure A-11. Tests passing*

# Adding Another Test

Let's move on to the next test, which will test that when given three numbers, the result coming back is correct. The following shows what the new test looks like:

```
[Test]
public void Add_returns_6_when_given_1_2_and_3()
{
    Assert.That(tMath.Add(1, 2, 3) == 6);
}
```

Now when we try to compile the solution, we get a compile error because the Add method we wrote does not take in three parameters. To get the compiler errors to go away, we need to refactor the existing Add method to accept three parameters. In fact, we should probably go ahead and set up the method so that it can take any number of parameters. Since we already have a test wrapped around this method, we can do this refactoring and feel confident that we are not breaking existing functionality. To save us some time, we will post what the method looks like when finished with this refactoring.

```
public decimal Add(params decimal[] numbers)
{
    return numbers.Sum();
}
```

When you run the NUnit client, your two tests should run and pass, as shown in Figure A-12.

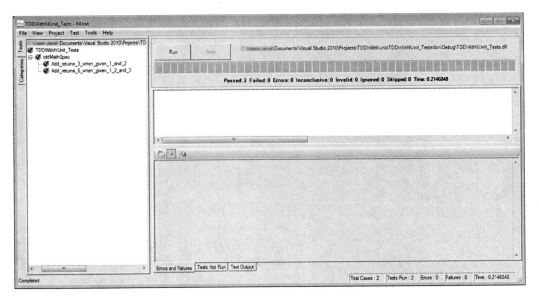

*Figure A-12. Multiple tests passing*

---

■ **Note** It is never a good idea to refactor a method that does not have any tests around it. The tests are your safety net in case you make a change that breaks existing functionality. If you need to refactor a method and it does not have any tests, write tests before you touch the method. These tests can be on anything, just create that safety net before you get on the high wire.

---

# Summary

This appendix provided a glimpse into TDD using the NUnit framework. We learned the following:

- How to install NUnit using either the .msi file from the nunit.org web site or NuGet.

- How to create a project that contains a test class.

- How to set up that test class to use the NUnit framework.

- How to write a test.

- After we write a test, we need to fix all the compiler errors before we can fail the test.

- Once we get the test failing (red), we add just enough code to the method that is being tested to get that test to pass (green).

- Once we get a passing test, we can move on to the next test. This next test may require us to refactor the existing method to get it to pass (refactor).

With this new-found knowledge, head back to the case-study section of this book to see how we use TDD and NUnit to write our blackjack application.

# BDD Primer with SpecFlow

When you start using test-driven development (TDD) in your work, you will feel empowered and secured in your development. After a while, however, the newness will wear off and you will want more out of your tests.

Behavior-driven development (BDD) is the next step in TDD. If you are not familiar with TDD, we suggest that you read Appendix A. BDD is centered on the behavior of a system. Where TDD was centered on the inner working of a system, BDD is concerned about the overall picture. BDD seeks a clearer understanding of the system by talking with the stakeholders of the system and understanding their desired behavior.

The test cases for BDD are written in a natural language. This allows the stakeholders and other non-developers to be a part of the system's development. The key to BDD is with its implementation of outside-in software development.

## Outside-In Software Development

Outside-in development focuses on the acceptance criteria as defined by the stakeholder. From the features and criteria defined by the stakeholders, you drive the design of your system and discover objects, as opposed to doing upfront design in which you are trying to design what the stakeholder might want. The goal of outside-in development is to produce software for the stakeholder that they want and need.

Figure B-1 shows the process of outside-in development, starting from selecting a user story to discovering low level classes via TDD.

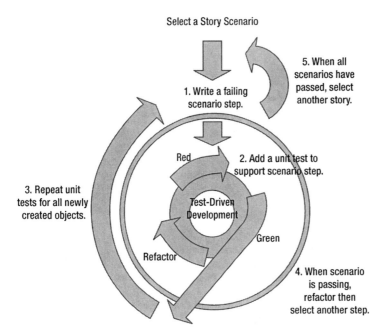

**Figure B-1.** *The outside-in development workflow*

The general flow of outside-in development is to start with a scenario (the outside part of outside-in development) and write a test for that. Once the test is written and fails, you step in one level deeper and write failing unit tests there. You keep going down a level at a time until you have reached the basic core method of the scenario. This core method usually is a simple method that takes basic inputs and returns a result. You then work yourself back up to the scenario by writing code that will make the tests pass in every level. Once you are done, you have a working behavior that is what the stakeholder expected. This suite of tests is also less brittle than just a set of unit tests.

## SpecFlow

The problem with BDD is that it is very hard, if not impossible, to turn the conversation with the stakeholders of a system into specific, detailed, code-level tests that the developer can use to create the story. In other words, how do we turn "meaningful" user requests into running code? This is where SpecFlow comes in.

SpecFlow is an open-source tool that allows a non-developer to define features or behaviors of the system in their own natural language (English, Russian, Chinese, etc.). A developer can then take those features and use SpecFlow to generate the scenarios for that feature. In essence, tests! A scenario is a unit test generated by SpecFlow from the feature. You can use any number of test runners to run these tests, for an example of this, refer to Appendix A.

The features are written in a format called the Gherkin language. The Gherkin language is a tool that was developed as an adjunct to Cucumber and works by placing the features in the format of Given/When/Then. Given refers to the setup of a test; When is the action performed by the test; and Then corresponds to the assertions that validate the test.

To install SpecFlow, navigate to `http://specflow.org/downloads/installer.aspx`, as shown in Figure B-2. Click the link and you will download an MSI installer file. Clicking the installation file will launch a typical installation wizard. Once this is installed, you will see SpecFlow templates that you can use in your application.

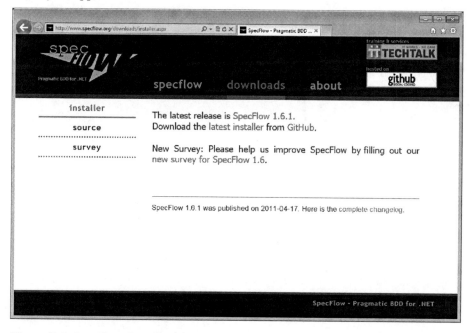

**Figure B-2.** *SpecFlow download page*

Another option is to use NuGet to download SpecFlow and add it to your project. As part of the walk-through in the next section, we will show you how to do this type of installation.

## BDD Walk-through

Now that you have been introduced to BDD and SpecFlow, you can begin writing code. In this walk-through we will show you a very simple example of using SpecFlow and BDD on an ASP.NET MVC solution. This is not a comprehensive walk-through, but we hope it will help you to see the benefit of using BDD in your projects, and how wonderful it is to have your customers and your developers speaking the same language.

The walk-through will consist of a feature with scenarios that pertain to a math-based web site. The feature will contain two scenarios and we will use BDD and TDD with NUnit (see Appendix A) to create the code needed to successfully implement this feature.

The first thing we need to do is create a new solution called MathSample. Once we have the empty solution, we need to start adding projects to it. The first thing we will do is add an ASP.NET MVC project to the solution called MathSample. This project will contain the web site in this example. Next, we will add a class library to the solution called MathSample.Specs. This project will contain all of our BDD and TDD tests. Now, on larger or more complicated projects, it is normal to split up the BDD and TDD aspects into their own projects in the solution with the BDD project labeled with .Specs and the TDD project labeled with .Tests, however, for simplicity in this appendix, we will combine the two into one project. We add the .Specs to the end of the project to remind us that we are writing specifications for the input the customer gave us in the way of features. When you are done, your solution should resemble the layout in Figure B-3.

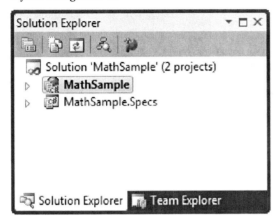

**Figure B-3.** *Your initial solution and projects*

Finally, we need to add references to SpecFlow and NUnit so we can write our tests. Using NuGet, this is a cinch. Begin by opening the Package Manager Console located under View   Other Windows   Package Manager Console, as shown in Figure B-4.

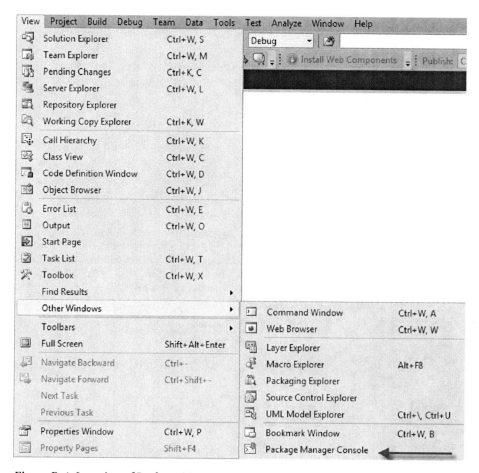

**Figure B-4.** *Location of Package Manager console*

With the console open, set the Default Project to MathSample.Specs. Type the following command to download SpecFlow and add a reference to it to the Specs project, as shown in Figure B-5.

```
PM> Install-Package SpecFlow
```

Now type the following command to download NUnit and add a reference to the Specs project as you see in Figure B-5.

```
PM> Install-Package NUnit
```

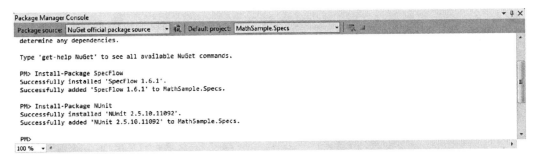

*Figure B-5. Using NuGet to install SpecFlow and NUnit*

## Writing Your Feature

With our solution structure set up, we can finally start to code. The feature we want to work on is giving the user the ability to add two numbers and see a result. To start, let's add a new folder to the MathSample.Specs project named Features. As you can guess, this folder will contain all the features that the customer gave us. Right-click on the newly created Features folder and add a new item. From the dialog box that appears, select the SpecFlow Feature File item as seen in Figure B-6.

*Figure B-6. The SpecFlow templates in Visual Studio*

Name the feature Addition.feature. Visual Studio will now create the feature and show a default template with a single scenario. Now that we have our feature file created, let's update the file to look like Figure B-7.

▓ **Note** For now, just add the first scenario (Navigation to MathPage) to the file. We will add the second scenario to the file later in the appendix.

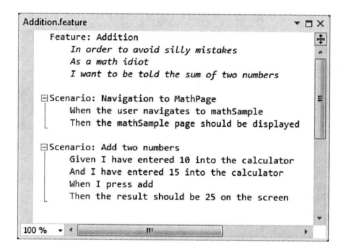

*Figure B-7. SpecFlow feature file*

If you take a closer look at the feature, you will see that it contains two scenarios. Another thing you will notice is that the wording is very conversational. It's like you are sitting down and actually talking to the customer. With the wording like this, you don't have to be a developer to understand what the system is doing.

## Scenario 1: Navigation to MathPage

Now that we have the feature file completed, compile the MathSample.Specs project. Once it is compiled, open up the NUnit client. If you have a question about how to run this client tool, see Appendix A. Once it is built, open up the NUnit client and load the DLL from the MathSample.Specs project. When you execute the test from the client, click on the Text Output tab and you will notice something strange, like that seen in Figure B-8.

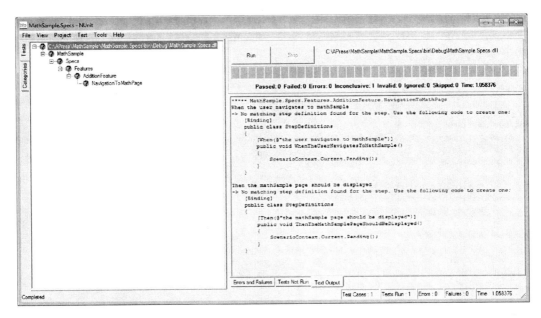

**Figure B-8.** *Step definition creation*

What you will notice is that the client said that the scenario test was inconclusive. It was inconclusive because there were no step definitions with this test, so it did not know how to run the test. The nice thing about the NUnit client tool is that it will actually generate the step definitions for you like you see in Figure B-8. What you see is that, based on the feature and the scenario we are testing, the system needs two steps to test it.

We need to copy these step definitions, so go to the MathSample.Spec project, right-click on it, and create a new folder called Steps. Once the new folder is created, right-click on it, and add a new class file to the folder called AdditionSteps.cs.

Copy the step definitions (do not include the classes) from the NUnit client tool and paste in the file created. You will need to remove the following line of code from each step:

```
ScenarioContext.Current.Pending();
```

We can continue by adding the necessary code to each of the steps. This code includes performing the action of going to the math page and asserting we are actually at the right page.

Next, add code to each method to test the app. You will also need to add a reference the MathSample project to the MathSample.Specs project so you can access the necessary controllers and views. When you are finished, your file should look like the following:

```
using System.Web.Mvc;
using MathSample.Controllers;
using MathSample.Models;
using NUnit.Framework;
using TechTalk.SpecFlow;

namespace MathSample.Specs.Steps

{
```

```
[Binding]
public class AdditionSteps
{
    ActionResult result;
    MathPageController mpController;

    [When(@"the user navigates to mathSample")]
    public void WhenTheUserNavigatesToMathSample()
    {
        mpController = new MathPageController();
        result = mpController.MathPage();
    }

    [Then(@"the mathSample page should be displayed")]
    public void ThenTheMathSamplePageShouldBeDisplayed()
    {
        Assert.IsInstanceOf<ViewResult>(result);
        Assert.AreEqual("Math Page", mpController.ViewData["Title"],
            "At the wrong page. Expected to be at the Math Page");
    }
}
}
```

There is one thing to note before we move on. The Binding attribute you see above the class is a SpecFlow attribute that allows SpecFlow to bind a step to the necessary methods. When you try to build the MathSample.Specs class, you will get numerous compile errors because the MathPageController and view are not created yet. Create the necessary file and objects to get the solution to compile.

Once you are able to compile the solution, run the NUnit client tool again and you will notice that there is no longer an inconclusive test, but a failed test, as shown in Figure B-9.

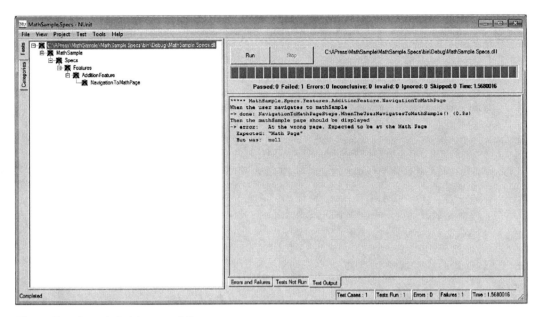

***Figure B-9.*** *Step definition test failure*

Now write the necessary code to get the test to pass, just like in TDD. To get the test to pass you need to do the following:

- Modify the method called MathPage() so that the method sets the title of the view before it returns the view

- Create a new view file located under Views  MathPage  MathPage.aspx

When this done, rerun the tests from the NUnit client and you will see that it passed, as shown in Figure B-10. Now, on to the next scenario!

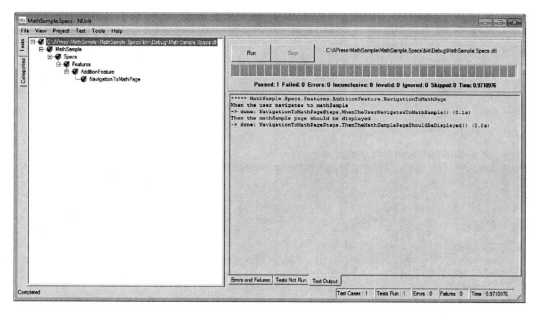

**Figure B-10.** *Step definition test success*

## Scenario 2: Add Two Numbers

We will handle this scenario just like the previous one. Go ahead and add this new scenario to the
Addition.feature file, as shown in Figure B-11. Once the scenario is added to the feature file, rerun
NUnit client and you will find that you have one test passed and one test inconclusive. You will also see
the step definitions for the inconclusive test. Copy the step definitions and paste them into the
AdditionSteps.cs file in the AdditionSteps class from the previous scenario.

```
Scenario: Add two numbers
    Given I have entered 10 into the page
    And I have entered 15 into the page
    When I press Add
    Then the result should be 25 on the screen
```

**Figure B-11.** *Add two numbers scenario*

The following is a list of the code that was added to the AdditionSteps class for this scenario. We will
talk about the model use in a minute.

```
MathPageModel mathPageModel = new MathPageModel();

[Given(@"I have entered 10 into the page")]
public void GivenIHaveEntered10IntoThePage()
{
    mathPageModel.FirstValue = 10;
}
```

```
[Given(@"I have entered 15 into the page")]
public void GivenIHaveEntered15IntoThePage()
{
    mathPageModel.SecondValue = 15;
}

[When(@"I press add")]
public void WhenIPressAdd()
{
    mpController = new MathPageController();
    result = mpController.MathPage(mathPageModel);
}

[Then(@"the result should be 25 on the screen")]
public void ThenTheResultShouldBe25OnTheScreen()
{
    var resultView = result as ViewResult;
    var model = (MathPageModel)resultView.ViewData.Model;

    Assert.IsNotNull(resultView, "View was Null");
    Assert.AreEqual(25, model.AdditionResult, "Addition was a failure");
}
```

Here is the code for the MathPageController that relates to this scenario.

```
[HttpPost]
public ActionResult MathPage(MathPageModel model)
{
    return ModelState.IsValid ? View(mathPageModel) : View();
}
```

One thing you will note is that we are using a Model in this test scenario. The data model is located under the Models folder and contains all the data that is to be bound to the view by the controller.

```
public class MathPageModel
{
    [DisplayName("Number 1")]
    public decimal FirstValue { get; set; }

    [DisplayName("Number 2")]
    public decimal SecondValue { get; set; }

    [DisplayName("Result")]
    public decimal AdditionResult { get { return FirstValue + SecondValue; } }
}
```

This code will take a model of the data and calculate the result and return the model to the view. From there we can test the model to make sure the controller handled it properly.

# Summary

This is a simple example, but it shows you the potential of what SpecFlow can do. If you are interested and would like to further you research of BDD and SpecFlow in particular, you can check out the following web sites:

- Introduction to BDD: `http://behaviour-driven.org/`

- Getting started with SpecFlow: `http://www.specflow.org/specflow/getting-started.aspx`

In this appendix we learned the following:

- BDD is the next step of TDD.

- The idea of outside-in software development is a key piece of BDD.

- How to install SpecFlow using either the installer from the web site or through NuGet.

- How to create a Specs project that contains the BDD tests.

- How to write a feature with multiple scenarios.

- How to create the step definitions needed to test each scenario with the NUnit client tool.

# Mocking with Moq

Moq (pronounced "Mock-you" or just "Mock"): what is it good for? With the evolution of automated testing, new challenges arise and mocking frameworks are one of these new challenges.

While other mocking frameworks exist—such as RhinoMocks (the framework we used in our case study) or TypeMock, to name a couple —Moq is the only mocking library for .NET to take full advantage of the .NET 3.0 and 3.5 Frameworks. Moq relies heavily on LINQ and lambda expressions, and its API is designed for developers new to mocking frameworks. While Moq relies on the .NET 3.0 and 3.5 language features, Moq does require .NET Framework 3.5 or higher.

We will explain why mocking is important and how it can save a developer time. We will also show you how to install Moq by either downloading the files or installing it through NuGet, and go through some practical examples to get you started.

## Why Mocking

There are a number of reasons to use mocking. It allows you to test the behavior of production code through automated tests. It also helps you to create one architecture layer before another; for example, you could write the business logic layer of an application before moving on to the data access layer.

Mocking is a valuable weapon to have in your arsenal when you want to create automated tests in which there are a number of dependencies. Rather than creating all the dependencies by hand, you want to "mock them out" to test a small piece of functionality. Mocking helps with this. Instead of implementing countless interfaces for the sole purpose of providing test functionality, use a mocking framework. We'll explain this in more detail later.

Another reason to use a mocking framework is if you're developing an application and want to focus on a particular module, such as the business logic, but you're not ready to implement the data layer yet. Mocking can be used to "mock out" the database using an interface, or even after having a working data layer, remove dependencies to interact with the database for testing purposes only. This is also useful if you have multiple developers developing on the same application. Instead of waiting for the data layer to get done, have the developers agree on an interface, and then the developers can use mocking to "fake out" data from the data layer and work independently from each other. This method eliminates a development dependency between having to first write the data layer, and allows quicker beginning parallel development.

Now that you have a better understanding of why you might want to use mocking, let's begin!

## Installation

Moq can be installed in two ways: through the web site and through NuGet.

# Web Page Installation

To install Moq you'll need to have .NET Framework 3.5 or higher with Visual Studio installed. The Moq project is hosted by `code.google.com` and can be downloaded from `http://code.google.com/p/moq/downloads/list`.

The latest version as of this writing is `Moq.4.0.10827.Final.zip`. After downloading, extract the file to the location of your choice. Once complete, copy the `Moq.dll` into the "Lib" folder of your project and reference this `dll`.

It really is that simple. Download the file, unzip it, add a reference to `Moq.dll`—and you are ready to start mocking!

# NuGet Installation

Another, more convenient option for installing Moq is through the NuGet Package Manager. NuGet is an open source development tool that integrates into Visual Studio and gives developers a simpler way of adding libraries into their projects. Think of NuGet as the Ruby Gems for .NET.

Installing NuGet is very simple. NuGet is available through the Extension Manager that is a part of Visual Studio (see Figure C-1). Simply search for "NuGet Package Manager" and click on the Download button; when it's finished, restart Visual Studio and you are done.

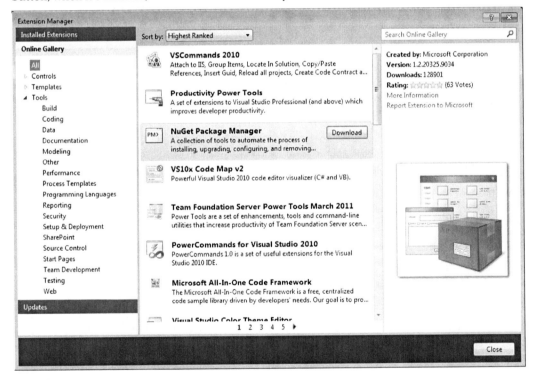

*Figure C-1. The Extension Manager window in Visual Studio*

Once NuGet is installed, we can access the Package Manager Console. This is where you will interact with NuGet. To get to the Package Manager Console, navigate to View   Other Windows   Package Manager Console (see Figure C-2).

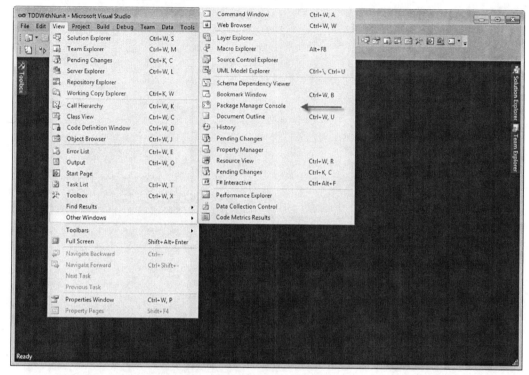

**Figure C-2.** *Navigating to the Package Manager Console*

To install the Moq package, first you need to have a solution open. We created a solution called MockingWithMoq, and inside that solution, a project called MoqExamples. We will talk more about this solution and the projects that make up the solution in a moment. From inside the Package Management Console window, run the following command:

```
PM> Install-Package Moq
```

This command goes to the web and pulls the latest version of Moq that NuGet knows of and installs it in the project. A "packages" folder will be created at the same level as your solution containing the package. NuGet will then add Moq references to the project that we specify in the Default Project dropdown. To verify that the install was successful and see what packages are installed on a project (as shown in Figure C-3), run the following command:

```
PM> Get-Package
```

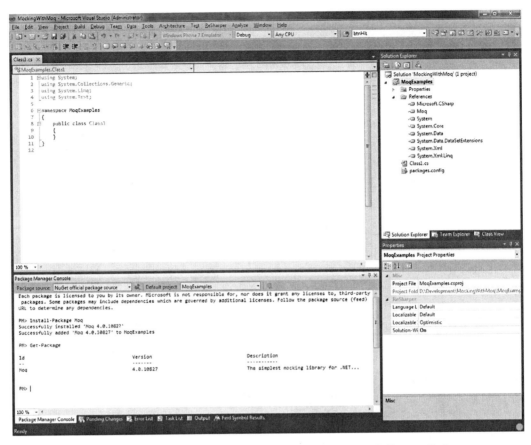

***Figure C-3.*** *Installing Moq through NuGet and verifying it was successfully installed*

## Moq Walk-through

Now that you have Moq installed, you can begin mocking objects! In this walk-through we are going to build a very simple Product class and show examples of how we can use mocking techniques with it.

### The Product Class

For our Moq examples, we've set up a solution called MockingWithMoq. In that solution, we've created two different class library projects, one containing the application code called SampleApp, and one containing the test code called MoqExamples. We have also set a project reference in the MoqExamples project to the SampleApp project. In the MoqExamples project, validate that a reference exists to both the Moq.dll and the nunit.framework.dll, since we'll be illustrating Moq through unit testing.

---

▓ **Note** If you need to install NUnit, refer to Appendix A.

---

Once the references are in place, add a class called Product.cs. The first thing we want to do is create a Product class that should look like the following:

```
    public class Product
{
    public int Id { get; set; }
    public string Name { get; set; }
    public decimal Price { get; set; }
    public decimal GetPriceWithExtendedWarranty (IWarrantyCalculator calculator)
    {
        return calculator.GetWarrantyPrice(Price) + Price;
    }
}
```

Notice that we've added a GetPriceWithExtendedWarranty property that is dependent upon the IWarrantyCalculator interface. We want IWarrantyCalculator to be an interface because we do not want to create a dependency and because it is irrelevant what implements this interface. This property could get its data from anywhere: the database, a configuration file—where it gets the data from is irrelevant. The IWarrantyCalculator will look as follows:

```
public interface IWarrantyCalculator
{
    decimal GetWarrantyPrice(decimal price);
}
```

Now that we have an object and an interface to work with, let's unit test the GetPriceWithExtendedWarranty property using Moq.

Let's create a new test method and call it verify_WarrantyCalculator_Equals_15.

```
[Test]
public void verify_WarrantyCalculator_Equals_15()
{
}
```

Inside this method, we want to create a Product object to test. We'll call it prod and the syntax is as follows:

```
Product prod = new Product {Id = 1, Name = "Product Name 1", Price = 10};
```

Next, we want to mock out the IWarrantyCalculator interface. With Moq, it's as simple as the following:

```
Mock<IWarrantyCalculator> fakeWarrantyCalculator = new Mock<IWarrantyCalculator>();
```

When you specify a Moq type you place the type you want to create within brackets and instantiate it. Even though we have created a mock instance, this of itself is not worth much. We need to configure this mock object. With our fakeWarrantyCalculator in place, we can setup fakeWarrantyCalculator as follows:

```
fakeWarrantyCalculator.Setup(warranty => warranty.GetWarrantyPrice(prod.Price)).Returns(5);
```

This is basically setting up the GetWarrantyPrice. We're passing the required prod.Price into the GetWarrantyPrice, which in our case is 10, and we set the property to return 5. Basically it's saying when we call this function, it will always return 5. We do have the option to configure this as a different value if we need to have different return values based on different input values, but currently it is configured to always return 5.

Now that we have the fakeWarrantyCalculator, we can tie that up to our prod object to get the prod.GetPriceWithExtendedWarranty and we pass in the fakeWarrantyCalculator object as follows:

```
decimal calculatedWarranty = prod.GetPriceWithExtendedWarranty(fakeWarrantyCalculator.Object);
```

With more complex mocking, such as having logic in the called class that may call different methods in the mocked interface, we may need to determine that the appropriate methods are being called. For situations such as this, Moq has a way to verify that the actual interface method was called, as follows:

```
fakeWarrantyCalculator.Verify(warranty => warranty.GetWarrantyPrice(prod.Price));
```

Now that we know we have mocked out the objects and verified that the method we expected was called, we are ready to write a unit test. The code thus far will get us the calculatedWarranty result, which should be 15 since we know that the price of the product is 10, the price of the extended warranty is 5, and the prod.GetPriceWithExtendedWarranty will just add those two together. With NUnit we can assert (verify) that this is the case, as follows:

```
Assert.AreEqual(calculatedWarranty, 15);
```

That's it! If you have TestDriven.Net installed, as explained in Appendix A, right-click in the test itself and click Run Test(s), and you should see the test pass.

Notice what you didn't have to do. You didn't have to hand-create a Moq interface, implement the GetWarrantyPrice method, and have it return fake data. Let Moq do all the hard lifting so that you can focus on testing the specific code you need to test.

Congratulations, you've written your first unit test with Moq!

# Summary

This was a small glimpse into using Moq and NUnit for mocking objects. The reason we mock is to eliminate having to write useless dependency code in order to create automated tests. We can save time and code by mocking-out dependencies and spending the time where we want: creating an automated test suite that tests code. We can also use mocking to build an architectural layer of an application before we move onto another.

In this appendix you learned the following:

- Why mocking is useful and the advantages of Moq.

- How to install Moq either from the web or from NuGet.
- How to mock-out a dependency with Moq and wrap unit tests around it.

# Manage a Product Backlog with Pivotal Tracker

One key component of agile is to be able to track manageable work items. In order to track these work items, we put information on Post-its and stick them on a board so that they are big and visible. It's an easy, low-tech way to manage a project, there's no overhead of a system to administer, it's visual, and it's simple.

However, there are times when we need to track this work electronically instead of exclusively using Post-its. For example, when we have remote workers who are not in the office, and thus, not able to see the board; when we need to capture more requirements than a single Post-it note will allow; or when we need to generate reports from user stories.

There are a variety of reasons to track work electronically and not just via Post-it notes. There are tools out there to aid in electronically managing user stories, swim lanes, and your overall agile workflow. In larger enterprise environments, you'd most likely see TFS (Visual Studio Team Foundation Server) from Microsoft, which also offers a Scrum Template to help manage workflow. TFS also has built-in integration between its tracking system and source code repository, which provides an added benefit than having individual products. It is a large, tightly-integrated system that can provide a lot of value in an enterprise environment.

This appendix will discuss an online agile management tool called Pivotal Tracker. While there are pricing plans available if you want to have Pivotal Tracker host private projects, public projects are hosted for the right price—free. Public projects allow others to see your user stories and, while publicly available to everyone, you can give rights to those you want to edit or join your project.

Public project hosting is intended for open-source projects that do not contain sensitive data. In order to use this product for a commercial use or a use that contains sensitive data, you need to register and pay as a private project.

We'll introduce you to Pivotal Tracker, create a public project, and show some of Pivotal Tracker's benefits and how you can use them to manage your agile project.

## Sign Up

To begin, go to Pivotal Tracker at `www.pivotaltracker.com` and sign up. You can also register using your Google account.

*Figure D-1. The Pivotal Tracker homepage*

# Create a Project

Once you've signed up, it's easy to create a project: just log in and you'll be presented with a dashboard that allows you to click on a Create Project button.

*Figure D-2. Creating a new project*

For the purpose of this appendix, we created a sample project called My Sample Project. After you create your project, you will see the dashboard shown in Figure D-3. The sample project contains sample data that helps you visualize how the data you input will be shown. It provides a clearer picture of a work-in-progress project, rather than an empty project. To have an empty project, go back to the previous step and create your own project name rather than the sample project.

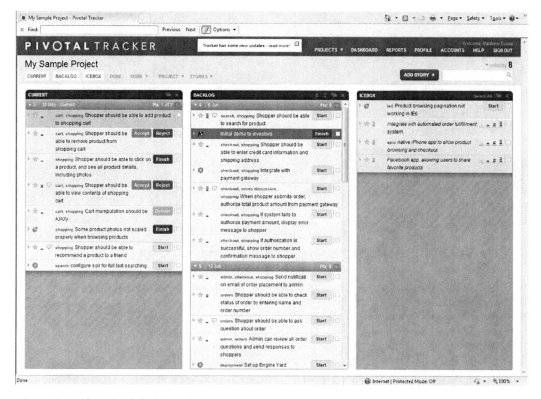

**Figure D-3.** *The initial dashboard*

The dashboard is your primary "home base." The default view lists the following panels:

- *Current:* The Current panel gives a quick glance of the status of things that are currently being worked on in the sprint. The status includes Start, Finish, Deliver, and once the demo is given, Accept/Reject.

- *Backlog:* This is an area for user stories that have already been prioritized and possibly sized, but the work is not yet in a sprint. The backlog is useful for the Release Planning items that we know we want in the product, but can't yet commit to the current sprint.

- *IceBox:* This is a term that Pivotal Tracker uses. Basically, these are user stories that are "on ice," meaning that they have not been prioritized, and most likely have not been sized. At this stage, these stories are nothing more than ideas.

This view is very flexible, as shown in Figure D-4. Pivotal Tracker has a number of different panels. You can turn panels on/off easily and display other ones.

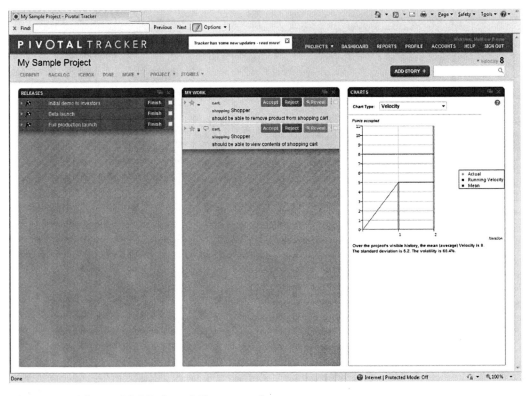

**Figure D-4.** *Releases, My Work, and Charts panels*

Some of the additional panels, which exist in the menu bar directly underneath the "My Sample Project" title, include the following:

- *Releases*: In this panel you can outline, at a high level, the goal or theme of each release. In this example there are three different releases, each with a theme. The Releases panel allows you to drag a story from another panel into a particular release on the panel.

- *My Work*: This panel shows the work that is currently assigned to you in the sprint. It will also display the status the work is in and you can click on the Reveal button to expand the ticker into more detail.

- *Charts*: There are different chart types that the team can view, including the following:

  - *Velocity*: This chart allows you to view the current velocity (the number of points the team is completing).

  - *Release Burn-Down*: This is a graphic of the number of points planned for the current release. It "burns down" the points that the team gets completed and calculates the completion date.

- *Current Iteration Burn-Up*: This report shows a "burn-up" chart based on the points that the team committed to for the sprint. The chart shows the expected and actual lines so that you can quickly assess where the team is in the sprint. The chart starts with 0 and increases upward as points are completed. (As a side note, iteration and sprint are interchangeable terms. *Sprint* comes from the Scrum methodology while the term *iteration* originated in the XP world.)

- *Story Type Breakdown*: This shows a list of the user stories to be implemented, whether that story is a feature, a chore, or a bug. This graphic helps reveal the new development or features being performed versus the number of bugs that need to be fixed.

These features are very useful in an agile environment.

## Keeping Things in Sync

While managing an agile project electronically is strongly encouraged, there's often a perception that it's doubling the work. Some of it may seem as "double work," but transparency is key not only within the team, but also for interested outside parties, that should have confidence that the team is accomplishing work.

Keep in mind that while the team needs to know the progress they are achieving, there are other interested parties, including the customer and management, who want to be apprised of the team's progress. In reality, it's different levels of work that need to be tracked. The low-tech way—the Post-its and the board—serves as a quick glance for members of your team, but more importantly, invested individuals outside the team, such as management and the customer, should also see the progress the team is making.

In the environments we've been in, we typically use both the low-tech way and the high-tech way. We mark the ticket number, or some ID that is associated with the system, with a brief description on the Post-it and walk the Post-it through the swim lanes as we complete the ticket. As we move the Post-its to different swim lanes, we also update the status in the system. While it's everyone's responsibility to keep the board up-to-date, the ScrumMaster serves as the key point of contact for questions, and resolves any outstanding syncing issues if the board and the system get out of sync.

At the beginning of our sprint retrospective, we go over the status of the board and the status in the system to verify that they reconcile. This doesn't take long and by doing it with each sprint, we discover that they are never very much out of sync.

## Summary

While Post-it notes and boards have their place and are useful in a collaborative environment, often the project needs to be managed electronically. In environments we've been in, typically the Post-it note provides the ticket number and a brief description of the ticket to be developed, and then we go into the system to get more details. Often you'll need to get further clarification, so you'll want to add that clarification to the system so that everyone is consistently on the same page.

This appendix provided a small glimpse of Pivotal Tracker, one tool that can manage a project via an agile methodology. While there are many tools out there, we hope this example generated ideas about electronically managing an agile project.

In this appendix you learned the following:

- Scenarios in which you may want to use a tool to electronically manage an agile project.

- The simplicity of signing up for a free public project using Pivotal Tracker.

- How to set up a project and how to view different panels from within Pivotal Tracker to see how the team is progressing from a user story point-of-view.

- Ways to keep items in sync between the low-tech and the high-tech way to track work progress.

# Web Testing with WatiN

With the evolution of web application development and automated testing, a testing framework called WatiN (pronounced as *What-in*) exists to get rid of the boring repetitive tasks of web testing. Web testing's purpose is to test the system from a user perspective. While these types of automated UI tests are slower and often a bit more cumbersome than unit tests, their importance exists to ensure the quality for an "end-to-end" perspective. With unit testing, we are testing smaller, individual blocks of code whereas with UI testing we are testing end-to-end functionality.

WatiN has become a standard for automated web testing in the .NET space. WatiN was patterned on Watir, a family of Ruby libraries that automate web browsers for testing, and is developed in C#. It focuses on automating your web tests using Internet Explorer or Firefox and the .NET language of your choice. This appendix shows you how to install WatiN, either through a web download or through NuGet. We will finish with a couple of simple WatiN tests to whet your appetite and show you how powerful this tool can be.

## Installation

WatiN can be installed in two ways: through the web site or through NuGet.

### Web Page Installation

To install WatiN you will need the following:

- Visual Studio 2005 or above. The installation contains binaries for .NET 2.0, 3.5, and 4.0 for the environment you are working in. For our example, we will assume that Visual Studio 2010 is installed.

- The latest version of WatiN located at http://watin.org.

- Please note that in order to get started with WatiN, you need to have, at a minimum, .NET Framework 2.0 installed. It won't matter if you are using a different version of the framework for your development.

You will need to go the WatiN web site and download the latest version using the Download button. At the time of this writing the latest release is WatiN 2.1 and is approximately 19.7MB.

After the .zip file downloads, extract the files to C:\WatiN then copy the "bin" content into your libs folder and reference WatiN.Care.dll in your project.

# NuGet Installation

A more convenient option for installing WatiN is through the NuGet Package Manager. NuGet is an open source development tool that integrates into Visual Studio and gives the developer a simpler way of adding libraries into their project. Think of NuGet as the Ruby Gems for .NET.

Installing NuGet is very simple. NuGet is available through the Extension Manager that is a part of Visual Studio (see Figure E-1). Simply click on the Download button and when it's finished, restart Visual Studio and you are done.

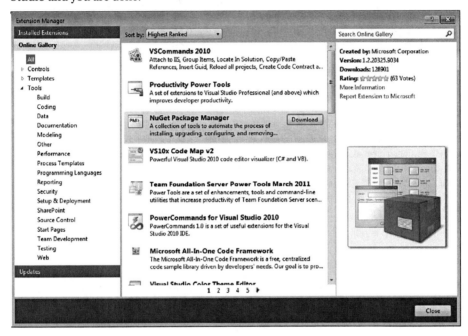

*Figure E-1. The Extension Manager window in Visual Studio*

Once NuGet is installed, we can access the Package Manager Console; this is where you will interact with NuGet. To get to the Package Manager Console navigate to View Other Windows Package Manager Console (see Figure E-2).

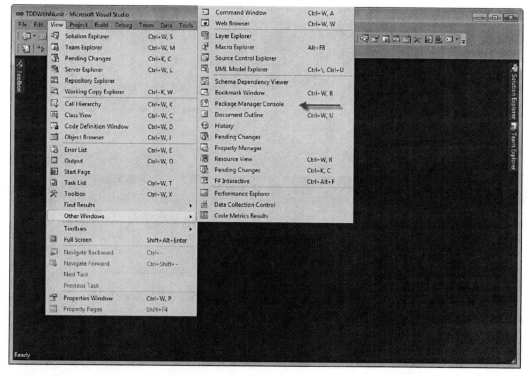

*Figure E-2. Navigating to the Package Manager console*

To install the WatiN package, first you need to have a solution open. We created a solution called "WebTestingWithWatiN," and inside that solution, a project called "WatiN_Tests." We will talk more about this solution and the projects that make up the solution in a moment. From inside the Package Management Console window, run the following command:

```
PM> Install-Package WatiN
```

This command goes to the web and pulls the latest version of WatiN that NuGet knows of and installs it in the project. NuGet will then add references to WatiN to the project that we specify in the Default Project dropdown. To verify that the install was successful, run the following command to see what packages are installed on a project (see Figure E-3).

```
PM> Get-Package
```

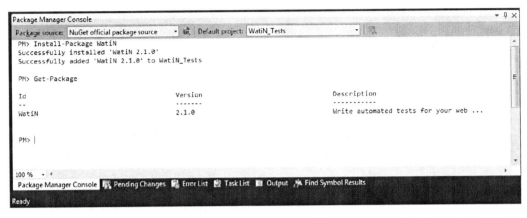

*Figure E-3. Installing WatiN through NuGet, as well as verifying to see that WatiN was installed successfully*

---

▪ **Note** WatiN is approximately 19.7MB. While installing WatiN, Visual Studio may become unresponsive. Be patient while it's downloading the files. Once it's completed, it'll say "Successfully installed," as Figure E-3 shows.

---

# WatiN Test Walk-through

Now that you have WatiN installed, you can begin to create automated web tests. Automated web testing allows developers to write test code that ensures the web application operates as expected. This dramatically reduces the amount of manual testing involved and can free up QA professionals to focus on other kinds of testing, automated or otherwise, including load, performance, and/or exploratory testing rather than performing the same, old, repetitive web tests.

In this walk-through, we are going to build a very simple test using a good .NET blog aggregator web site called DotNetKicks (www.dotnetkicks.com). We'll walk through a few "configuration gotchas" and validate that a simple test on a remote site can be run. We'll then expand that knowledge and create our own simple web application called "HelloWebApp," which takes an input parameter and displays that same parameter. Using this simple web application, we can test this with WatiN.

## Remote WatiN Test

In the WatiN_Tests project, validate that a reference exists to both the WatiN.Core.dll and the nunit.framework.dll.

---

▪ **Note** If you need to install NUnit, refer to Appendix A.

---

Once the references are in place, add a class called `RemoteWebSiteTest.cs`. This class should look like the following:

```csharp
using NUnit.Framework;
using WatiN.Core;

namespace WatiN_Tests
{
    public class RemoteWebSiteTest
    {
        [Test]
        public void verify_DotNetKicksWebSite_Title_Says_DotNetKicks()
        {
            using (var ie = new IE("http://www.dotnetkicks.com", true))
            {
                Assert.IsTrue(ie.Title.Contains("DotNetKicks"));
            }

        }
    }
}
```

Notice we've set up a class and there exists one test named `verify_DotNetKicksWebSite_Title_Says_DotNetKicks`. It's a good idea to give the test a meaningful name, typically in the format of <action>_<Test>_<ExpectedResult>. Giving tests meaningful names saves time to note what exactly you're looking for in a test when it fails and a starting point on how to fix it.

The code is mostly self-documenting. There is one primary tidbit, which is the `IE` object. We pass in the URL but we always want to run the test in a new process, which is why we pass in true. After the test has finished, we want to close out of IE, which is why we wrap the ie variable in a using block.

Since we've got the class set up, before we run the tests, there are two configuration notes to be aware of that need to occur on any type of WatiN test project:

1. Copy the `Interop.SHDocVw.dll` file that came with WatiN to the debug directory. Not doing this results in a "FileNotFound" exception when running the tests. If NuGet was used to install WatiN, then this is already done for us.

2. If using Internet Explorer as your browser to test, add an `app.config` file to the test project with the following configurations:

```xml
<configSections>
    <sectionGroup name="NUnit">
      <section name="TestRunner" type="System.Configuration.NameValueSectionHandler"/>
    </sectionGroup>
  </configSections>
  <NUnit>
    <TestRunner>
      <!-- WatiN can only host IE in STA mode -->
      <add key="ApartmentState" value="STA"/>
    </TestRunner>
  </Nunit>
```

This configuration is needed because IE needs to run in single-threaded apartment (STA) mode because Internet Explorer is not thread-safe. This is also true if testing in Firefox 3. When running WatiN tests, verify that Visual Studio is running as Administrator. Running as Administrator is also necessary if running WatiN tests from an external test runner like the NUnit test runner.

Now that we have the class creating, our configuration is now correct, we are now ready to run the test. We'll use the free TestDriven.Net Visual Studio plugin (see Figure E-4) to run the test. You can download TestDrive.Net from (`http://testdriven.net`).

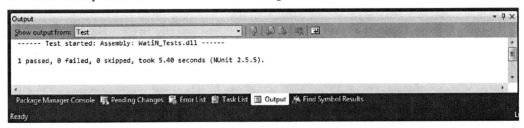

**Figure E-4.** *TestDriven.Net*

Once TestDriven.NET is installed, place your cursor in the body of the test function and in your right-click context menu, there will be a Run Test(s) button. Once you click this, the test will run. Figure E-5 shows what you should see as a result of running that test.

*Output*

```
------ Test started: Assembly: WatiN_Tests.dll ------

1 passed, 0 failed, 0 skipped, took 5.40 seconds (NUnit 2.5.5).
```

Package Manager Console  🔩 Pending Changes  🔩 Error List  📋 Task List  🔲 Output  🔍 Find Symbol Results
Ready

**Figure E-5.** *Test output*

This is how simple it is to get started with WatiN for automated web testing. What we've done is created an instance of Internet Explorer and pointed that instance to a specific URL. Once on the URL, we assert (test) that the title of the browser window contains the text DotNetKicks. While this is a simpler test, it demonstrates what a framework like WatiN has to offer and how to set it up for a remote web site. Next, we'll cover automated testing for local web applications.

# Testing WatiN for Local Web Applications

It's common to use WatiN and tie that in with your Continuous Integration (CI) server to run automated tests. The advantage is that after a build, the automated tests will run with no human interaction and the CI server will produce a report showing you the number of tests that passed/failed. In this section, we'll create a simple ASP.NET MVC web application and then create tests in our WatiN_Tests project that tests the application we just created without having to manually run the project.

First, let's add an ASP.NET MVC 2 Application to our WatiN_Tests solution and call it "HelloWebApp." As shown in Figure E-6, the HelloWebApp is a simple web application where some text is entered into a text box; there's a submit button that displays the input that was in the textbox.

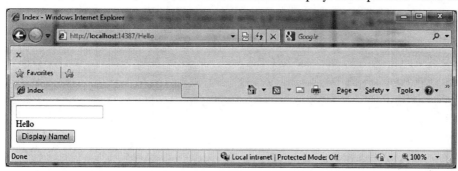

***Figure E-6.*** *HelloWebApp screenshot*

Notice that we have an application that has a virtual path of "Hello." We can type a string in the textbox, click the Display Name! button, and the application will display "Hello + name." We want our automated test to do the following seven things:

1. Start up a web server

2. Instantiate an instance of the browser and navigate to the Hello view

3. Type "Matthew" in the text box

4. Click the Display Name! button

5. Assert that the page contains the string "Hello Matthew"

6. Close the browser

7. Shut down the web server

# CassiniDev

In this example, we'll use CassiniDev, which is a web server that can be used independently of IIS and can run ASP.NET web applications. You can download Cassini from CodePlex (`http://cassinidev.codeplex.com/`). At the time of this writing, the version we'll be using is Cassini 3.5/4.0 Developers Edition.

First, download the CassiniDev project and extract to a location of your choice. Copy the CassiniDev-lib into the "libs" folder of your solution and set a reference in your test project. Now we are ready to create the SetUp and TearDown portions of the test.

The test SetUp portion should look like the following code snippet:

```
using WatiN.Core;
using NUnit.Framework;
using CassiniDev;


[TestFixture]
public class Hello_Tests
{
    private CassiniDevServer _hostServer;

    #region Setup
    [TestFixtureSetUp]
    public void TestFixtureSetUp()
    {
        _hostServer = new CassiniDevServer();

        // assuming your test project and web project or site are in the same parent directory
        const string applicationPath = @"..\..\..\HelloWebApp\";

        // Will start specified application as "localhost" on loopback and first available
        // port in the range 8000-10000 with vpath "/"
        _hostServer.StartServer(applicationPath);
    }

    #endregion
}
```

We create a _hostServer variable that will hold our CassiniDevServer object and then we assume that the test site is in the same parent directory. In the TestFixtureSetup we need to only start the server, which is accomplished using the _hostServer.StartServer(applicationPath); command.

Now that we have the server started, we want to write a TearDown procedure that shuts the server down when we are either done with the tests or the tests have failed. The TearDown procedure looks like the following:

```
[TestFixtureTearDown]
public void TestFixtureTearDown()
{
    _hostServer.StopServer();
}
```

This code should be self-explanatory; we are just stopping the server.

Now that we have the SetUp and TearDown methods, let's focus on creating our test. In our test, we want to do the following five things:

1. Navigate to the Hello page

2. Type "Matthew" in the text box

3. Click on the Display Name! button

4. Assert that the browser contains the following text: "Hello Matthew"

5. Close the browser

First, let's create a name for our test. Let's follow the <action>_<Test>_<ExpectedResult> format. We want to verify that when entering a name and clicking the Display Name! button we expect certain text. So let's name this function verify_EnterNameAndClickingButton_Contains_HelloName.

This function should look like the following code:

```
[Test]
    public void Verify_EnterNameAndClickingButton_Contains_HelloName()
    {
        string url = _hostServer.NormalizeUrl("Hello/");
        string name = "World";

        using (var ie = new IE(url, true))
        {
            ie.TextField(Find.ByName("Name")).TypeText(name);
            ie.Button(Find.ByName("btnDisplayName")).Click();

            Assert.IsTrue(ie.ContainsText("Hello " + name));
        }

    }
```

For the most part, the code should be self-explanatory. Here we've introduce a couple new methods off of the ie object: the TextField method and the Button Method. The TextField method you want to use when dealing with a TextField or TextBox control. This statement finds the textbox by name and proceeds to enter the value of the name variable. Likewise with the Button method, we have the ability to search for a button name, in this instance called btnDisplayName, and click on that button.

Run the test and the output window should look like Figure E-7—showing that the test passed!

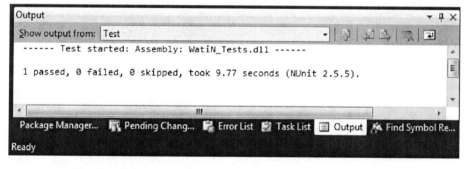

*Figure E-7. Showing the test passed*

Congratulations on writing your first test that can be run fully automated from a DLL. Using the CassiniDev web server and pointing to a web site or web application, this framework could easily be hooked up to the CI Server and your automated web test suite could be run at the click of a button—or even scheduled!

## Summary

This was a small glimpse into using WatiN and NUnit for automated web testing. In this appendix we learned the following:

- How to install WatiN using either the .zip file from the WatiN.org web site or NuGet.

- How to create a simple test using WatiN on an existing remote web site.

- How to create an isolated, automated environment to test a local web application using CassiniDev.

With this new found knowledge, head back to the case study section of the book to see how we use WatiN to test our BlackJack application.

# APPENDIX F

# Source Control with SVN

A source control system (SCS) is a storage and revision repository for all of the source code, tools, libraries, tests, and documents that are required to build, run, test, and document your application. You can think of SCS as a way to see the history of your application and go back in time to any point in that history and examine the code as it was. Any SCS worth its salt will allow you to create branches of your source code. It will also let you go back to any previous configuration or build and fix bugs in it, or create a tangent branch and try and solve a problem in a different manner without having to undo a lot of code.

Apache Subversion (SVN) is an SCS that has evolved originally from Concurrent Versions System (CVS) and is now one of the most popular open-source SCS on the market. In this appendix, we show you how to set up and use your own SVN repository so you never have to lose precious code again. We also introduce a couple of online SVN hosting sites that handle the hassle of managing your SVN repository.

## Distributed Systems vs. Centralized Systems

When talking about SCS, you need to know that there are two main types of systems: distributed control systems and centralized control systems. A distributed system works under the premise that each developer has his own repository and there is no one central repository for everyone to pull from. You can think of a distributed system as a peer-to-peer system. Distributed control systems are typically used by open-source projects due to the fact that a typical open-source project may have developers scattered all over the world and one centralized repository does not make sense in that environment. Some popular source control systems of this type are Git and Mercurial. You can find more information about them at http://git-scm.com/ and http://mercurial.selenic.com/ respectively.

The tool we will use in the book, SVN, is a centralized SCS. A centralized system works under the premise that there is one central master repository on a server somewhere and each developer will pull down a working copy of that repository, from which they can work from. When they are done making changes, they can push those changes back to the central master repository. Think of a centralized system as a client server system. In addition to SVN, other popular centralized systems include CVS and proprietary offerings such as Microsoft Visual SourceSafe, Microsoft Team Foundation Server (TFS), and SourceGear Vault.

The reason for using SVN as opposed to other centralized systems or even distributed systems was purely author preference. You can use any SCS that you like to house and maintain your source code.

## Installation

When setting up SVN, there are two things you need to install: the server that houses your source control repository and a client that you will use to make check ins and check outs against that repository.

## Server Installation

VisualSVN is a software package that contains both a client and a server component. The client component is purchased software, but the server component is a free download. For this, we are going to install the VisualSVN Server.

To install VisualSVN Server, you will need to get the installation program from www.visualsvn.com/server/, shown in Figure F-1, where you can get the latest version of the tool.

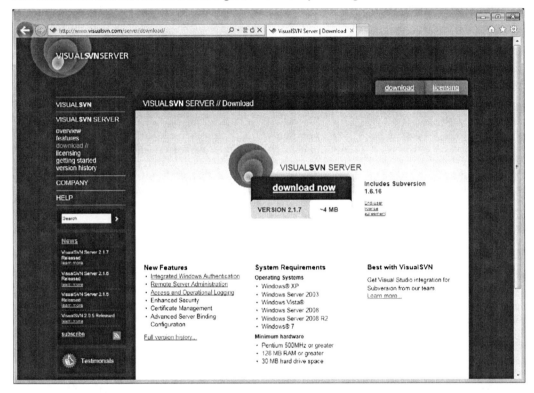

*Figure F-1. VisualSVN Server download page*

Clicking on the downloaded .msi file will launch a typical installation wizard. One thing to note is that when you are installing the server, select VisualSVN Server and Management Console when the wizard gets to the Select Components step in the installation, as shown in Figure F-2.

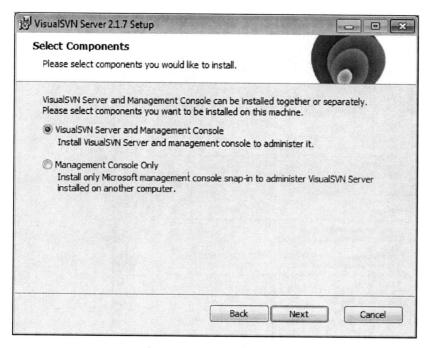

*Figure F-2. VisualSVN Server installation*

For everything else in the installation, you can select the default options. One thing to note is that source control is not about the security of your code. You don't set up a SCS because you want to limit who can access your code. It is about keeping a history of your code. Having said this, there are ways to lock down repositories to certain developers. We will talk about this briefly in a moment. Once the installation has finished, the Management Console will launch as shown in Figure F-3.

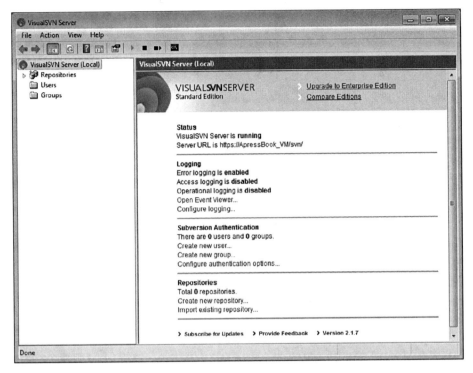

*Figure F-3. VisualSVN Server management console running*

From within the Management Console, right-click on the Repositories icon and select Create New Repository. When selected, you will see the Create New Repository window, as shown in Figure F-4. For this demo, we will call ours ApressAgile, but of course you can call yours whatever you want. You may want to give it a more specific name, based on how you plan on setting up your projects.

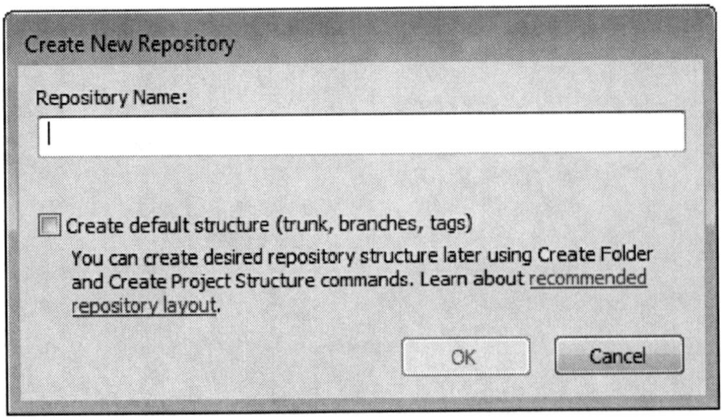

*Figure F-4. Creating a new repository*

If this is your first repository, check the "Create default structure" checkbox. This will create a new repository with the default structure. The default structure would be for three subfolders under the following repository names: trunk, tags, and branches. The tags folder would contain your software releases, where trunk would house the current development of your software. The branches folder is the area where you would store branches of your software from trunk. Once this is done, the server part of the process is complete. Now to install the client.

By default, everyone has access to this repository, meaning that anybody can commit changes to the repository. This is probably not such a great idea, so to resolve this, right-click on the newly-created ApressAgile repository and select Properties. A security dialog will pop up with the security tab selected; from here you can set the permissions for the repository. Select the "everyone" group and select "no access" as the permission. Now add yourself as a user, either through Windows Authentication or a separate VirtualSVN Server account, and give yourself read/write privileges.

This completes setting up the server part of SVN. As a rule of thumb, you need to balance out the difference of who can access the repository with the ability to have everything in the repository. You don't want to hinder the productivity of a development team because of the fact that they did not have access to the repositories that they needed to do their job.

## Client Installation

You can interact with the SVN server in a number of ways. The most basic way is via the command line, but there are tools out there that can make the interaction easier if you are not accustomed to working with the command line. There is a tool called TortoiseSVN that integrates very nicely with Windows Explorer. In this example, however, we want to talk about the client tools that integrate into Visual Studio. There are a couple of tools that offer the Visual Studio integration—some free and some not free. We are going to show you how to install AnkhSVN, one of the free tools.

You can install AnkhSVN from inside Visual Studio by using the Extensions Manager. Simply open the Extensions Manager and do a search inside the Online Gallery for AnkhSVN, as shown in Figure F-5. From there, simply click on the provider and install. Clicking Install will open a web site from CollabNet, which asks you to register for openCollabNet; this is not required to install AnkhSVN. Simply click the "Skip registration and download the software" link.

***Figure F-5.*** *Installing AnkhSVN through the Extensions Manager*

Clicking the .msi file will launch a typical installation wizard. AnkhSVN supports Visual Studio 2005/2008/2010, so the default options will work just fine. You can change which versions of Visual Studio that it will integrate by clicking on the Advance button and going through a custom installation.

Once the installation is complete, you will need to restart Visual Studio for the changes to take effect. With that, you have installed the client. Now you need to set up the client to talk to the server.

## Communicating from Client to Server

With both the client and the server installed, you are half way to using a SCS to protect your source code. Now, you need to set up the client software so that it can communicate with the server.

Once Visual Studio has been restarted to handle the installation of the client, you will have a couple new menu options available. One of these menu options is called the Repository Explorer that is located under the View menu option, as shown in Figure F-6.

**Figure F-6.** *Opening the Repository Explorer*

The Repository Explorer is your connection to the SVN server. From this window you can connect to multiple SVN servers, as well as add/edit/delete each repository. To start, we need to connect to a SVN server.

Clicking on the globe with the plus-sign in the upper left of the window will open the Browse Repository dialog. Here we need to enter in the URL of our SVN server and in particular the repository that we created earlier, `https://localhost/svn/ApressAgile/`, as shown in Figure F-7. Once you click the OK button, it will ask you for your SVN credentials. This is where you need to enter the credentials for the SVN that you created on the SVN server earlier.

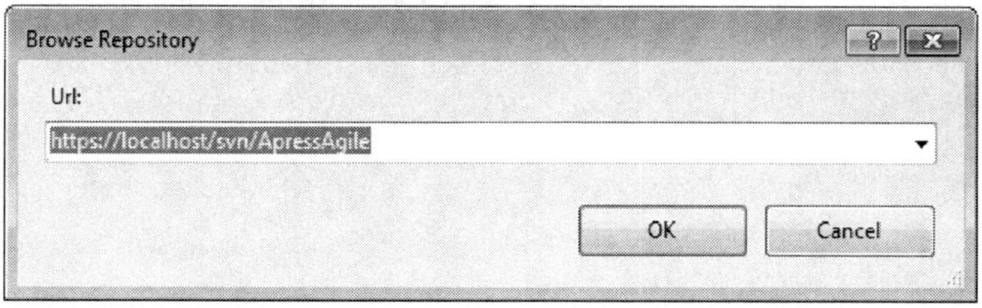

**Figure F-7.** *Browsing to the repository*

# Working Folder

You have the client installed and connected to the repository. Now is time to set up your working folder. The working folder is your local copy of the source code. The working folder contains a copy of everything that is in the repository; when you check out a file, the file will be pulled down to this location from the repository.

To set up your working folder, click the repository name underneath your server name. With that highlighted, click the Checkout from Subversion button, as shown in Figure F-8.

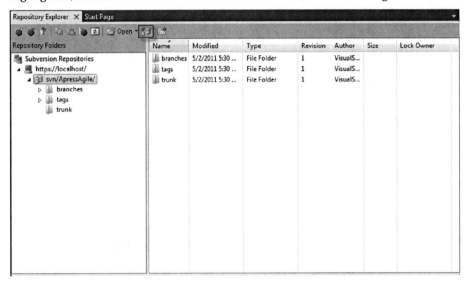

**Figure F-8.** *Setting up the working folder*

Clicking the button will pull up the Checkout from Subversion window, shown in Figure F-9. This window will show you what repository you are pulling from, as well as what version of the code you are getting. It will also show you where you are going to store these files locally. The path is where you can set up your working folder.

Inside the path textbox, enter a location where you want to store your copy of the repository. If the location where you want to store the repository is not already created, it will create the location as part of pulling down the repository. When you are finished, click OK. This will pull down the latest version of the repository that you created to the location that you specified. The first time you do this it may seem confusing to checking out a repository that has no code in it. The reason you are doing this is to create the repository structure in your working folder.

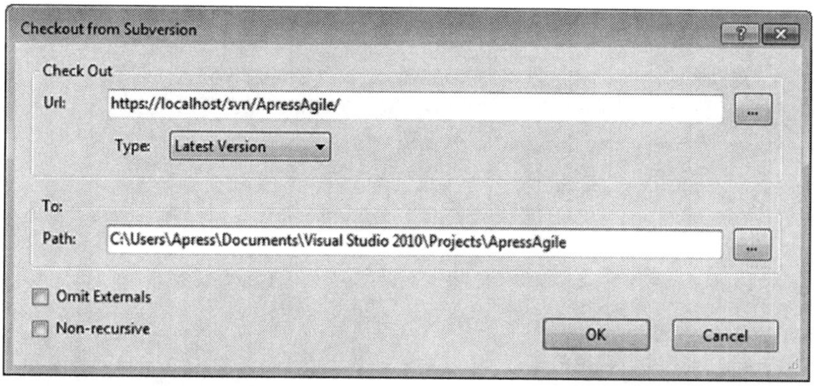

*Figure F-9. Checkout from SVN*

Now whenever you create a new project in Visual Studio, you will be given the option to add that project to SVN. When you click the checkbox to add it to SVN, an additional dialog window will appear, allowing you to specify which repository to add the project to, as well as where in the repository to store the project.

This is how you create a new project and store it into SVN. If you have an existing folder structure that you want to add to SVN, however, you don't want to re-create the entire thing—you want to import it into the repository. Next, we will talk about using another SVN client tool, TortoiseSVN to handle the importing.

## Importing into SVN with TortoiseSVN

TortoiseSVN is a great client tool that integrates into Windows Explorer. With TortoiseSVN, you don't need to have an IDE like Visual Studio. In fact, with TortoiseSVN you can store files other than source code into a repository.

To download TortoiseSVN, go the TortoiseSVN site located at `http://tortoisesvn.tigris.org/`, as shown in Figure F-10. Once TortoiseSVN has downloaded the correct installation file (32-bit or 64-bit), run the installation program and select the default installation options. TortoiseSVN works by integrating tightly into Windows Explorer. When you install TortoiseSVN, you will need to restart your computer for the installation to take effect.

*Figure F-10. TortoiseSVN site*

After you have restarted, navigate to your solution structure and right-click the root of the folder you wish to import. You should now see the TortoiseSVN options presented within the context sensitive menu. Select TortoiseSVN Import. What the import does is copy the folder structure that you specify into the SVN repository that you specify.

The URL of your repository should be `http://localhost/svn/nameOfRepository`, in our case the name of the repository is ApressAgile. Add a message in the import dialog box, as shown in Figure F-11, as a way to let other people know what you checked in, and hit OK.

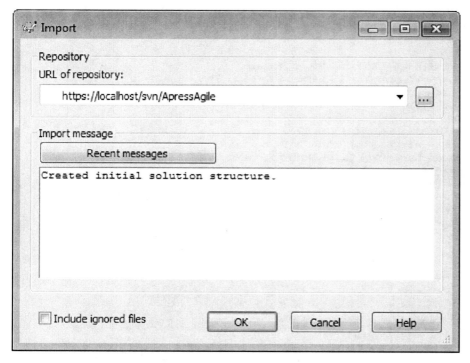

*Figure F-11. Importing a solution into SVN*

You will be prompted to enter the SVN credentials that you created when you installed the SVN server. Once past security, your initial folder structure will be committed to the repository as shown in Figure F-12.

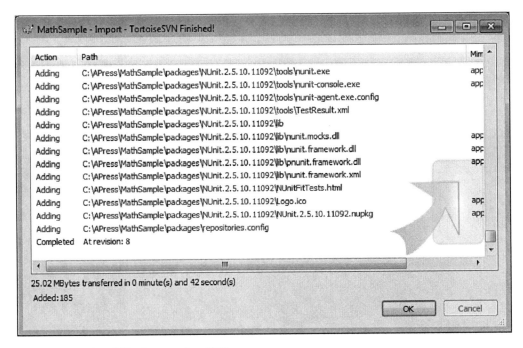

*Figure F-12. List of files imported to SVN*

With your solution structure imported into SVN, you will need to check it out so that you can start adding to it. Right-click your ApressAgile folder and select the SVN Checkout option from the context-sensitive menu. The code check out form will appear, as shown in Figure F-13, and ask you which repository you want to check out and where you want to check it out to. Confirm that the correct repository is selected and hit OK.

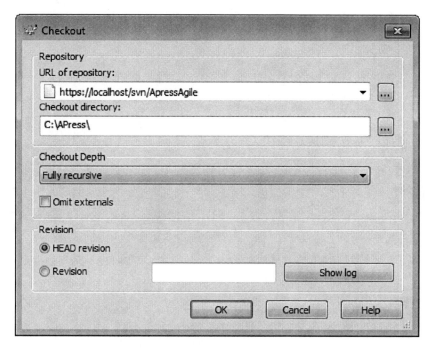

*Figure F-13. TortoiseSVN code checkout dialog*

A dialog box will warn you that the destination folder isn't empty, but don't worry about that because this is a one-time process. Once you have checked out all of the items, you will find that the icons for the folders change, as seen in Figure F-14. The green tick signifies that the item has not been changed. As you start to work with the code base, you will see icons applied to signify that they are not under source control or that they have been modified since you last checked out.

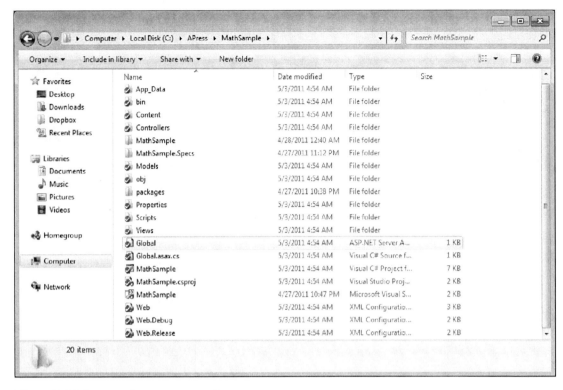

*Figure F-14. Items under source control*

## Online SVN Hosting

We have just shown you how to set up your own SVN server locally. There are online hosting options, however, that handle the hassle of maintaining the hardware requirements for your SVN server. Sites like CodeSpaces (www.codespaces.com) offer you SVN hosting, as well as project management and bug tracking, for a fee. There are also free options available. One site in particular is CodePlex (www.codeplex.com), which offers free SVN hosting for open-source projects only.

Setting up your own SVN server is relatively painless, but there are other options available if you don't want to maintain your own server.

## Summary

This appendix was a general overview of SVN, in which you learned the following:

- The difference between distributed and centralized control systems

- How to install the VisualSVN Server

- How to install the AnkhSVN client that integrates into Visual Studio

- How to import an existing folder structure into SVN through TortoiseSVN

- SVN hosting options

We can't stress enough the priority of getting your code backed-up to a repository. You never know when a piece of hardware will fail or if a software change will wreck your application; with this solution in place, you won't lose all the hard work you put into your code.

# Continuous Integration with Cruise Control.NET

Unless you are a team of one, you will have come across the situation of multiple developers frequently checking code changes into a source repository. With all these developers checking in code, it can be hard to maintain a working build of your product. To ensure you have that working build, you need a tool that will verify, every time a developer checks in code to the source repository, that the latest changes did not break the build and the product still compiles successfully. A continuous integration (CI) server is that tool.

## Continuous Integration

CI is a cornerstone of the agile process. Its focal point is the idea of continuously integrating code that every developer creates into the main code base. On a project you will have developers constantly checking in small changes. CI makes sure those changes do not break existing functionality in the product. This verification is done by compiling and testing the code base each time changes are made. This provides feedback to the team as early as possible to warn of any potential issues in the code base. By getting this information earlier in the process, developers can fix small problems before they become roadblocks. CI can also provide a level of confidence to developers that the code is working as expected, especially when they are refactoring a portion of the code base.

## CruiseControl .NET

A CI server coordinates continuous integration with the help of your source control repository and builds manager. Every time a developer checks code into the source repository, the CI server catches this check in. The server will then get the latest version of the code from the source repository and compile and test the code. Another responsibility of a CI server is to provide feedback on the integration process. Figure G-1 will refresh your memory on the job that the CI server does.

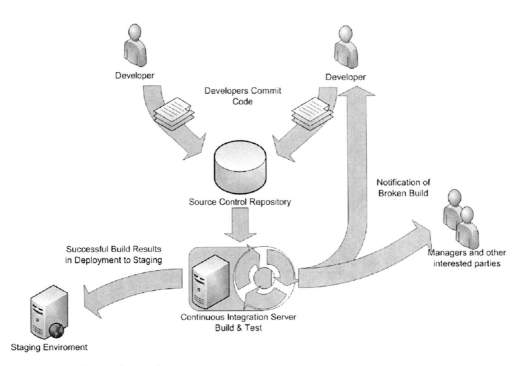

*Figure G-1.* *The continuous integration process*

One thing to note is that deploying successful builds to a staging environment is not always an automated task. This will vary based on the environment that you are working in.

In this scenario, we will be using CruiseControl.NET (CCNET) from ThoughtWorks. It is an open-source piece of software that is configured via XML. Through the configuration, you can set up CCNET to talk to a variety of source control repositories and use a number of testing frameworks to test the code. You can also set up CCNET to notify people via e-mail when a build is broken.

Now before you worry, using the configuration file is not as bad as you may have heard. It is simply laid out in XML. An added benefit to using a configuration file is that you can store the CCNET configuration file under source control. Then you need never worry about permanently damaging CCNET because you can always roll back to a good configuration setup. Let's get started with how to install CCNET.

# Installation

To get started with CCNET, navigate to http://ccnet.thoughtworks.com and download the latest version, as shown in Figure G-2. One thing to note before you start, the machine that you will install CCNET on must have Microsoft's web server Internet Information Services (IIS) installed on it. If IIS is not installed, then that needs to be done before you continue with the CCNET installation.

▨ **Note** If you are installing IIS as a pre-requisite for CCNET, remember to install ASP.NET along with it. You can do this through "Turn Windows features on or off" in the Control Panel applet Programs and Features. Once there, navigate to Internet Information Services   World Wide Web Services   Application Development Features and click the checkbox next to ASP.NET. Another way to install IIS is through the Web Platform Installer available from Microsoft. Using the Platform Installer you can select IIS Recommended Configuration, which will install a good set of the service. Trust us, this will save you hours.

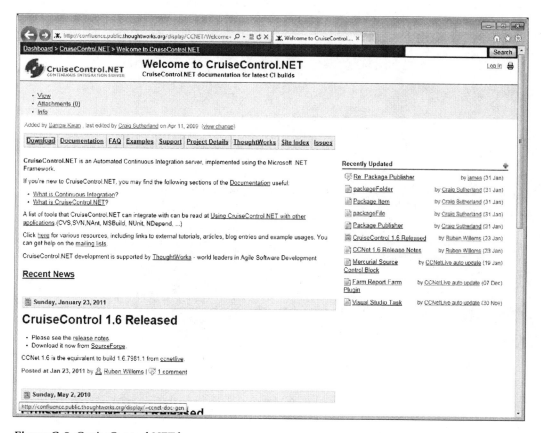

*Figure G-2. CruiseControl.NET homepage*

Once CCNET is downloaded, you will be presented with a common installation wizard. The defaults will suffice for most installations, but the following are some things that you need to make certain are selected when installing:

- "Web Dashboard" is selected; it should be selected as the default

- CCNET is installed as a Windows service

- "Create Virtual Directory in IIS for Web Dashboard" is selected

Once the installation has completed, you are able to run CCNET as a Windows service or as a stand-alone application.

## Stand-Alone Application

The easiest way to start CCNET is to run it as a stand-alone application. During the installation process, a shortcut is placed on the desktop by the installer. To get CCNET running, all you need to do is double-click the shortcut. On double-click, a console window will open and show you what is happening with CCNET, as demonstrated in Figure G-3.

*Figure G-3. CCNET running as a stand-alone application*

From this point on, CCNET will behave normally. There is only one difference between this mode and running it as a service. If the machine happens to reboot for any reason, you need to log in and restart CCNET manually.

## Windows Service

Another way to run CCNET is as a Windows service. If you chose to install CCNET as a Windows service during the installation process, then there will be a service on the machine for CCNET. At this time, however, the service is not started. Open your services and look for the service named *CruiseControl.NET Server*. Right-click on the entry and select Properties. You will see something like Figure G-4.

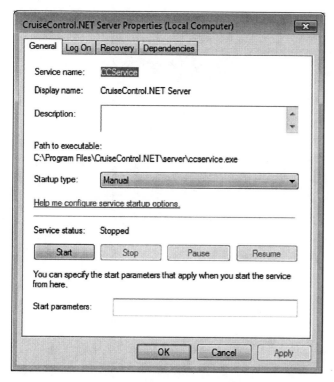

*Figure G-4. Setting up CCNET to run as a Windows service*

From this window, set the Startup Type to Automatic and click the Start button. What this will do is start the service immediately and tell Windows to start the service every time the system is started in the future.

On the Log On tab you may want to change the service's account to an account with elevated privileges if you intend CruiseControl.NET to change files on the server. For now, since we are not setting up CruiseControl.NET to change files, we can keep it as is; but it's something to keep in mind when you get to the deployment stage of successful code.

The only difference between the two running modes is what happens when the system is rebooted. Now that we have the application installed, let's set it up.

# CruiseControl.NET Web Dashboard

Now that you have CCNET installed and the service running, you will want to verify that the installation was a success. To do that, navigate to `http://localhost/ccnet` with a web browser. If the default web page appears, as shown in Figure G-5, CruiseControl.NET installed successfully.

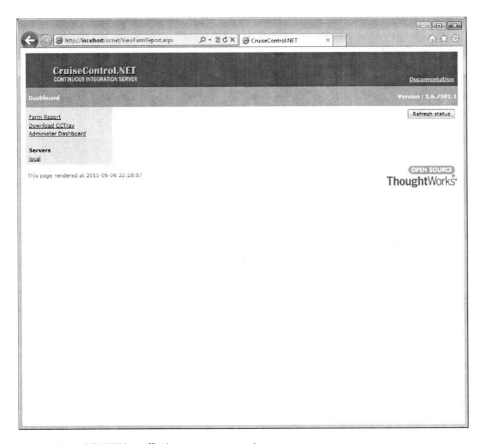

*Figure G-5. CCNET installation was a success!*

The next thing you may want to do is install some packages onto CCNET. Packages are small applications that bolt onto CCNET and give it extra functionality. Since the packages are installed via the web interface, the web interface must have permissions to move files within the web dashboard directory. The app pool that is related will have to have at least the Modify permission in the web dashboard directory.

To install the packages, navigate in a web browser to http://localhost/ccnet. Click the Administrator Dashboard link. The first time you do this, you may see an error on the page, as shown in Figure G-6. If so, you will need to set the administrator password.

**Dashboard Administration**

⚠ **Error:** Administration password may not be empty. Update dashboard.config, section administrationPlugin.

The administration console is password protected, please enter your password:

[                    ]  [ Enter ]

*Figure G-6. An administration password must be specified.*

To set the password, navigate to the folder where you installed CCNET. By default, it is installed into the `C:\Program Files\CruiseControl.NET\` (`C:\Program Files(x86)\CruiseControl.NET\` if your system is 64-bit) directory. From there, navigate to the web dashboard folder and open the `dashboard.config` file. To edit this file you will need to do this as an administrator (i.e. run Notepad as an administrator). By default, users do not have permissions to modify this file. Inside this config file you will find an XML node like the following:

```
<administrationPlugin password="" />
```

This is where you set the password. Set the password to whatever you wish. Once that is done, save and close the config file. One last thing you need to do is restart IIS after these changes have been made. Open a command prompt and enter the following command:

```
C:\> iisreset
```

Once this is done, refreshing the page will allow you to enter the password you just set. Once the password is entered, you will be taken to package screen, as shown in Figure G-7.

## Dashboard Administration

### Remote Servers

local
[tcp://localhost:21234/CruiseManager.rem]

### Packages

CodeIt.Right Analysis

Duplicate Finder Results

Final Build Status

Fitnesse Results

FxCop Results

Gendarme Results

Liquid Blue Theme

Modification History

Modifications

ModificationsByChangeNumber

MSBuild Results

MSTest Results

NAnt Results

NCover Results

NDepend Results

Note worthy Theme

NUnit Results

Ohloh

Package List

Project Configuration Display

Project Statistics

Project Timeline

Queue Status Display

Security Configuration Display

Server Configuration Display

Server Information Display

Server Log Display

Simian Results

StyleCop Results

User List

Web Dashboard Administration [Installed]

### Commands

[ Add New Server ]   [ Load Package ]   [ Reload dashboard ]   [ Logout ]

*Figure G-7. The list of packages you can install*

To install a package, you simply need to click it. This will produce a popup window, as shown in Figure G-8, where you can simply click the Install button. To verify that the package has installed correctly, as shown in Figure G-9, click on the View Log button.

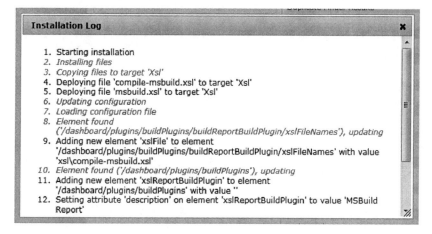

**Package details**                                      ✖

**Name:**        MSBuild Results
**Description:**   Display the results of a MSBuild build.

[  Install  ]    [  Remove  ]    [  Close  ]

*Figure G-8. Installing a package*

**Installation Log**                                     ✖

1. Starting installation
2. *Installing files*
3. *Copying files to target 'Xsl'*
4. Deploying file 'compile-msbuild.xsl' to target 'Xsl'
5. Deploying file 'msbuild.xsl' to target 'Xsl'
6. *Updating configuration*
7. *Loading configuration file*
8. *Element found ('/dashboard/plugins/buildPlugins/buildReportBuildPlugin/xslFileNames'), updating*
9. Adding new element 'xslFile' to element '/dashboard/plugins/buildPlugins/buildReportBuildPlugin/xslFileNames' with value 'xsl\compile-msbuild.xsl'
10. *Element found ('/dashboard/plugins/buildPlugins'), updating*
11. Adding new element 'xslReportBuildPlugin' to element '/dashboard/plugins/buildPlugins' with value ''
12. Setting attribute 'description' on element 'xslReportBuildPlugin' to value 'MSBuild Report'

*Figure G-9. The package install is complete.*

There are numerous packages that you can install to CCNET, but the following is a list of some packages that you may find useful:

- NUnit Results

- Project Statistics

- Server Log Display

- Project Configuration Display

While these packages are not technically required by CCNET, you will not be able to add projects or do the work in the rest of this appendix without them. With these packages installed, it's time to configure CCNET to grab your source code and compile it.

# CruiseControl.NET Configuration and Setup

The configuration file for CCNET is located in the directory where the application was installed. By default, it is located at `C:\Program Files\CruiseControl.NET\server\`. The file is also available through the Start Menu in Windows through Program Files CruiseControl.NET. Once there, open the `ccnet.config` file. This contains all the setup needed for CCNET to access your source control, pull down the latest code, compile, and test it.

## Adding a Project

Open the `ccnet.config` file through a text editor. The group of related config settings in this file is called a project.

---

⬛ **Caution** When opening the config file in a text editor, be sure to run the editor as an administrator.

---

The following is an example of a project in the config file that will go to the designated source control, pull down all the code, and then compile and test it. This way, the customer can have access to the results.

```
<cruisecontrol xmlns:cb="urn:ccnet.config.builder">
  <project name="Math Cards" webURL="http://localhost/ccnet">
    <sourcecontrol type="svn">
            <trunkUrl>svn://svn.servername.com/MathCards/trunk</trunkUrl>
            <workingDirectory>c:\dev\ccnet</workingDirectory>
    </sourcecontrol>
    <tasks>
        <devenv solutionfile="c:\dev\MathCards\MathCards.sln" configuration="debug" />
        <nunit path="C:\Program Files\NUnit 2.2\bin\nunit-console.exe">
            <assemblies>
                    <assembly>c:\dev\MathCards\bin\Debug\MathCards.Specs.exe</assembly>
            </assemblies>
        </nunit>
    </tasks>
    <publishers>
      <xmllogger logDir="log" />
    </publishers>
  </project>
</cruisecontrol>
```

Now that you have added a project to CCNET, click the dashboard link in the upper-left and it will take you back to the main page. The first time you add a project to CCNET, you will always see the projects laid out this way, as in Figure G-10.

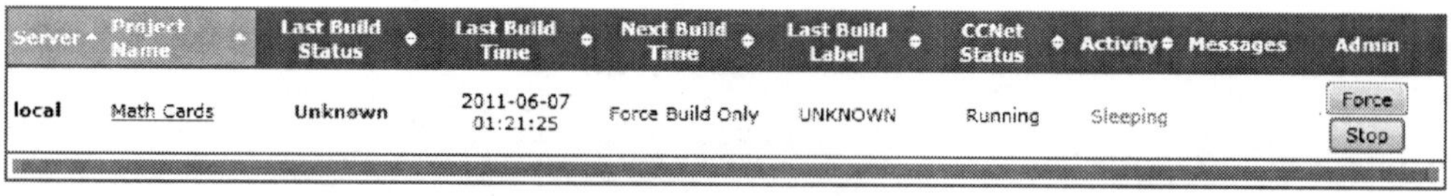

| Server ▲ | Project Name | Last Build Status | Last Build Time | Next Build Time | Last Build Label | CCNet Status | Activity ◆ | Messages | Admin |
|---|---|---|---|---|---|---|---|---|---|
| local | Math Cards | Unknown | 2011-06-07 01:21:25 | Force Build Only | UNKNOWN | Running | Sleeping | | Force Stop |

*Figure G-10. You have successfully added a project to CCNET.*

Further details are beyond the scope of this appendix, but the CCNET documentation should answer any questions you have. At the time of writing, it can be found at http://confluence.public.thoughtworks.org/display/CCNET/Documentation. Feel free to experiment with the different project settings and nodes.

## Setting up CCTray

One way you can stay updated on the status of the build from CCNET is a small application called CCTray that runs in your windows tray and gives you feedback at regular intervals. To download CCTray, simply click on the Download CCTray link that is located on the main page of the web dashboard.

When you install the application, the default settings will be more than enough. Once installed, you will be able to right-click the CCTray icon in your windows tray and select settings from the popup menu.

To let CCTray know about your project, from the settings dialog window select the Build Projects tab, then hit Add; a new project window will display. Hit Add Server from this window and you will be shown the Build Server window as shown in Figure G-11. Keep the default "Connect directly using .NET remoting option" selected, enter the URL of the CCNET server, and then hit OK. Your project is now set up within CCTray and you are able to use this to force a build. You will also be alerted to the status of the build.

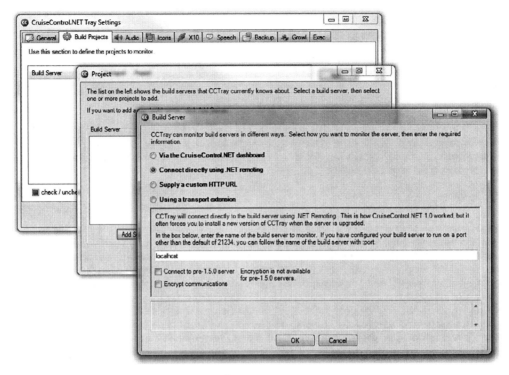

*Figure G-11. Setting up the CruiseControl tray*

Now, when a build is run by CruiseControl you will see CCTray alert you to the status of it, as shown in Figure G-12.

*Figure G-12. Alert display from the CruiseControl tray*

## Summary

In this appendix, you learned a few things about continuous integration and discovered a tool called CruiseControl.NET, which can help you implement continuous integration. We also showed you the following:

- How to install CCNET

- How to run CCNET as a stand-alone application

- How to run CCNET as a Windows service

- How to set up the web dashboard

- How to set up the administrator password for CCNET

- How to install packages to CCNET

- How to set up your first project in CCNET

- How to install CCTray

We just scratched the surface of all CCNET can do. We hope that you see that a CI server is a great tool for allowing a team to be aware of the state of their code base at any time. It is one way developers can get a quick feedback loop about the code they are writing. There are numerous places on the web (beginning with the documentation) that you can find information about CCNET, so the fun does not have to stop now.

Happy integrating!

# Index